INTRODUCING MARKETING

INTRODUCING MARKETING

JOHN BURNETT
University of Denver

JOHN WILEY & SONS, INC.

Acquisitions Editor   *Jeff Marshall*
Editorial Assistant   *Michael Brennan*
Marketing Manager   *Charity Robey*
Senior Production Editor   *Norine M. Pigliucci*
Senior Designer   *Dawn Stanley*
Photo Researcher   *Elyse Rieder*
Photo Editors   *Sara Wight and Hilary Newman*
Cover Photo   *©Hugh Sitton/STONE*
Production Management Services   *Argosy Publishing*

This book was set in *Times Roman* by *Argosy Publishing* and printed and bound by *Hamilton Printing*.
The cover was printed by *Phoenix Color Corp.*

The book is printed on acid-free paper. ∞

ISBN 0-471-39531-5 (pbk)

Library of Congress Cataloging-in-Publication Data
Burnett, John, 1944–
    Introducing marketing / John Burnett.
        p. cm.
    Includes bibliographical references.
    ISBN 0-471-39531-5 (pbk. : alk. paper)
1. Marketing. I. Title.

    HF5415 .B7727 2001
    658.8—dc'21

                                                                    2001045644

To order books please call (800) 225-5945.

Printed in the United States of America

10 9 8 7 6 5 4 3 2 1

PREFACE

Through good economic times and bad, marketing remains the pivotal function in any business. Determining and satisfying the needs of customers through products that have value and accessibility and whose features are clearly communicated is the general purpose of any business. It is also a fundamental definition of marketing. This text introduces students to the marketing strategies and tools that practitioners use to market their products.

BALANCED COVERAGE

To emphasize how various marketing areas work together to create a cohesive strategy, I define and explain the various marketing areas and their comparative strengths and weaknesses, as well as stress how to best "mix" marketing tools in a strategic, integrated plan. The book begins with a discussion of the marketing planning process, continues with a discussion of the preliminary tasks of developing the plan, and concludes with the tactics available to the marketing planner. This complete coverage ensures that students will learn how to plan, execute, and evaluate a marketing program that is effective and efficient from start to finish.

INTERNATIONAL AND TECHNOLOGY COVERAGE

Introducing Marketing recognizes the impact of the global community on marketing practices. International implications are discussed in Chapter 6 and are also integrated into the text through relevant examples.

Technology is altering many marketing practices. The World Wide Web, databases, tracking devices, and market simulations are only a few examples of the ways technology has affected marketing strategies. Technology coverage is woven throughout the text, features, and end-of-chapter materials of this book. (Note that because technology is changing so rapidly, it is virtually impossible for a text such as this to remain absolutely current.)

CURRENT EXAMPLES FROM ALL TYPES AND SIZES OF BUSINESS

This book demonstrates how companies use marketing. Specific examples appear not only in text discussions, but also in the chapter openers, the Integrated Marketing and Newsline boxes, and the end of chapter cases. Examples and stories bring theory to life, demonstrating the relevance of the reading. The example subjects are vivid, current, and varied. They range from Fortune 500 companies to smaller, privately held businesses. The text also focuses on international companies of all sizes.

Learning is not always about success stories. Diagnosing problems and failures is an important aspect of critical thinking, and examples of such are introduced to challenge students to learn from others' mistakes and better manage real-world problems.

A CLEAR, EFFECTIVE ORGANIZATION

Time is a precious commodity to instructors and students. Market feedback revealed that instructors want an introductory marketing text that (1) covers the basics well and (2) omits unnecessary detail. Careful selection of topics, appropriate depth of coverage, and concise writing helped us meet those two objectives. Instead of the typical 20–25 chapters, this text offers 10 chapters of manageable length.

HELPFUL PEDAGOGY

We introduce several features to reinforce learning and help students build business skills that they can use on the job. Our comprehensive learning system enables students to master materials quickly and thoroughly. Some features of that system include opening vignettes, performance-based learning objectives, concept reviews, Integrated Marketing boxes, Newsline boxes, end-of-chapter projects, and end-of chapter cases.

SUPPLEMENTS OF THE BOOK

- The Instructor's Manual with Test Questions provides helpful teaching ideas, advice on course development, sample assignments and chapter-by-chapter text highlights, learning objectives, lecture outlines, class exercises and more. This manual also includes multiple choice, true/false, and short answer text questions for each chapter.
- PowerPoint Presentations are available for download via the text web site (www.wiley.com/college/burnett). These slides contain lecture outlines for each chapter of the text.
- A computerized version of the Test Bank is available to instructors for customization of their exams.
- Additional online resources are available to instructors via the text web site. These resources include: *In Practice* exercises for each chapter, which relate directly to the Wall Street Journal articles on-line; an interactive Study Guide; interactive web-based cases; on-line chapter summaries; a Reading Room containing on-line articles from the Wall Street Journal, which correlate with key concepts and topics within each chapter of the text; and more.

ACKNOWLEDGMENTS

Introducing Marketing, First Edition benefits from insights provided from marketing educators around the country that carefully read and critiqued draft chapters. I am pleased to express my appreciation to the following colleagues for their contributions:

Joe K. Ballenger
Stephen F. Austin State University

Dong Jin Lee
State University of New York (SUNY), Binghamton

Amit Bhatnagar
University of Wisconsin, Milwaukee

Thomas L. Ainscough
College of William and Mary

Jeffrey B. Schmidt
University of Illinois at Urbana-Champaign

James V. Spiers
Arizona State University

I would also like to thank the Wiley team including my editor, Jeff Marshall, marketing manager, Charity Robey, production editor, Norine Pigliucci, Cindy Rhoads, Dawn Stanley, Mike Brennan, and Elyse Rieder for their hard work and support of this project. A great deal of thanks also goes to my friend and colleague, Pallab Paul, for his outstanding contributions to the web site.

CONTENTS

CHAPTER ONE   *INTRODUCING MARKETING*   **1**

Introduction   **2**
Marketing: Definition and Justification   **3**
   Defining Marketing   **3**
   Justification for Study   **6**
   Characteristics of a Marketing Organization   **7**
   The Role of Marketing in the Firm:
      A Basis for Classification   **12**
   Strategic Components of Marketing   **17**
Keys to Marketing Success   **22**
Summary   **24**
Marketer's Vocabulary   **24**
Discussion Questions   **24**
Project   **25**
Case Application: The Hog Is Alive and Well   **25**
References   **26**

CHAPTER TWO   *UNDERSTANDING AND APPROACHING THE MARKET*   **27**

Introduction   **28**
Defining the Market   **28**
   The Market Is People   **28**
   The Market Is a Place   **29**
   The Market Is an Economic Entity   **29**
Types of Markets   **30**
   Consumer Markets   **30**
   Industrial Markets   **30**
   Institutional Markets   **30**
   Reseller Markets   **30**
Approaching the Market   **31**
   The Undifferentiated Market (Market Aggregation)   **32**
   Product Differentiation   **33**
   The Segmented Market   **34**
   The Strategy of Market Segmentation   **45**
Summary   **49**
Marketer's Vocabulary   **49**
Discussion Questions   **50**
Project   **51**
Case Application: Rolling Rock Finds Its Niche   **51**
References   **52**

CHAPTER THREE   *MARKETING RESEARCH: AN AID TO DECISION MAKING*   **53**

Introduction   **53**
The Nature and Importance of Marketing Research   **54**
What Needs Researching in Marketing?   **55**
Procedures and Techniques in Marketing Research   **57**
   Making a Preliminary Investigation   **57**
   Creating the Research Design   **59**
Conducting the Research   **67**
Processing the Data   **67**
The Value of Marketing Research   **67**
Summary   **70**
Marketer's Vocabulary   **70**
Discussion Questions   **71**
Project   **71**
Case Application: Research Saves the Day at Case   **72**
References   **72**

CHAPTER FOUR   *UNDERSTANDING BUYER BEHAVIOR*   **73**

Introduction   **74**
Buyer Behavior and Exchange   **74**
Buyer Behavior as Problem Solving   **75**
   The Decision Process   **76**
   Influencing Factors of Consumer Behavior   **82**
Organizational Buyer Behavior   **91**
   Characteristics of Organizational Buying   **91**
   Stages in Organizational Buying   **93**
Summary   **98**
Marketer's Vocabulary   **98**
Discussion Questions   **99**
Project   **99**
Case Application: Customer Satisfaction Still Matters   **99**
References   **100**

CHAPTER FIVE   *EXTERNAL CONSIDERATIONS IN MARKETING*   **101**

Introduction   **102**
External Factors that Affect Planning   **103**
   External Surprises   **104**
   Competitors   **104**

Legal/Ethical Factors   **106**
Economic/Political Issues   **110**
Technology   **113**
Social Trends   **115**
Forecasts of the Future   **120**
Summary   **123**
Marketer's Vocabulary   **123**
Discussion Questions   **123**
Project   **124**
Case Application   **124**
References   **125**

CHAPTER SIX   *MARKETING IN GLOBAL MARKETS*   **126**

Introduction   **127**
Defining International Marketing   **127**
Standardization and Customization   **128**
Reasons for Entering International Markets   **129**
Reasons to Avoid International Markets   **130**
The Stages of Going International   **130**
Exporting   **131**
Licensing   **131**
Joint Ventures   **132**
Direct Investment   **132**
U.S. Commercial Centers   **132**
Trade Intermediaries   **133**
Alliances   **133**
The International Marketing Plan   **133**
The Corporate Level   **134**
The Business Level   **134**
The Functional Level   **136**
The International Marketing Environment   **139**
The Social/Cultural Environment   **139**
The Political/Legal Environment   **142**
The Technological Environment   **144**
The Economic Environment   **145**
The Competitive Environment   **145**
Summary   **148**
Marketer's Vocabulary   **148**
Discussion Questions   **149**
Project   **149**
Case Application: Unilever's Global Brand   **149**
References   **150**

CHAPTER SEVEN   *INTRODUCING AND MANAGING THE PRODUCT*   **151**

Introduction   **152**
Defining the Product   **152**
Classification of Products   **154**
Consumer Goods and Industrial Goods   **155**
Goods Versus Services   **157**

Product Planning and Strategy Formulation   **159**
The Determination of Product Objectives   **159**
The Product Plan   **160**
Product Strategies   **161**
Strategies for Developing New Products   **168**
Step 1: Generating New Product Ideas   **173**
Step 2: Screening Product Development Ideas   **175**
Step 3: Business Analysis   **176**
Step 4: Technical and Marketing Development   **178**
Step 5: Manufacturing Planning   **178**
Step 6: Marketing Planning   **178**
Step 7: Test Marketing   **178**
Step 8: Commercialization   **180**
Summary   **182**
Marketer's Vocabulary   **182**
Discussion Questions   **183**
Project   **183**
Case Application: Hershey Chocolate Milk   **183**
References   **184**

CHAPTER EIGHT   *COMMUNICATING TO MASS MARKETS*   **185**

Introduction   **186**
The Role of IMC   **187**
Primary Tasks   **187**
Integrated Marketing Communication   **189**
The Meaning of Marketing Communication   **189**
The Objectives of Marketing Communication   **190**
How We Communicate   **191**
Basic Elements of Communication   **191**
Types of Communication Systems   **193**
Marketing Communications   **194**
Designing an IMC Strategy   **194**
The Promotion Mix   **197**
The Campaign   **198**
Understanding Advertising   **199**
The Organization of Advertising   **199**
The Advertising Agency   **200**
Developing the Creative Strategy   **200**
Developing the Media Plan   **201**
Banner Advertisements   **202**
Sales Promotion and Public Relations   **204**
Sales Promotion: A Little Bit of Everything   **204**
Public Relations: The Art of Maintaining Goodwill   **207**
Personal Selling and the Marketing Communication Mix   **211**
Strengths and Weaknesses of Personal Selling   **218**
The Sales Force of the Future   **219**
Summary   **222**
Marketer's Vocabulary   **222**
Discussion Questions   **223**

Project **224**
Case Application: The Microrecorder **224**
References **225**

CHAPTER NINE *PRICING THE PRODUCT* **226**

Introduction **227**
Price Defined: Three Different Perspectives **227**
  The Customer's View of Price **227**
  Price from a Societal Perspective **228**
  Rational Man Pricing: An Economic Perspective **229**
  Irrational Man Pricing: Freedom Rules **230**
  The Marketer's View of Price **230**
Pricing Objectives **230**
Developing a Pricing Strategy **231**
  Nonprice Competition **232**
  Competitive Pricing **234**
New Product Pricing **235**
Price Lines **237**
Price Flexibility **237**
  Discounts and Allowances **237**
Price Bundling **240**
Psychological Aspects of Pricing **240**
Alternative Approaches to Determining Price **242**
  Cost-Oriented Pricing: Cost-Plus and Mark-Ups **242**
  Break-Even Analysis **243**
  Target Rates of Return **244**
  Demand-Oriented Pricing **244**
  Value-Based Pricing **244**
The Future of Pricing **246**
Summary **248**
Marketer's Vocabulary **248**
Discussion Questions **248**
Project **249**
Case Application: United Techtronics **249**
References **250**

CHAPTER TEN *CHANNEL CONCEPTS: DISTRIBUTING THE PRODUCT* **252**

Introduction **253**
The Dual Functions of Channels **253**
The Evolution of the Marketing Channel **254**
Flows in Marketing Channels **255**
Functions of the Channel **256**
Channel Institutions: Capabilities and Limitations **257**
  Producer and Manufacturer **257**
  Retailing **258**
  Wholesaling **263**
  Physical Distribution **264**

Organizing the Channel **267**
  Conventional Channels **267**
  Vertical Marketing Systems **268**
  Horizontal Channel Systems **268**
The Channel Management Process **269**
  Analyze the Consumer **269**
  Establish the Channel Objectives **270**
  Specify Distribution Tasks **270**
  Evaluate and Select from Channel Alternatives **271**
  Evaluating Channel Member Performance **272**
The Human Aspect of Distribution **273**
  Role **273**
  Communication **273**
  Conflict **274**
  Power **274**
Summary **276**
Marketer's Vocabulary **276**
Discussion Questions **277**
Project **277**
Case Application: Connecting Channel Members **277**
References **278**

PHOTO CREDITS **279**

INDEX **281**

CHAPTER 1

INTRODUCING MARKETING

LEARNING OBJECTIVES

As you read the chapter, you should develop an understanding of the following key marketing concepts:

- The important role marketing can play in the success of an organization.
- Organizations that correctly employ marketing have several common characteristics.
- The various kinds of marketing.
- the strategic workings of marketing components.

ELVIS—ALIVE AND WELL

It's Elvis week in Memphis, and all over town they've got banners: "'20 years/Still Rocking.'" Is it just us, or is it weird to wax so upbeat about the twentieth anniversary of a death? You can't help but feel that the world's got the Elvis Presley it wanted: a changeless, ageless object of contemplation and veneration. Elvis Week culminates in an event called *Elvis—The Concert 2000* in which the man himself, resurrected by video technology, will sing with his living ex-band mates and the Memphis Symphony Orchestra. Who wouldn't secretly prefer this fail-safe digitized spectacle to a weary 62-year-old grinding out "If I Can Dream" one more time?

Twenty years ago, no one close to Elvis could have imagined that his fans would spend over $250 million annually on Elvis dolls, plates, key chains, towels, and wigs—to name just a few items. Two years after Elvis's death, his estate was worth less on paper than it owed in taxes. Then, in 1979, Priscilla Presley, Elvis's ex-wife, was named an executor of the estate for her daughter. The family's crown jewels—Elvis's recordings—had been sold off years earlier and Priscilla had just one chance to save the legacy. She gambled that Elvis's name, image, and likeness were worth something. And she turned his home into a roadside attraction to finance a legal war, fighting for control of all that was Elvis.

Priscilla concluded that there was only one way to save Graceland: sell tickets to the hundreds of gawkers who daily pressed their faces against Elvis's gates. Meanwhile, why not sell some gewgaws to the fans that were already buying cheesy trinkets at the strip mall across the street? Buoyed by an initial investment of $560,000, Graceland's doors were opened to the public in 1982. It took 38 days to recoup their investment; 350,000 visitors walked through the house the first year. "I felt I was betraying Elvis," says Priscilla, recalling her decision to enter the amusement business. "Graceland was

© Elvis Presley Enterprises, Inc.

his pride and joy. But it came down to the reality that I had to open it up for my daughter's future."

Today 750,000 people visit Graceland each year—52% of them under 35, which suggests this is a business with a future. The mansion has upgraded its public facilities many times over the years, but there still are no vending machines on the grounds and the lawns have never been turned into a parking lot. The original 24 acres have been expanded into an 80-acre compound and Priscilla intends to add a hotel to the complex. There are also plans for a casino in Las Vegas—perhaps with an Elvis wedding chapel— and an international chain of Hard Rock Café–style restaurants called *Elvis Presley's Memphis*. Finally, a staff of ten lawyers is employed full-time by Elvis Presley Enterprises simply to protect Elvis's image from interlopers.

Sources: Corie Brown, "Look Who's Taking Care of Business," *Newsweek*, August 18, 1997, p. 62. Karen Schoemer, "Burning Love," *Newsweek*, August 18, 1997, pp. 58–61. G. Brown, "More Early Elvis Unearthed," *The Denver Post*, August 15, 1997, p. 9F. Greg Hassell, "King of Trees Rises From Graceland," *Houston Chronicle*, Dec. 8, 1999, p. 11. Duncan Hughes, "Elvis is Back From the Dead Financially," *Sunday Business*, August 15, 1999, p. 23.

INTRODUCTION

The success of Elvis Presley Enterprises was a result of the insights and courage of Priscilla Presley. Despite her lack of formal training in marketing, she exhibited a creative approach toward doing business that will become more and more necessary as the 21st century continues. Innovative thinking has become a prerequisite for success in today's global environment, which is saturated with near clone products being sold by millions of comparable competitors. The status quo will no longer suffice. The need for constant change paired with clear strategies is now essential.

Marketing constitutes just one of the functions available to every business. Along with research, production, finance, accounting, and a myriad of other functions, marketing contributes to the ability of a business to succeed. In many businesses, marketing may be deemed of highest importance; in others, it may be relegated to a lesser role. The very existence of business depends upon successful products and services, which in turn rely on successful marketing. For this reason, every business person will benefit from even basic marketing knowledge. Moreover, marketing principles have been effectively applied to several nonbusiness institutions for more than 30 years. Bankers, physicians, accounting firms, investment analysts, politicians, churches, architectural firms, universities, and the United Way have all come to appreciate the benefits of marketing.

A word of warning: there is a long-standing myth that marketing is easy. After going through this book you may conclude that marketing is interesting, fun, challenging—even vague—but it is not easy. Whether you like numbers or hate numbers, like people or hate people, like doing the same thing every day or like constant change, there are opportunities for you in marketing.

MARKETING: DEFINITION AND JUSTIFICATION

Defining Marketing

Noted Harvard Professor of Business Theodore Levitt, states that the purpose of all business is to "find and keep customers." Furthermore, the only way you can achieve this objective is to create a *competitive advantage*. That is, you must convince buyers (potential customers) that what you have to offer them comes closest to meeting their particular need or want at that point in time. Hopefully, you will be able to provide this advantage consistently, so that eventually the customer will no longer consider other alternatives and will purchase your product out of habit. This loyal behavior is exhibited by people who drive only Fords, brush their teeth only with Crest, buy only Dell computers, and have their plumbing fixed only by "Samson Plumbing—On Call 24 hours, 7 days a week." Creating this blind commitment—without consideration of alternatives—to a particular brand, store, person, or idea is the dream of all businesses. It is unlikely to occur, however, without the support of an effective marketing program. In fact, the specific role of marketing is to *provide assistance in identifying, satisfying, and retaining customers.*

While the general tasks of marketing are somewhat straightforward, attaching an acceptable definition to the concept has been difficult. A textbook writer once noted, "Marketing is not easy to define. No one has yet been able to formulate a clear, concise definition that finds universal acceptance." Yet a definition of some sort is necessary if we are to lay out the boundaries of what is properly to be considered "marketing." How do marketing activities differ from nonmarketing activities? What activities should one refer to as marketing activities? What institutions should one refer to as marketing institutions?

Marketing is advertising to advertising agencies, events to event marketers, knocking on doors to salespeople, direct mail to direct mailers. In other words, to a person with a hammer, everything looks like a nail. In reality, marketing is a way of thinking about business, rather than a bundle of techniques. It's much more than just selling stuff and collecting money. It's the connection between people and products, customers and companies. Like organic tissue, this kind of connection—or relationship—is always growing or dying. It can never be in a steady state. And like tissue paper, this kind of connection is fragile. Customer relationships, even long-standing ones, are contingent on the last thing that happened.

Tracing the evolution of the various definitions of marketing proposed during the last thirty years reveals two trends: 1) expansion of the application of marketing to non-profit and non-business institutions; e.g., charities, education, or health care; and 2) expansion of the responsibilities of marketing beyond the personal survival of the individual firm, to include the betterment of society as a whole. These two factors are reflected in the official American Marketing Association definition published in 1988.

> *"Marketing is the process of planning and executing the conception, pricing, promotion, and distribution of ideas, goods, and services to create exchanges that satisfy individual (customer) and organizational objectives."*[1]

While this definition can help us better comprehend the parameters of marketing, it does not provide a full picture. Definitions of marketing cannot flesh out specific transactions and other relationships among these elements. The following propositions are offered to supplement this definition and better position marketing within the firm:

1. The overall directive for any organization is the mission statement or some equivalent statement of organizational goals. It reflects the inherent business philosophy of the organization.

2. Every organization has a set of functional areas (e.g., accounting, production, finance, data processing, marketing) in which tasks that are necessary for the success of the organization are performed. These functional areas must be managed if they are to achieve maximum performance.

3. Every functional area is guided by a philosophy (derived from the mission statement or company goals) that governs its approach toward its ultimate set of tasks.

4. Marketing differs from the other functional areas in that its primary concern is with exchanges that take place in markets, outside the organization (called a *transaction*).

5. Marketing is most successful when the philosophy, tasks, and manner of implementing available technology are coordinated and complementary.

Perhaps an example will clarify these propositions: L.L. Bean is an extremely successful mail order company. The organization bases much of its success on its longstanding and straightforward mission statement: "Customer Satisfaction: An L.L. Bean Tradition" (Proposition 1). The philosophy permeates every level of the organization and is reflected in high quality products, fair pricing, convenience, a 100% satisfaction policy and—above all—dedication to customer service (Proposition 2). This philosophy has necessitated a very high standard of production, efficient billing systems, extensive and responsive communication networks, computerization, innovative cost controls, and so forth. Moreover, it has meant that all of these functional areas have to be in constant communication, must be totally coordinated, and must exhibit a level of harmony and mutual respect that creates a positive environment in order to reach shared goals (Proposition 3). The L.L. Bean marketing philosophy is in close harmony with its mission statement. Everything the marketing department does must reinforce and make real the abstract concept of "consumer satisfaction" (Proposition 4). The price-product-quality relationship must be fair. The product must advertise in media that reflects this high quality. Consequently, L.L. Bean adver-

AD 1.1   The website for L.L. Bean represents the newest form of marketing communication.

tises through its direct-mail catalogue and through print ads in prestigious magazines (e.g., *National Geographic*). It also has one of the most highly regarded websites (Ad 1.1). Product selection and design are based upon extensive research indicating the preferences of their customers. Since product delivery and possible product return is critical, marketing must be absolutely sure that both these tasks are performed in accordance with customers' wishes (Proposition 5). While one might argue that the marketing function must be the most important function at L.L. Bean, this is not the case. L.L. Bean is just as likely to lose a customer because of incorrect billing (an accounting function) or a flawed hunting boot (a product function) as it is from a misleading ad (a marketing function).

Admittedly, marketing is often a critical part of a firm's success. Nevertheless, the importance of marketing must be kept in perspective. For many large manufacturers such as Proctor & Gamble, Microsoft, Toyota, and Sanyo, marketing represents a major expenditure, and these businesses depend on the effectiveness of their marketing effort. Conversely, for regulated industries (such as utilities, social services, or medical care or small businesses providing a one-of-a-kind product) marketing may be little more than a few informative brochures. There are literally thousands of examples of businesses—many quite small—that have neither the resources nor the inclination to support an elaborate marketing organization and strategy. These businesses rely less on research than on common sense. In all these cases, the marketing program is worth the costs only if it fits the organization and facilitates its ability to reach its goals.

NEWSLINE: PICTURE YOUR MISSION

Artist Linda Armantrout, owner of Armantrout Graphic Design and Illustration, works with businesses to help them picture their goals—literally—through a "pictorial mission statement."

As opposed to the typical written mission statement that is handed down to employees from management, Armantrout creates a bright watercolor picture of the statement, after receiving input from both employees and managers. The final result is usually a collage of sorts that depicts what is important to the staff and the business—such as clients, products, services, and ethics.

The mission statement picture that Armantrout designs is framed and hung at the company to remind employees of their goals. The pictorial statements also can be put on coffee mugs, jackets, and desktop posters, or turned into screen savers.

One of Armantrout's clients, BancOne Leasing Corporation, came up with a colorful image of a globe surrounded by images representing its clients and services. Drawings of airplanes and buses represent what the company leases and the globe represents its national presence.

Sources: Katie Ford, "Picture Your Goals in Color," *The Denver Business Journal*, March 17–18, 1999, pp. 33A, 35A. Shirleen Holt, "Mission Possible," *Business Week*, August 16, 1999, p. F-12. Teri Lammers, "The Effective and Indispensable Mission Statement," *Inc.*, August, 1999, p. 75.

Justification for Study

This task of determining the appropriateness of marketing for a particular business or institution serves as a major justification for learning about marketing. Although marketing has clearly come of age during the decades of the 1970, 1980s, and 1990s, there is still a great deal of misunderstanding about the meaning and usefulness of marketing. For most of the global public, marketing is still equated with advertising and personal selling. While marketing is both of those, it is also much more.

The business community can attribute a partial explanation for this general lack of understanding about marketing to the uneven acceptance and adoption of marketing. Some businesses still exist in the dark ages when marketing was defined as "the sales department will sell whatever the plant produces." Others have advanced a bit further, in that they have a marketing officer and engage in market research, product development, promotion, and have a long list of marketing activities. More and more businesses firmly believe that the aim of marketing is to make selling superfluous, meaning that the marketer knows and understands the customer so well that the product or service is already what's wanted and sells itself. This does not mean that marketers ignore the engineering and production of the product or the importance of profits. It does suggest, however, that attention to customers—who they are and who they are going to be—is seen to be in the best long-term interest of the company. As a student interested in business, it is beneficial for you to have an accurate and complete comprehension of the role marketing can and should play in today's business world.

There are also several secondary reasons to study marketing. One we have already alluded to in our discussion on definitions: The application of marketing to more nonprofit and nonbusiness institutions is growing. Churches, museums, the United Way, the U.S. Armed Forces, politicians, and others are hiring individuals with marketing expertise. This has opened up thousands of new job opportunities for those with a working knowledge of marketing.

Even if you are not getting a degree in marketing, knowing about marketing will pay off in a variety of careers. Consider the following individuals:

- Paul Moore, an engineer specializing in earth moving equipment, constantly works with product development and sales personnel in order to create superior products.
- Christy Wood, a CPA, is a top tax specialist who spends much of her time maintaining customer relationships, and at least three days a month seeking new customers.
- Steve Jacobson, a systems analyst and expert programmer, understands that his skills must be used to find the right combination of hardware and software for every one of his customers.
- Doris Kelly, a personnel manager, must be skilled at finding, hiring, and training individuals to facilitate her organization's marketing efforts.
- Craig Roberts, an ex-Microsoft engineer, has recently started a dot-com company and is in the process of raising capital.

There are two final factors that justify the study of marketing for nearly every citizen. First of all, we are all consumers and active participants in the marketing network. Understanding the rudiments of marketing will make us better consumers, which in turn will force businesses to do their jobs better. Second, marketing has an impact on society as a whole. Concepts such as trade deficit, embargo, devaluation of a foreign currency, price fixing, deceptive advertising, and product safety take on a whole new meaning when we view them in a marketing context. This knowledge should make you a more enlightened citizen who understands what such social and political issues mean to you and to our society.

Marketing capsules summarize the information throughout this text.

Characteristics of a Marketing Organization

As noted earlier, the application of marketing in a particular organization varies tremendously, ranging from common-sense marketing to marketing departments with thousands of staff members and multimillion-dollar budgets. Yet both may have a great deal in common in respect to how they view the activity called marketing. We refer to these common characteristics as the *Cs of Marketing*. They are your clues that a business understands marketing.

MARKETING CAPSULE *1.1*

1. The purpose of marketing is to help find and keep customers by creating a competitive advantage.
2. Marketing, one of several functions operating in an organization, is directed by the mission statement of the organization and provides certain tools to reach objectives.
3. The value of marketing must be kept in perspective: it must contribute to the growth of the firm.

4. The primary reasons for studying marketing are:
   a. It is important to assess the role marketing should play in the firm.
   b. Marketing offers growing career opportunities.
   c. Marketing enhances our chances of becoming more effective consumers and citizens.

Consumer Content

What makes the existence of any organization possible is that there are a significant number of people who need the product or service offered by that organization. As soon as that group becomes too small, or the need no longer exists, or some other organization can satisfy that need better, the organization will be eliminated. That is the way of a free economy. Thus, a politician doesn't get re-elected, an inner-city church closes its doors, the money needed to cure AIDS is not allocated, and the Vail Ski Resort files for bankruptcy.

In the case of business organizations, and marketing organizations in particular, the people with the needs are called *consumers* or *customers*. In marketing, the act of obtaining a desired object from someone by offering something of value in return is called the *exchange process*. Moreover, the exchange between the person with the need (who gives money or some other personal resource) and the organization selling this need-satisfying thing (a product, service, or idea) is inherently economic, and is called a *transaction*. There tends to be some negotiation between the parties. Individuals on both sides attempt to maximize rewards and minimize costs in their transactions so as to obtain the most profitable outcomes. Ideally, all parties achieve a satisfactory level of reward.

In each transaction, there is an underlying philosophy in respect to how the parties perceive the exchange. Sometimes deception and lying permeate the exchange. Other exchanges may be characterized as equitable, where each party receives about the same as the other—the customer's need is satisfied and the business makes a reasonable profit. With the emergence of the Internet and e-commerce during the 1990s, the nature of the exchange for many businesses and customers has changed dramatically. Today's consumers have access to far more and far better information. They also have many more choices. Businesses must provide a similar level of information and must deal with new competitors that are quicker, smarter, and open 24 hours a day.

An organization that employs marketing correctly knows that keeping customers informed is easier if they keep in constant contact with the customer. This does not necessarily mean that they write and call regularly, although it could. Rather, it more likely means that a marketing organization knows a great deal about the characteristics, values, interests, and behaviors of its customers, and monitors how these factors change over time. Although the process is not an exact science, there is sufficient evidence that marketers who do this well tend to succeed.

When this attempt to know as much about the consumer as possible is coupled with a decision to base all marketing on this information, it is said that the organization is *consumer-oriented* or has adopted the *marketing concept*. It means working back from the customers' needs, rather than forward from the factory's capabilities.

Both historically and currently, many businesses do not follow the marketing concept. Companies such as Texas Instruments and Otis Elevator followed what has been labeled a *production orientation*, where the focus is on technology, innovation, and low production costs. Such companies assume that a technically superior or less expensive product sells itself. There are also companies, such as Amway, where sales and marketing are essentially the same thing. This *sales orientation* assumes that a good salesperson has the capability to sell anything. Often, this focus on the selling process may ignore the consumer or view the consumer as someone to be manipulated. Insightful businesses acknowledge the importance of production and sales, but realize that a three-step process is most effective: (1) continuously collect information about customers' needs and competitors' capabilities; (2) share the information across departments; and (3) use the information to create a competitive advantage by increasing value for customers. This is true marketing.

Company Capabilities

All marketing organizations try to objectively compare their existing capabilities with their ability to meet the consumer's needs now and in the future. Moreover, when deficiencies are found, a good marketing organization must be willing to make changes as quickly as possible. When Toyota realized that their products were not connecting with consumers aged 35 and younger, it decided to take direct action. In 1999, it gathered eight people in their 20s and 30s from around the company into a new, ethnically diverse marketing group called "genesis." Their first assignment was to launch three cars meant to pull in younger buyers: the entry-level ECHO subcompact, a sporty new two-door Celica, and the MR2 Spyder, a racy convertible roadster.[2]

Although assessing company capabilities often begins in the marketing area, all the business functions must be assessed. Do we have the technical know-how to produce a competitive product? Do we have the plant capacity? Do we have the necessary capital? Do we have good top management? A "no" to any of these questions may stymie the marketing effort. Conversely, a strong advantage in cost control or dynamic leadership may provide the company with a competitive marketing advantage that has little to do with marketing, but everything to do with the business succeeding.

Communication

Few doubt that the secret of success in any relationship is communication. This is especially true in a marketing relationship, where the attitude of both parties is frequently skeptical, the nature of the contact is hardly intimate, and the message delivery system tends to be impersonal and imprecise. It's because of these factors that communication plays such an important role in a marketing organization.

Marketers know that consumers are constantly picking up cues put out by the organization, or about the organization, that they use to form attitudes and beliefs about the organization. Many of these message-laden cues are controlled by the organization, including factors such as product design, product quality, price, packaging, outlet selection, advertising, and the availability of coupons. In this case, marketers follow basic communication principles that are discussed throughout this book. Most notably, there is a constant attempt to make sure that all of these elements deliver a consistent message, and that this message is understood and interpreted in the same way by the various consumers.

On the other hand, there are many message-laden cues that are not under the control of the marketer, yet may be more powerful in the minds of consumers, and that must be anticipated and dealt with by the marketers. A recent report that United Air Lines had the worst customer satisfaction scores created a downturn in both United's stock and customer reservations. Although there are many sources delivering such information, the three most prominent are employees, competitors, and the media.

Employees, from the president on down, are all considered representatives of the organization for which they work. Consumers often assume that the behavior, language, or dress of an employee is an accurate reflection of the entire organization. Making employees— and possibly even former employees—positive ambassadors of the organization has become so important that a new term has emerged—*internal marketing*.

Competitors say a great deal about one another, some truths, some boldface lies. A marketing organization must be cognizant of this possibility and be prepared to respond. The automobile industry has used *comparison messaging* for over thirty years. Coke and Pepsi have been attacking and counter-attacking for about the same length of time. Negative political messages appear to be very effective, even though few politicians admit to the strategy.

Finally, the media (editors and reporters working for newspapers, TV and radio stations, and magazines) looms as one of the greatest communication hurdles faced by marketers. In a large marketing organization, the responsibility of communicating with the media is assigned to a public relations staff. Public relations people write press release stories about their organization that they hope the media will use. If the press releases are not used, the marketer attempts to ensure that whatever the media says about the organization is accurate and as complementary as possible. For smaller companies, dealing with the media becomes everyone's responsibility. Many businesses now face a new media, the Internet: chat rooms, websites, and propaganda campaigns intended to destroy a business have become commonplace. Companies that are willing to focus on communication as a means of doing business engage in *relationship marketing*—a type of marketing that builds long-standing positive relationships with customers and other important stakeholder groups. Relationship marketing identifies "high value" customers and prospects and bonds them to the brand through personal attention.

Competition

We have already mentioned the importance that competition plays in a marketing organization. At a minimum, marketing companies must thoroughly understand their competitors' strengths and weaknesses. This means more than making sweeping generalizations about the competitors. It means basing intelligent marketing decisions on facts about how competitors operate and determining how best to respond.

Often the identification of competitors is fairly straightforward. It is the supermarket on the next block, or the three other companies that manufacture replacement windshields. There are instances, however, when the identification of a competitor is not clear. Marketing expert Theodore Levitt coined the term "marketing myopia" several years ago to describe companies that mis-identify their competition.[3] Levitt argued, for example, that the mistake made by the passenger train industry was to restrict their competition to other railroads instead of all mass transit transportation alternatives, including automobiles, airlines, and buses. Today we see the same mistake being made by companies in the entertainment industry (movie theaters, restaurants, and resorts), who assume that their only competition is like-titled organizations.

Since practically no marketer operates as a monopoly, most of the strategy issues considered by a marketer relate to competition. Visualize a marketing strategy as a huge chess game where one player is constantly making his or her moves contingent on what the other player does. Some partners, like Coke and Pepsi, McDonald's and Burger King, and Ford and General Motors, have been playing the game so long that a stalemate is often the result. In fact, the relative market share owned by Coke and Pepsi hasn't changed by more than a percentage or two despite the billions of dollars spent by each on marketing.

The desire of companies to accurately gauge competitors has led to the growing popularity of a separate discipline—*competitive intelligence*. This field involves gathering as much information about competitors through any means possible, usually short of breaking the law. More is said about this process in the Integrated Marketing (IM) box that follows.

Cross-Functional Contact

One of the first mistakes an organization might make is to allow the various functional areas to become proprietary. Whenever a marketing department considers itself most important to the success of the organization and self-sufficient without need for accounting, manufacturing, or human resources, it ceases to be a reliable marketing group. True marketers know that they cannot be any better than their weakest link. Lack of understanding and trust between marketing and manufacturing, for instance, could mean that a product sold by marketing is not delivered when promised or with the right features. Marketers should consider their peers in engineering, who might not be able to produce an ambitious product requested by marketing at the cost desired. Likewise, human resources might not be able to locate the individual "with ten years of experience in package goods marketing" requested by the marketing manager.

The point is that marketing is far more likely to be successful if its staff relate intelligently and honestly with members of the other functional areas. In some organizations, the walls of parochialism have been standing so long that tearing them down is almost impossible. Nevertheless, creating inter-departmental connections is critical.

With downsizing and other cost-cutting activities prevalent during the last decade, the need for inter-related and harmonious business functions has become even more important. In the field of marketing, the term *integrated marketing* has been coined, suggesting that individuals working in traditional marketing departments are no longer specialists, but must become knowledgeable about all the elements of the business that currently or potentially have an impact on the success of marketing. At the corporate level, all managers should share a corporate vision, and there should be an organizational structure that makes it possible for departments or divisions to share information and participate in joint planning.

This approach represents the direction in which many companies are moving, including giants like Kraft and Disney. To be truly integrated, though, every decision at each level of the business should support decisions made at all the other levels. To illustrate, let's say that the corporate goal is to maximize profit. A marketing plan objective to increase sales by marketing new products matches the goal. The previous IM box also illustrates this point.

Community Contact

Most marketers are curious; they enjoy observing and noting what's happening in their community. Although the word "community" usually denotes a city, town, or neighborhood, we use the word here in a much broader sense. "Community" refers to the environment in

---

INTEGRATED MARKETING *1.1*

SPYING TO STAY COMPETITIVE

Most corporate detectives avoid terms like spying and espionage, preferring the more dignified label "competitive intelligence," but whatever they call it, snooping on business rivals has become an entrenched sub-industry.

Nearly every large U.S. company has an intelligence office of some kind. Some, like Motorola, Inc., have units sprinkled in almost all of their outposts around the world. Their assignment is to monitor rivals, sniff out mergers or new technologies that might affect the bottom line, even to keep tabs on morale at client companies. A veteran of the Central Intelligence Agency formed Motorola's intelligence unit, viewed as a model in the business, in 1982.

Corporate intelligence relies on a slew of tools—some sophisticated, many quite basic. On the simpler end of the spectrum, business sleuths do everything from prowling trade-show floors to combing through rivals' web sites and patent office filings. They keep their ears open in airports and aboard flights. But sometimes they go further. They take photographs of competitive factories, and, increasingly, they rely on new data-mining software that permits them to scan the Internet at high speeds for snippets about their rivals.

Sources: Neil King, Jr. and Jess Bravin, "Call It Mission Impossible Inc.—Corporate Spying Firms Thrive," *The Wall Street Journal*, Monday, July 3, 2000, pp. B1, B4; Norm Brodsky, "The First Step," *Inc.*, August, 2000, pp. 37–38; "Spy Practice," *Sunday Times (London)*, July 23, 2000, p. 89; "Competitive Intelligence is Not Corporate Espionage," *Financial News*, June 30, 2000, p. A6.

which the marketer operates. For Esther and Jim Williams, who operate an A&W drive-in in Mattoon, Illinois, community is quite small. For Verizon Communication, community encompasses practically the entire world, extending even to outer space.

Regardless of the scope of the marketer's community, maintaining contact with it is essential. Contact could mean reading the local newspaper and listening to the local gossip. Or it could mean subscribing to information releases of several marketing research firms that monitor world events 24 hours a day, every day. Either might do the job, although the differences in financial costs would be great. In Chapter 3 we discuss some of the more important trends in the world community. Esther and Jim would find this discussion interesting, but not very useful.

Ultimately, to be considered a responsible citizen in the environments in which it operates, marketers have the ongoing task of engaging in only pro-societal activities and conducting business in an ethical manner. There are many marketing companies that donate millions of dollars or land to communities, clean lakes and rivers, revamp deteriorating neighborhoods, give free product to the needy, manage recycling activities, and so forth. There is no doubt that the need for marketing to continue such activities will increase.

The Role of Marketing in the Firm: A Basis for Classification

Marketing is an individualized and highly creative process. Despite the availability of high-powered computers and sophisticated software capable of analyzing massive amounts of data, marketing is still more of an art rather than a science. Each business must customize its marketing efforts in response to its environment and the exchange process. Consequently, no two marketing strategies are exactly the same.

This requirement of marketing to play slightly different roles, depending upon some set of situational criteria, has in turn provided us with a division of marketing into a number of different categories. This is not to imply, however, that there aren't general marketing principles that work in most businesses—there are. There is a right and wrong way to design a package. There are certain advertising strategies that tend to work more often than others. Rather, we are saying that because of certain factors, a business's approach toward marketing and the ensuing strategy will require some modification from the basic plan.

Shown in Table 1.1 are the most common types of marketing categories. Since these various types of marketing will be discussed throughout this text, a brief introduction is provided at this point.

Macromarketing Versus Micromarketing

The division of marketing into macromarketing and micromarketing is a fairly recent one. Initially, the division was a result of the controversy concerning the responsibility of marketing. Should marketing be limited to the success of the individual firm, or should marketing consider the economic welfare of a whole society? Accepting the later, or "macro," point of view dramatically changes the way marketing is carried out. In this light, every marketing decision must be evaluated with regard to how it might positively or negatively affect each person and institution operating in that society. In 1982, Hunt and Burnett surveyed the academic community in order to define more precisely the distinction between macro- and mircomarketing.[4] Their findings suggest that the separation depends upon "what is being studied," "whether it is being viewed from the perspective of society or the firm," and "who receives the consequences of the activity." Examples of macromarketing activities are studying the marketing systems of different nations, the consequences on society of certain marketing actions, and the impact of certain technologies on the marketing trans-

AD 1.2 The pharmaceutical industry tries to maintain contact with consumers.

action. The use of scanners in supermarkets and automatic teller machines in banking illustrates the last example. Micromarketing examples include determining how Nikon Steel should segment its market, recommending how National Jewish Hospital should price their products, and evaluating the success of the "Just Say No" anti-drug campaign.

Service Marketing Versus Goods Marketing

The distinction between services and goods products is not always clear-cut. In general, service products tend to be intangible, are often consumed as they are produced, are difficult

AD 1.3   Hot dogs are goods products and, as such, are marketed differently.

to standardize because they require human labor, and may require the customer to partic-ipate in the creation of the service product.

Goods products tend to be just the opposite in terms of these criteria. Consequently, marketers of service products usually employ a marketing strategy quite different from that of goods marketers. For example, a local family physician creates tangibility by providing an environment: waiting room, examination rooms, diplomas on the walls, that convinces patients that they are receiving good health care. Conversely, coffee producers create intan-gibility in order to appear different from competitors. This is done through colorful pack-

TABLE 1.1 Kinds of Marketing

CLASSIFICATION	EXAMPLE	FACTORS
Macromarketing	The devaluation of the yen	Emphasis of study
Micromarketing	A pricing strategy for Wal-Mart	Perspective, receiver of consequences
Goods marketing	Nabisco International	Tangibility, standardization,
Service marketing	Chase Manhattan Bank	storage, production, involvement
For-profit marketing	Otis Elevator	Concerns for profits
Nonprofit marketing	New York Museum of Art	Tax status
Mass marketing	Sony	Nature of contact,
Direct marketing	*Time* magazine	information,
Internet marketing	trip.com	process for purchasing and delivery
Local marketing	Imperial Garden Restaurant	Proximity of customers,
Regional marketing	Olympia Brewery	geographic area,
National marketing	American Red Cross	extent of distribution,
International marketing	Ford Motor Company	network, marketing
Global marketing	Qwest	variation commitment to country
Consumer goods marketing	Kraft Foods	Nature of customer
Business-to-business marketing	IBM	Product function

aging and advertisements showing people who are successful because they start each day with a cup or two or ten of Starbuck's coffee.

For-profit Marketing Versus Nonprofit Marketing

As the terms connote, the difference between for-profit and nonprofit marketing is in their primary objective. For-profit marketers measure success in terms of profitability and their ability to pay dividends or pay back loans. Continued existence is contingent upon level of profits.

Nonprofit institutions exist to benefit a society, regardless of whether profits are achieved. Because of the implicit objectives assigned to nonprofits, they are subject to an entirely different additional set of laws, notably tax laws. While they are allowed to generate profits, they must use these monies in specific ways in order to maintain their nonprofit status. There are several other factors that require adjustments to be made in the marketing strategies for nonprofits.

Mass Marketing, Direct Marketing, and Internet Marketing

Mass marketing is distinguished from direct marketing in terms of the distance between the manufacturer and the ultimate user of the product. Mass marketing is characterized as having wide separation and indirect communication. A mass marketer, such as Nike, has very little direct contact with its customers and must distribute its product through various retail outlets alongside its competitors. Communication is impersonal, as evidenced by its national television and print advertising campaigns, couponing, and point-of-purchase displays. The success of mass marketing is contingent on the probability that within the huge audience exposed to the marketing strategy, there exist sufficient potential customers interested in the product to make the strategy worthwhile.

Direct marketing establishes a somewhat personal relationship with the customer by first allowing the customer to purchase the product directly from the manufacturer and then communicating with the customer on a first-name basis. This type of marketing is experiencing tremendous growth. Apparently, marketers have tired of the waste associated with mass marketing and customers want more personal attention. Also, modern mechanisms for collecting and processing accurate mailing lists have greatly increased the effectiveness of direct marketing. Catalogue companies (Spiegel, J.C. Penney), telecommunications companies (Sprint), and direct mail companies (Publishers Clearing House) are example of direct marketers. A modified type of direct marketing is represented by companies that allow ordering of product by calling a toll-free number or mailing in an order card as part of an advertisement.

Although (officially), Internet marketing is a type of direct marketing, it has evolved so quickly and demanded the attention of so many companies that a separate section here is warranted. Essentially, Internet technology (which changes by the moment) has created a new way of doing business. In the Internet age, the way consumers evaluate and follow through on their purchase decisions has changed significantly. "Call now!" is no longer an effective pitch. Consumers have control over how, when, and where they shop on the Inter-

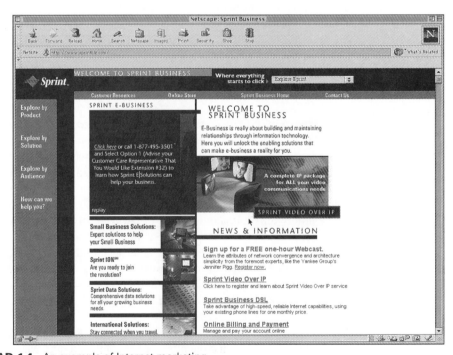

AD 1.4 An example of Internet marketing.

net. The Internet has all but eliminated the urgency of satisfying the need when the opportunity is presented. Internet marketing will be discussed in detail in a later chapter.

Local, Regional, National, International, and Global Marketers

As one would expect, the size and location of a company's market varies greatly. Local marketers are concerned with customers that tend to be clustered tightly around the marketer. The marketer is able to learn a great deal about the customer and make necessary changes quickly. Naturally, the total potential market is limited. There is also the possibility that a new competitor or environmental factor will put a local marketer out of business.

Regional marketers cover a larger geographic area that may necessitate multiple production plants and a more complex distribution network. While regional marketers tend to serve adjoining cities, parts of states, or entire states, dramatic differences in demand may still exist, requiring extensive adjustments in marketing strategy.

National marketers distribute their product throughout a country. This may involve multiple manufacturing plants, a distribution system including warehouses and privately owned delivery vehicles, and different versions of the marketing "mix" or overall strategy. This type of marketing offers tremendous profit potential, but also exposes the marketer to new, aggressive competitors.

International marketers operate in more than one country. As will become clear later in this book, massive adjustments are normally made in the marketing mix in various countries. Legal and cultural differences alone can greatly affect a strategy's outcome. As the U.S. market becomes more and more saturated with U.S.-made products, the continued expansion into foreign markets appears inevitable.

Global marketing differs from international marketing in some very definite ways. Whereas international marketing means a company sells its goods or services in another country, it does not necessarily mean that the company has made any further commitments. Usually the product is still manufactured in the home country, sold by their people, and the profits are taken back to that country. In the case of Honda Motors, for example, it means building manufacturing plants in the U.S., hiring local employees, using local distribution systems and advertising agencies, and reinvesting a large percentage of the profits back into the U.S.

Consumer Goods Marketing and Business-to-Business (Industrial) Marketing

Consumer goods marketers sell to individuals who consume the finished product. Business-to-business marketers sell to other businesses or institutions that consume the product in turn as part of operating the business, or use the product in the assembly of the final product they sell to consumers. Business-to-business marketers engage in more personal selling rather than mass advertising and are willing to make extensive adjustments in factors such as the selling price, product features, terms of delivery, and so forth.

For the consumer goods marketer, the various marketing components are relatively fixed. In addition, consumer goods marketers might employ emotional appeals and are faced with the constant battle of getting their product into retail outlets.

Strategic Components of Marketing

A necessary and useful starting point for the study of marketing is consideration of the management process. The management of marketing serves as the framework for the process of marketing. Marketing management also serves as a central link between marketing and the societal level and everyday consumption by the general public. Although there are many variations of the marketing process, the one shown in Figure 1.1 will be employed in this book. Our process begins with corporate-level considerations, which dictate the direction the entire organization will take. The three corporate-level considerations listed here (mission, objectives, and strategy) are more precisely basic management topics, but are addressed in passing in the following sections.

Functional-Level Considerations

If a marketing firm is to adopt the customer-centered orientation discussed earlier, it must also extend this philosophy to the other functions/institutions with which it must interact. These functions, and the institutions that perform the functions, can be categorized as nonmarketing institutions and marketing institutions.

Nonmarketing institutions can exist within the organization or outside the organization. The former include accounting, financial planning, human resources, engineering, manufacturing, research and development, and so on. Marketing must be familiar with the capabilities of each of these functions and plan accordingly. Establishing and maintaining rapport with leaders in these other functional areas is a challenge for every marketer. Nonmarketing institutions outside the firm facilitated the marketing process by providing expertise in areas not directly related to marketing. Examples include financial institutions that lend marketers necessary funds; regulatory institutions that pass laws to allow marketers to perform an activity; and the press, which tells the public about the activities of the marketer.

The Marketing Plan

To a great extent, the same sequence of activities performed at the corporate level is repeated at the marketing level. The primary difference is that the marketing plan is directly influenced by the corporate plan as well as the role of the other functions within the organization. Consequently, the marketing plan must always involve monitoring and reacting to changes in the corporate plan.

Apart from this need to be flexible to accommodate the corporate plan, the marketing plan follows a fairly standardized sequence. The marketing plan begins with a mission. A mission reflects the general values of the organization. What does it stand for? How does it define integrity? How does it view the people it serves? Every organization has an explicit

MARKETING CAPSULE 1.2

The characteristics of a marketing organization include:

1. Maintenance of contact with consumers
2. Objective comparison of existing capabilities with ability to meet present and future consumer needs
3. Maintenance of a consistent message from all marketing elements to all consumer groups
4. Thorough understanding of strengths and weaknesses of competitors
5. Understanding of the capabilities of other nonmarketing functions
6. Attempts at familiarity with the community

The types of marketing:

1. Macromarketing and micromarketing
2. Service marketing and goods marketing
3. For-profit marketing and nonprofit marketing
4. Mass marketing, direct marketing, and Internet marketing
5. Local, regional, national, and international marketing
6. Consumer goods marketing and business-to-business marketing

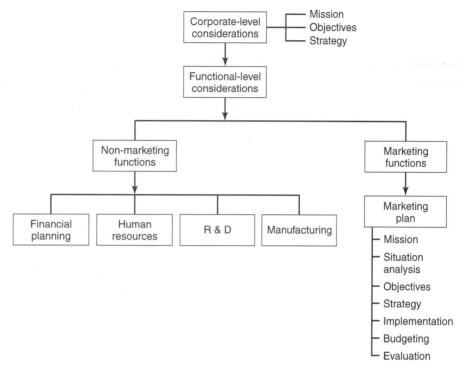

FIGURE 1.1 The marketing process

or implicit mission. The corporate mission might contain words such as "quality," "global," "profitability," and "sacrifice." The marketing-level mission should extend the corporate mission by translating the latter into a marketing context. For example, a corporate mission that focuses on technology might be accompanied by a production-oriented marketing mission. A corporation that stresses stockholders/dividends may result in a sales-orientation in marketing. A corporate mission that concentrates on value or quality reflects a consumer-oriented marketing mission. Once the mission is established, the situation analysis follows.

A marketing plan's *situation analysis* identifies factors, behaviors, and trends that have a direct bearing on the marketing plan. Much of this information is usually collected simultaneously with the corporate information. However, collecting information about potential and actual customers tends to be the concern of marketers. This is an ongoing activity and represents a great deal of the marketer's time and money. (Chapter 2 describes the process of marketing research.)

The situation analysis helps produce a relevant set of marketing objectives. At the corporate level, typical objectives include profitability, cost savings, growth, market share improvement, risk containment, reputation, and so on. All these corporate objectives can imply specific marketing objectives. "Introducing a certain number of new products usually" may lead marketers to profitability, increased market share, and movement into new markets. Desire to increase profit margins might dictate level of product innovation, quality of materials, and price charged.

The Marketing Mix

Once the objectives are established, the marketer must decide how to achieve these objectives. This produces a set of general strategies that must be refined into actionable and achievable activities. The *marketing mix*—product, price, promotion, and distribution—represents the way in which an organization's broad marketing strategies are translated into marketing programs for action.

Product   Products (and services)—the primary marketing mix element that satisfied customer wants and needs—provide the main link between the organization and its customers. Marketing organizations must be ready to alter products as dictated by changes in competitive strategies or changes in other elements of the organization's environment. Many organizations have a vast array of products in their mix. Ideally, each of the products is profitable. But this is often not the case, so some tough decisions must be made concerning the length of time an unsuccessful product is kept on the market.

Distribution   The organization's distribution system moves the product to the final consumer. Because there are many alternatives when selecting a distribution channel, marketing management must have a clear understanding of the types of distributors, of the trends influencing those distributors, and of how those distributors are perceived by customers.

Communication (Promotion)   The product's benefits must be communicated to the distributors and to the final customers. Therefore, the marketing organization must provide marketing information that is received favorably by distributors and final customers. Marketing organizations, through promotion, provide information by way of advertising, sales promotions, salespeople, public relations, and packaging.

Price   Finally, marketers must price their products in such a way that customers believe they are receiving fair value. Price is the primary means by which customers judge the attractiveness of a product or service. Moreover, price is a reflection of all the activities of an organization. Finally, price is a competitive tool, in that it is used as a basis for comparison of product and perceived value across different organizations.

Decisions about the marketing mix variables are interrelated. Each of the marketing mix variables must be coordinated with the other elements of the marketing program. Consider, for a moment, a situation in which a firm has two product alternatives (deluxe and economy), two price alternatives ($6 and $3), two promotion alternatives (advertising and couponing), and two distribution alternatives (department stores and specialty stores). Taken together, the firm has a total of 16 possible marketing mix combinations. Naturally, some of these appear to be in conflict, such as the "deluxe" product/low price combination. Nevertheless, the organization must consider many of the possible alternative marketing programs. The problem is magnified by the existence of competitors. The organization must find the right combination of product, price, promotion, and distribution so that it can gain a differential advantage over its competitors. (All the marketing mix elements will be discussed in more detail in later chapters of this book.)

Even a well-designed marketing program that has been through a thorough evaluation of alternatives will fail if its implementation is poor. *Implementation* involves such things as determining where to promote the product, getting the product to the ultimate consumer, putting a price on the product, and setting a commission rate for the salespeople. Once a decision is made, a marketing manager must decide how to best implement the terms of the plan.

Scandinavian Airlines (SAS) provides a good example of an organization that has successfully implemented their marketing strategy. SAS had good on-time performance, a good safety record, and many services designed to make flying easier for its customers. However, these were not enough to improve SAS revenue. Other things had to be done to attract business-class customers. The approach taken by SAS was largely symbolic in nature. They put everyone who bought a full-price ticket in "Euroclass," entitling them to use a special boarding card, an executive waiting lounge, designer steel cutlery, and a small napkin clip that could be taken as a collector's item. These and other values were provided at no extra cost to the customer. The approach was very successful; business class passengers flocked to SAS, since they appreciated the perceived increase in value for the price of a ticket.

The Budget

Marketing mix components must be evaluated as part of an overall marketing strategy. Therefore, the organization must establish a marketing budget based on the required marketing effort to influence consumers. The marketing budget represents a plan to allocate expenditures to each of the components of the marketing mix. For example, the firm must establish an advertising budget as part of the marketing budget and allocate expenditures to various types of advertising media—television, newspapers, magazines. A sales promotion budget should also be determined, allocating money for coupons, product samples, and trade promotions. Similarly, budgets are required for personal selling, distribution, and product development.

How much should be spent? Consider the following example. A common question that marketers frequently ask is, "Are we spending enough (or too much) to promote the sale of our products?" A reasonable answer would revolve around another consideration: "What do we want to accomplish? What are our goals?" The discussion should next turn to the methods for achievement of goals and the removal of obstacles to these goals. This step is often skipped or avoided.

Usually, when the question is asked, "Are we spending enough?" an automatic answer is given, in terms of what others spend. Knowing what others in the same industry spend can be important to an organization whose performance lags behind the competition or to an organization that suspects that its expenditures are higher than they need to be. But generally, knowing what others spend leads to an unproductive "keeping-up-with-the-Joneses" attitude. It also assumes that the others know what they are doing.

Evaluating Results

No marketing program is planned and implemented perfectly. Marketing managers will tell you that they experience many surprises during the course of their activities. In an effort to ensure that performance goes according to plans, marketing managers establish controls that allow marketers to evaluate results and identify needs for modifications in marketing strategies and programs. Surprises occur, but marketing managers who have established sound control procedures can react to surprises quickly and effectively.

Marketing control involves a number of decisions. One decision is what functions to monitor. Some organizations monitor their entire marketing program, while others choose to monitor only a part of it, such as their sales force or their advertising program. A second set of decisions concerns the establishment of standards for performance; e.g., market share, profitability, or sales. A third set of decisions concerns how to collect information for making comparisons between actual performance and standards. Finally, to the extent that discrepancies exist between actual and planned performance, adjustments in the marketing program or the strategic plan must be made.

Once a plan is put into action, a marketing manager must still gather information related to the effectiveness with which the plan was implemented. Information on sales, profits, reactions of consumers, and reactions of competitors must be collected and analyzed so that a marketing manager can identify new problems and opportunities.

KEYS TO MARKETING SUCCESS

A prime guideline for marketing success is to realize that establishing customer satisfaction should be the company's number-one priority. The only people who really know what customers want are the customers themselves. A company that realizes this will develop a marketing mentality that facilitates information gathering and maintains effective communication with the primary reason for the company's existence: the customer.

A second guideline is to establish a company image that clearly reflects the values and aspirations of the company to employees, customers, intermediaries, and the general public. Philips Petroleum has done this for years with their advertising campaign that focuses on how their company benefits society.

Third, while marketing requires work that is clearly distinct from other business activities, it should be central to the entire organization. Marketing is the aspect of the business that customers see. If they see something they do not like, they look elsewhere.

Fourth, the business should develop a unique strategy that is consistent with the circumstances that it faces. The marketer must adapt basic marketing principles to the unique product being sold. This means that what General Foods does may not work for GTE because one is inherently a goods product and the other a service product. And neither will work for the State of Kentucky's Parks and Recreation Department, because that is a public, nonprofit organization. In other words, imitating what other organizations do without fully understanding one's own situation is a dangerous strategy.

Finally, technological progress dictates how marketing will be performed in the future. Because of computer technology inventiveness, both consumers and businesses are better informed. Knowledge is the most important competitive advantage. The world is one market, and information is changing at light-speed.

MARKETING CAPSULE *1.3*

1. The components of marketing management are as follows:
   a. Corporate-level considerations include the organization's mission and objectives.
   b. Functional-level considerations include nonmarketing institutions and marketing institutions.
   c. Marketing-level considerations include the mission, the situation analysis, objectives, strategy, implementation, budget, and evaluation.
   d. The marketing mix includes the primary tools available to the marketer: product, distribution, promotion, and price.

2. The keys to marketing success are:
   a. Satisfy the customer.
   b. Establish a clear company image.
   c. Make marketing central to the organization.
   d. Be proactive.
   e. Develop a strategy consistent with the situation.

THE WALL STREET JOURNAL.

IN PRACTICE

Marketing plays a critical role in the success of business organizations: it helps them create a competitive advantage. By continuously collecting information about customers' needs and competitors' capabilities and by sharing this information across departments, business organizations can create a competitive advantage by increasing value for customers.

Individuals working in marketing departments must be knowledgeable about all the elements of the business that impact the success of marketing efforts. Marketing objectives are directed by an organization's mission statement, and marketers use a set of strategies to achieve these objectives.

Implementation is critical to a marketing plan's success; therefore, the marketing budget allocates expenditures for each of the components of the marketing mix. Marketing success depends on several factors, the most important of which is establishing customer satisfaction as the #1 priority.

TAKE A TOUR

The Front Section of the Interactive Journal (wsj.com) is similar to the front page of the newspaper version of *The Wall Street Journal*. The left column displays the menu selection, with the five major sections listed at the top. These five sections are:

1. Front Section
2. Marketplace
3. Money & Investing
4. Tech Center
5. Personal Journal

The menu remains on the page as you navigate through the site, allowing you to return to the Front Section at any time.

Articles related to marketing are typically found in the **Marketplace** section. Click on **Marketplace** now to view today's articles. Just below the main menu on the left side, a smaller menu titled **In this Section . . .** appears, listing main header topics in **Marketplace**. One of the topics is **Marketing/Media**. Visit this section now to read today's articles.

Chapter 1, *Introducing Marketing*, provides and overview of the importance and functions of marketing in business organizations. Marketing takes many forms, and evolves with new technologies. Marketing on the Internet, also known as e-commerce marketing, provides challenges and opportunities for marketers. Visit Volkswagen's website, www.vw.com, to see how the company has extended its marketing efforts from television and print to its website.

DELIVERABLE

Search the Interactive Journal for articles about e-commerce marketing. Under **Journal Atlas**, click on **Search** to conduct a search using key words like e-commerce, Internet, and marketing. Use the **Business Index** feature to search for articles on specific companies. Search the **Business Index** now to find articles on Volkswagen.

DISCUSSION QUESTIONS

1. Some marketers believe the Internet will become the most effective avenue for marketing products to consumers. Do you agree or disagree?

2. Recently, the effectiveness of online marketing efforts has been questioned. What can marketers do to measure the success of online marketing?

3. What advantages does receiving the *Wall Street Journal* online provide for users? Specifically, marketers?

SUMMARY

This introductory chapter described marketing as one of the major strategic tools available to the business organization. It began with a basic definition and expanded to a set of propositions of marketing. Simply, marketing is based on the mission statement of the organization; is dependent on the effective management of other functional areas; contains a functional area guided by its own philosophy; is the functional area that is concerned with market exchanges; and is likely to be successful when the philosophy, tasks, and manner of implementing available technology are coordinated and complimentary.

The chapter also discussed several characteristics shared by organizations that correctly implement marketing. Referred to as the Cs of marketing, they include consumer contact, company capabilities, communication, cross-functional contact, and community contact. Companies share these characteristics; the following factors divide marketing into specific types: macromarketing and micromarketing; services and goods marketing; for-profit and nonprofit marketing; mass and direct marketing; local, regional, national, and international marketing; and consumer goods and business-to-business marketing.

The chapter concluded with a discussion of the four levels of strategic management with considerations applicable to marketing: corporate, functional, marketing, and marketing mix.

MARKETER'S VOCABULARY

Marketing   The process of planning and executing the conception, pricing, and distribution of ideas, goods, and services to create exchanges that satisfy individual and organizational objectives.

Consumer/customers   Individuals who have needs/wants that can be satisfied by the marketer's product or service.

Transaction   An exchange between the person with the need and the organization selling the need-satisfying thing, inherently economic-based.

Internal marketing   Attempting to ensure that all employees are positive ambassadors of the organization.

Competitive advantage   Convince buyers (potential customers) that what you have to offer them comes closest to meeting their particular want or need at that point in time.

Marketing concept   Understanding the consumer and working from the customer back rather than factory forward.

DISCUSSION QUESTIONS

1. How would you have defined marketing before you read this chapter? How does that definition differ from the definition provided?

2. Can you think of another organization that demonstrates the propositions of marketing as well as L.L. Bean? Provide a similar discussion using that organization.

3. What are the factors to consider in maintaining consumer contact? Community contact?

4. Why is it so important to understand your competition? Company functions?

5. Contrast macro- and micromarketing. Contrast services and goods marketing.

6. Demonstrate how the corporate mission can directly influence marketing.

7. What is the difference between the internal and external environment? Provide five examples of each.[2]

8. What is a competitive advantage? How does marketing contribute to the creation of a competitive advantage?

9. Discuss the reasons for studying marketing.

10. Give examples of how marketing communication differs from personal communication.

PROJECT

Survey 10 nonbusiness students and ask them to provide a definition of marketing. Analyze these answers with respect to how they differ and why people differed in their understanding of this topic. Write a five-page report explaining.

CASE APPLICATION

THE HOG IS ALIVE AND WELL

After making a remarkable comeback in the 1980s, motorcycle manufacturer Harley-Davidson had two-year-long waiting lists all over the country. But the success placed the company in a familiar quandary. Should Harley expand and risk a market downturn or should it stay the course, content with its good position in the industry?

"To invest or not to invest, that was the question," notes Frank Cimermancic, Harley's Director of Business Planning. "Dealers were begging us to build more motorcycles. But you have to understand our history. One of the things that caused past problems was lack of quality, and that was the result of a too-rigid expansion. We did not want to relive that situation."

In 1989, the reputation of Harley-Davidson was excellent. Harley shipped 30,000 motorcycles in 1985; just four years later it shipped 44,000. Harley's market share in the heavyweight bike category went from 27% to 57% during the same time period. It was regularly turning a profit—$53 million in 1989.

At the same time, however, the market for heavyweight bikes was shrinking. Harley-Davidson needed to know whether its growth could continue. "We were doing fine, but look at the market," said Cimermancic. "Maybe, we thought, we could reverse these trends and become an industry leader, something we hadn't been for years."

A new kind of customer seemed to hold the key to market growth. White-collar motorcycle enthusiasts, or "Rubbies" (rich urban bikers), started to shore up Harley sales in the mid-1980s, adding to the company's success and image. But whether these people were reliable, long-term customers was another question. Harley also needed to know if it should market its product differently to different audiences. A core clientele of traditional "bikers" had kept Harley afloat during its leanest years, and they could not be alienated.

From their research, Harley identified seven core customer types: the Adventure-Loving Traditionalist, the Sensitive Pragmatist, the Stylish Status-Seeker, the Laid-Back Camper, the Classy Capitalist, the Cool-Headed Loner, and the Cocky Misfit. All of them appreciated Harley-Davidson for the same reasons: independence, freedom, and power constituted the universal Harley appeal. Also, owners were very loyal.

Loyalty meant the company could build and sell more motorcycles without having to overextend itself. In 1990, Harley expanded to build 62,800 bikes; in 2000, it built more than 180,000. Based on research and the still-expanding waiting lists, Harley expects its phenomenal growth to continue. In addition, Harley is expanding its product line. In early 2000, the company introduced a $4,400 bike called the Blast, aimed at first-time riders and women.

Sources: Ian P. Murphy, "Aided by Research, Harley Goes Whole Hog," *The Marketing News*, December 2, 1996, p. 16; Richard A. Melcher, "Tune-up Time for Harley," *Business Week*, April 8, 1996, pp. 90, 94; Kelly Barron, "Hog Wild," *Forbes*, May 15, 2000, pp. 68–70.

Questions:

1. Identify the ways in which Harley-Davidson exhibits the propositions discussed in this chapter.

2. Would you consider Harley to be a marketing organization? Why or why not?

REFERENCES

1. *Dictionary of Marketing Terms*, Peter D. Bennett, Ed., American Marketing Association, 1988, p. 54.
2. "A New Recipe for the Family Dinner," *Adweek*, April 27, 1992, p. 46.
3. Theodore Levitt, "Marketing Myopia," *Harvard Business Review*, July–August, 1960, pp. 45–66.
4. Shelby D. Hunt and John J. Burnett, "The Macromarketing/Micromarketing Dichotomy: A Taxonomical Model," *Journal of Marketing*, Summer, 1982, pp. 11–26.

UNDERSTANDING AND APPROACHING THE MARKET

LEARNING OBJECTIVES

After studying this chapter, you should be able to:

- Understand the role of the market in the exchange process.
- Distinguish between the basic kinds of markets.
- Appreciate the differences between the undifferentiated and segmental approach toward markets.
- Understand the various bases for market segmentation.
- Translate segmentation concepts into the activity of selecting a target market.

THE WEB SEGMENT

Online advertising is still a relatively tiny market, but an increasing number of companies are vying for the right to tell advertisers and their ad agencies where and how to responsibly spend their limited pool of Web ad dollars.

Easier said than done. No reliable measurements exist for determining the size of the Web audience, leaving advertisers to sort through a dizzying number of competing claims from different web sites. The creator of a system that catches on with advertisers has a big opportunity: the chance to become the Nielsen of the Internet.

The latest entrant in the race to accurately count Web viewers: Relevant.Knowledge, an Atlanta-based company founded by former Turner Broadcasting executives and staffed with research executives with experience counting eyeballs in traditional media like television and radio. This company provides standardized, detailed demographic data and faster feedback about Web viewing, among other services. Relevant.Knowledge has been delivering data on a test basis to companies including CNN, Sony, c|NET, and Microsoft's MSN Network.

Relevant.Knowledge is taking aim at one of the biggest issues bedeviling online advertisers and publishers: a dearth of reliable information that advertisers can use to justify buying ads on the Web. So far, advertisers have been caught in a culture clash between technology buffs and traditional researchers. The result: not enough data that can be applied to multiple web sites. Individual sites provide information about the number of visitors they receive, but such results can't easily be compared to what other sites may be supplying. And most sites can't distinguish one person visiting the same site over and over again from a new visitor. Instead, media buyers have had to rely on more primitive tools, like reports about what competitors are spending and where.

Sources: Al Urbansky, "Escape To The Net," *Promo*, February 2000, pp. 21–22; Heather Green, "Getting Too Personal," *Business Week e.biz*, February 7, 2000, p. EB14; "You've got Spam," *American Demographics*, September 1999, p. 22; Christine LeBeau, "Cracking the Niche," *American Demographics*, June 2000, pp. 38–39.

INTRODUCTION

Knowing your market accurately and completely is a prerequisite for successful marketing. This task is made even more difficult for companies trying to advertise on the Web. Yet, as noted earlier, this trend toward using the Internet will continue. Three important concepts related to the topic of markets are presented in this chapter: defining the nature of markets, identifying the types of markets, and a discussion of product differentiation and market segmentation.

DEFINING THE MARKET

The market can be viewed from many different perspectives, and, consequently, is impossible to define precisely. In order to provide some clarity, we provide a basic definition of a market: *A group of potential buyers with needs and wants and the purchasing power to satisfy them.* Rather than attempting to cut through the many specialized uses of the term, it is more meaningful to describe several broad characteristics and use this somewhat ambiguous framework as the foundation for a general definition.

The Market Is People

Since exchange involves two or more people, it is natural to think of the market as people, individuals, or groups. Clearly, without the existence of people to buy and consume goods, services, and ideas, there would be little reason for marketing. Yet this perspective must be refined further if it is to be useful.

People constitute markets only if they have overt or latent wants and needs. That is, individuals must currently recognize their need or desire for an existing or future product, or have a *potential* need or desire for an existing or future product. While the former condition is quite straightforward, the latter situation is a bit more confusing, in that it forces the marketer to develop new products that satisfy unmet needs. Potential future customers must be identified and understood.

When speaking of markets as people, we are not concerned exclusively with individual ultimate consumers. Although individuals and members of households do constitute the most important and largest category of markets, business establishments and other organized behavior systems also represent valid markets. People, individually or in groups, businesses, and institutions create markets.

However, people or organizations must meet certain basic criteria in order to represent a valid market:

1. There must be a true need and/or want for the product, service, or idea; this need may be recognized, unrecognized, or latent.

2. The person/organization must have the ability to pay for the product via means acceptable to the marketer.

3. The person/organization must be willing to buy the product.

4. The person/organization must have the authority to buy the product.

5. The total number of people/organizations meeting the previous criteria must be large enough to be profitable for the marketer.

All five criteria must be met for an aggregate group of people or organizations to equate to a market. Failure to achieve even one of the criteria may negate the viability of a market. An interesting example is the pharmaceutical industry. There are several serious human diseases that remain uncured only because they have not been contracted by a large enough number of people to warrant the necessary research. The excessive research costs required to develop these drugs necessitates that companies are assured a certain level of profitability. Even though the first four criteria may be met, a small potential customer base means no viable market exists.

The Market Is a Place

Thinking of the market as a place—"the marketplace"—is a common practice of the general public. Such locations do exist as geographical areas within which trading occurs. In this context, we can think of world markets, international markets, American markets, regions, states, cities, and parts of cities. A shopping center, a block, a portion of a block, and even the site of a single retail store can be called a market.

While not as pervasive as the "people" component of the market, the "place" description of a market is important too. Since goods must be delivered to and customers attracted toward particular places where transactions are made, this identification of markets is useful for marketing decision-making purposes. Factors such as product features, price, location of facilities, routing salespeople, and promotional design are all affected by the geographic market. Even in the case of unmeasurable fields, such as religion, a marketplace might be Yankee Stadium, where Billy Graham is holding a revival. Finally, a market may be somewhere other than a geographical region, such as a catalogue or ad that allows you to place an order without the assistance of a marketing intermediary or an 800 number.

The Market Is an Economic Entity

In most cases, a market is characterized by a dynamic system of economic forces. The four most salient economic forces are supply, demand, competition, and government intervention. The terms *buyer's market* and *seller's market* describe different conditions of bargaining strength. We also use terms such as *monopoly*, *oligopoly*, and *pure competition* to reflect the competitive situation in a particular market. Finally, the extent of personal freedom and government control produces free market systems, socialistic systems, and other systems of trade and commerce.[1]

Again, placing these labels on markets allows the marketer to design strategies that match a particular economic situation. We know, for instance, that in a buyer's market, there is an abundance of product, prices are usually low, and customers dictate the terms of sale. U.S. firms find that they must make tremendous strategy adjustments when they sell their products in Third World markets. The interaction of these economic factors is what creates a market.

There is always the pressure of competition as new firms enter and old ones exit. Advertising and selling pressure, price and counterprice, claim and counterclaim, service and extra service are all weapons of competitive pressure that marketers use to achieve and protect market positions. Market composition is constantly changing.

TYPES OF MARKETS

Now that we have defined markets in a general sense, it is useful to discuss the characteristics of the primary types of markets: (1) consumer markets, (2) industrial markets, (3) institutional markets, and (4) reseller markets. It should be noted that these categories are not always clear-cut. In some industries, a business may be in a different category altogether or may even encompass multiple categories. It is also possible that a product may be sold in all four markets. Consequently, it is important to know as much as possible about how these markets differ so that appropriate marketing activities can be developed.

Consumer Markets

When we talk about *consumer markets*, we are including those individuals and households who buy and consume goods and services for their own personal use. They are not interested in reselling the product or setting themselves up as a manufacturer. Considering the thousands of new products, services, and ideas being introduced each day and the increased capability of consumers to afford these products, the size, complexity, and future growth potential of the consumer market is staggering. The next chapter, Chapter 3, touches on many of these issues.

Industrial Markets

The *industrial market* consists of organizations and the people who work for them, those who buy products or services for use in their own businesses or to make other products. For example, a steel mill might purchase computer software, pencils, and flooring as part of the operation and maintenance of their business. Likewise, a refrigerator manufacturer might purchase sheets of steel, wiring, shelving, and so forth, as part of its final product.[2] These purchases occur in the industrial market.

There is substantial evidence that industrial markets function differently than do consumer markets and that the buying process in particular is different.

Institutional Markets

Another important market sector is made up of various types of profit and nonprofit institutions, such as hospitals, schools, churches, and government agencies. *Institutional markets* differ from typical businesses in that they are not motivated primarily by profits or market share. Rather, institutions tend to satisfy somewhat esoteric, often intangible, needs. Also, whatever profits exist after all expenses are paid are normally put back into the institution. Because institutions operate under different restrictions and employ different goals, marketers must use different strategies to be successful.

Reseller Markets

All intermediaries that buy finished or semi-finished products and resell them for profit are part of the *reseller market*. This market includes approximately 383,000 wholesalers and 1,300,000 retailers that operate in the U.S. With the exception of products obtained directly from the producer, all products are sold through resellers. Since resellers operate under unique business characteristics, they must be approached carefully. Producers are always cognizant of the fact that successful marketing to resellers is just as important as successful marketing to consumers.

AD 2.1 The Olympus camera is part of the consumer market.

APPROACHING THE MARKET

All the parties in an exchange usually have the ability to select their exchange partner(s). For the customer, whether consumer, industrial buyer, institution, or reseller, product choices are made daily. *For a product provider, the person(s) or organization(s) selected as potential customers are referred to as the **target market**.* A product provider might ask: given that my product will not be needed and/or wanted by all people in the market, and given that my

AD 2.2   An example of an institutional ad.

organization has certain strengths and weaknesses, which target group within the market should I select? The process is depicted in Figure 2.1.

For a particular product, marketing organizations might follow an undifferentiated, segmentation, or combination approach toward a market. These concepts are explained in the following sections.

The Undifferentiated Market (Market Aggregation)

The undifferentiated approach occurs when the marketer ignores the apparent differences that exist within the market and uses a marketing strategy that is intended to appeal to as

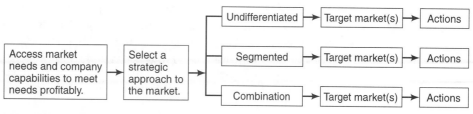

FIGURE 2.1 Approaches to the market

many people as possible. In essence, the market is viewed as a homogeneous aggregate. Admittedly, this assumption is risky, and there is always the chance that it will appeal to no one, or that the amount of waste in resources will be greater than the total gain in sales.

For certain types of widely consumed items (e.g., gasoline, soft drinks, white bread), the undifferentiated market approach makes the most sense. One example was the campaign in which Dr. Pepper employed a catchy general-appeal slogan, "Be A PEPPER!", that really said nothing specific about the product, yet spoke to a wide range of consumers. Often, this type of general appeal is supported by positive, emotional settings, and a great many reinforcers at the point-of-purchase. Walk through any supermarket and you will observe hundreds of food products that are perceived as nearly identical by the consumer and are treated as such by the producer—especially knock-off or generic items.

Identifying products that have a universal appeal is only one of many criteria to be met if an undifferentiated approach is to work. The number of consumers exhibiting a need for the identified product must be large enough to generate satisfactory profits. A product such as milk would probably have universal appeal and a large market; something like a set of dentures might not. However, adequate market size is not an absolute amount and must be evaluated for each product.

Two other considerations are important: the per unit profit margin and the amount of competition. Bread has a very low profit margin and many competitors, thus requiring a very large customer base. A product such as men's jockey shorts delivers a high profit but has few competitors.

Success with an undifferentiated market approach is also contingent on the abilities of the marketer to correctly identify potential customers and design an effective and competitive strategy. Since the values, attitudes, and behaviors of people are constantly changing, it is crucial to monitor these changes. Introduce numerous cultural differences, and an extremely complex situation emerges. There is also the possibility that an appeal that is pleasing to a great diversity of people may not then be strong or clear enough to be truly effective with any of these people.

Finally, the competitive situation might also promote an undifferentiated strategy. All would agree that Campbell's dominates the canned soup industry, and that there is little reason for them to engage in much differentiation. Clearly, for companies that have a very large share of the market, undifferentiated market coverage makes sense. For a company with small market share, it might be disastrous.[3]

Product Differentiation

Most undifferentiated markets contain a high level of competition. How does a company compete when all the product offerings are basically the same and many companies are in fierce competition? The answer is to engage in a strategy referred to as *product differentiation*. It is an attempt to tangibly or intangibly distinguish a product from that of all competitors in the eyes of customers. Examples of tangible differences might be product features, performance, endurance, location, or support services, to name but a few. Chrysler once differentiated their product by offering a 7-year/70,000-mile warranty on new models. Pepsi has convinced many consumers to try their product because they assert that it really does taste better than Coke. Offering products at a lower price or at several different prices can be an important distinguishing characteristic, as demonstrated by Timex watches.

Some products are in fact the same, and attempts to differentiate through tangible features would be either futile or easily copied. In such cases, an *image* of difference is created through intangible means that may have little to do with the product directly. Soft drink companies show you how much fun you can have by drinking their product. Beer companies suggest status, enjoyment, and masculinity. Snapple may not taste the best or have the fewest calories, but may have the funniest, most memorable commercials. There tends to be a heavy emphasis on the use of mass appeal means of promotion, such as advertising, when differentiated through intangibles. Note the long-term use of Bill Cosby by Jell-O to create an image of fun. Microsoft has successfully differentiated itself through an image of innovation and exceptional customer service.

There are certain risks in using product differentiation. First, a marketer who uses product differentiation must be careful not to eliminate mention of core appeals or features that the consumer expects from the product. For example, differentiating a brand of bread through its unique vitamin and mineral content is valid as long as you retain the core freshness feature in your ad. Second, highlighting features that are too different from the norm may prove ineffective. Finally, a product may be differentiated on a basis that is unimportant to the customer or difficult to understand. The automobile industry has learned to avoid technical copy in ads since most consumers don't understand it or don't care.

However, there is a flip-side to product differentiation, an approach toward the market called *market segmentation*.[4]

The Segmented Market

While product differentiation is an effective strategy to distinguish your brand from competitors', it also differentiates your own products from one another. For example, a company such as Franco-American Spaghetti has differentiated its basic product by offering various sizes, flavors, and shapes. The objective is to sell more product, to more people, more often. Kraft has done the same with their salad dressings; Xerox with its multitude of office products. The problem is not competition; the problem is the acknowledgement that people within markets are different and that successful marketers must respond to these differences.

This premise of *segmenting* the market theroizes that people and/or organizations can be most effectively approached by recognizing their differences and adjusting accordingly. By emphasizing a segmentation approach, the exchange process should be enhanced, since a company can more precisely match the needs and wants of the customer. Even the soft drink manufacturers have moved away from the undifferentiated approach and have introduced diet, caffeine-free, and diet-caffeine-free versions of their basic product.[5]

While it is relatively easy to identify segments of consumers, most firms do not have the capabilities or the need to effectively market their product to all of the segments that can be identified. Rather, one or more target markets (segments) must be selected. In reality, market segmentation is both a disaggregation and aggregation process. While the market is initially reduced to its smallest homogeneous components (perhaps a single individual), business in practice requires the marketer to find common dimensions that will allow him to view these individuals as larger, profitable segments. Thus, market segmentation is a twofold process that includes: (1) identifying and classifying people into homogeneous groupings, called *segments*, and (2) determining which of these segments are viable target markets. In essence, the marketing objectives of segmentation analysis are:

1. To reduce risk in deciding where, when, how, and to whom a product, service, or brand will be marketed
2. To increase marketing efficiency by directing effort specifically toward the designated segment in a manner consistent with that segment's characteristics

Segmentation Strategies

There are two major segmentation strategies followed by marketing organizations: a concentration strategy and a multisegment strategy.

An organization that adopts a *concentration strategy* chooses to focus its marketing efforts on only one market segment. Only one marketing mix is developed. For example, the manufacturer of Rolex watches has chosen to concentrate on the luxury segment of the watch market. An organization that adopts a concentration strategy gains an advantage by being able to analyze the needs and wants of only one segment and then focusing all its efforts on that segment. This can provide a differential advantage over other organizations that market to this segment but do not concentrate all their efforts on it. The primary disadvantage of concentration is related to the demand of the segment. As long as demand is strong, the organization's financial position will be strong. But if demand declines, the organization's financial position will also decline.

The other segmentation strategy is a *multisegment strategy*. When an organization adopts this strategy, it focuses its marketing efforts on two or more distinct market segments. The organization does so by developing a distinct marketing mix for each segment. They then develop marketing programs tailored to each of these segments. Organizations that follow a multisegment strategy usually realize an increase in total sales as more marketing programs are focused at more customers. However, the organization will most likely experience higher costs because of the need for more than one marketing program.[6]

Bases of Segmentation

There are many different ways by which a company can segment its market, and the chosen process varies from one product to another. Further, the segmentation process should be an ongoing activity. Since markets are very dynamic, and products change over time, the bases for segmentation must likewise change. (See Figure 2.2.)

MARKETING CAPSULE 2.1

1. Defining the market
   a. The market is people
   b. The market is a place
   c. The market is an economic entity
2. Types of markets
   a. Consumer markets
   b. Industrial markets

   c. Institutional markets
   d. Reseller markets
3. Approaching the market
   a. The undifferentiated market (market aggregation)
   b. Product differentiation
   c. The segmented market
      1. Strategies: concentration, multisegment

	Bases for Segmentation	
Primary Dimension	**Consumer Market**	**Industrial Market**
Characteristics of person or organization	Geography, age, sex, race, income, life cycle, personality, lifestyle	Industry (SIC), location, size, technology, profitability, legal, buying situation
Purchase situation	Purpose, benefits, purchase approach, choice criteria, brand loyalty, importance	Volume, frequency, application, choice criteria, purchasing procedure, importance

FIGURE 2.2 Bases for Segmenting Markets: Consumer and Industrial Markets

In line with these basic differences we will first discuss the bases for segmenting ultimate consumers followed by a discussion of the factors used to segment industrial users.

Segmenting Ultimate Consumers

Geographic Segments Geography probably represents the oldest basis for segmentation. Regional differences in consumer tastes for products as a whole are well-known. Markets according to location are easily identified and large amounts of data are usually available. Many companies simply do not have the resources to expand beyond local or regional levels; thus, they must focus on one geographic segment only. Domestic and foreign segments are the broadest type of geographical segment.

Closely associated with geographic location are inherent characteristics of that location: weather, topography, and physical factors such as rivers, mountains, or ocean proximity. Conditions of high humidity, excessive rain or draught, snow or cold all influence the purchase of a wide spectrum of products. While marketers no longer segment markets as being east or west of the Mississippi River, people living near the Mississippi may constitute a viable segment for several products, such as flood insurance, fishing equipment, and dredging machinery.

Population density can also place people in unique market segments. High-density states such as California and New York and cities such as New York City, Hong Kong, and London create the need for products such as security systems, fast-food restaurants, and public transportation.

Geographic segmentation offers some important advantages. There is very little waste in the marketing effort, in that the product and supporting activities such as advertising, physical distribution, and repair can all be directed at the customer. Further, geography provides a convenient organizational framework. Products, salespeople, and distribution networks can all be organized around a central, specific location.

The drawbacks in using a geographic basis of segmentation are also notable. There is always the obvious possibility that consumer preferences may (unexpectedly) bear no relationship to location. Other factors, such as ethnic origin or income, may overshadow location. The stereotypical Texan, for example, is hard to find in Houston, where one-third of the population has immigrated from other states. Another problem is that most geographic areas are very large, regional locations. It is evident that the Eastern seaboard market contains many subsegments. Members of a geographic segment often tend to be too heterogeneous to qualify as a meaningful target for marketing action.

Demographic Segments Several demographic characteristics have proven to be particularly relevant when marketing to ultimate consumers. Segmenting the consumer market by age groups has been quite useful for several products. For example, the youth market (approximately 5 to 13) not only influences how their parents spend money, but also make

AD 2.3 The focus is on the pre-teen to young adult segment, assuming they will test product features at the store.

purchases of their own. Manufacturers of products such as toys, records, snack foods, and video games have designed promotional efforts directed at this group. More recently, the elderly market (age 65 and over) has grown in importance for producers of products such as low-cost housing, cruises, hobbies, and health care.

Gender has also historically been a good basis for market segmentation. While there are some obvious products designed for men or women, many of these traditional boundaries are changing, and marketing must apprise themselves of these changes. The emergence of the working women, for instance, has made determination of who performs certain activities in the family (e.g., shopping, car servicing), and how the family income is spent more difficult. New magazines such as *Men's Guide to Fashion*, *Modern Black Man*, *Sportswear International*, *NV*, and *Vibe* indicate how media is attempting to subsegment the male segment. Thus, the simple classification of male versus female may be useful only if several other demographic and behavioral characteristics are considered as well.

Another demographic trait closely associated with age and sex is the *family life cycle*. There is evidence that, based on family structure (i.e., number of adults and children), families go through very predictable behavioral patterns. For example, a young couple who have one young child will have far different purchasing needs than a couple in their late fifties whose children have moved out. In a similar way, the types of products purchased by a newly married couple will differ from those of a couple with older children.[7]

Income is perhaps the most common demographic basis for segmenting a market. This may be partly because income often dictates who can or cannot afford a particular product. It is quite reasonable, for example, to assume that individuals earning minimum wage could not easily purchase a $25,000 sports car. Income tends to be a better basis for segmenting markets as the price tag for a product increases. Income may not be quite as valuable for products such as bread, cigarettes, and motor oil. Income may also be helpful in examining certain types of buying behavior. For example, individuals in the lower-middle income group are prone to use coupons. *Playboy* recently announced the introduction of a special edition aimed at the subscribers with annual incomes over $45,000.

Several other demographic characteristics can influence various types of consumer activities. *Education*, for example, affects product preferences as well as characteristics demanded for certain products. *Occupation* can also be important. Individuals who work in hard physical labor occupations (e.g., coal mining) may demand an entirely different set of products than a person employed as a teacher or bank teller, even though their incomes are the same. *Geographic mobility* is somewhat related to occupation, in that certain occupations (e.g., military, corporate executives) require a high level of mobility. High geographic mobility necessitates that a person (or family) acquire new shopping habits, seek new sources of products and services, and possibly develop new brand preferences. Finally, *race and national origin* have been associated with product preferences and media preferences. Black Americans have exhibited preferences in respect to food, transportation, and entertainment, to name a few. Hispanics tend to prefer radio and television over newspapers and magazines as a means for learning about products. The following Integrated Marketing box discusses how race may be an overlooked segment.[8,9]

Even *religion* is used as a basis for segmentation. Several interesting findings have arisen from the limited research in this area. Aside from the obvious higher demands for Christian-oriented magazines, books, music, entertainment, jewelry, educational institutions, and counseling services, differences in demand for secular products and services have been identified as well. For example, the Christian consumer attends movies less frequently than consumers in general and spends more time in volunteer, even non-church-related, activities.

Notwithstanding its apparent advantages (i.e., low cost and ease of implementation), considerable uncertainty exists about demographic segmentation. The method is often misused. A typical misuse of the approach has been to construct "profiles" of product users. For example, it might be said that the typical consumer of Mexican food is under 35 years of age, has a college education, earns more than $10,000 a year, lives in a suburban fringe of a moderate-size urban community, and resides in the West. True, these characteristics do describe a typical consumer of Mexican food, but they also describe a lot of other consumers as well, and may paint an inaccurate portrait of many other consumers.

Usage Segments   In 1964, Twedt made one of the earliest departures from demographic segmentation when he suggested that the heavy user, or frequent consumer, was an important basis for segmentation. He proposed that consumption should be measured directly, and that promotion should be aimed directly at the heavy users. This approach has become very popular, particularly in the beverage industry (e.g., beer, soft drinks, and spirits). Considerable research has been conducted with this particular group, and the results suggest that finding other characteristics that correlate with usage rate often greatly enhances marketing efforts.[10]

Four other bases for market segmentation have evolved from the usage-level criteria. The first is *purchase occasion*. Determining the reason for an airline passenger's trip, for

INTEGRATED MARKETING *2.1*

SEEKING THE AFRICAN-AMERICAN WEB COMMUNITY

Silas Myers is a new millennium African-American. He's 31, holds an MBA from Harvard University, works as an investment analyst for money manager Hotchkeo & Wiley, and pulls in a salary close to six figures. And he spends about 10 hours a week online, buying everything from a JVC portable radio to Arm & Hammer deodorant. "Maybe I'm nuts," he says, "but shopping online is so much easier to me."

Millions of African-Americans are online. They're younger, more affluent, and better educated than their offline kin. And they're not tiptoeing onto the Net. They're right at home. Five million blacks now cruise through cyberspace, nearly equaling the combined number of Hispanic, Asian, and Native American surfers, according to researcher Cyber Dialogue.

True, Net use among African-Americans continues to lag behind the online white population: 28% of blacks as opposed to 37% for whites. But it's time to take a closer look at the digital divide. While those who don't have Net access tend to be poor and undereducated, there's a large group of African-Americans who are spending aggressively on the Web. "We're looking at a tidal wave coming of African-American-focused content and online consumers," says Omar J. Wasow, executive director of BlackPlanet.com, a black-oriented online community. "You ignore it at your peril."

With good reason, African-Americans have become smitten with the ability to compare prices and find bargains online. Melvin Crenshaw, manager of *Kidpreneurs* magazine, recently used the Travelocity Web site to save $300 on a ski trip to Denver. "I really liked the value," he says.

It's a shame, then, that so few sites market to such an attractive group. Almost every bookstore on the street has a section in African-American or ethnic literature. So it's shocking that e-commerce giants like Amazon.com don't have ethnic book sections. The solution is easy. Web merchants can create what the National Urban League's B. Keith Fulton calls "micro bundles"—Web categories within a site's merchandise that resemble the inner-city black bookstore or clothier. "You want blacks to click on a button and feel like they're in virtual Africa or virtual Harlem," says Fulton, the Urban League's director of Technology programs and policy. To attract blacks, he recommends decorating that corner of the site in *kinte* cloth patterns.

Sources: Roger O. Crockett, "Attention Must Be Paid," *Business Week e-biz*, February 7, 2000, p. 16; Kate Fitzgerald, "Connection Confirmation," *Advertising Age*, November 29, 1999, p. S-3; "African-Americans Online," *Advertising Age*, November 29, 1999, p. S-14.

---

instance, may be the most relevant criteria for segmenting airline consumers. The same may be true for products such as long-distance calling or the purchase of snack foods. The second basis is *user status*. It seems apparent that communication strategies must differ if they are directed at different use patterns, such as nonusers versus ex-users, or one-time users versus regular users. New car producers have become very sensitive to the need to provide new car buyers with a great deal of supportive information after the sale in order to minimize unhappiness after the purchase. However, determining how long this information is necessary or effective is still anybody's guess. The third basis is *loyalty*. This approach places consumers into loyalty categories based on their purchase patterns of particular brands. A key category is the brand-loyal consumer. Companies have assumed that if they can identify individuals who are brand loyal to their brand, and then delineate other characteristics these people have in common, they will locate the ideal target market. There is still a great deal of uncertainty as to how to correctly measure brand loyalty. The final characteristic is *stage of readiness*. It is proposed that potential customers can be segmented as follows: unaware, aware, informed, interested, desirous, and intend to buy. Thus if a marketing manager is aware of where the specific segment of potential customers is, he/she can design the appropriate market strategy to move them through the various stages of readiness. Again, these stages of readiness are rather vague and difficult to accurately measure.

Psychological Segments   Research results show that the concept of segmentation should recognize psychological as well as demographic influences. For example, Phillip

Morris has segmented the market for cigarette brands by appealing psychologically to consumers in the following way:

- Marlboro: the broad appeal of the American cowboy
- Benson & Hedges: sophisticated, upscale appeal
- Parliament: a recessed filter for those who want to avoid direct contact with tobacco
- Merit: low tar and nicotine
- Virginia Slims: appeal based on "You've come a long way, baby" theme

Evidence suggests that attitudes of prospective buyers towards certain products influence their subsequent purchase or non-purchase of them. If persons with similar attitudes can be isolated, they represent an important psychological segment. *Attitudes* can be defined as predispositions to behave in certain ways in response to given stimulus.[11]

Personality is defined as the long-lasting characteristics and behaviors of a person that allow them to cope and respond to their environment. Very early on, marketers were examining personality traits as a means for segmenting consumers. None of these early studies suggest that measurable personality traits offer much prospect of market segmentation. However, an almost inescapable logic seems to dictate that consumption of particular products or brands must be meaningfully related to consumer personality. It is frequently noted that the elderly drive big cars, that the new rich spend disproportionately more on housing and other visible symbols of success, and that extroverts dress conspicuously.[12]

Motives are closely related to attitudes. A motive is a reason for behavior. A buying motive triggers purchasing activity. The latter is general, the former more specific. In theory, this is what market segmentation is all about. Measurements of demographic, personality, and attitudinal variables are really convenient measurements of less conspicuous motivational factors. People with similar physical and psychological characteristics are presumed to be similarly motivated. Motives can be positive (convenience), or negative (fear of pain). The question logically arises: why not observe motivation directly and classify market segments accordingly?

Lifestyle refers to the orientation that an individual or a group has toward consumption, work, and play and can be defined as a pattern of attitudes, interests, and opinions held by a person. Lifestyle segmentation has become very popular with marketers, because of the availability of measurement devices and instruments, and the intuitive categories that result from this process.[13] As a result, producers are targeting versions of their products and their promotions to various lifestyle segments. Thus, companies like All State Insurance are designing special programs for the good driver, who has been extensively characterized through a lifestyle segmentation approach.[14,15]

Lifestyle analysis begins by asking questions about the consumer's activities, interests, and opinions. If a man earns $40,000–$50,000 per year as an executive, with a wife and four children, what does he think of his role as provider versus father? How does he spend his spare time? To what clubs and groups does he belong? Does he hunt? What are his attitudes toward advertising? What does he read?

AIO (activities, interests, opinions) inventories, as they are called, reveal vast amounts of information concerning attitudes toward product categories, brands within product categories, and user and non-user characteristics. Lifestyle studies tend to focus upon how people spend their money; their patterns of work and leisure; their major interests; and their opinions of social and political issues, institutions, and themselves. The popularity of lifestyles as a basis for market segmentation has prompted several research firms to specialize in this area. However, few have achieved the success of VALS and VALS 2 developed by SRI International.

Introduced in 1978, the original VALS (Values, Attitudes, and Lifestyle) divided the American population into nine segments, organized along a hierarchy of needs. After several years of use, it was determined that the nine segments reflected a population dominated by people in their twenties and thirties, as the U.S. was ten years ago. Moreover, businesses found it difficult to use the segments to predict buying behavior or target consumers. For these reasons, SRI developed an all-new system, VALS 2. It dropped values and lifestyles as its primary basis for its psychographic segmentation scheme. Instead, the forty-three questions ask about unchanging psychological stances rather than shifting values and lifestyles.

The psychographic groups in VALS 2 are arranged in a rectangle (see Figure 2.3). They are stacked vertically by their resources (minimal to abundant) an horizontally by their self-orientation (principle, status, or action-oriented).

An annual subscription to VALS 2 provides businesses with a range of products and services. Businesses doing market research can include the VALS questions in their questionnaire. SRI will analyze the data and VALS-type the respondents.

Segmenting Organizational Markets

It is also important for the marketing manager to understand how business or organization customers can be segmented. Many firms sell not to ultimate consumers but to other businesses. Although there are many similarities between how consumers and businesses behave, there are also several differences, as mentioned earlier. Recall that business buyers differ as follows: (1) most business buyers view their function as a rational (problem-solving) approach; (2) the development of formal procedures, or routines, typifies most business buying; (3) there tend to be multiple purchase influences; (4) in industrial buying it is necessary to maintain the correct assortment of goods in inventory; and (5) it is often the responsibility of the purchasing executive to dispose of waste and scrap.

A number of basic approaches to segmenting organizational markets exist. An industrial marketing firm must be able to distinguish between the industries it sells to and the different market segments that exist in each of those industries. There are several basic approaches to segmenting organizational markets: (1) types of customers; (2) the Standard Industrial Classification; (3) end use; (4) common buying factors; and (5) buyer size and geography.[2, 16]

Type of Customer   Industrial customers, both present and potential, can be classified into one of three groups.

1. Original Equipment Manufacturers (OEMs), such as Caterpillar in the road equipment industry.
2. End users, such as farmers who use farm machinery produced by John Deere and OEMs.
3. Aftermarket customers, such as those who purchase spare parts for a piece of machinery.

Similarly, industrial products can be classified into one of three categories, each of which is typically sold to only certain types of customers:

1. Machinery and equipment (e.g., computers, trucks, bulldozers): these are end products sold only to OEM and end user segments.
2. Components or subassemblies (e.g., switches, pistons, machine tool parts): these are sold to build and repair machinery and equipment and are sold in all three customer segments.
3. Materials (e.g., chemicals, metals, herbicides): these are consumed in the end-user products and are sold only to OEMs and end users.

Old & New

The nine original VALS psychographic segments have been replaced by eight new psychographic groups. In the new system, the groups are arranged vertically by their resources and horizontally by their self-orientation.

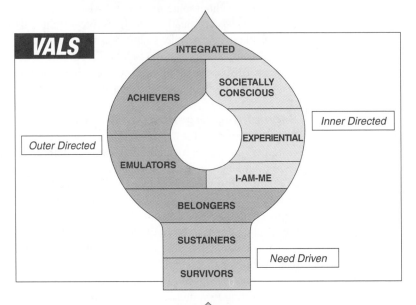

VALS

INTEGRATED

SOCIETALLY CONSCIOUS

ACHIEVERS

Inner Directed

EXPERIENTIAL

Outer Directed

EMULATORS

I-AM-ME

BELONGERS

SUSTAINERS

Need Driven

SURVIVORS

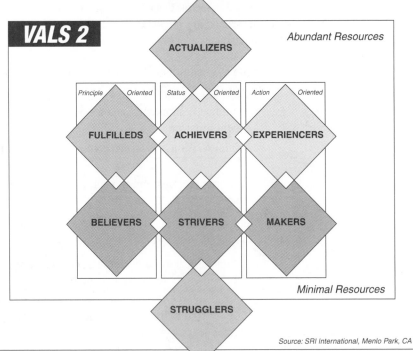

VALS 2

Abundant Resources

ACTUALIZERS

Principle *Oriented* | *Status* *Oriented* | *Action* *Oriented*

FULFILLEDS | ACHIEVERS | EXPERIENCERS

BELIEVERS | STRIVERS | MAKERS

Minimal Resources

STRUGGLERS

Source: SRI International, Menlo Park, CA

FIGURE 2.3 VALS and VALS2 are two segmentation techniques.

The Standard Industrial Classification (SIC)   A second industrial segmentation approach employs the Standard Industrial Classification (SIC) codes published by the U.S. Government. The SIC classifies business firms by the main product or service provided. Firms are classified into one of ten basic SIC industries. Within each classification, the major groups of industries can be identified by the first two numbers of the SIC code. For example, SIC number 22 are textile mills, SIC number 34 are manufacturers of fabricated metals, and so on. An industrial producer would attempt to identify the manufacturing groups that represent potential users of the products it produces and sells. Figure 2.4 takes the two-digit classification and converts it to three-, four-, five-, and seven-digit codes. As you can see in Figure 2.4, use of the SIC code allows the industrial manufacturer to identify the organizations whose principal request is, in this case, pliers.

Based upon this list of construction machinery and equipment products, it is possible to determine what products are produced by what manufacturers by consulting one of the following sources:

1. Dun's Market Identifiers—computer-based records of three million United States and Canadian business establishments by four-digit SIC.

2. Metalworking Directory—a comprehensive list of metalworking plants with 20 or more employees, as well as metal distributors, by four-digit SIC.

3. Thomas Register of American Manufacturers—a directory of manufacturers, classified by products, enabling the researcher to identify most or all of the manufacturers of any given product.

4. Survey of Industrial Purchasing Power—an annual survey of manufacturing activity in the United States by geographic areas and four-digit SIC industry groups; reports the number of plants with 20 or more and 100 or more employees, as well as total shipment value.

End uses   Sometimes industrial marketers segment markets by looking at how a product is used in different situations. When employing end-use segmentation, the industrial marketer typically conducts a cost/benefit analysis for each end-use application. The manufacturer must ask: What benefits does the customer want from this product? For example, an electric motor manufacturer learned that customers operated motors at different speeds. After making field visits to gain insight into the situation, he divided the market into slow-speed and high-speed segments. In the slow-speed segment, the manufacturer emphasized a competitively priced product with a maintenance advantage, while in the high-speed market product, superiority was stressed.

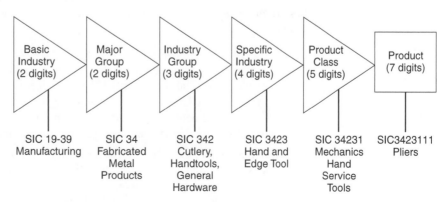

FIGURE 2.4   SIC two-digit to seven-digit classification

Common Buying Factors Some industrial marketers segment markets by identifying groups of customers who consider the same buying factors important. Five buying factors are important in most industrial buying situations: (1) product performance, (2) product quality, (3) service, (4) delivery, and (5) price.[2] Identifying a group of customers who value the same buying factors as important is difficult, as industrial organizations' and resellers' priorities often change.

Buyer Size and Geography If organizations' markets cannot be easily segmented by one of the previous approaches, market advantages may still be realized by segmenting based on account size or geographic boundaries. Sales managers have done this for years, but only recently have organizations learned to develop several pricing strategies for customers that are both close and far away geographically. Similarly, different strategies can be developed for large, medium, and small customers.

Single-Base and Multi-Base Segmentation

So far, we have talked about the use of individual bases for market segmentation. The use of a *single-base segmentation strategy* is a simple way to segment markets, and is often very effective. Clearly, the use of bases such as sex (cosmetics), or age (health care products, music), or income (automobiles), provides valuable insights into who uses what products. But the use of a single base may not be precise enough in identifying a segment for which a marketing program can be designed. Therefore, many organizations employ *multi-base segmentation strategies*, using several bases to segment a total market. For example, the housing market might be segmented by family size, income, and age.

American Log Home, for example, offers a wide variety of packages and options to its customers based on their needs, incomes, skills, family size, and usage. Packages range from one-room shelters designed primarily for hunters to a 4,000 square-foot unit complete with hot tub, chandeliers, and three decks. Customers can select to finish part of the interior, part of the exterior, or to have the entire structure finished by American Log Home.

The resulting huge array of products is a disadvantage of multi-base segmentation as a strategy. Using several bases that vary in importance, considering all to be equal, could produce misdirected efforts.

Qualifying Customers in Market Segments

Clearly, it is important to employ appropriate factors to identify market segments. Equally important is qualifying the customers who make up those segments. Qualifications involves judgment. Marketers must be able to differentiate between real prospects and individuals or firms who have some similar characteristics but cannot be converted to purchasers.

It should be clear that not all market segments present desirable marketing opportunities. Traditionally, five criteria have been employed to gauge the relative worth of a market segment:[16]

1. *Clarity of identification*: The degree to which we can identify who is in and who is outside the segment. Part of this process also involves the delineation of demographic and social characteristics that make it easier to measure and track the identified segment. Unfortunately, obtaining segment data is not always easy, especially when the segment is defined in terms of behavioral or benefit characteristics. Sex is a clear basis for segmenting a product such as brassieres.

2. *Actual or potential need*: Needs that reflect overt demands for existing goods and services, or needs that can be transformed into perceived wants through educa-

tion or persuasion, constitute a segment. It is further assumed that this need exists in a large enough quantity to justify a separate segmentation strategy. This criterion requires the ability to measure both the intensity of the need and the strength of the purchasing power supporting it. A 40-story building has a clear need for elevators.

3. *Effective demand*: It is not enough for an actual or potential need to exist; purchasing power must also exist. Needs plus purchasing power create effective demand. The ability to buy stems from income, savings, and credit. Purchasing power derived from one or more of these three sources must belong to the members of a market segment in order for it to represent a meaningful marketing opportunity. The possession of a valid Visa or other credit card meets this criteria for most products.

4. *Economic accessibility*: The individuals in a market segment must be reachable and profitable. For example, segments could be concentrated geographically, shop at the same stores, or read the same magazines. Regrettably, many important segments—those based on motivational characteristics, for instance—cannot be reached economically. The elderly rich represent such a segment.

5. *Positive response*: A segment must react uniquely to marketing efforts. There must be a reason for using different marketing approaches in the various segments. Different segments, unless they respond in unique ways to particular marketing inputs, hardly justify the use of separate marketing programs.

The Strategy of Market Segmentation

During the last two decades, a more complete and concise understanding of market segmentation has emerged. This is not to say that there are not still unsettled issues, measurement problems, and other issues to consider. The most severe problem remains the difficulty of defining precisely the basis for segmentation. A great deal of knowledge about the market and considerable experience with it are highly desirable. Research into consumer motivation is essential. This does not mean that historical, descriptive data about consumers are no longer important. Nevertheless, the ultimate purpose of going through the process of delineating market segments is to select a target market or markets: otherwise, the segmentation process is worthless.

The segmental approach will be described throughout the text in greater detail. At this point, it is sufficient to know that the segmentation strategy is the primary marketing approach used by a majority of producers. Combined with product differentiation, it is the essence of a contemporary marketing strategy. The activity of selecting a target market involves five steps:

1. Identify relevant person/organization and purchase situation variables beyond the core product variable. (For Minolta's Maxxum SLR Camera, the core product variable would be fool-proof photographs, and other relevant variables might be age, income, family composition, occasion for use, and photographic experience.)

2. Collect and analyze other related data about potential segments (e.g., characteristics of neophyte camera users, price perceptions of these potential users, size of group, trends, minimum product features).

3. Apply criteria of a good segment.

4. Select one or more segments as target markets (e.g., neophyte photographers, frustrated with neccessary adjustments for a 35mm camera, income of $35,000 or more, family, between 25-45 years of age, male).

5. Develop appropriate action programs to reach target segment(s) (e.g., price at $350; distribute through discount stores, camera stores, and department stores; promote through TV and magazine ads). This type of effective action program is demonstrated in the Newsline that follows.

NEWSLINE: YOUTH SEGMENTS

It takes more than just traditional advertising to appeal to the ever-elusive teenage market. One company that has discovered the right formula to reach this group is High Frequency Marketing (HFM), a youth marketing firm founded by Ron Vos. Since its inception in 1995, HFM has grown significantly in terms of cross-industry reach, marketing network, and revenue (which has tripled in the past two years). Vos attributes the company's success to its unconventional promotional campaigns.

As a youth marketing start-up, Vos's energies were initially focused on the music industry. He appealed to his target market of 12- to 26-year-olds by using grassroots marketing efforts and specializing in "takin' it to the streets." Back in 1995, street marketing had not become the cliché that it is now. Yet, Vos's key to success is the adaptability of his firm to youth culture and technology. As he likes to say, "As soon as a marketing concept becomes mainstream, it's history."

When asked to pinpoint a breakthrough campaign for his company, Vos immediately mentions *The Wedding Singer.* Hired by New Line Cinema in 1998 to promote the film, HFM developed the concept of a "karaoke jam contest" in the malls of 24 cities. The campaign was immensely successful, opening doors for HFM to the whole entertainment industry.

Another successful campaign took place in 2000, when Food.com approached HFM with the concept of partnering with Second Harvest (a national food bank) to sponsor a national food drive on college campuses, using the incentive of awarding the campus that collected the most food at a big concert. HFM had to go back to the company and say that "you can put a carrot on the end of a stick, but the stick can't be too long." In other words, Food.com needed a more tangible campaign, something with instant feedback to "show (the students) that it's real, that it's there." Vos and his creative marketing team came up with a compilation CD entitled "Music 4 Food," which was distributed free of charge to students who donated food (they also received a ticket to a nearby concert).

Sources: Debra Goldman, "S&SI Markets the Tried and True to Teen Boys: Misogyny," *Adweek*, May 15, 2000, p. 24; Jinnefer Gilbert, "New Teen Obsession," *Advertising Age*, February 14, 2000, p. 38; Christina Merrill, "The Ripple Effect Reaches Gen Y," *American Demographics*, November 1999, pp. 15–16; Lauren Goldstein, "The Alpha Teenager," *Fortune*, December 20, 1999, pp. 201–203.

The Concept of Positioning

Both product differentiation and market segmentation result in a perceived position for the company or organization. From the intelligent marketing organization, there should be an attempt to create the desired position, rather than wait for it to be created by customers, the public, or even competitors. *Positioning* is defined as the act of designing the company's offering and image to occupy a distinctive place in the target market's mind. The end result of positioning is the successful creation of a market-focused value proposition, a cogent reason why the target market should buy the product.

Since positioning is a strategy that starts with the product, we expand our discussion of positioning in the Product Chapter.

The Future of the Marketplace

As the spread of the global marketplace continues, aided by satellites, the World Wide Web, and univeral problems, it will also become increasingly difficult to effectively assess the market. In fact, there is solid evidence that the market will often consist of a single person or company. Customized product design, relationship marketing, and one-on-one marketing suggests that marketing has gone full circle. Like the first half of the twentieth century, when the corner grocer knew all of his customers personally, marketing in the rest of the twenty-first century may look very similar.

MARKETING CAPSULE 2.2

1. Bases of segmentation
   a. Ultimate Consumers
      1. Geographic
      2. Demographics
      3. Usage
      4. Psychological
   b. Organizations
      1. Type of customer
      2. End uses
      3. Common buying factors
      4. Size and geography
   c. Single-base versus multi-base
   d. Qualify people into segments
      1. Clarity of identification
      2. Actual or potential need
      3. Effective demand
      4. Economic accessibility
      5. Positive response
   e. Segmentation process

THE WALL STREET JOURNAL.

IN PRACTICE

What is the market? It depends on your product but, generally, all markets possess similar, basic characteristics. The market is people, either individuals or groups, businesses or institutions. The market is also a place, as in marketplace, where transactions take place. Finally, the market is an economic entity, influenced by financial pressures and government regulations.

In order to sell a product, marketers must know their market and know it well. Four primary markets exist, but they are not mutually exclusive. Consumer, industrial, institutional, and reseller markets all have characteristics specific to their consumers, but they also overlap in many instances. As a result, most successful companies segment their markets. By segmenting markets, a company can match the needs and wants of consumers to its product.

Print magazines and their online counterparts are excellent examples of market segmenting. The Interactive Journal targets the business community, while Outside Magazine (www.outsidemag.com), clearly targets outdoor enthusiasts.

You are able to customize the Interactive Journal to your personal preferences. On the Front Section, click on **Personal Journal** on the main menu. From here you will be directed to the **Setup Center**. Here, you can create folders in three separate areas:

1. News
2. Favorites
3. Portfolio

In the **News** section, you can search for news items in the Interactive Journal using key words, company names, and industry type. Articles meeting the criteria you specify will be listed automatically on a daily basis. Set up your own **News** folder now.

In the **Favorites** section, you can track regularly running columns and features in the major sections such as Marketplace and Tech Center. Create your own **Favorites** folder now.

In the **Portfolio** section, you can track your purchases and sales of specific stocks.

DELIVERABLE

Identify three to five companies with segmented markets. Visit their websites for specific information about the companies and their products. Also search the Interactive Journal for more information about the companies you have identified. For each company, identify the segmented market and list specific characteristics about that market.

DISCUSSION QUESTIONS

1. What are the advantages of identifying and selling to segmented markets versus broader, general markets?
2. How do companies identify the market most likely to buy their products?
3. Describe why market segmenting helps the companies you identified in your Deliverable sell their products.
4. How can you use the Interactive Journal to learn more about markets?

SUMMARY

The concept of a market was examined in this chapter. It was defined from three perspectives: people, place, and economic activity. In addition, the four types of markets were discussed. The bulk of this chapter dealt with the two general marketing approaches toward the market: undifferentiated (aggregated) and segmental. The former was defined as the assumption that the market is homogeneous and developing separate strategies is unnecessary. The latter was defined as the acknowledgement that markets contain submarkets known as segments, which must be evaluated as potential target markets. The remainder of the chapter highlighted various bases for segmenting markets and delineating the criteria employed in assessing the value of a segment.

MARKETER'S VOCABULARY

Market aggregation (undifferentiated marketing)   Treating an entire market uniformly, making little or no attempt to differentiate marketing effort.

Product differentiation   A marketing strategy that emphasizes distinctive product features without recognizing diversity of consumer needs.

Market segmentation   Dividing a total market into several submarkets or segments, each of which is homogeneous in all significant aspects, for the purpose of selecting one or more target markets on which to concentrate marketing effort.

Concentration strategy   Used by an organization that chooses to focus its marketing efforts on only one market segment.

Multisegment strategy   Used by an organization that chooses to focus its marketing effort on two or more distinct segments.

Ultimate user   An individual or organization that buys and/or uses products or services for their own personal consumption.

Industrial user   An organization that buys products or services for use in their own businesses, or to make other products.

Demographic characteristics   Statistical characteristics of a population often used to segment markets, such as age, sex, family lifecycle, income, or education.

Usage rate   A segmentation base that identifies customers on the basis of the frequency of use of a product.

Purchase occasion   A segmentation base that identifies when they use the product.

User status   A segmentation base that identifies customers on the basis of patterns of use, such as one-time or regular use.

Loyalty   A segmentation base that identifies customers on the basis of purchase patterns of particular brands.

Stage of readiness   A segmentation base that identifies customers on the basis of how ready a customer is to buy.

Psychological segmentation   The use of attitudes, personality, motives, and lifestyle to identify customers.

Attitude   A predisposition to behave in a certain way to a given stimuli.

Personality   All the traits of a person that make him/her unique.

Motive   A reason for behavior.

Lifestyle   A pattern of attitudes, interests, and opinions held by a person.

Organizational markets   A market consisting of those organizations who buy products or services for their businesses, for use in making other products, or for resale.

Standard industrial classification (SIC)   A U.S. government publication that classifies business firms by the main product or service provided.

Single-base segmentation strategy   The use of a single base to segment markets.

Multi-base segmentation strategy   The use of two or more bases to segment markets.

Clarity of identification   The degree to which one can identify those inside and those outside the market segment.

Actual need   Overt demand for existing goods or services.

Potential need   A need that can be changed into perceived wants through such means as education or persuasion.

Effective demand   Actual or potential needs existing along with purchasing power (income, savings, and credit) belonging to members of a market segment.

Economic accessibility   Members of a market segment must be reachable and profitable.

DISCUSSION QUESTIONS

1. What makes the concept of market segmentation different from that of product differentiation?

2. What are the advantages that market segmentation has over aggregate or mass marketing?

3. What criteria would you use to determine whether the toothpaste market should be grouped into a "drinker's toothpaste" segment? A "business person's toothpaste" segment?

4. Why is demographic segmentation alone not always a sufficient means of target market identification? Suggest a better method.

5. Assume that you have been hired by a firm to segment the market for replacement tires. What segmentation bases would you use? What pitfalls should you be suspicious of?

6. List the steps in the market segmentation process.

7. Describe the means by which industrial reseller markets can be segmented.

8. Segmentation is really an aggregation process. Explain.

9. Is a multi-base segmentation approach always better than the use of a single segmentation base?

10. Do you think that there are distinct market segments for personal computers? If so, what are the characteristics? If not, why not?

PROJECT

Go through a cross-section of consumer and business magazines. Clip out ads that you feel represent at least five bases for segmentation. Select one and apply the criteria of a valid segment. Write a two-page report.

CASE APPLICATION

ROLLING ROCK FINDS ITS NICHE

On the back of each long-neck bottle of Rolling Rock beer, a bold but simple "33" stands out. Plain white on the dark green glass, the number sits enclosed in quotation marks, squarely below a block of type, daring the drinker to discover its meaning.

Since 1939, when the brew from Latrobe, Pennsylvania, made its debut, that "33" has been capturing the imagination of consumers. Fans of the beer steadily wrote Latrobe Brewing Co., trying to discern the significance of the number. Theories abound, but if anybody knows the real story, they haven't told—which only adds to the "33" mystique.

This natural marketing hook, however, remained untapped for most of the beer's history. The company rarely ran promotions and its advertising did little to bolster the "33" myth. Rolling Rock was just another beer saddled with a blue-collar image, and in the white-collar 1980s sales began to decline steadily.

Things began to change for Rolling Rock in mid-1987, when Labatt's USA acquired Latrobe Brewing. The new owner, who recognized a good thing, brought in a Dallas-based promotions agency, The Marketing Continuum, and ad agency, Hill, Holliday, Connors, Cosmopulous, to take advantage of the "33" legend.

The agencies believed that by playing up the number, they could preserve the brand's unique personality. They also sought to reposition Rolling Rock as a super-premium brand and saw "33" as the vital link to its long history, distinctive packaging, and special aura.

How successful has the new strategy been? Sales during the first two months climbed fifteen percent from the same period a year earlier. The repositioning has also paid off nicely. The brand's primary audience is no longer college students and blue-collar workers. The demographic on today's average Rolling Rock consumer shows a 21 to 35-year-old white-collar male earning $40,000 or more per year.

David Mullen, executive at TMC, says it was clear early in his company's relationship with Rolling Rock that the kind of "me too" bikini advertising, which has homogenized so many of the major beers, would be a poor direction for this brand. That's because Rolling Rock was a niche brand trying to capture the attention of consumers and distributors in a saturated market. The marketing minds behind Rolling Rock, Mullen says, saw a window of opportunity in the super-premium segment, where brands like Michelob and Lowenbrau were losing their allure with consumers who wanted something unique. So Mullen and his cohorts devised a successful program that continues to stress the "specialness" of the brand.

Source: Kathy Thacker, "Solutions: Winning Number," *Adweek* (October 28, 1999): pp. 40–41.

Questions:

1. Despite the apparent success of this new marketing strategy designed by TMC, there are potential problems with the segmentation approach employed. Discuss these problems.
2. Discuss other possible bases for segmentation that Rolling Rock could have used.

REFERENCES

1. Alvin A. Achenbaum, "Advertising Doesn't Manipulate Consumerism," *Journal of Advertising Research*, April 1972, p. 7.
2. B. Charles Ames and James D. Hlavacek, *Managing Marketing for Industrial Firms*, New York, N.Y.: Random House, pp. 96–103.
3. Ames, p. 102.
4. Betsy D. Belb, "Discovering the 65+ Consumer," *Business Horizons*, May–June 1982, pp. 42–46.
5. Alfred S. Boote, "Market Segmentation by Personal Values and Salient Product Attributes," *Journal of Advertising Research*, Vol. 21, No. 1, February 1981, pp. 29–35.
6. Kenneth Boulding, *Economic Analysis*, New York, N.Y.: Harper & Row, Inc., 1995, pp. 608–615.
7. William R. Darden, W.A. French, and R.D. Howell, "Mapping Market Mobility: Psychographic Profiles and Media Exposure," *Journal of Business Research*, Vol. 7, No. 8, 1979, pp. 51–74.
8. Duane L. Davis and Ronald S. Rubin, "Identifying the Energy-Conscious Consumer: The Case of the Opinion Leader," *Journal of the Academy of Marketing Science*, Spring 1983, p. 185.
9. Terry Elrod and Russel S. Winer, "An Empirical Evaluation of Aggregation Approaches for Developing Market Segments," *Journal of Marketing*, Vol. 46, No. 4, Fall 1982, pp.32–34.
10. Ronald Frank, William Massey, and Yoram Wind, *Market Segmentation*, Englewood Cliffs, N.J.: Prentice-Hall, 1972.
11. Martha Farnsworth, "Psychographics for the 1990s," *American Demographics*, July 1989, pp. 25, 28–30.
12. H.H. Kassarjian, "Personality and Consumer Behavior: A Review," *Journal of Marketing Research*, Vol. 8, November 1971.
13. William D. Wells, "Psychographics: A Critical Review," *Journal of Marketing Research*, May 1975, pp. 196–213.
14. Joseph T. Plummer, "The Concept and Application of Life Style Segmentation," *Journal of Marketing*, January 1974, p. 33.
15. David J. Reibstein, Christopher H. Lovelock, and Ricardo de P. Dobson, "The Direction of Causality Between Perceptions, Affect, and Behavior: An Application to Travel Behavior," *Journal of Consumer Research*, Vol 6., March 1980, pp. 370–376.
16. Benson P. Shapiro and Thomas V. Bonoma, "How to Segment Industrial Markets," *Harvard Business Review*, May–June 1984, pp. 104–110.

CHAPTER 3

MARKETING RESEARCH: AN AID TO DECISION MAKING

LEARNING OBJECTIVES

Having completed this chapter, you should:
- Understand the role of marketing research.
- Understand the marketing research process and the techniques employed.

DISCOVERING WHY THEY CHEW

Juicy Fruit Gum, the oldest brand of the Wm. Wrigley Jr. Company, wasn't chewing up the teen market, gum's top demographic. In 1997, the company found itself under pressure from competitors. Sales and market share were down. How could Wrigley make more kids chomp on Juicy Fruit?

What qualities about Juicy Fruit might appeal to teens? Wrigley went to the source to find out. It found kids who chew five sticks or more of Juicy Fruit each week and promptly gave them a homework assignment. Find pictures that remind them of the gum and write a short story about it. From the focus group, Wrigley learned that teens chew Juicy Fruit because it's sweet. It refreshes and energizes them.

Their ad agency, BBDO, confirmed what the teens were saying. BBDO asked more than 400 heavy gum chewers to rate various brands by attributes that best represented them. For Juicy Fruit, respondents picked phrases such as "has the right amount of sweetness" and "is made with natural sweetness."

Another study by BBDO looked into why teens chew gum. Was it because they're stressed out—or because they forgot to brush their teeth before going to school? Nearly three out of four kids said they stick a wad into their mouth when they crave something sweet. And Juicy Fruit was the top brand they chose to fulfill that need (Big Red was a distant second).

Sources: "How Sweet It Is," *American Demographics*, March 2000, p. S18; "Flavor du Jour," *American Demographics*, March 2000, p. S10; Erika Rasmusson, "Cool for Sale," *Sales & Marketing Management*, March 1998, pp. 20–22.

INTRODUCTION

Although the marketing research conducted by the Wrigley Co. was fairly simple, it provided a new direction for their marketing strategy. BBDO developed four TV commercials

FIGURE 3.1 The marketing planning process

with the "Gotta Have Sweet" theme. Roughly 70 percent of respondents voluntarily recalled the Juicy Fruit name after watching the commercial (the average recall for a brand of sugar gum is 57 percent). Sales of 100-stick boxes of Juicy Fruit rose 5 percent after the start of the ad campaign, reversing a 2 percent decline prior to it. Juicy Fruit's market share also increased from 4.9 percent to 5.3 percent, the biggest gain of any established chewing gum brand during the year following the campaign.

Marketing research addresses the need for quicker, yet more accurate, decision making by the marketer. The impetus for this situation is the complex relationship between the business firm and the ever-changing external environment. In particular, most marketers are far removed from their customers; yet must know who their customers are, what they want, and what competitors are doing. Often the marketer relies on salespeople and dealers for information, but more and more the best source of information is marketing research.

It should be noted that most marketing decisions are still made without the use of formal marketing research. In many cases, the time required to do marketing research is not available. In other cases, the cost of obtaining the data is prohibitive or the desired data cannot be obtained in reliable form. Ultimately, successful marketing executives make decisions on the basis of a blend of facts and intuition.

In this chapter, we provide an overview of the marketing research process. We start the discussion with a look at business information. As noted in Figure 3.1, marketing research is applicable throughout the marketing planning process.

THE NATURE AND IMPORTANCE OF MARKETING RESEARCH

Informal and, by today's standards, crude attempts to analyze the market date back to the earliest days of the marketing revolution. Only in recent years, however, has the role of research as it relates to management been clearly recognized.

Reflecting this change in orientation, the following definition of marketing research is offered: *marketing research* is the scientific and controlled gathering of nonroutine marketing information undertaken to help management solve marketing problems. There is often hearty disagreement over the answer to the question of whether marketing research is a science. One's answer depends on the employed definition of "science." To be specific, a research activity should use the scientific method. In this method, hypotheses (tentative statements of relationships or of solutions to problems) are drawn from informal observations. These hypotheses are then tested. Ultimately, the hypothesis is accepted, rejected, or modified according to the results of the test. In a true science, verified hypotheses are turned into "laws." In marketing research, verified hypotheses become the generalizations upon which management develops its marketing programs. (To simplify our discussion, we will use "questions" as a synonym of "hypothesis.")

The mechanics of marketing research must be controlled so that the right facts are obtained in the answer to the correct problem. The control of fact-finding is the responsibility of the research director, who must correctly design the research and carefully supervise its execution to ensure that it goes according to plan. Maintaining control in marketing research is often difficult because of the distance that separates the researcher and the market and because the services of outsiders are often required to complete a research project.[1]

WHAT NEEDS RESEARCHING IN MARKETING?

An easy, and truthful, answer to this question is "Everything." There is no aspect of marketing to which research cannot be applied. Every concept presented in this marketing text and every element involved in the marketing management process can be subjected to a great deal of careful marketing research. One convenient way to focus attention on those matters that especially need researching is to consider the elements involved in marketing management. Many important questions relating to the consumer can be raised. Some are:

- Who is/are the customer(s)?
- What does he/she desire in the way of satisfaction?
- Where does he/she choose to purchase?
- Why does he/she buy, or not buy?
- When does he/she purchase?
- How does he/she go about seeking satisfaction in the market?

Another area where research is critical is *profits.* Two elements are involved. First, there is the need to forecast sales and related costs—resulting in profits. Second, there is the necessity to plan a competitive marketing program that will produce the desired level of sales at an appropriate cost. Sales forecasting is the principal tool used in implementing the profit-direction element in the marketing management concept. Of course, the analysis of past sales and interpretation of cost information are important in evaluation of performance and provide useful facts for future planning.

A great deal of marketing research is directed toward rather specialized areas of management. These activities are broken down into five major areas of marketing research. Briefly, these activities are:

1. *Research on markets*—market trends, market share, market potentials, market characteristics, completion, and other market intelligence.
2. *Research on sales*—sales analysis, sales forecasting, quota-setting, sales territory design, sales performance measurement, trade channels, distribution costs, and inventories.

3. *Research on products*—new product research, product features, brand image, concept tests, product tests, and market tests. (See the following Newsline.)

4. *Research on advertising and promotion*—promotion concepts, copy research, media research, merchandising, packaging, advertising effectiveness measurement.

5. *Research on corporate growth and development*—economic and technological forecasting, corporate planning inputs, corporate image, profitability measurement, merger and acquisition studies, and facilities location.

NEWSLINE: HOW EXECS USE RESEARCH

Creating and introducing new products is the most important research priority among marketing executives. The Marketing Science Institute of Cambridge, Massachusetts, surveyed 160 executives from its sponsoring organizations. The executives, representing 60 major consumer and industrial goods and services corporations, were asked to divide 100 points among several research areas.

After successful new product introductions, the executives said that market orientation and customer relationships are the next most important areas. Those issues displaced improving the use of marketing information and measuring brand equity as the second- and third-highest concerns, respectively, in the previous survey.

"The new research priorities indicate that a shift is taking place in marketing practice," notes Donald Lehmann, executive director of the institute. "Market orientation has taken hold and the increasing power of the consumer is apparent in the movement away from product-driven strategies. Marketers also realize that they need to make choices about who their customers should be and whose needs they are best equipped to meet . . . and most significantly, they are looking for better ways to anticipate adoption and diffusion of really new products." Said Marni Clippenger, communications director at MSI, "Companies seem to be shifting away from using the brand to really figuring out what customers want."

Source: Rachel Rosenthal, "New Products Reign as Research Priority," *Advertising Age*, August 8, 1994, p. 26; Robert McMath, "To Test or Not To Test," *American Demographics*, June 1998, p. 64; John McManus, "Mission Invisible," *American Demographics*, March 1999, p. 6.

MARKETING CAPSULE *3.1*

1. Marketing research is the scientific and controlled gathering of nonroutine marketing information undertaken to help management solve marketing problems.

2. Any business that is consumer-oriented will benefit from marketing research.

3. Research can be applied to every facet of marketing.

Sales forecasts	Demographic trends
Cost forecasts	Legislative impact
Product testing	Price testing
Consumer needs	Marketing communication testing
Consumer attitudes	Channel locations
Consumer product usage	Competition
Market size/trends	Psychographic trends
Product replacement	Environmental trends

FIGURE 3.2 Areas of research application

PROCEDURES AND TECHNIQUES IN MARKETING RESEARCH

Considering the relatively short span of time in which marketing research has developed since the 1930s, it is quite remarkable that so sophisticated and thorough a collection of procedures and techniques should have been developed. In many respects, marketing research has advanced faster than any other specialized area in marketing management. In view of the highly specialized nature of marketing research, it is not possible in this discussion to present more than an outline of the basic procedures and techniques.

It is important for a marketing manager to be familiar with the basic procedures and techniques of marketing research. It is true that many businesspeople will never have occasion to engage personally in marketing research. However, it is quite likely that they will be faced with a need either to supervise an internal marketing research activity or to work with an outside marketing research firm. The manager who understands the research function is in a position to judge intelligently the proposals made by research specialists and to evaluate their findings and recommendations. Occasionally, the manager herself will have to seek solutions to marketing problems. It may not be possible to obtain the services of marketing research specialists. The manager familiar with the basic procedures of fact-finding in marketing should be able to supervise a reasonably satisfactory search for the information required.

There is no single set of steps in a market research procedure that is accepted by all. Indeed, each marketing research problem requires, to some degree, its own peculiar procedure. However, there is general agreement that four major activities should be performed in a thorough marketing research project. These are: (1) making a preliminary investigation; (2) creating the research design; (3) conducting the investigation; and (4) processing the data/reporting results (see Figure 3.3).[2]

Making a Preliminary Investigation

There are two phases of activity in the preliminary investigation. The first of these involves the determination of the purpose and scope of the research. The second involves an investigation into the marketing environment called the informal assessment.

Determining the Purpose and Scope of the Research

The basic and critical problem in marketing research is seldom the problem that appears on the surface. It is therefore necessary to explore beneath the surface to ascertain the nature and size of the problem. This is the vital first step and *must* be done correctly, since every subsequent phase of the project is directed at solving the basic problem. For the research

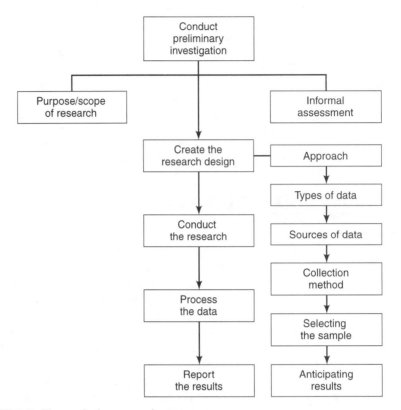

FIGURE 3.3 The marketing research process

to be worthwhile (indeed, for it not to be a waste of resources), the problem must be stated clearly and correctly. Failure to do so is the most serious of mistakes in this project.

Correctly defining the research problem should lead to the establishment of the research parameters. A research study could be restricted by function (advertising); customer group (heavy users); market (Far East); and time frame (1999–2001). Because research is so costly, it is imperative that parameters are established and maintained.

The Informal Assessment

The second important phase of the preliminary investigation is called the *informal assessment*. This is an unstructured search of the marketing environment. It enables the researcher to become familiar with the problem setting. This is particularly important for the outside consultant who needs to become acquainted with the company, its customers, its products, and all of the marketing conditions surrounding the problems. But it is also wise for the company researcher to refresh his/her knowledge of those internal factors bearing on the problem and also to discover the external elements involved.

The informal investigation goes beyond merely "getting acquainted" with the problem and its marketing setting, however. The final result of the preliminary investigation is the creation of a set of research questions. In marketing research, theses questions can be stated as a tentative explanation of the problem that the research is designed to solve. For example, if a marketing manager is trying to solve a problem that involves an important loss of market share in a particular area of the country, an informal investigation might reveal three possible reasons for the decline in market position. These reasons, until verified by thorough study, can best be stated as research statements:

1. The decline in market share is the result of increased competitive advertising in the area.

2. The decline in market share is the result of the test marketing of a new product by a major competitor.

3. The decline in market share is the result of "stock outs" at the retail level caused by a trucking strike in the area.

In attempting to verify one or more of these hypothetical statements, the researcher examines company records to uncover new sources of information or to discover relationships in old data with bearing on the current problem. Interviews with company executives and operating personnel are often conducted. Interviews are also conducted with various persons outside the company whose opinions might be expected to have some relevance to the problem. The preliminary search is always limited to obtaining an insight into the problem and into possible solutions for it.

In the final phase of the preliminary investigation, the researcher analyzes the results he has so far obtained and restates them in the form of research questions to be tested in the subsequent research steps.

Creating the Research Design

The design of a marketing research project is the plan proposed for testing the research questions as well as collecting and processing information. The administration of the project according to the design insures that the fact-finding process will be adequately controlled. "Design" means more than simply using good market research procedures. Every research project should be individually designed to produce the kinds of information needed to solve a particular problem. For this reason, no two market research projects are ever exactly alike.[3]

Six steps are involved in creating a research design: choosing the approach, determining types of data needed, locating data sources, choosing a method of collecting data, selecting the sample, and anticipating/collecting the results.

Choosing the Approach Three alternative approaches are possible in creating a research design. They are not mutually exclusive, but in most cases, the design of a research plan is limited to the use of one of the three.

The first approach is the *experimental approach*. This approach requires that certain procedural rules must be followed. Essentially, the variable of interest—e.g., price, message—must be manipulated and everyone participating in the experiment must have a known and equal chance of being selected.

In a market experiment, information relating to the basic problem is obtained through the use of a small-scale simulated program designed to test a specific research hypothesis. Suppose, for example, that we wish to test the question that *families of similar size and economic characteristics living in three different cities purchase different amounts of a particular formula of a soft drink, such as Dr. Pepper.* The first step would be to establish the research question: "For a given time period, the average fluid ounces of a Formula A, B, or C purchase in each city were the same." Next, a sample of the families in each city would be selected and randomly assigned either A, B, or C. Next, a survey would be taken to determine the number of ounces purchased by each family. Once this was done, a statistical test would be used to test the research question. If statistically significant differences in purchases of Formula A, B, or C of Dr. Pepper were noted, it could be concluded that taste does influence the amount of this soft drink purchased by families with the same social and economic characteristics. Of course, other hypotheses about soft drink purchasing could also have been tested using a slightly different method. For example, the effect of television advertising on the purchase of Dr. Pepper might have been studied by inspecting purchases in two or more cities that are in the same general area of the country (such as the Southwest) but in which different levels of television advertising had been used.

The second approach is the *historical.* In this approach, reliance is placed on past experiences in seeking solutions to marketing problems. Historical marketing facts are relevant only to the degree that they can be projected into the future. Fortunately, in many areas of marketing, this can be done with a good deal of confidence. Certain types of changes, such as populations and income distribution, come about rather slowly. The day-to-day effect of these changes on marketing is almost imperceptible. Projections of future population, gross national product, and consumer purchasing power are practically foolproof. Historical analyses of such factors as consumer behavior, competitive selling tactics, and distributors' buying practices tend also to be fairly reliable indicators of future behavior by these same marketing components. Often, it is possible to trace the experience of organizations similar to yours and assess how they dealt with similar problems. There are literally hundreds of case studies on companies such as Microsoft that are useful to many business functions. Learning from the mistakes of others makes good business sense.

The third approach that can be used in designing a marketing research plan is the *survey approach.* In the survey approach, marketing information is collected either from observation or by questionnaire or interview. In contrast to the experimental and historical methods, in which the data are more or less directly related to the problem, the survey approach necessarily involves far more subjectivity and intuition on the part of the researcher. Watching a customer make a purchase of a new TV reveals something about his motives; simply asking him why he is buying it is much better. Drawing conclusions from either observations of behavior or from the opinions offered by a respondent create important insights. The survey method is flexible. It can be adapted to almost any type of research design. For this reason, and because of the difficulties in creating marketing experiments and in collecting pertinent historical data, the survey approach is the most often used in marketing research.

Determining the Types of Data Needed   Three types of data are used: facts, opinions, and motivational information. The types of data required are partly identified by the nature of the problem to be solved. For instance, if the problem relates to production and inventory scheduling, the *facts* that are needed relate to market and sales potential. On the other hand, if the problem revolves around the choice between two new products, the *opinions* of potential customers are important considerations. Finally, if a problem involves the choice of an appropriate selling appeal, buyers' *motivations* are probably be most important. Facts are quantitative or descriptive information that can be verified. Opinions are ideas relating to a problem that are expressed by people involved in the solution. Motivations are basic reasons, recognized or unrecognized, that explain action. They are extremely difficult to discover.

Locating the Sources of Data   There are two general sources of data, *secondary* sources and *primary* sources.

Secondary source information has been previously published and can be either internal or external. Company records and previously prepared marketing research reports are typical of internal secondary source material. External secondary sources are widely available and can be found outside the organization. Excellent bibliographies of secondary data sources are available, especially online. There are eight primary sources of secondary market information:

1. Public libraries.
2. Universities—library facilities and bureaus of business and economic research.
3. Government agencies—especially departments of commerce, agriculture, and labor.
4. Professional and trade associations.
5. Commercial publishers—especially trade publications.
6. Research and nonprofit organizations.
7. Conferences and personal contact.
8. Computer-provided search systems.

There are tremendous advantages in using data from secondary sources. In the first place, the expense of gathering information from secondary sources is a fraction of the cost of collecting primary data. The time required to collect data is also less. Frequently, the information required to solve a management problem must be obtained quickly. Thanks to computer technology, it is now possible to gather, merge, and reformulate many secondary sources of data. This capability has made secondary data even more attractive.

The inherent limitations of using secondary sources data are twofold. First, the information is frequently dated. Second, seldom are secondary data collected for precisely the same reasons that the information is sought to solve the current marketing problem. In spite of these limitations, the advantages of secondary research are so great that it is a common procedure not to proceed with the collection of primary data until after a thorough search of secondary information source has been completed.

Primary information is obtained directly from its source. It involves data that are not available in published form or in company records. It is gathered specifically to answer your research question. The sources of primary information, however, cannot be as easily identified as can the sources of secondary market data. Having identified the information required to help management solve a problem, it is usually possible to identify the person or persons possessing the information desired. In some cases, the information can be obtained from one of several sources. In other situations, the information can be obtained only by contacting specific sources. For example, a manufacturer of vitamins for children discovered that it was necessary to obtain information from the users (children), purchasers (parents), sellers (for the most part, druggists), and purchase influencers (pediatricians). Similarly, a manufacturer of feed for dairy cattle found it desirable to seek market information from farmers, feed dealers, and dairy specialists. Obviously, it is expensive to collect marketing information from multiple sources, and often it is rather time-consuming. These two disadvantages are offset by the fact that the information so obtained is tailored to the specific problem at hand. Ultimately, the question as to which source of market information to use depends on the value of the information in relationship to the time and cost required to gather it.[4]

Choosing the Method of Collecting Data   There are various methods of collecting data, both secondary and primary. Secondary sources of information, listed earlier, can be gathered through a number of means. A company may establish a data-gathering/storage system as part of their computer system. Sales, expenses, inventory, returns, and customer complaints are then gathered automatically. Or a company can subscribe to one or more public research companies that gather relevant information. Finally, a company can obtain information on a problem-by-problem basis.

There are three common methods used to collect primary information: observation, questionnaire, and self-report. *Observational data collection* may be the oldest method. Since the beginning of commerce, merchants have been watching their customers and noncustomers engage in a variety of behaviors. Examples include shopping, purchase, return, complaint behavior, and so forth. A local fast food manager might simply observe the expression on customers' faces as they eat a new sandwich. More formal observation techniques are also employed. Video cameras or audio systems can be targeted at customers. Researchers can also be hired to do license plate surveys in parking lots or simply record observations in a prescribed manner. There are even observational techniques that are quite intrusive. For instance, in the case of a *pantry (cabinet) audit*, the researcher comes to the consumer's home and actually takes an inventory of products found. *Ethnography* requires that the researcher practically move in with the consumer and observe various relevant behaviors. This technique is illustrated in the Newsline box that follows.

NEWSLINE: WHERE'S THE BEEF?

A woman in suburban Baltimore is shopping for her family's meals for the week. She cruises past the poultry section, stopping only momentarily to drop a couple of packages of boneless chicken breasts into her cart. Then, the dreaded sea of red looms before her. Tentatively, she picks up a package of beef. "This cut looks good, not too fatty," she says, juggling her two-year-old on her hip. "But I don't know what it is. I don't know how to cook it," she confesses, and trades it for a small package of sirloin and her regular order of ground beef.

Scenes like these are replayed daily in supermarkets across the country. But this time, it's being captured on videotape by New York City–based PortiCo Research, part of a recent ethnographic study of beef consumers for the National Cattleman's Beef Association (NCBA) and major grocery retailers. And due in part to the trepidation of this one mother in Baltimore, many grocers' meat cases are now being rearranged to display beef by cooking method, rather than by cuts of meat. Simple, three-step cooking instructions will soon be printed on the packages.

Ethnographic research, which combines intense observation with customer interviews, shows companies how people live with products—how they purchase and use them in their everyday lives. Knowing what consumers do with beef is vital to the NCBA. The study cost the NCBA approximately $60,000 (studies might range from $5,000 to $800,000). PortiCo videotaped consumer's purchasing behavior as well as their preparation habits at home. The researchers interviewed them each step of the way what they thought about beef, why they did (or didn't) select particular cuts, and how they prepared the family meal. The retailers couldn't believe how little consumers knew about something that seemed as familiar to them as sliced bread or soft drinks.

Sources: Kendra Parker, "How Do You Like Your Beef?" *American Demographics,* January 2000, pp. 35–38; Jennifer Lach, "Meet You in Aisle Three," *American Demographics,* April 1999, pp. 41–42.

The observation technique can provide important research insights, especially if consistent patterns are noted. This method is relatively inexpensive and can be implemented and completed quickly. Unfortunately, interpreting an observation is still very subjective and mistakes are made.

Gathering information through a *questionnaire* format reflects the most popular research technique. There are two interrelated issues: the design of the questionnaire and the administration of the questionnaire.

There are several rules of thumb that should be followed when designing a questionnaire. For example, a good questionnaire should be like a well-written story: it should be logical, relevant, easy to follow, and interesting to the reader/respondent. There are also a host of techniques and related guidelines. For example, Figure 3.4 illustrates the forms questions can take. A yes/no question is considered a closed-ended dichotomous question; i.e., respondent *must* check one of two possible answers. Questions 4 and 5 are two types of scaled questions. Questions 6–8 are open-ended, in that respondent can provide any answer desired. Closed-ended questions are best used when the researcher desires a particular set of answers or feels the respondent is unlikely to come up with an original answer. Open-ended questions allow the respondent to come up with personal answers. Of course, there is a risk that the respondent will have no answer.

Other considerations are whether to place the easier questions at the beginning of the questionnaire, group similar questions, or place demographic questions at the end of the questionnaire. Again, the goal is to enable the respondent to answer the questionnaire easily and accurately.

The design of a questionnaire is a function of how the questionnaire is administered, and vice versa. Four techniques for administering a questionnaire are currently used: mail, telephone, personal interview, and online. In the *mail technique*, the questionnaire is distributed and returned through the mail. A typical packet might contain a cover letter explaining the purpose of the research, a copy of the questionnaire, a stamped self-addressed return envelope, and an incentive for compliance (cash, merchandise, contribution to charity, or copy of report). Mail questionnaires allow the researcher to ask a large number of questions over a broad range of topics. They also allow the respondent to answer the questionnaire at their leisure. Finally, the standardized format does not allow for subjective bias. Unfortunately, these advantages can become limitations. The longer the questionnaire, the less likely the individual will respond. In fact, a response rate of 10–20% is common without an incentive. Control is lost through the mail process. Did the targeted person answer the questionnaire? Did the respondent understand the questions? Did she/he complete the questionnaire? Was the questionnaire returned on time? The loss of control also means that the interviewer cannot probe further into an interesting or controversial answer.

A more convenient and faster way of gathering marketing information is to conduct a *telephone survey*. Names and related telephone numbers can be obtained directly from a telephone directory or from an internally or externally generated database. Telephone surveys are limited in several important ways, such as the difficulty of reaching the correct respondent, the problem of completing the interview if the respondent decides to hang up, and the inability to eliminate the bias introduced by not interviewing those without phones or individuals with unlisted numbers. Also, 10–15 questions are likely to be the maximum number to be asked. Therefore, only a limited number of topics can be addressed. In spite of these limitations, the telephone survey method has grown in popularity. The costs are relatively low, research companies can provide well-trained and technically supported interviewers, and the technique works if the research questions are limited and require a quick answer. Still, it would be better if they didn't call while you were eating dinner.

Although often very costly and time-consuming, *personal interviews* may constitute the best way of collecting survey information. Once compliance is gained, the well-trained interviewer can make sure the right person is answering, ask as many questions as necessary,

A. DIRECT QUESTIONS/CLOSED-ENDED

1. HAVE YOU PURCHASED A NEW AUTOMOBILE SINCE JANUARY 1 OF THIS
   YEAR:

   ☐ YES   ☐ NO

2. IF YOU HAVE PURCHASED A NEW AUTOMOBILE, WHAT MAKE AND
   MODEL DID YOU BUY?

   MAKE:_____ MODEL:_____

3. IF YOU HAVE NOT PURCHASED A CAR SINCE JANUARY 1, DO YOU NOW
   PLAN TO BUY A NEW AUTOMOBILE BEFORE DECEMBER 31 OF THIS
   YEAR?

   ☐ YES   ☐ NO   ☐ NOT DECIDED

4. IF YOU HAVE NOT DECIDED WHETHER OR NOT YOU WILL BUY A NEW
   AUTOMOBILE, DO YOU NOW THINK THAT IT IS

   __EXTREMELY LIKELY

   __QUITE LIKELY

   __UNLIKELY

   __EXTREMELY UNLIKELY

   THAT YOU WILL BUY A NEW AUTOMOBILE BETWEEN NOW AND
   DECEMBER 31?

5. I TEND TO RELY HEAVILY ON THE REPUTATION OF A CAR BRAND

   DISAGREE   AGREE

        1   2   3   4   5

B. DEPTH QUESTIONS/OPEN-ENDED

6. IF YOU HAVE NOT PURCHASED A NEW AUTOMOBILE, WHAT IS THE MOST
   IMPORTANT REASON FOR YOUR DECISION NOT TO BUY A NEW CAR?

   _____
   _____

7. THAT IS VERY INTERESTING. TELL ME MORE ABOUT THAT.

   _____
   _____

8. ANY OTHER REASONS?

   _____
   _____

FIGURE 3.4   Examples of questions used in marketing research

make sure questions are understood, probe in order to address new issues, and encourage
the respondent to complete the questionnaire. With freedom comes bias. It is sometimes
difficult for an interviewer to maintain objectivity. Asking questions with a certain intona-
tion, changing the wording, or changing the ordering of questions can all modify responses.

There are several *online* information-gathering techniques that allow the respondent more freedom in providing answers. As one would expect, there has been a recent rapid technological evolution in this area. Online questionnaires can help web site sponsors to gauge customer satisfaction, profile visitors, and provide a way to measure traffic for advertisers beyond banner click-throughs. By using research tools such as exit surveys, e-tailers can find out why people are leaving their sites—and why they might not come back.

There are four popular types of online research. *Pop-up surveys* occur when visitors are intercepted when they leave certain pages of the web site. A questionnaire then appears in a box on top of their main browser screens asking for responses. With *e-mail/web surveys*, a company sends an e-mail message asking the recipient to complete a survey. Sometimes the survey is embedded in the e-mail itself. Other times the e-mail lists either a passworded location to visit or a unique location that only the addressee can access to fill out the survey. *Online groups* are much like traditional focus groups, but are conducted in a web-based chat room where select individuals are invited by the company or its research firm. Finally, in the case of *moderated e-mail groups*, discussions take place over a period of time with a group communicating by e-mail. A moderator compiles the answers and sends the summary back to the group for comments and follow-up.

The third technique used to gather research information is *self-reporting*. This technique allows the respondent to deliver the information in a somewhat unstructured format. One very popular version of this technique is the *focus group*. A focus group takes place in a room where approximately 8–10 individuals and a trained moderator gather to discuss a particular business problem or set of problems. Often, the room contains a two-way mirror, which the sponsors of the research sit behind in order to observe the process. The proceedings are audiotaped and/or videotaped. Focus groups have been an extremely popular type of data collecting for a long time. A great deal of diverse information can be gathered quickly (assuming there is a well-trained moderator). However, there are serious limitations. It's still a subjective process and interpretation is necessary. It is also expensive; often several thousand dollars per focus group. Finally, it is difficult to control the behavior of the participants. Some dominate and some say nothing. And some become the equivalent of professional focus group members and no longer are able to provide the hoped-for spontaneity.

According to a psychologically proven premise, it is possible by impersonalizing questions to obtain information from a respondent that he would not, or could not, otherwise provide. This method involves the use of the *projective technique*, and represents a second type of self-report technique. The intent of the projective technique is to give respondents an opportunity to answer questions without the embarrassment or confusion created by direct involvement. Several projective techniques are employed:

1. Word association tests. In the word association test, the respondent is asked to say the first word that comes into his mind upon the presentation of another word stimulus. The most obvious applications of this test are in research on brand recognition, company image, and advertising appeals.

2. Sentence completion tests. In a sentence completion test, the respondent is asked to complete a number of sentences with the first words that come to mind. A series of sentence completion questions used by a supermarket chain were: (a) I like to shop in an AG supermarket because . . .; (b) I think that food prices are . . .; (c) The thing that bothers me most about food shopping in an AG store is . . . .

   The sentence completion test is relatively simple to administer and easy to interpret. It is usually difficult, however, to reduce the finding from a sentence completion test to statistical form.

3. Psychodrama. In the psychodramatic type of question, the respondent is asked to project himself into an artificial marketing situation. The obvious artificiality of the situation makes the psychodrama a "role-playing" experiment in which the respondent provides information based on his *personal* attitudes through his explanation of the artificial situation.

Perhaps the greatest deficiency of projective techniques is the difficulty of presenting the findings. The identification of attitudes, motives, opinions, and so forth is not difficult; however, it is extremely hard to measure the importance of these factors.

Selecting the Sample   In most marketing research, it is seldom necessary to conduct a complete census; i.e., to talk to 100% of the target segment. To do so is time-consuming and expensive. For this reason most marketing surveys make use of samples. A *sample* is a group of elements (persons, stores, financial reports) chosen from among a "total population" or "universe." The value of a research project is directly affected by how well the sample has been conceived and constructed.[5]

The selection of the sample to be investigated requires a master list, or a framework, from which they may be selected. The sampling frame is the "population" or statistical "universe" from which the sample units will be selected. The frame for a survey of attitudes of credit customers of a department store would be the company's list of customers using charge accounts.

Although there are many kinds of sample designs, all of them can be classified as either *probability* samples or *nonprobability* samples. In a probability sample, each unit has a known chance of being selected for inclusion in the sample. Its simplest version is the *simple random* sample, in which each unit in the sample frame has exactly the same chance of selection. Examples of this include flipping a fair coin, whose sides have a 50% chance of turning up, and throwing an unloaded die, whose sides have a 16 2/3% chance of turning up. This same principle can be applied to the previous department store example. A sample of names could be selected from the company's list of charge customers according to a random process, such as that of using a table of random digits.

While in a *probability* sample the sampling units have a known chance of being selected, in a *nonprobability* sample the sampling units are selected arbitrarily. To return to our department store example, instead of using a table of random numbers to select a sample of charge customers, an arbitrary and more convenient method would be to take the first fifty or sixty names on the list.

Anticipating the Results/Making the Report   The research plan should provide for: (1) procedures for processing the data; (2) procedures for interpretation and analysis of the findings; and (3) an outline of the final report. In reaching these decisions, it is usually helpful to work from the form and content of the final report. The report should present a summary of findings and recommendations for management action drawn up in the light of the reasons for the research. The kinds of facts to be presented and the manner of their presentation dictates the type of analysis to be undertaken. The kinds of analysis will, in turn, often suggest the method of data processing. *Data processing* in general refers to the procedures for sorting, assembling, and reporting data. It can be done manually by the use of work sheets or by computer programming. The method of data processing has important bearing upon the manner in which the data are collected and reported. Thus, the design of the project is often expedited by a thorough consideration of the kinds of results that are expected and how they will be handled in the final report.

Anticipating the results of the project and preparing a "dummy" final report has another advantage. It is often helpful to use the results of this step in the research design to demonstrate to management the kind of project that is going to be undertaken. Agreement by the management group that the kinds of information anticipated will assist in the solving of a marketing problem is helpful in obtaining approval for the project and in restraining management expectations as to the scope and purpose of the project.

CONDUCTING THE RESEARCH

The attention devoted in the previous paragraphs to the design of the research plan might leave the impression that once a marketing research project has been carefully designed, the job is almost done. Clearly, this is not the case. The implementation of a research plan is seldom an easy task. Often a research program requires extra effort from already-busy personnel in the company. In other cases, outsiders must be recruited, hired, and trained. In either situation, carrying out a marketing research plan is difficult and requires very close supervision and control. To the extent that the plan has been well conceived, supervision and control are restricted to making sure that the research activities called for in the plan are carried out according to schedule and in the manner prescribed.

PROCESSING THE DATA

Processing the data obtained in a market survey involves transforming the information obtained into a report to be used by management. Four steps are involved: (1) editing the data; (2) tabulating the data; (3) interpreting the data; and (4) presenting the report. If, in the *anticipation of the results* of the survey, the procedures for handling the data have been sent forth and the form of the final report conceived, these final four steps in the research procedure may be quite mechanical. A good plan for the analysis and interpretation of the data is of immense assistance in bringing a project to a successful conclusion, but it should never limit the kinds of interpretations that eventually are made or restrict the content of the final report.

The final report of a marketing research study should ordinarily be written. Since vast amounts of data often are involved, the written report is the only appropriate method of presenting these findings. The written report also has the advantage of being permanent, thus permitting management to study the findings carefully and to refer to them in the future. Unfortunately, many marketing research projects are never translated into management action—sometimes because the research conclusions do not directly contribute to the solution of the problem, sometimes because the report is too technical and difficult to understand, and sometimes because the report writer has not offered specific suggestions as to how the report should be translated into management strategy.

THE VALUE OF MARKETING RESEARCH

It is important to point out that it is not always necessary to conduct research before attempting to solve a problem in marketing management. The manager may feel that he already knows enough to make a good decision. In a few instances, there may be no choice among alternatives and hence no decision to make. It is rather pointless to study a problem if there is only one possible solutions. But in most business situations, the manager must make a choice among two or more courses of action. This is where fact-finding enters in to help make the choice.

But even if a manager would like more information in order to make a decision, it is not always wise for her to conduct the research that would be required. One reason is that the time involved may be too great. Another more compelling reason is that the cost of the research may exceed its contribution. In principle, it is easy to understand how such a cost test might be applied. If the cost of conducting the research is less than its contribution to the improvement of the decision, the research should be carried out. If its cost is greater, it should not be conducted. The application of this principle in actual practice is somewhat more complex. Finally, good research should help integrate marketing with the other areas of the business.

INTEGRATED MARKETING *3.1*

RESEARCH BRINGS IT TOGETHER

It's the bane of modern business: too many data, not enough information. Computers are everywhere, accumulating gigabytes galore. Yet it only seems to get harder to find the forest for the trees—to extract significance from the blizzard of numbers, facts, and stats. But help is on the way, in the form of a new class of software technology known broadly as data-mining. First developed to help scientists make sense of experimental data, this software has enough smarts to "see" meaningful patterns and relationships—to see patterns that might otherwise take tens of man-years to find. That's a huge leap beyond conventional computer databases, which are powerful but unimaginative. They must be told precisely what to look for. Data-mining tools can sift through immense collections of customer, marketing, production, and financial data, and, using statistical and artificial intelligence techniques, identify what's worth noting and what's not.

The payoffs can be huge, as MCI Communications is learning. Like other phone companies, MCI wants to keep its best customers. One way is to identify early those who might be considering jumping to a rival. If it can do that, the carrier can try to keep the customer with offers of special rates and services, for example.

How to find the customers you want to keep from among the millions? MCI's answer has been to comb marketing data on 140 million households, each evaluated on as many as 10,000 attributes—characteristics such as income, lifestyle, and details about past calling habits. But which set of those attributes is the most important to monitor, and within what range of values? A rapidly declining monthly bill may seem like a dead give-away, but is there a subtler pattern in inter-national calling to be looking for, too? Or in the number of calls made to MCI's customer-service lines?

To find out, MCI regularly fires up its IBM SP/2 supercomputer—its "data warehouse"—which identifies the most telling variables to keep an eye on. So far, the SP/2 has compiled a set of 22 detailed—and highly secret—statistical profiles based on repeated crunching of historical facts. None of them could have been developed without data-mining programs, says Lance Boxer, MCI's Chief Information Officer.

Data-mining in itself is a relatively tiny market: sales of such programs will grow to maybe $750 million by 2001. But the technology is crucial in getting a big payoff from what information technology executives think will be an immensely important growth area in coming years: *data warehousing*. There are the enormous collections of data—sometimes trillions of bytes—compiled by mass marketers, retailers, or service companies as they monitor transactions from millions of customers. Data warehouses, running on ultrafast computers with specialized software, are the basis on which companies hope to operate in real time—instantly adjusting product mix, inventory levels, cash reserves, marketing programs, or other factors to changing business conditions.

Source: John W. Verity, "Coaxing Meaning out of Raw Data," *Business Week*, February 3, 1997, pp. 134–138; "Researchers Integrate Internet Tools in Their Work," *R&D Magazine*, June 2000, vol. 24, No. 6, p. E13; "Smarter Kids. Com Chooses Quadstons—The Smartest Customer Data Mining Solution," *Business Week*, July 31, 2000.

THE WALL STREET JOURNAL.

IN PRACTICE

Marketing research is a scientific and controlled process, but ultimately, decisions are based on a blend of facts and intuition. Understanding marketing research allows managers to intelligently evaluate findings and recommendations.

Determining the purpose and scope of the research is the first critical activity in any marketing research project. All subsequent decisions are results of this process. Creating the research design, conducting the investigation, and processing the data are the remaining critical activities. Both primary and secondary data are accumulated when conduction research. Using this information to produce good research allows managers to integrate marketing with other areas of the business.

Secondary sources of data online include associations and business information sites. Check out the American Marketing Association's website at www.ama.org/resource for a list of resources and guides. For links to business directories, media sites, and marketing-related resources, check out A Business Researcher's Interests at www.brint.com.

Your subscription to the Interactive Journal allows you to access articles in various Dow Jones publications. Under **More Dow Jones Sites** in the left menu, click on **Dow Jones & Co.** From here you will be able to access **Dow Jones Web Links** which offers you links to dozens of business and news websites. Click on several of these links now.

Return to the Interactive Journal's **Front Section**. Under **Tools** in the left menu, select **WSJ Yogi**. The WSJ Yogi is a free software application that works like a personal assistant, automatically suggesting relevant content to you as you browse the web. The WSJ Yogi will gather links to related stories as you read. Download the WSJ Yogi now.

Return again to the Interactive Journal's **Front Section**. Under **Resources** in the left menu, select **Special Reports**. This section offers links to special reports that have appeared as supplements to The Wall Street Journal print edition. These reports provide a thorough analysis and review of various topics such as e-commerce, Small Business, and World Business. Review recent **Special Reports** now.

DELIVERABLE

With the information provided in this section about web resources, use the Interactive Journal and relevant web links to conduct market research on recent trends in e-commerce. Find at least five sources of secondary data online that will help you identify relevant trends in e-commerce advertising, marketing, and business strategies.

DISCUSSION QUESTIONS

1. How can marketing research help managers create successful product lines and customer relationships?
2. Most people conduct research when buying certain "big ticket" items like cars or computers. How do you conduct marketing research for these types of items?
3. How has the Internet impacted consumers and their purchase decisions? What about the impact on companies?

MARKETING CAPSULE *3.2*

1. The following steps are involved in conducting marketing research:
   a. Making a preliminary investigation
   b. Creating the research design

   c. Conducting the investigation
   d. Processing the data/deliver the results

SUMMARY

Four major elements are involved in undertaking marketing research. The first element is a preliminary investigation. This initial study permits the researcher to determine the purpose and scope of his research as well as to identify tentative questions.

Creating a research design to test the questions is the most important and most complicated aspect of marketing research. It commences with the selection of the approach to be taken. The three most commonly used are the experimental, the observational, and the survey approaches. Any given project may use one or more of the three.

It is also necessary to determine the types of data that will be needed to solve the marketing problem and to locate sources where this information can be obtained. Data sources are generally classified as either primary or secondary. Secondary data are made up of previously collected information and are obtained from historical records, publications, government documents, and the like. Primary data are gathered for the first time. The survey method is probably the most frequently used method for collecting primary data. Data are by gathered by mail, by telephone, by personal interviewing, and online.

Another critical aspect of most marketing research projects is the selection of the sample. A probability sample involves the selection of respondents in such a way that every unit in the pool has the same chance of being selected. One method of drawing a probability sample is by the use of a table of random digits. A nonprobability sample is drawn on a judgmental basis; the respondents are selected because they are considered to be representative of the group from which they are drawn.

The final aspect of the research design is the anticipation of the results and the decision as to how the data will be summarized and reported. It is becoming more and more common in large marketing research projects to make use of a computer for the processing and tabulation of the research results. Some problems usually arise, however, and careful supervision and control of the data-collection activities are important. It is particularly critical to guard against various kinds of survey bias that can creep into a project.

MARKETER'S VOCABULARY

Marketing research   The scientific and controlled gathering of nonroutine marketing information undertaken to help management solve marketing problems.

Informal assessment   An unstructured search of the marketing environment.

Research design   Plan proposed for testing the research questions as well as collecting and processing information.

Experimental approach   Variable interest must be manipulated and everyone participating in the experiment must have a known and equal chance of being selected.

Historical/case method   Reliance is placed on past experiences in seeking solutions to current marketing problems.

Survey approach   Marketing information is collected either from observation or by questionnaire or interview.

Secondary source data   Information that has been previously published and can come from within or outside the business.

Primary information   Information gathered to address a particular problem.

Data processing   Procedures for sorting, assembling, and reporting data.

DISCUSSION QUESTIONS

1. Marketing research is sometimes referred to as a "problem-solving tool." Explain what is meant by this statement.

2. It is often argued that only such fields as physics, chemistry, and mathematics are really "scientific" and that marketing research, as common with all behavioral research, cannot be scientific. How would you respond to someone who stated this opinion?

3. Do you think that a distinction can be made between "pure" and "applied" research in marketing?

4. Select a local or campus enterprise with which you are familiar. Identify a marketing problem that it faces. (You may need to interview the manager of the establishment.) Translate this marketing problem into its informational elements. Conduct a small-scale informal investigation:
   (a) What tentative hypotheses can you develop?
   (b) What types of research design do you believe would be necessary to test these hypotheses?

5. A small manufacturer of highly specialized medical laboratory equipment and a manufacturer of a proprietary (nonprescription) cold remedy need information to assist in planning new product introductions. What would be the advantages and drawbacks of using primary versus secondary marketing information for each firm?

6. You are the advertising manager of a company that manufactures professional baseball equipment. Your firm employs fifty field salespeople who make periodic calls on sporting goods dealers, large schools and colleges, and professional athletic organizations. You also place full-page advertisements in a trade publication for the sporting goods industry, *Scholastic Coach*. The president of your company has questioned the use of this publication and has asked you to find out how effective it is in increasing awareness about your products and in stimulating sales. How would you go about this task?

7. In 1970, Ford Motor Co. introduced its subcompact automobile, the Pinto. Suppose you had been a marketing research analyst working for another car manufacturer. What kinds of primary and secondary marketing research would you have conducted to evaluate the success of this new product introduction?

PROJECT

Design a short questionnaire (no more than 10 questions) intended to reveal whether or not another student is a good prospect for a new laptop computer. Assume the purpose of this questionnaire is to obtain information that could be used to help increase sales of laptops to college students. Would you use the same questions on a mail questionnaire as in a personal interview? If not, what questions would you use if you were going to mail the questionnaires?

CASE APPLICATION

RESEARCH SAVES THE DAY AT CASE

In today's combative marketplace, making any significant progress against skillful and large rivals is nothing short of a colossal achievement. Case Corporation, a manufacturer of construction and farm equipment, can make such a claim, but only after spending two years digging itself out of decline— operating losses for 1991 and 1992 reached $900,000—and finally showing growth. Case's net income increased more than 300% in 1994 to $165 million, with a 14% sales increase, and 1995 revenues reached $4.2 billion.

Significant headway toward recovery began in 1994 when new CEO Jean-Pierre Rosso launched a new era at Case. His matter-of-fact pronouncement, "We need to be asking what the farmer and contractor need," triggered the company's turnaround and kindled a new respect from its customers.

Basic as it may seem, for most of the 1980s, "asking" was not a part of Case's product-driven orientation. Result: Underperforming products such as low-horsepower tractors entered the marketplace, fueled by low prices and sales incentives.

Worse yet, when market demand eventually plummeted, dealers found themselves stuck with a glut of unsold Case equipment. To further aggravate the situation, relationships with dealers were increasingly greeted with suspicion.

In the face of those dire conditions, Rosso issued his market-driven directive that pressed Case managers to determine the wants and needs of its customers. One incident showcases the process they used to obtain reliable customer feedback: A contractor was flown in to Case's Burlington, Iowa test site and put to work for three days testing a piece of Case equipment and comparing its performance with that of comparable Caterpillar and Deere machines. Each day managers grilled the customer about features, benefits, and problems.

In another approach, Case sent teams of engineers and marketing personnel to talk to key customers and users of competitors' equipment. Applying what they learned from the feedback, engineers developed prototype machines and shipped them to hundreds of participating users for evaluation. The engineers then incorporated actual field data into final prototypes.

The bottom line: All this market-driven "asking" is a far cry from the Case's reputation during the 1980s of being one of the most mismanaged companies in the field.

Questions

1. Although things seem to be going well for Case, can you identify any potential mistakes they made in doing their research?
2. How could they gather secondary data on this product category?

REFERENCES

1. Ralph H. Sprague, Jr. and Hugh J. Watson, *Decision Support Systems: Putting Theory Into Practice*, Englewood Cliffs, N.J.: Prentice-Hall, 1986, p. 1.
2. Claire Selitz, Lawrence S. Wrightsman, and Stuart W. Cook, *Research Methods in Social Relations*, New York: Holt, Reinhart and Winston, 1976, pp. 114–115.
3. Ian P. Murphy, "Research with Bottom Line in Mind Only," *Marketing News*, March 3, 1997, p. 10.
4. Pamela L. Alreck and Robert B. Settle, *The Survey Research Handbook*, Richard D. Irwin, Inc., 1995.
5. Seymour Sudman, *Applied Sampling*, New York: Academic Press, 1976.

CHAPTER 4

UNDERSTANDING BUYER BEHAVIOR

LEARNING OBJECTIVES

Having read this chapter, you should be able to:

- Understand the behavior of the individual consumers in the marketplace.
- Examine the many factors that influence consumer behavior.
- Recognize the various principles of psychology, sociology, and social psychology that are of value in explaining consumer behavior.
- Examine the relationship of consumer behavior to marketing management decisions—particularly, target market selection and the design of the marketing mix.
- Understand how organizational market behavior differs from consumer market behavior.
- Examine how organizations make purchase decisions.

TILL DEATH DO US PART

At **1:58 P.M.** on Wednesday, May 5, in Houston's St. Luke's Episcopal Hospital, a consumer was born. Her name was Alyssa J. Nedell, and by the time she went home three days later, some of America's biggest marketers were pursuing her with samples, coupons, and assorted freebies. Proctor & Gamble hoped its Pampers brand would win the battle for Alyssa's bottom. Johnson & Johnson offered a tiny sample of its baby soap. Bristol-Myers Squibb Co. sent along some of its Enfamil baby formula.

Like no generation before, Alyssa enters a consumer culture surrounded by logos, labels, and acts almost from the moment of birth. As an infant, Alyssa may wear Sesame Street diapers and miniature pro-basketball jerseys. By the time she's 20 months old, she will start to recognize some of the thousands of brands flashed in front of her each day. At age 7, if she's anything like the typical kid, she will see some 20,000 TV commercials a year. By the time she's 12, she will have her own entry in the massive data banks of marketers. Multiply Alyssa by 30 million—the number of babies born in this country since 1990—and you have the largest generation to flood the market since the baby boom. More impressive than their numbers, though, is their wealth. The increase in single-parent and dual-earner households means that kids are making shopping decisions once left to Mom. Combining allowance, earnings, and gifts, kids aged 14 and under will directly spend an estimated $20 billion this year, and will influence another $200 billion.

No wonder they have become the target of marketing campaigns so sophisticated as to make the kid-aimed pitches of yore look like, well, Mickey Mouse.

Marketers who had long ignored children now systematically pursue them—even when the tykes are years away from being able to buy their products. "Ten years ago it was cereal, candy, and toys. Today it's also computers and airlines and hotels and banks," says Julie Halpin, general manager of Saatchi & Saatchi Advertising's Kid Connection Division. "A lot of people are turning to a whole segment of the population they haven't been talking to before."

Those businesses that have always targeted kids, such as fast-food restaurants and toymakers, have stepped up their pitches, hoping to reach kids earlier and bind them more tightly. Movies, T-shirts, hamburger wrappers, and dolls are all part of the cross-promotional blitz aimed at convincing kids to spend. The cumulative effect of initiating children into a consumerist ethos at an early age may be profound. As kids take in the world around them, many of their cultural encounters—from books to movies to TV—have become little more than sales pitches. Even their classrooms are filled with corporate logos. To quote clinical psychologist Mary Pipher, "Instead of transmitting a sense of who we are and what we hold important, today's marketing-driven culture is instilling in them the sense that little exists without a sales pitch attached and that self-worth is something you buy at a shopping mall."

Some wonder if marketers are creating a relationship with consumers too soon and for all the wrong reasons.

Sources: David Leonhardt, "Hey Kid, Buy This," *Business Week*, June 30, 1997, p. 65–67; Larry Armstrong, "Pssst! Come Into My Web," *Business Week*, June 30, 1997, p. 67; Tom McGee, "Getting Inside Kids Heads," *American Demographics*, January 1997, pp. 53–59; "Kids These Days," *American Demographics*, April 2000, pp. 9–10; Joan Raymond, "Kids Just Wanna Have Fun," *American Demographics*, February 2000, pp. 57–61.

INTRODUCTION

As noted, many of the parents of today's kids are the baby boomers marketers have been tracking for over forty years. Primarily, their importance is based on their group's enormous size. Just as important, however, is that they have a great deal in common; some demographics, such as age, income, and health; some shared concerns such as college for their children, retirement, and diminishing health; and some behaviors such as voting Republican, eating out, and buying expensive walking shoes. Nevertheless, they still remain individuals who were brought up in a unique family and retain a personal way of thinking and behaving. The ultimate challenge facing marketers is to understand the buyer both as an individual and as a member of society so that the buyer's needs are met by the product offered by the marketer. The purpose of this chapter is to present a discussion of several of the key buyer behaviors considered important to marketers.

BUYER BEHAVIOR AND EXCHANGE

As noted in an earlier chapter, the relationship between the buyer and the seller exists through a phenomenon called a *market exchange.* The exchange process allows the parties to assess the relative trade-offs they must make to satisfy their respective needs and wants. For the marketer, analysis of these trade-offs is guided by company polices and objectives. For example, a company may engage in exchanges only when the profit margin is 10% or greater. The buyer, the other member in the exchange, also has personal policies and objectives that guide their responses in an exchange. Unfortunately, buyers seldom write down their personal policies and objectives. Even more likely, they often don't understand what prompts them to behave in a particular manner. This is the mystery or the "black box" of buyer behavior that makes the exchange process so unpredictable and difficult for marketers to understand.

Buyers are essential partners in the exchange process. Without them, exchanges would stop. They are the focus of successful marketing; their needs and wants are the reason for marketing. Without an understanding of buyer behavior, the market offering cannot possibly be tailored to the demands of potential buyers. When potential buyers are not satisfied, exchange falters and the goals of the marketer cannot be met. As long as buyers have free choice and competitive offerings from which to choose, they are ultimately in control of the marketplace.

A *market* can be defined as a group of potential buyers with needs and wants and the purchasing power to satisfy them. The potential buyers, in commercial situations, "vote" (with their dollars) for the market offering that they feel best meets their needs. An understanding of how they arrive at a decision allows the marketer to build an offering that will attract buyers. Two of the key questions that a marketer needs to answer relative to buyer behavior are:

1. How do potential buyers go about making purchase decisions?
2. What factors influence their decision process and in what way?

The answers to these two questions form the basis for target market selection, and, ultimately, the design of a market offering.

When we use the term "buyer," we are referring to an individual, group, or organization that engages in market exchange. In fact, there are differences in the characteristics of these three entities and how they behave in an exchange. Therefore, individuals and groups are traditionally placed in the *consumer* category, while *organization* is the second category. Let us now turn to consumer decision making.

BUYER BEHAVIOR AS PROBLEM SOLVING

Consumer behavior refers to buyers who are purchasing for personal, family, or group use. Consumer behavior can be thought of as the combination of efforts and results related to the consumer's need to solve problems. Consumer problem solving is triggered by the identification of some unmet need. A family consumes all of the milk in the house or the tires on the family care wear out or the bowling team is planning an end-of-the-season picnic. This presents the person with a problem which must be solved. Problems can be viewed in terms of two types of needs: physical (such as a need for food) or psychological (for example, the need to be accepted by others).

Although the difference is a subtle one, there is some benefit in distinguishing between needs and wants. A need is a basic deficiency given a particular essential item. You need food, water, air, security, and so forth. A want is placing certain personal criteria as to how that need must be fulfilled. Therefore, when we are hungry, we often have a specific food item in mind. Consequently, a teenager will lament to a frustrated parent that there is nothing to eat, standing in front of a full refrigerator. Most of marketing is in the want-fulfilling business, not the need-fulfilling business. Timex doesn't want you to buy just any watch, they want you to want a Timex brand watch. Likewise, Ralph Lauren wants you to want

Polo when you shop for clothes. On the other hand, the American Cancer Association would like you to feel a need for a check-up and doesn't care which doctor you go to. In the end, however, marketing is mostly interested in creating and satisfying wants.

The Decision Process

Figure 4.1 outlines the process a consumer goes through in making a purchase decision. Each step is illustrated in the following sections of your text. Once the process is started, a potential buyer can withdraw at any stage of making the actual purchase. The tendency for a person to go through all six stages is likely only in certain buying situations—a first-time purchase of a product, for instance, or when buying high priced, long-lasting, infrequently purchased articles. This is referred to as *complex decision making.*

   For many products, the purchasing behavior is a routine affair in which the aroused need is satisfied in a habitual manner by repurchasing the same brand. That is, past reinforcement in learning experiences leads directly to buying, and thus the second and third stages are bypassed. This is called *simple decision making.* However, if something changes appreciably (price, product, availability, services), the buyer may reenter the full decision process and consider alternative brands. Whether complex or simple, the first step is need identification.[1]

Need Identification

Whether we act to resolve a particular problem depends upon two factors: (1) the magnitude of the discrepancy between what we have and what we need, and (2) the importance of the problem. A consumer may desire a new Cadillac and own a five-year old Chevrolet. The discrepancy may be fairly large, but relatively unimportant compared to the other prob-

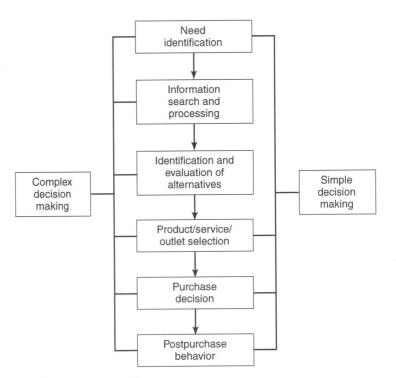

FIGURE 4.1 The consumer decision process

lems he/she faces. Conversely, an individual may own a car that is two years old and running very well. Yet, for various reasons, he/she may consider it extremely important to purchase a car this year. People must resolve these types of conflicts before they can proceed. Otherwise, the buying process for a given product stops at this point, probably in frustration.

Once the problem is recognized, it must be defined in such a way that the consumer can actually initiate the action that will bring about a relevant problem solution. Note that, in many cases, problem recognition and problem definition occur simultaneously, such as a consumer running out of toothpaste. But consider the more complicated problem involved with status and image—how we want others to see us. For example, you may know that you are not satisfied with your appearance, but you may not be able to define it any more precisely than that. Consumers will not know where to begin solving their problem until the problem is adequately defined.

Marketers can become involved in the need recognition stage in three ways. First, they need to know what problems consumers are facing in order to develop a marketing mix to help solve these problems. This requires that they measure problem recognition. Second, on occasion, marketers want to activate problem recognition. Public Service Announcements espousing the dangers of cigarette smoking is an example. Weekend and night shop hours are a response of retailers to the consumer problem of limited weekday shopping opportunities. This problem has become particularly important to families with two working adults. Finally, marketers can also shape the definition of the need or problem. If a consumer needs a new coat, does he define the problem as a need for inexpensive covering, a way to stay warm on the coldest days, a garment that will last several years, warm covering that will not attract odd looks from his peers, or an article of clothing that will express his personal sense of style? A salesperson or an ad may shape his answers.

Information Search and Processing

After a need is recognized, the prospective consumer may seek information to help identify and evaluate alternative products, services, and outlets that will meet that need. Such information can come from family, friends, personal observation, or other sources, such as *Consumer Reports*, salespeople, or mass media. The promotional component of the marketers offering is aimed at providing information to assist the consumer in their problem-solving process. In some cases, the consumer already has the needed information based on past purchasing and consumption experience. Bad experiences and lack of satisfaction can destroy repeat purchases. The consumer with a need for tires may look for information in the local newspaper or ask friends for recommendation. If he has bought tires before and was satisfied, he may go to the same dealer and buy the same brand.

Information search can also identify new needs. As a tire shopper looks for information, she may decide that the tires are not the real problem, that the need is for a new car. At this point, the perceived need may change, triggering a new informational search.

Information search involves mental as well as the physical activities that consumers must perform in order to make decisions and accomplish desired goals in the marketplace. It takes time, energy, money, and can often involve foregoing more desirable activities. The benefits of information search, however, can outweigh the costs. For example, engaging in a thorough information search may save money, improve quality of selection, or reduce risks. As noted in the Integrated Marketing box, the Internet is a valuable information source.

Information Processing

When the search actually occurs, what do people do with the information? How do they spot, understand, and recall information? In other words, how do they process information? This broad topic is important for understanding buyer behavior in general as well as effective communication with buyers in particular, and it has received a great deal of study. Assessing how a person processes information is not an easy task. Often observation has served as the basis. Yet there are many theories as to how the process takes place. One widely accepted theory proposes a five step sequence.[2]

1. *Exposure*. Information processing starts with the *exposure* of consumers to some source of stimulation such as watching television, going to the supermarket, or receiving direct mail advertisements at home. In order to start the process, marketers must attract consumers to the stimulus or put it squarely in the path of people in the target market.

2. *Attention*. Exposure alone does little unless people pay attention to the stimulus. At any moment, people are bombarded by all sorts of stimuli, but they have a limited capacity to process this input. They must devote mental resources to stimuli in order to process them; in other words, they must pay *attention*. Marketers can increase the likelihood of attention by providing informational cues that are relevant to the buyer.

3. *Perception*. *Perception* involves classifying the incoming signals into meaningful categories, forming patterns, and assigning names or images to them. Perception is the assignment of meaning to stimuli received through the senses. (More will be said about perception later.)

4. *Retention*. Storage of information for later reference, or *retention*, is the fourth step of the information-processing sequence. Actually, the role of retention or memory in the sequence is twofold. First, memory holds information while it is being processed throughout the sequence. Second, memory stores information for future, long-term use. Heavy repetition and putting a message to music are two things marketers do to enhance retention.

5. *Retrieval and Application*. The process by which information is recovered from the memory storehouse is called *retrieval*. *Application* is putting that information

INTEGRATED MARKETING *4.1*

KIDS ARE HOOKED ONLINE

These days, practically even the tiniest of tykes is tech-savvy. And it's no wonder. There are computers in elementary schools, computer games, and, of course, there is educational software.

Kids spend a lot of time online, not just at school, but also at home, for social interaction and entertainment. According to market researcher Teen Research Unlimited, 62% of teenagers say they log on at home for 4.2 hours a week, while 46% spend 2.3 hours a week using a computer outside the home. Teens say they spend most of their online time doing research (72%), sending and reading email (63%), playing games (28%), and checking out things to buy or making purchases (23%).

Internet consultancy Cyber Dialogue Data reveals the number of teenagers going online at least once a month grew by nearly 270% between 1998 and 1999. That frequency, coupled with the fact that 19% of these kids have a credit card in his or her own name and 9% have access to a parent's card to shop online, adds up to a huge customer base for Internet marketers.

Snowball.com is a portal that claims to serve both Gen Y and Gen X youth. It includes ChickClick.com for young women, IGN.com for young men, Power Students.com for high school and college students, and InsideGuide.com for college students. The portal has inked deals with major marketers, including Sony, Toyota, and Pillsbury. The site also has received a lot of interest from the entertainment world.

Sources: Jennifer Gilbert, "New Teen Obsession," *Advertising Age*, February 14, 2000, p. 8; "School Daze," *American Demographics*, August 1999, p. 80; Krestina Filiciano, "Just Kidding," *Adweek*, May 1, 2000, p. 58.

into the right context. If the buyer can retrieve relevant information about a product, brand, or store, he or she will apply it to solve a problem or meet a need.

Variations in how each step is carried out in the information-processing sequence also occur. Especially influential is the degree of elaboration. *Elaborate processing*, also called *central processing*, involves active manipulation of information. A person engaged in elaborate processing pays close attention to a message and thinks about it; he or she develops thoughts in support of or counter to the information received. In contrast, *nonelaborate,* or *peripherial*, processing involves passive manipulation of information.[3] It is demonstrated by most airline passengers while a flight attendant reads preflight safety procedures. This degree of elaboration closely parallels the low-involvement, high-involvement theory, and the same logic applies.

Identification and Evaluation of Alternatives

After information is secured and processed, alternative products, services, and outlets are identified as viable options. The consumer evaluates these alternatives, and, if financially and psychologically able, makes a choice. The criteria used in evaluation varies from consumer to consumer just as the needs and information sources vary. One consumer may consider price most important while another puts more weight upon quality or convenience.

The search for alternatives and the methods used in the search are influenced by such factors as: (1) time and money costs; (2) how much information the consumer already has; (3) the amount of the perceived risk if a wrong selection is made; and (4) the consumer's predisposition toward particular choices as influenced by the attitude of the individual toward choice behavior. That is, there are individuals who find the selection process to be difficult and disturbing. For these people there is a tendency to keep the number of alternatives to a minimum, even if they haven't gone through an extensive information search to find that their alternatives appear to be the very best. On the other hand, there are individuals who feel it necessary to collect a long list of alternatives. This tendency can appreciably slow down the decision-making function.

Product/Service/Outlet Selection

The selection of an alternative in many cases will require additional evaluation. For example, a consumer may select a favorite brand and go to a convenient outlet to make a purchase. Upon arrival at the dealer, the consumer finds that the desired brand is out-of-stock. At this point, additional evaluation is needed to decide whether to wait until the product comes in, accept a substitute, or go to another outlet. The selection and evaluation phases of consumer problem solving are closely related and often run sequentially, with outlet selection influencing product evaluation, or product selection influencing outlet evaluation.

The Purchase Decision

After much searching and evaluating, or perhaps very little, consumers at some point have to decide whether they are going to buy. Anything marketers can do to simplify purchasing will be attractive to buyers. In their advertising marketers could suggest the best size for a particular use, or the right wine to drink with a particular food. Sometimes several decision situations can be combined and marketed as one package. For example, travel agents often package travel tours.

To do a better marketing job at this stage of the buying process, a seller needs to know answers to many questions about consumers' shopping behavior. For instance, how much effort is the consumer willing to spend in shopping for the product? What factors influence when the consumer will actually purchase? Are there any conditions that would prohibit or delay purchase? Providing basic product, price, and location information through labels, advertising, personal selling, and public relations is an obvious starting point. Product sampling, coupons, and rebates may also provide an extra incentive to buy.

Actually determining how a consumer goes through the decision-making process is a difficult research task. As indicated in the Newsline box, there are new research methods to better assess this behavior.

NEWSLINE: FOLLOW THE CONSUMER AND SEE WHAT HAPPENS

It seems that traditional market research no longer works with an increasingly diverse and fickle customer base. The methods marketers have relied on for decades—perfunctory written and phone surveys—merely skim the surface of the shifting customer profile. Says Larry Keeley, president of the Doblin Group, a Chicago-based design and consulting firm: "The surveys are nothing more than tracking studies designed to measure if customers are a little more or a little less pleased with you than they were last year."

Surely there must be a better way. Wise heads in the arcane world of customer research are onto something called *storytelling*. These folks advocate far more probing research than ever before, advising companies to elicit real-life stories from customers about how they behave and what they truly feel. The notion may seem like a leap into the unknown, but some companies have discovered that these storytelling methods work. Great service and, ultimately, breakthrough products have resulted. Kimberly-Clark built a new $500-million diaper market using in-depth customer research. At Intuit, storytelling customers helped its software writers revolutionize the way people all over the U.S. handle their money. Clothing maker Patagonia, soliciting true tales about how customers live and use their gear, manages to keep its product ahead of the curve.

At the heart of this new brand of customer research is a search for subtle insight into human behavior—not only emotion-laden anecdotes, but also unspoken impulses. Just think, for example, of the last time you made eye contact with an attractive stranger. A whole range of feelings washed over you, and at that moment it would be hard to argue with the notion that at least 80% of all human communication is nonverbal.

At Patagonia, an outdoor-sports apparel company in Ventura, California, customer storytellers surf at the "Point" right outside the front door of headquarters. Founder Yoon Chouinard, who spends at least six months a year at the ends of the earth testing his company's gear himself, has made a point of hiring several of these customers so they could share their war stories in-house. He refers to them affectionately as his "dirtbags," people who spend so much time outside that it shows under their fingernails.

Patagonians collect such war stories from far-flung customers as well and use them as a marketing tool. Many of their wares are sold through a biennial catalogue that is unique among its peers. Instead of spending millions to shoot glossy spreads of unthinkably beautiful models, the company relies on its customers to pose while wearing Patagonia duds in exotic locales. This pictorial road map of customer adventures makes for great reading, but it has another role as well.

The placement of customers' stories front and center proves that their opinions and experience are valued, and they respond in droves. "We have trained them to believe that we are serious about responding to their feedback and improving our products," notes Randy Howard, the company's director of quality.

Sources: Joanne Gordon, "Shrink Rap," *Fortune*, February 7, 2000, pp. 110–111; Ronald B. Liebier, "Storytelling: A New Way to Get Close to the Customer," *Fortune*, February 3, 1997, pp. 102–105; Kendra Darko, "Zooming In On What's Important," *American Demographics*, August 1999, pp. 46–47.

Postpurchase Behavior

All the behavior determinants and the steps of the buying process up to this point are operative before or during the time a purchase is made. However, a consumer's feelings and evaluations after the sale are also significant to a marketer, because they can influence repeat sales and also influence what the customer tells others about the product or brand.

Keeping the customer happy is what marketing is all about. Nevertheless, consumers typically experience some postpurchase anxiety after all but the most routine and inexpensive purchases. This anxiety reflects a phenomenon called *cognitive dissonance*. According to this theory, people strive for consistency among their cognitions (knowledge, attitudes, beliefs, values). When there are inconsistencies, dissonance exists, which people will try to eliminate. In some cases, the consumer makes the decision to buy a particular brand already aware of dissonant elements. In other instances, dissonance is aroused by disturbing information that is received after the purchase.[4] The marketer may take specific steps to reduce postpurchase dissonance. Advertising that stresses the many positive attributes or confirms the popularity of the product can be helpful. Providing personalized reinforcement has proven effective with big-ticket items such as automobiles and major appliances. Salespeople in these areas may send cards or may even make personal calls in order to reassure customers about their purchase.

MARKETING CAPSULE *4.1*

1. Buyer behavior takes place in an exchange setting and addresses two questions:
   a. How do potential buyers go about making purchase decisions?
   b. What factors influence their decision process and in what way?
2. Buyer behavior is a problem-solving process and entails the following decisions:
   a. Need identification
      1. Determined by the discrepancy between what we have and what we want
      2. Determined by the relative importance of the problem

   b. Information search and processing is a five-step sequence:
      1. Exposure
      2. Attention
      3. Reception
      4. Retention
      5. Retrieval and application
   c. Identification and evaluation of alternatives
   d. Product/service/outlet selection
   e. The purchase decision
   f. Postpurchase behavior

Influencing Factors of Consumer Behavior

While the decision-making process appears quite standardized, no two people make a decision in exactly the same way. As individuals, we have inherited and learned a great many behavioral tendencies: some controllable, some beyond our control. Further, the ways in which all these factors interact with one another ensures uniqueness. Although it is impossible for a marketer to react to the particular profile of a single consumer, it is possible to identify factors that tend to influence most consumers in predictable ways.

The factors that influence the consumer problem-solving process are numerous and complex. For example, the needs of men and women are different in respect to cosmetics; the extent of information search for a low-income person would be much greater when considering a new automobile as opposed to a loaf of bread; a consumer with extensive past purchasing experience in a product category might well approach the problem differently from one with no experience. Such influences must be understood to draw realistic conclusions about consumer behavior.

For purposes of discussion, it may be helpful to group these various influences into related sets. Figure 4.2 provides such a framework. Situational, external, and internal influences are shown as having an impact on the consumer problem solving process. *Situation influences* include the consumer's immediate buying task, the market offerings that are available to the consumer, and demographic traits. *Internal influences* relate to the consumer's learning and socialization, motivation and personality, and lifestyle. *External influences* deal with factors outside the individual that have a strong bearing on personal behaviors. Current purchase behavior is shown as influencing future behavior through the internal influence of learning. Let us now turn to the nature and potential impact of each of these sets of influences on consumer problem solving. Figure 4.2 focuses on the specific elements that influence the consumer's decision to purchase and evaluate products and services.

Situational Influences

Buying Task   The nature of the buying task has considerable impact on a customer's approach to solving a particular problem. When a decision involves a low-cost item that is

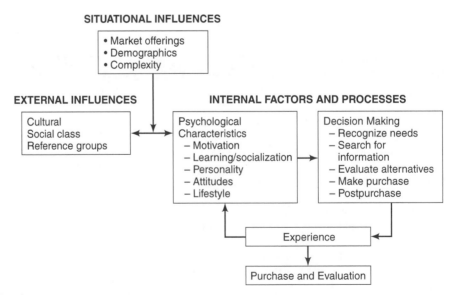

FIGURE 4.2   A model of consumer behavior

frequently purchased, such as bread, the buying process is typically quick and routinized. A decision concerning a new car is quite different. The extent to which a decision is considered complex or simple depends on (1) whether the decision is novel or routine, and on (2) the extent of the customers' involvement with the decision. A great deal of discussion has revolved around this issue of involvement. *High-involvement decisions* are those that are important to the buyer. Such decisions are closely tied to the consumer's ego and self-image. They also involve some risk to the consumer; financial risk (highly priced items),

Now you can get rid of annoying commercials and your annoying cable company at the same time.

With DishPVR from DISH Network, you can skip recorded commercials, record up to 35 hours without videotape pause live TV and never have to wait for your cable guy again. DishPVR Plan offers you this personal video recorder, 165 channels including your locals, the satellite TV system with 2nd-room receiver and free standard Professional Installation – for just $59.99 a month. Another reason why DISH IS IT.

Requires 12-month commitment and a $49.99 Activation Fee that includes first month's Plan payment. Valid major credit card required.

Promo Code RPVR

AD 4.1 Ordering DishPVR is a high-involvement decision.

social risk (products important to the peer group), or psychological risk (the wrong decision might cause the consumer some concern and anxiety). In making these decisions, it is worth the time and energies to consider solution alternatives carefully. A complex process of decision making is therefore more likely for high-involvement purchases. *Low-involvement decisions* are more straightforward, require little risk, are repetitive, and often lead to a *habit*; they are not very important to the consumer.[5] Financial, social, and psychological risks are not nearly as great. In such cases, it may not be worth the consumer's time and effort to search for information about brands or to consider a wide range of alternatives. A low-involvement purchase therefore generally entails a limited process of decision making. The purchase of a new computer is an example of high involvement, while the purchase of a hamburger is a low-involvement decision.

When a consumer has bought a similar product many times in the past, the decision making is likely to be simple, regardless of whether it is a high- or low-involvement decision. Suppose a consumer initially bought a product after much care and involvement, was satisfied, and continued to buy the product. The customer's careful consideration of the product and satisfaction has produced *brand loyalty*, which is the result of involvement with the product decision.

Once a customer is brand-loyal, a simple decision-making process is all that is required for subsequent purchases. The consumer now buys the product through *habit*, which means making a decision without the use of additional information or the evaluation of alternative choices.

Market Offerings   Another relevant set of situational influences on consumer problem solving is the available market offerings. The more extensive the product and brand choices available to the consumer, the more complex the purchase decision process is likely to be.

For example, if you already have purchased or are considering purchasing a DVD, you know there are many brands to choose from—Sony, Samsung, Panasonic, Mitsubishi, Toshiba, and Sanyo, to name several. Each manufacturer sells several models that differ in terms of some of the following features—single or multiple event selection, remote control (wired or wireless), slow motion, stop action, variable-speed scan, tracking control, and so on. What criteria are important to you? Is purchasing a DVD an easy decision? If a consumer has a need that can be met by only one product or one outlet in the relevant market, the decision is relatively simple. Either purchase the product or let the need go unmet.

This is not ideal from the customer's perspective, but it can occur. For example, suppose you are a student on a campus in a small town many miles from another marketplace. Your campus and town has only one bookstore. You need a textbook for class; only one specific book will do and only one outlet has the book for sale. The limitation on alternative market offerings can clearly influence your purchase behavior.

As you saw in the DVD example, when the extent of market offerings increases, the complexity of the problem-solving process and the consumers' need for information also increases. A wider selection of market offerings is better from the customer's point of view, because it allows them to tailor their purchases to their specific needs. However, it may confuse and frustrate the consumer so that less-than-optimal choices are made.

Demographic Influences   An important set of factors that should not be overlooked in attempting to understand and respond to consumers is demographics. Such variables as age, sex, income, education, marital status, and mobility can all have significant influence on consumer behavior. One study showed that age and education have strong relationships to store selection by female shoppers. This was particularly true for women's suits or dresses, linens and bedding, cosmetics, and women's sportswear.

DeBeers Limited, which has an eighty percent share of the market for diamonds used in engagement rings, employed a consumer demographic profile in developing their promotional program. Their target market consists of single women and men between the ages of 18 and 24. They combined this profile with some lifestyle aspects to develop their promotional program.

People in different income brackets also tend to buy different types of products and different qualities. Thus various income groups often shop in very different ways. This means that income can be an important variable in defining the target group. Many designer clothing shops, for example, aim at higher-income shoppers, while a store like K-mart appeals to middle- and lower-income groups.

External Influences

External factors are another important set of influences on consumer behavior. Among the many societal elements that can affect consumer problem solving are culture, social class, reference groups, and family.

Culture   A person's *culture* is represented by a large group of people with a similar heritage. The American culture, which is a subset of the Western culture, is of primary interest here. Traditional American culture values include hard work, thrift, achievement, security, and the like. Marketing strategies targeted to those with such a cultural heritage should show the product or service as reinforcing these traditional values. The three components of culture—beliefs, values, and customs—are each somewhat different. A *belief* is a proposition that reflects a person's particular knowledge and assessment of something (that is, "I believe that . . ."). *Values* are general statements that guide behavior and influence beliefs. The function of a value system is to help a person choose between alternatives in everyday life.

Customs are overt modes of behavior that constitute culturally approved ways of behaving in specific situations. For example, taking one's mother out for dinner and buying her presents for Mother's Day is an American custom that Hallmark and other card companies support enthusiastically.

The American culture with its social values can be divided into various subcultures. For example, African-Americans constitute a significant American subculture in most U.S. cities. A consumer's racial heritage can exert an influence on media usage and various other aspects of the purchase decision process.

Social Class   *Social class*, which is determined by such factors as occupation, wealth, income, education, power, and prestige, is another societal factor that can affect consumer behavior. The best-known classification system includes upper-upper, lower-upper, upper-middle, lower-middle, upper-lower, and lower-lower class. Lower-middle and upper-lower classes comprise the mass market.

The upper-upper class and lower-upper class consist of people from wealthy families who are locally prominent. They tend to live in large homes furnished with art and antiques. They are the primary market for rare jewelry and designer originals, tending to shop at exclusive retailers. The upper-middle class is made up of professionals, managers, and business owners. The are ambitious, future-oriented people who have succeeded economically and now seek to enhance their quality of life. Material goods often take on major symbolic meaning for this group. They also tend to be very civic-minded and are involved in many worthy causes. The lower-middle class consists of mid-level white-collar workers.

These are office workers, teachers, small business people and the like who typically hold strong American values. They are family-oriented, hard-working individuals. The upper-lower class is made up of blue-collar workers such as production line workers and service people. Many have incomes that exceed those of the lower-middle class, but their values are often very different. They tend to adopt a short-run, live-for-the-present philosophy. They are less future-oriented than the middle classes. The lower-lower class consists of unskilled workers with low incomes. They are more concerned with necessities than with status or fulfillment.

People in the same social class tend to have similar attitudes, live in similar neighborhoods, dress alike, and shop at the same type stores. If a marketer wishes to target efforts toward the upper classes, then the market offering must be designed to meet their expectations in terms of quality, service, and atmosphere. For example, differences in leisure—concerts are favored by members of the middle and upper classes, while fishing, bowling, pool, and drive-in movies are more likely to involve members of the lower social classes.

Reference Groups   Do you ever wonder why Pepsi used Shaquille O'Neal in their advertisements? The teen market consumes a considerable amount of soft drinks. Pepsi has made a strong effort to capture a larger share of this market, and felt that Shaquille represented the spirit of today's teens. Pepsi is promoted as "the choice of a new generation" and Shaquille is viewed as a role model by much of that generation. Pepsi has thus employed the concept of reference groups.

A *reference group* helps shape a person's attitudes and behaviors. Such groups can be either formal or informal. Churches, clubs, schools, notable individuals, and friends can all be reference groups for a particular consumer. Reference groups are characterized as having individuals who are opinion leaders for the group. *Opinion leaders* are people who influence others. They are not necessarily higher-income or better educated, but perhaps are seen as having greater expertise or knowledge related to some specific topic. For example, a local high school teacher may be an opinion leader for parents in selecting colleges for their children. These people set the trend and others conform to the expressed behavior. If a marketer can identify the opinion leaders for a group in the target market, then effort can be directed toward attracting these individuals. For example, if an ice cream parlor is attempting to attract the local high school trade, opinion leaders at the school may be very important to its success.

The reference group can influence an individual in several ways:[6]

1. Role expectations: The role assumed by a person is nothing more than a prescribed way of behaving based on the situation and the person's position in the situation. Your reference group determines much about how this role is to be performed. As a student, you are expected to behave in a certain basic way under certain conditions.

2. Conformity: Conformity is related to our roles in that we modify our behavior in order to coincide with group norms. *Norms* are behavioral expectations that are considered appropriate regardless of the position we hold.

3. Group communications through opinion leaders: We, as consumers, are constantly seeking out the advice of knowledgeable friends or acquaintances who can provide information, give advice, or actually make the decision. For some product categories, there are professional opinion leaders who are quite easy to identify—e.g., auto mechanics, beauticians, stock brokers, and physicians.

Family   One of the most important reference groups for an individual is the family. A consumer's family has a major impact on attitude and behavior. The interaction between husband and wife and the number and ages of children in the family can have a significant effect on buying behavior.

One facet in understanding the family's impact on consumer behavior is identifying the decision maker for the purchase in question. In some cases, the husband is typically dominant, in others the wife or children, and still others, a joint decision is made. The store choice for food and household items is most often the wife's. With purchases that involve a larger sum of money, such as a refrigerator, a joint decision is usually made. The decision on clothing purchases for teenagers may be greatly influenced by the teenagers themselves. Thus, marketers need to identify the key family decision maker for the product or service in question.

Another aspect of understanding the impact of the family on buying behavior is the *family lifecycle*. Most families pass through an orderly sequence of stages. These stages can be defined by a combination of factors such as age, marital status, and parenthood. The typical stages are:

1. The bachelor state; young, single people.

2. Newly married couples; young, no children.

3. The full nest I and II; young married couples with dependent children:
   a. Youngest child under six (Full nest I)
   b. Youngest child over six (Full nest II)

4. The full nest III; older married couples with dependent children.

5. The empty nest I and II; older married couples with no children living with them:
   a. Adults in labor force (Empty nest I)
   b. Adults retired (Empty nest II)

6. The solitary survivors; older single people:
   a. In labor force
   b. Retired

Each of these stages is characterized by different buying behaviors. For example, a children's clothing manufacturer would target its efforts primarily at the full nest I families. Thus, the family cycle can be helpful in defining the target customers.

Internal Influences

Each customer is to some degree a unique problem solving unit. Although they can be grouped into meaningful segments, in order to fully appreciate the totality of the buying process, a marketer needs to examine the internal forces that influence consumers. They are learning/socialization, motivation and personality, and lifestyle.

Learning and Socialization   As a factor influencing a person's perceptions, *learning* may be defined as changes in behavior resulting from previous experiences. However, learning does not include behavior changes attributable to instinctive responses, growth, or temporary states of the organism, such as hunger, fatigue, or sleep. It is clear that learning is an ongoing process that is dynamic, adaptive, and subject to change. Also, learning is an *experience* and *practice* that actually brings about changes in behavior. For example, in order to learn how to play tennis, you might participate in it to gain experience, be exposed to the different skills required, the rules, and so forth. However, the experience does not have to be an actual, physical one. It could be a conceptualization of a potential experience. In other words, you could learn to play tennis by reading about how to play without actually doing it. This is called *nonexperiential learning.*

Nonexperiential learning is particularly relevant in consumer behavior. For example, assume you are considering purchasing a bottle of Zinfandel wine. You ask the salesclerk what it tastes like, and he tells you it tastes like a strong ginger ale. Not liking the taste of ginger ale, you reject the purchase. Thus you have learned that you do not like Zinfandel wine without having a direct taste experience. A great deal of our learning is of this type. This may be one reason why marketers try to identify opinions leaders who in turn tell others in the market about the benefits of the product.

Another characteristic of learning is that the changes may be immediate or anticipated. In other words, just because we do not see immediate evidence that learning has taken place is no reason to assume that learning has not occurred. We can store our learning until it is needed, and frequently do this in terms of making purchase decisions. For example, we are willing to learn about many product attributes even though we do not expect to buy the product in the near future.

As new information is processed and stored over time, consumer learning takes place. There are several theories of learning; one of the most useful to marketers is that of socialization. *Socialization* refers to the process by which persons acquire the knowledge, skills, and dispositions that make them more or less able members of their society. The assumption made is that behavior is acquired and modified over the person's lifecycle.

The social learning approach stresses sources of influence—"socialization agents" (i.e., other people)—that transmit cognitive and behavioral patterns to the learner. In the case of consumer socialization, this takes place in the course of the person's interaction with other individuals in various social settings. Socialization agents might include any person, organization, or information source that comes into contact with the consumer.

Consumers acquire this information from the other individuals through the processes of modeling, reinforcement, and social interaction. *Modeling* involves imitation of the agent's behavior. For example, a teenager may acquire a brand name preference for Izod from friends. Marketers can make use of this concept by employing spokespersons to endorse their products and services who have strong credibility with their target consumers, as in the case of Bill Cosby (Jell-O). *Reinforcement* involves either a reward or a punishment mechanism used by the agent. A parent may be reinforced by good product performance, excellent post-purchase services, or some similar rewarding experience. The *social interaction* mechanism is less specific as to the type of learning involved; it may include a combination of modeling and reinforcement. The social setting within which learning takes place can be defined in terms of variables such as social class, sex, and family size.

These variables can influence learning through their impact on the relationship between the consumer and others. It should be noted that an individual who promotes learning can be anyone—such as parent, friend, salesperson, or television spokesperson.

Motivation   Motivation is a concept that is difficult to define. In fact, the difficulty of defining motives and dealing with motivation in consumer research accounts for its limited application. For the most part, the research in motivation involves benefit segmentation and patronage motives. *Patronage motives* typically concern the consumer's reasons for shopping at a particular outlet. Consumers are classified, for example, as price-conscious, convenience-oriented, service-oriented, or in terms of some other motivating feature.

A *motive* is the inner drive or pressure to take action to satisfy a need. To be motivated is to be a goal-oriented individual. Some goals are positive, some are negative, some individuals have a high level of goal orientation, some have a very low level. In all cases, the need must be aroused or stimulated to a high enough level so that it can serve as a motive.

It is possible (and usual) to have needs that are latent (unstimulated) and that therefore do not serve as the motive of behavior. The sources of this arousal may be internal (people get hungry), environmental (you see an ad for a Big Mac), or psychological (just thinking about food can cause hunger). It is possible (and usual) to have needs that are latent (unstimulated) and that therefore do not serve as the motive of behavior.

For motivation to be useful in marketing practice, a marketing manager must understand what motives and behaviors are influenced by the specific situation in which consumers engage in goal-directed, problem-solving behavior.

Motivation flows from an unmet need, as does all consumer problem solving. Perhaps the best known theory dealing with individual motivation is provided in the work of A.H. Maslow. One of the most important parts of Maslow's theory is his development of a model consisting of several different levels of needs that exist in a human being and relate to each other via a "need hierarchy." Maslow has differentiated between five levels of needs. The first of these concerns itself with physiological needs; that is, hunger, thirst, and other basic drives. All living beings, regardless of their level of maturity, possess physiological needs. Physiological needs are omnipresent and are of a recurrent nature.[7]

Safety and security needs are second in Maslow's hierarchy. The difference between physiological needs and safety and security needs is somewhat hazy. Safety and security imply a continued fulfillment of physiological needs. This is an extension of the more basic needs.

Third in Maslow's hierarchy of needs are the love needs. These are the needs for belonging and friendship. They involve a person's interaction with others. The fourth level of needs in Maslow's hierarchy is the esteem needs. These are needs related to feeling good about oneself and having a positive self-image.

The fifth and highest level in Maslow's needs hierarchy is the need for self-actualization or self-fulfillment. This need can be defined as the need of a person to reach his full potential in terms of the application of his own abilities and interest in functioning in his environment.

It is important in discussing these levels of Maslow's hierarchy to point out two additional factors. First, Maslow has clearly indicated that these five levels of needs operate on an unconscious level. That is, the individual is probably not aware of concentration upon one particular need or one assortment of needs. One of the misunderstandings associated with Maslow's theory is that he believes the five needs to be mutually exclusive. That, in fact, is not the intent of Maslow. To the contrary, several of these needs may occur simultaneously for any one individual; the relative importance of each need for any one individual determines the hierarchy involved.

When we attempt to integrate Maslow's needs hierarchy with the concept of segmentation, we can see that a manager might find certain subgroups that fit together because of some homogeneity of needs. For example, a marketer may target a group with strong self-esteem needs in designing a promotional program for cosmetics. Appeals to higher-order needs are important for many products and services, even basic commodities.

Personality is used to summarize all the traits of a person that make him/her unique. No two people have the same traits, but several attempts have been made to classify people with similar traits. Perhaps the best-known personality types are those proposed by Carl Jung, as is a variation on the work of his teacher, Sigmund Freud. His personality categories are *introvert* and *extrovert*. The *introvert* is described as defensive, inner-directed, and withdrawn from others. The *extrovert* is outgoing, other-directed, and assertive. Several other more elaborate classifications have also been devised.

Various personality types, like people with various motives, are likely to respond in different ways to different market offerings. For example, an extrovert may enjoy the shopping experience and rely more on personal observation to secure information; thus, in-store promotion would become an important communication tool. Knowing the basic personality traits of target customers can be useful information for the manager in designing the marketing mix. Marketers have, however, found personality to be difficult to apply in developing marketing strategy. The primary reason for this is the lack of good ways to measure personality traits. Most available measures were developed to identify people with problems that needed medical attention. These have little value with consumers who are mentally healthy. As a result, most marketers have turned to lifestyle analysis.

Lifestyle   One of the newer and increasingly important set of factors that is being used to understand consumer behavior is lifestyle. *Lifestyle* has been generally defined as the attitudes, interests, and opinions of the potential customer. Such variables as interest in hunting, attitude toward the role of women in society, and opinion on the importance of dressing well can be used to better understand the market and its behavior.

It is the multifaceted aspect of lifestyle research that makes it so useful in consumer analysis. A prominent lifestyle researcher, Joseph T. Plummer, summarizes the concept as follows:

> . . . life style patterns, combines the virtues of demographics with the richness and dimensionality of psychological characteristics. . . . Life style is used to segment the marketplace because it provides the broad, everyday view of consumers life style segmentation and can generate identifiable whole persons rather than isolated fragments.[8]

A useful application of the lifestyle concept relates to consumer's *shopping orientation*. Different customers approach shopping in very different ways. They have different attitudes and opinions about shopping and different levels of interest in shopping. Once people know their alternatives, how do they evaluate and choose among them? In particular, how do people choose among brands of a product? Current description of this process emphasizes the role of attitudes. An *attitude* is an opinion of a person, idea, place, or thing. Attitudes range based on a continuum from very negative to very positive. Traditionally, an attitude is broken down into three components: cognitive, affective, and behavioral. That is, an attitude is first what we know/believe, followed by what we feel, and ending with an action. Thus, we have learned that a particular company has been polluting a local river; we feel very strongly that business shouldn't do this and feel very angry; and we boycott the product made by that company.

A great deal of marketing strategy is based on the idea that the cognitive, affective, and behavioral components of an attitude tend to be consistent. Thus, if it is possible to change what people believe about Yamaha CD players, their feelings and their actions may eventually change as well. However, this relationship among the three components of an attitude seems to be situation- or even product-specific. For example, attitudes tend to predict behavior better in high-involvement decisions. Thus, if someone has a strong attitude about wearing stylish clothes, then it is possible to predict that the person will restrict purchases to a particular set of brands. Furthermore, we do not react to products in isolation. The situation, or our attitude toward the situation, plays an important role in how well attitudes predict behavior. For example, assume that a consumer likes pizza but doesn't like Pizza Inn pizza. In a social setting where everyone wants to go to Pizza Inn for pizza, this person might eat this brand rather than not have pizza at all.

Despite limitations on the predictive power of attitudes, attitudes can help us understand how choices are made. However, we need to carefully assess the validity of the attitude–behavior relationships for each situation and product.

1. The following factors influence consumer behavior:
   a. Situational influences
      1. The buyer task: high-involvement vs. low-involvement
      2. Market offerings
      3. Demographics
   b. External influences
      1. Culture
      2. Social class
      3. Reference groups
      4. Family
   c. Internal influences
      1. Learning and socialization
      2. Motivation
      3. Personality
      4. Lifestyle
      5. Attitudes

Given the hypothesis that attitudes influence buying behavior, how can a company bring its products and consumers' attitudes into a consistent state; that is, into a situation where consumers evaluate a given product or brand as satisfying their need? Marketers have two choices: either they can change consumers' attitudes to be consistent with their product, or they can change the product to match attitudes. It is easier to change the product than to change consumers' attitudes. Nevertheless, attitudes can sometimes be modified. Modifying attitudes might be the only reasonable choice, as when a firm is introducing a truly new product or an unusual new use for an existing one. Marketers should nevertheless face the fact that it is extremely difficult to change consumers' attitudes. If there is to be change, it is most likely to occur when people are open-minded in their beliefs or when an existing attitude is of weak intensity; that is, when there is little information to support the attitude or very little ego involvement on the individual's part. The stronger a person's loyalty to a certain brand, for example, the more difficult it is to change that attitude.

ORGANIZATIONAL BUYER BEHAVIOR

Those who supply goods and services to consumer markets are themselves in need of goods and services to run their business. These organizations—producers, resellers, and government—make up vast marketing organizations that buy a large variety of products, including equipment, raw material, and labor and other services. Some organizations sell exclusively to other organizations and never come into contact with consumer buyers.

Despite the importance of organizational markets, far less research has been conducted on factors that influence their behavior than on factors that influence consumers. However, we can identify characteristics that distinguish organizational buying from consumer buying and typical steps in the organizational buying process.

Characteristics of Organizational Buying

Many elements of the sociocultural environment discussed earlier influence organizational as well as consumer buying, but some additional forces are salient only in the organizational setting. In particular, each organization has its own business philosophy that guides its actions in resolving conflicts, handling uncertainty and risk, searching for solutions, and adapting to change. For example, Peabody Coal, which is part of a declining industry, relies on a conservative purchase strategy in an attempt to maintain their status quo.

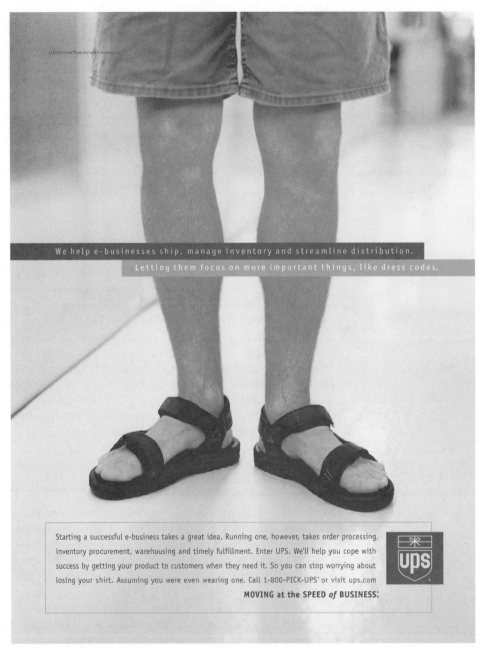

AD 4.2   This ad illustrates organization behavior decision criteria.

Five characteristics mark the organizational buying process:

1. In organizations, many individuals are involved in making buying decisions.
2. The organizational buyer is motivated by both rational and quantitative criteria dominant in most organizational decisions; the decision makers are people, subject to many of the same emotional criteria used in personal purchases.

3. Organizational buying decisions frequently involve a range of complex technical dimensions. A purchasing agent for Volvo Automobiles, for example, must consider a number of technical factors before ordering a radio to go into the new model. The electronic system, the acoustics of the interior, and the shape of the dashboard are a few of these considerations.

4. The organizational decision process frequently spans a considerable time, creating a significant lag between the marketer's initial contact with the customer and the purchasing decision. Since many new factors can enter the picture during this lag time, the marketer's ability to monitor and adjust to these changes is critical.

5. Organizations cannot be grouped into precise categories. Each organization has a characteristic way of functioning and a personality.[10]

The first item in this list of characteristics has important implications. Unlike the consumer buying process, organizational buying involves decision making by groups and enforces rules for making decisions. These two characteristics greatly complicate the task of understanding the buying process. For example, to predict the buying behavior of an organization with certainty, it is important to know who will take part in the buying process, what criteria each member uses in evaluating prospective suppliers, and what influence each member has. It is also necessary to understand something not only about the psychology of the individuals involved but also how they work as a group. Who makes the decision to buy depends in part on the situation. Three types of buying situations have been distinguished: the straight rebuy, the modified rebuy, and the new task.

The *straight rebuy* is the simplest situation: The company reorders a good or service without any modifications. The transaction tends to be routine and may be handled totally by the purchasing department. With the *modified rebuy*, the buyer is seeking to modify product specifications, prices, and so on. The purchaser is interested in negotiation, and several participants may take part in the buying decision. A company faces a *new task* when it considers buying a product for the first time. The number of participants and the amount of information sought tend to increase with the cost and risks associated with the transaction. This situation represents the best opportunity for the marketer.

Stages in Organizational Buying

The organizational buying process contains eight stages, or key phrases, which are listed in Figure 4.3. Although these stages parallel those of the consumer buying process, there are important differences that have a direct bearing on the marketing strategy. The complete process occurs only in the case of a new task. Even in this situation, however, the process is far more formal for the industrial buying process than for the consumer buying process.

Most of the information an industrial buyer receives is delivered through direct contacts such as sales representatives or information packets. It is unlikely that an industrial buyer would use information provided through a trade ad as the sole basis for making a decision.

1. **Problem recognition.** The process begins when someone in the organization recognizes a problem or need that can be met by acquiring a good or service. Problem recognition can occur as a result of internal or external stimuli. External stimuli can be a presentation by a salesperson, an ad, or information picked up at a trade show.

2. **General need description.** Having recognized that a need exists, the buyers must add further refinement to its description. Working with engineers, users, purchasing

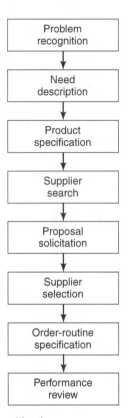

FIGURE 4.3   Stages of organizational buying

agents, and others, the buyer identifies and prioritizes important product characteristics. Table 4.1 lists several sources of information for many industrial customers. Armed with extensive product knowledge, this individual is capable of addressing virtually all the product-related concerns of a typical customer. To a lesser extent, trade advertising provides valuable information to smaller or isolated customers. Noteworthy is the extensive use of direct marketing techniques (for example, toll-free numbers and information cards) in conjunction with many trade ads. Finally, public relations plays a significant role through the placement of stories in various trade journals.

3. **Product specification.** Technical specifications come next. This is usually the responsibility of the engineering department. Engineers design several alternatives, depending on the priority list established earlier.

4. **Supplier search.** The buyer now tries to identify the most appropriate vendor. The buyer can examine trade directories, perform a computer search, or phone other companies for recommendations. Marketers can participate in this stage by contacting possible opinion leaders and soliciting support or by contacting the buyer directly. Personal selling plays a major role at this stage.

5. **Proposal solicitation.** Qualified suppliers are next invited to submit proposals. Some suppliers send only a catalog or a sales representative. Proposal development is a complex task that requires extensive research and skilled writing and presentation. In extreme cases, such proposals are comparable to complete marketing strategies found in the consumer sector.

TABLE 4.1   Industrial Buyer Information Sources

Source	Description
Salespeople	Sales personnel representing manufacturers or distributors of the product in question.
Technical sources	Engineering types of personnel internal or external to the subject's firm.
Personnel in buyer's firm	Peer group references (e.g., other purchasing agents in the subject's firm).
Purchasing agents in other companies	Peer group references external to the buyer's firm.
Trade association	Cooperatives voluntarily joined by business competitors designed to assist its members and industry in dealing with mutual problems (e.g., National Association of Purchasing Management).
Advertising in trade journals	Commercial messages placed by the manufacturer or distributor of the product in question.
Articles in trade journals	Messages relating to the product in question but not under the control of the manufacturer or distributor.
Vendor files	Information pertaining to the values of various sources of supply as developed and maintained by the buyer's firm.
Trade registers	Buyer guides providing listings of suppliers and other marketing information (e.g., *Thomas' Register*).
Product literature	Specific product and vendor information supplied by the manufacturing or distributing firm.

6. **Supplier selection.** At this stage, the various proposals are screened and a choice is made. A significant part of this selection is evaluating the vendor. One study indicated that purchasing managers felt that the vendor was often more important than the proposal. Purchasing managers listed the three most important characteristics of the vendor as delivery capability, consistent quality, and fair price. Another study found that the relative importance of different attributes varies with the type of buying situations.

   For example, for routine-order products, delivery, reliability, price, and supplier reputation are highly important. These factors can serve as appeals in sales presentations and in trade ads.

7. **Order-routine specification.** The buyer now writes the final order with the chosen supplier, listing the technical specifications, the quantity needed, the warranty, and so on.

8. **Performance review.** In this final stage, the buyer reviews the supplier's performance. This may be a very simple or a very complex process.

NEWSLINE: THE FUTURE OF THE CONSUMER

Experts say consumers in the new millennium will throw some surprising twists and turns into the business of target marketing, overturning some of the traditional thinking about what we'll buy, how we'll live, and where we'll work. "The 21st century will be the century of the consumer," says Roger Blackwell, a professor of marketing. "Marketers will have to push their understanding beyond knowing what people buy to knowing why they buy." The 2010s will be the "Linked Decade," defined by a busy, mature, ethnically heterogeneous group of consumers who are confident in their ability to read anything, buy anything, and experience anything.

Several fundamental demographic changes will serve as the underpinning for this new consumer mind-set: the aging of the baby boom generation, the increasing importance of children as consumers, a growing chasm between society's haves and have-nots, and the world's increasingly diverse population.

Given that demographic backdrop, what will be the most powerful values shaping the consumer mind-set? The following possibilities have been proposed:

- The Shrinking Day—Harried baby boomers will create a time famine for themselves by working more hours and committing to more family and community obligations.

- The Connectedness Craze—The urge to connect will pervade all aspects of consumers' lives and increasingly consumers will turn to the World Wide Web for a sense of community between buyers and sellers, information suppliers and consumers, and friends and family.

- The Body vs. Soul Conundrum—Consumers will continue their obsession with fitness and spirituality, while at the same time consuming record amounts of take-out food.

- The Triumph of Individualism—Work, family, and purchase processes will reflect the consumer's need to be treated as a unique individual.

MARKETING CAPSULE 4.3

1. Organizational buyer behavior is different from consumer behavior:
   a. Many individuals make the buying decision
   b. Behavior is motivated by both rational and emotional factors
   c. Decisions include a range of complex technical decisions
   d. Lag time exists between contact and actual decision
   e. Organizations cannot by grouped into precise categories

2. The following stages are involved in the organizational buying decision:
   a. Problem recognition
   b. General need description
   c. Product specification
   d. Supplier's research
   e. Proposal solicitation
   f. Supplier selection
   g. Order-routine specification
   h. Performance review

IN PRACTICE

Understanding buyer behavior is a complicated process, with many factors influencing the process. Why and what products are purchased baffles marketers as much as understanding why certain products are not purchased. Ultimately, understanding buyer behavior influences the marketing mix used for a product.

Marketers must be able to answer two critical questions when assessing consumer and organizational buyer behavior: (1) How do buyers make purchase decisions? and (2) What factors influence decisions and in what way? Answering these questions correctly impacts the success of any product.

Consumer and organizational buyer behavior differ significantly. While considerable research about consumer purchasing decisions has been conducted, minimal research has been done about organizational buyer behavior. Marketers must understand the different factors and influences affecting each group and the impact of these on purchase decisions.

Cisco Systems, Inc., provides networking solutions that connect computer devices and networks for businesses. Check out Cisco's Web site at www.cisco.com. Under **Solutions for Your Network**, click on **Overview**. A menu will appear to the left with information for customers such as Large Enterprises, Small and Medium Businesses, and Government entities. Click on one of those links now to read about product offerings for these customers.

The **Business Focus** section of **Marketplace** provides information about various business activities, including purchasing. On the **Marketplace** home page, click on **Business Focus** on the left menu.

For information about consumer buying behavior, go to the Interactive Journal's **Front Section** and click on **Marketplace**. Click on **Marketing/Media**. Look for articles in the Advertising section. These articles discuss examples of advertising efforts that various companies employ to influence consumer buying decisions. Information about retail sales can also be found in **Marketing/Media**.

DELIVERABLE

Using the Interactive Journal's **Business Index** feature under **Journal Atlas** on the left menu, select a consumer products company featured in today's Interactive Journal. Visit that company's website and search the Interactive Journal for information that will help you identify the Situational and External Influences for customers purchasing the company's product(s).

DISCUSSION QUESTIONS

1. How can marketers use the Internet to influence consumer buyer behavior? Organizational buyer behavior?
2. How has business-to-business (B2B) commerce affected purchasing transactions?
3. What new factors or influences do you foresee impacting consumer buyer behavior? Organizational buyer behavior?
4. What ethical considerations (if any) do advertisers face when they try to influence buyer behavior?

SUMMARY

In this chapter, the rudiments of buyer behavior were presented. The chapter is divided into two parts: consumer behavior and organizational behavior. In the case of consumer behavior, the discussion began with six stages in the consumer decision-making process. These stages include need identification, information search and processing, evaluation of alternatives, product/service/outlet selection, purchase, and postpurchase behavior.

Following the material was a discussion of the factors that influence this decision-making process. The situational influences consist of the complexity, market offerings, and demographics. External influences include the culture, social class, reference groups, and the family. Finally, the internal influences identified were learning/socialization, motivation, personality, lifestyles, and attitudes.

The final section of the chapter dealt with issues germane to how organizations make buying decisions compared to how consumers make buying decisions. Discussion began with a description of the characteristics of organizational buying. The section concluded with a description or the stages followed in organizational buying. These stages were problem recognition, general need description, product specification, supplier's search, proposal solicitation, supplier selection, order-routine specification, and performance review.

MARKETER'S VOCABULARY

Market   A group of potential buyers with needs and wants and the purchasing power to satisfy them.

Need   A basic deficiency given a particular situation.

Want   Placing certain personal criteria as to how a need should be fulfilled.

Information search   Involves the mental as well as physical activities that consumers must perform in order to make decisions and accomplish desired goals in the marketplace.

Attitude   An opinion we hold toward a person, idea, place, or thing.

Cognitive dissonance   Negative feelings the consumer has after purchase.

High-involvement decisions   Decisions that are important to the buyer because they are closely tied to self-image and have an inherent risk.

Low-involvement decisions   Decisions that are not very important to the buyer because ego is not involved and risk is low.

Culture   A large group of people with a similar heritage.

Social class   People grouped together because of similar occupation, wealth, income, education, power, and prestige.

Reference groups   Individuals who share common attitudes and behavior.

Family lifecycle   Predictable stages experienced by families.

Learning   Changes in behavior resulting from previous experiences.

Socialization   The process by which persons acquire the knowledge, skills, and dispositions that make them more or less able members of their society.

Motivation   An inner drive or pressure to take action to satisfy a need.

Personality   A term used to summarize all the traits of a person that makes him/her unique.

Lifestyle   A profile of an individual as reflected in their attitudes, interests, and opinions.

DISCUSSION QUESTIONS

1. Discuss several reasons why marketers continue to have a hard time understanding, predicting, and explaining consumer behavior.

2. Based on your understanding of motives, develop some general guidelines or directives for practicing marketing.

3. How can marketers influence a person's motivation to take action? How can they facilitate learning?

4. Define an attitude. Discuss the components of an attitude. What are the implications for marketing?

5. Distinguish between high-involvement and low-involvement decision making.

6. Present a diagram of the consumer decision process. What is the role of marketing in each stage of this process?

7. What are the differences between the consumer decision-making process and organizational decision-making process?

8. Assume that you are training a salesperson to sell industrial products. Although this salesperson has a strong track record, she has been selling consumer products. What would you emphasize during training?

9. Explain how complexity of the product influences the buying decision process.

10. Why are opinion leaders so important to marketers? Discuss how marketers could use this type of individual in prompting a decision.

PROJECT

Locate an individual who has purchased a new automobile during the last year. Using the six-step decision-making process, ask this person to indicate how he or she accomplished each step.

CASE APPLICATION

CUSTOMER SATISFACTION STILL MATTERS

To many American travelers, airline quality is an oxymoron. Ted J. Kredir, director of hobby sales for Dallas-based trading card company, Pinnacle Brands, Inc., complains of frequent flight cancellations, late arrivals, and lousy food. To the surprise of skeptical passengers, the gripes aren't falling on deaf ears. After years of focusing on paring expenses, such major airlines as American, Delta, and Continental are stepping up their quality efforts. Cost-cutting "diverted our attention from the nuts and bolts of out business," concedes American Airlines Chief Executive Robert L. Crandall. "Our customers have noticed."

American, which once dubbed itself the "on-time machine," placed a dismal ninth among 10 carriers in on-time rankings for the third quarter of 1996. So Crandall told managers at the next meeting that leading all industry-quality ratings is their top job for 1997. An American spokesperson won't provide specifics, but says: "We're talking about a lot of operational things like customer comfort onboard airplanes."

At Delta Air Lines, Inc., customer complaints have nearly doubled since 1994; CEO Ronald W. Allen blames the pursuit of lower costs. "In some cases we did cut too deeply," he says. Trans World Airlines, Inc., now in the cellar for on-time and customer complaint rankings by the Transportation

Department, is getting the message too. After on-time arrivals dropped under 50% during the holidays and cancellations climbed, managers warned workers to get back to basics.

Underscoring the quality drive is the stunning turnaround at Continental Airlines, Inc., where for two years CEO Gordon M. Bethune has hammered away at the theme. Once near the bottom of transportation rankings, Continental now has one of the best ratings for on-time performance, baggage handling, and customer complaints. And in 1996, they won the prestigious J.D. Power & Associates, Inc., award for the highest customer satisfaction on long-haul flights. Bethune claims to be grabbing marketing share among business travelers from American and others. "We've been kicking their butts," boasts Bethune.

Jaded coach passengers, however, aren't expecting first-class treatment anytime soon. "The product is bad, and it's going to stay that way as near as I can tell," says Ed Perkins, editor of *Consumer Reports Travel Letters*. It's up to the airlines to prove such doubters wrong.

Questions

1. What risk do airlines take when all of them have the same goal—improving service quality?
2. Should the airlines focus on business travelers or consumers? Why?

REFERENCES

1. Henry Assael, *Consumer Behavior and Marketing Action*, 3rd ed., Boston: Kent Publishing, 1987, p. 84.
2. James Bettman, *An Information Processing Theory of Consumer Choice*, Reading, Mass: Addison Wesley, 1979.
3. Richard E. Petty, John T. Cacioppo, and David Schumann, "Central and Peripheral Routes to Advertising Effectiveness: The Moderating Role of Involvement," *Journal of Consumer Research* 10, September 1983, pp. 135–146.
4. L. Festinger, *A Theory of Cognitive Dissonance*, Stanford, Calif.: Stanford University Press, 1957.
5. Richard Petty and John T. Cacioppo, "Issue Involvement as a Moderator of the Effects on Attitude Advertising Content and Context,"
in *Advances in Consumer Research*, ed. K. B. Monroe, Vol. 8, Ann Arbor, Mich., 1981.
6. William O. Bearden and Michael G. Etzel, "Reference Group Influence on Product and Brand Choice," *Journal of Consumer Research*, September 1982, pp. 183–194.
7. C. N. Coffer and M. H. Appley, *Motivation: Theory Research*, New York: John Wiley & Sons, 1964.
8. Martha Farnsworth Riche, "Psychographics for the 1990's," *American Demographics*, July 1989, pp. 25–6, 30–2.
9. William A. Dempsey, "Vendor Selection and the Buying Process," *Industrial Marketing Management* 7, 1978, pp. 257–67.

CHAPTER *5*

EXTERNAL CONSIDERATIONS IN MARKETING

LEARNING OBJECTIVES

As you read through this chapter, you should develop an understanding of the external considerations in marketing planning. Specifically, you should:

■ Understand the importance of analyzing the organization's external environment and the impact that the external environment has on strategic marketing planning.

■ Realize that marketing organizations often work with external agencies that perform some of these marketing activities. These agencies include distributors, retailers, market research suppliers, advertising agencies, and materials suppliers.

■ Appreciate the external factors that have an impact on marketing activities, including external agencies, competitors, legal/ethical issues, economic/political issues, technology, and social trends.

■ Relate these external factors to the marketing planning process.

THE CAR INDUSTRY AND TECHNOLOGY

The **EV1** is an electric car built by General Motors, marketed under the Saturn brand. The EV1 was introduced to California and Arizona in 1996 with an estimated $25 million marketing campaign.

In 1997, a clean air mandate went into effect in three states—California, Massachusetts, and New York. The mandate requires that each year, a certain percentage of vehicles sold must be zero-emission vehicles. California has since pushed its deadline to the year 2003, but requires that ten percent of all vehicles sold be zero-emission. General Motors stayed with the original date and won acclaim for the zero-emission technology. General Motors is not the only company with an interest in developing electric-powered vehicles. Here are several other electric projects that are underway:

- Honda EV Plus, introduced in 1997 and marketed to families of four
- Chrysler EPIC
- Nissan Prairie Jay minivan
- Ford Ranger EV
- Chevy S-10 pickups
- Toyota RAV4-EV sport-utility vehicle

Production of electric vehicles was undertaken in response to *voter mandates*, a factor external to the firm. Now, auto producers are introducing electric vehicles in part to learn about customer reactions. And there is still much to learn about electric-powered technology. Today, there are concerns about things like range, price, and refueling of electric vehicles. This is quite a drastic change from typical customer concerns like car phones, cup holders, and other frills associated with gas-powered vehicles. A few other facts about General Motors' EV1:

- It leases for between $399 and $549 monthly.
- Monthly payments on a typical purchase are around $500.
- They have limited range (about 120 miles between changes).
- Recharging takes several hours.
- They are currently best as a second vehicle.

Sources: "GM's Advanced Auto Technologies Showcased at Democratic National Convention," *Financial News*, August 13, 2000; Jon Pepper, "California Mandate for Electric Cars Means GM Has a Lot to Explain," *The Detroit News*, August 23, 2000, p. 1; Paul Rogers, "California Air Officials Want Auto Makers to Deliver Electric Cars in Two Years," *San Jose Mercury News*, September 9, 2000.

INTRODUCTION

When marketing organizations plan strategically, the key question is, "Does the strategic planning process raise the overall level of the organization's effectiveness, and does it provide the new strategic direction that is required for the future?" A good strategic plan must help marketing organizations recognize the interrelationships among various forces in the business environment. These interrelationships must be accounted for if the organization is to be capable of implementing its vision.

It is important to recognize that most existing planning processes have an internal focus. Internal planning processes ask questions like, "What are our strengths and weaknesses?", "What comparative cost advantages do we have?" and "What product features provide us with an advantage?"

The external planning approach asks these same questions but also attempts to understand how all of the elements of the marketplace relate to each other. In this chapter, we focus on the external environmental factors that have an impact on the organization, especially the marketing function. In the chapters that follow, we consider the marketplace and its behavior.

As shown in Figure 5.1, marketing managers are confronted with many environmental concerns, including technology: customer; competitor; ethical/legal; and economic, political, demographic, and social trends. All organizations should continuously appraise their situation and adjust their strategy to adapt to the environment.

One technique used by organizations to monitor the environment is known as *environmental scanning*, which refers to activities directed toward obtaining information about events and trends that occur outside the organization and that can influence the organization's decision making. In a sense, such data collection scanning acts as an early warning system for the organization. It allows marketers to understand the current state of the environment and to predict trends. A formal but simple strategic information scanning system can enhance the effectiveness of the organization's environmental scanning efforts.[1] An information system (part of marketing research) organizes the scanning effort so that information related to specific situations can be more readily obtained and used.

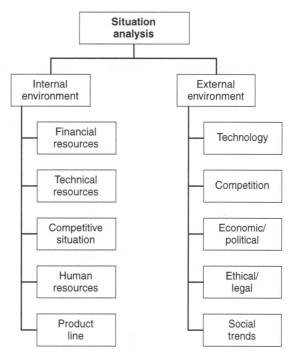

FIGURE 5.1 Environmental factors affecting the organization

A good strategic plan requires careful monitoring of the marketing organization's external environment. The external environment represents sources of opportunities and threats. If the marketing organization is to align its capabilities and resources with opportunities and threats, it must know what those threats are. It is important that marketing organizations have a strategy to uncover relevant strategic opportunities and threats early. As threats and opportunities appear, marketing organizations should develop strategies to deal with them.

Another problem is that at any one time, there may appear to be a great many opportunities and threats looming. Marketers must be able to prioritize these opportunities and threats according to such factors as their relevance to the organization, the cost effectiveness of strategies to deal with the threats and opportunities, and the urgency of the threat or opportunity. Organizations are inundated with information and must therefore have an effective mechanism for sorting out that information which is relevant to the organization.

Only after the marketing environment is thoroughly understood can an organization spot trends and determine whether they represent market opportunities or market threats.

EXTERNAL FACTORS THAT AFFECT PLANNING

There are many marketplace changes occurring that marketers cannot control but affect what marketers do. Faced with these environmental uncertainties, successful marketers will be those who recognize the changes that are occurring and who make effective adjustments.

There are a number of external factors that constitute the external environment. Our approach is to attempt to present an all-encompassing view of the elements of the external environment. Rather, it is to briefly describe each of the components and show how external factors affect marketing strategy.

External Suprises

Carol Wolfe and Jane Barnes have been friends for six years, sharing carpool responsibilities, a common love of sewing, and a belief that being self-employed would be a dream come true. After two years of tinkering, they produced a child carrier that they felt would appeal to devoted moms who wanted their baby to be physically attached to the parent in a secure and comfortable manner. They knew they would need lots of help getting this business off the ground, but never realized how difficult and complicated it would be to obtain such assistance.

They contacted the chairman of the marketing department at a local college and were told they could be considered as a student project for the capstone marketing course. One month later, they were given a preliminary report. The report began by listing the various agencies and intermediaries they would need to contact in order to start their business. The list included the following: personal attorney, patent attorney, accountant, commercial banker, raw materials providers (e.g., denim, thread, staples), distributors (wholesalers and retailers), advertising agency, marketing research firm, and fulfillment house. Further, they would have to understand the capabilities, options, and costs associated with each agency/intermediary.

Since they lived in a relatively small city (population 185,000), many of these agencies/intermediaries were not readily available. A local attorney put them in touch with a patent attorney and a marketing research company in a nearby large city. The estimated cost of doing the patent search was $5,500, while the cost of preliminary research was $9,300. Their combined savings totalled $18,000. Clearly, they were underfunded. A quick call to the local bank produced another list of requirements they would have to meet in order to qualify for a business loan, including a business plan, a *pro forma* statement, and so forth.

The initial business plan developed by the student group indicated that there were several competitors selling a product very similar to Carol and Jane's baby carrier. Also, the sources for denim were limited and required a minimum purchase of 500 bolts of fabric. Finally, because most retailers selling similar products were already committed to other manufacturers, it was unlikely that they would find retail distributors. The expected cost of manufacturing and marketing 30,000 units the first year was $1.4 million, with a maximum possible profit of $146,000. Carol and Jane gave up on their idea.

While this scenario is quite depressing, it is not that unusual. It is critical that a business identify and evaluate the various agencies and intermediaries that it must deal with. Throughout this book, we will constantly identify these external agencies and attempt to assess their influence on a marketing organization.

Competitors

As with other external forces, management must also prioritize the importance of the factors that affect competition. The relationships between these elements and competition must be understood if the organization is to be able to develop and sustain a competitive advantage.

Competitive analysis focuses on opportunities and threats that may occur because of actual or potential competitive changes in strategy. It starts with identifying current and potential competitors. For example, who are General Motors competitors? If you named companies like Toyota, Ford, Chrysler, and Honda, you are right, but you've just begun. Table 5.1 outlines some of General Motors' competitors and Table 5.2 does the same with Nintendo's competitors.

It is essential that the marketer begin this assessment by answering the following question: "What criteria can be used to identify a salient set of competitors?"

TABLE 5.1 Analysis of General Motors' Competitors

Transportation		After-Market	
Autos	**Other**	**Repairs**	**Parts**
Toyota	Schwinn	Auto dealers	Pep-Boys
Ford	Delta Airlines	Sears	NAPA
Chrysler	American Airlines	K-Mart	
Honda	Honda motorcycles	Local repair shops	
Audi	Mass transit		

TABLE 5.2 Analysis of Nintendo's Competitors

Video Games			Entertainment	
Game Suppliers	**Game Providers**	**In-Home**	**Out-of-Home**	**Hobbies**
Sega	The Tilt	Family time	Plitt Theaters	Hunting, fishing,
Atari	Video game parlor	Parker Brothers	The New York Mets	golf, Little League,
Genesis	Mazzio's	Blockbuster Video	Six Flags	baseball, Girl Scouts

It is clear from these two examples that an accurate accounting of competitors is much broader than the obvious. If we define our competitors too narrowly, we risk the chance that an unidentified competitor will take market share away from us without our knowledge. For example, General Motors obviously competes against Ford, Chrysler, Toyota, and other auto manufacturers. But they also compete against Sears in the repair market, the subway in large cities, the airlines, and Schwinn, among people for whom bicycle riding is popular. Nintendo competes against Sega in the video game market. But they also compete against Blockbuster Video, the local gym, board games, the theater, and rock concerts. Competition focuses on the wants and needs being satisfied, not the product being produced. General Motors, then, is competing to satisfy your need for transportation. Nintendo is competing to satisfy your need for entertainment.

In addition to identifying a competitor from the perspective of the customer, other criteria might be the geographic location of competitors, relative size, history, channels of distribution, and common tactics.

A second question to consider is the following: "What criteria do we need to use to make sure that our competitors are 'correctly' identified?" One way of answering this question is to track the customer's perceptions of product groupings and substitution. Do they change over time? Likewise, tracking expected competitors over time may prove insightful.

Once competitors are correctly identified, it is helpful to assess them relative to factors that drive competition: entry, bargaining power of buyers and suppliers, existing rivalries, and substitution possibilities. These factors relate to a firm's marketing mix decisions and may be used to create a barrier to entry, increase brand awareness, or intensify a fight for market share.

Barriers to entry represent business practices or conditions that make it difficult for new or existing firms to enter the market. Our entrepreneurs Carol and Jane faced several barriers to entry. Typically, barriers to entry can be in the form of capital requirements, advertising expenditures, product identity, distribution access, or switching costs. Japan has been accused of having unofficial cultural-based barriers to the Japanese market.

In industries such as steel, automobiles, and computers, the *power of buyers and suppliers* can be very high. Powerful buyers exist when they are few in number, there are low switching costs, or the product represents a significant share of the buyer's total costs. This is common for large retailers such as Wal-Mart and Home Depot. A supplier gains power when the product is critical to the buyer and when it has built up the switching costs. Examples include Microsoft and BMW.

Existing competitors and *possible substitutes* also influence the dynamics of the competition. For example, in slow-growth markets, competition is more severe for any possible gains in market share. High fixed costs also create competitive pressures for firms to fill production capacity. For example, hospitals are increasing their advertising in a battle to fill beds, which represents a high fixed cost.

Legal/Ethical Factors

Every marketing organization's activities are influenced by ethical and legal factors that establish the rules of the game. These laws, agencies, policies, and behavioral norms are established to ensure that marketers compete legally and ethically in their efforts to provide want and need satisfying products and services. The various legal issues with which marketers must be knowledgeable include the following:

1. *Monetary and fiscal policy*—Marketing decisions are affected by factors like tax legislation, the money supply, and the level of government spending. The tendency of a Republican Congress to spend on defense materials and not on the environment is an example.

2. *Federal legislation*—Federal legislation exists to ensure such things as fair competition, fair pricing practices, and honesty in marketing communications. Antitobacco legislation affects the tobacco and related industries.

3. *Government/industry relationships*—Agriculture, railroads, shipbuilding, and other industries are subsidized by government. Tariffs and import quotas imposed by government affect certain industries (e.g., automobile). Other industries are regulated (or no longer regulated) by government (e.g., rail, trucking, and airlines). Deregulating the utilities industry had a tremendous negative effect on the California power industry in 2001.

4. *Social legislation*—Marketers' activities are affected by broad social legislation like the civil rights laws, programs to reduce unemployment, and legislation that affects the environment (e.g., water and air pollution). The meat processing industry has spent billions of dollars trying to comply with water pollution legislation.

5. *State laws*—State legislation affects marketers in different ways. For example, utilities in Oregon can spend only $\frac{1}{2}\%$ of their net income on advertising. California has enacted legislation to reduce the energy consumption of refrigerators and air conditioners. And in New Jersey, nine dairies have paid the state over $2 million dollars to settle a price-fixing lawsuit.

6. *Regulatory agencies*—State regulatory agencies (e.g., the Attorney General's Office) actively pursue marketing violations of the law. But federal agencies like the Federal Trade Commission and the Consumer Product Safety concern themselves with all facets of business.

Literally every facet of business is affected by one or more laws. It would be impossible to adequately cover them all in the space allotted. However, we will briefly discuss the three areas receiving the most notice in marketing: product liability, deregulation, and consumer protection.

Product Liability

The courts are increasingly holding sellers responsible for the safety of their products. The courts generally hold that the producer of a product is liable for any product defect that causes injury in the course of normal use. Liability can even result if a court or a jury decides that a product's design, construction, or operating instructions and safety warnings make the product unreasonably dangerous to use.[2]

> *Two Maryland men decided to dry their hot air balloon in a commercial laundry dryer. The dryer exploded, injuring them. They sued the manufacturer and won.*
>
> *A two-year-old child being treated for bronchial spasms suffered brain damage from a drug overdose. The hospital staff had clearly exceeded the dosage level prescribed by the drug manufacturer. The child's parents successfully sued the manufacturer.*
>
> *In Australia, about 20,000 kangaroos are killed or injured by motor vehicles each year. Vehicles are equipped with bullbars to limit damage to kangaroos. The problem is that the bullbars often confuse computer sensors, causing airbags to deploy unnecessarily. To solve the problem, General Motors–Holden's Automotive is experimenting with Robo-roo, a crash dummy that is made in the image of a 60-kg. kangaroo. Robo-roo is used to test various bullbars in an effort to find one that prevents injury to the kangaroos and is often safe with regard to airbags.[3]*

While examples such as these are devastating, many feel that product liability law is now as it should be—in favor of the injured product user. Consumer advocates like Ralph Nader argue that for too long, product liability favored producers at the expense of the product user. They claim that the threat of lawsuits and huge settlements and restitutions force companies to make safe products. While a discussion of all aspects of products liability is beyond the scope of this text, it is clear that liability has and will continue to have tremendous impact on consumers and manufacturers alike. And these two groups are not the only ones affected. Retailers, franchises, wholesalers, sellers of mass-produced homes, and building site developers and engineers are all subject to liability legislation.

Deregulation

Deregulation means the relaxation or removal of government controls over industries that were thought to be either "natural monopolies," such as telephones, or essential public services like airlines and trucking. When regulated, industries got protection against renegade competition. For 40 years, the Civil Aeronautics Board barred the creation of any major new airline. And carriers could fly only over routes awarded them by the CAB.

With time, the bargain grew increasingly bad. Insulated from competition, regulated industries had little reason to lower costs. They concentrated on influencing the regulators to make favorable decisions. There was an unhealthy tension and costs rose, industries sought price increases, and regulators resisted, often depressing industry profits. That, in turn, reduced new investment and perpetuated high costs and poor service.

Industries such as the airlines, banking railroads, communications, and trucking have long been subject to government regulation. A marketplace shockwave hit these industries as they were deregulated. Each of these industries saw the birth of many new competitors attempting to take advantage of market opportunities uncovered by deregulation. For example, US Airways, Midway, People Express, AirCal, Golden West, Muse Air and Texas Air all started after the airline industry was deregulated. Not all of them survived. The result was that competition intensified, prices were lowered (sometimes below cost), and many once-stable organizations suffered huge financial losses.

As deregulation unfolded—new competition was permitted, rate regulation was loosened or abandoned—the vicious cycle began to reverse itself. For example, AT&T had been slow to adopt fiber-optic cable. In 1985, there were only 136,000 miles of it in AT&T's system. Sprint and MCI had more. AT&T responded. By 1994, it had 1.3 million miles of fiber cable (slightly more than MCI and Sprint). Airlines, freed of the CAB's routine restrictions, organized "hub and spoke" systems—routing passengers via major transfer points—that provided more connections. In 1978, about 14% of all passengers had to change airlines to reach their destination; by 1995, this number fell to about 1%.[4]

Consumer Protection

Since the beginning of the twentieth century, there has been a concerted effort to protect the consumer. For example, the *Food, Drug, and Cosmetic Act* (1938) was aimed principally at preventing the adulteration or misbranding of the three categories of products. The various federal consumer protection laws include more than 30 amendments and separate laws relating to food, drugs, and cosmetics, such as the *Infant Formula Act* (1980) and the *Nutritional Labeling and Education Act* (1990). Perhaps the most significant period in consumer protection was the 1960s, with the emergence of *consumerism*. This was a grass-roots movement intended to increase the influence, power, and rights of consumers in dealing with the institutions. The *Consumer Product Safety Act* (1972) established the Consumer Product Safety Commission.

Ethics is generally referred to as the set of moral principles or values that guide behavior. There is a general recognition that many, if not most, business decisions involve some ethical judgement. Consider the following dilemma. An athletic shoe company is considering whether to manufacture shoes in a country with a very poor record on human rights. The new facility will improve the company's competitive position, but the host government will also make a considerable profit, a profit that will be enjoyed by the ruling elite, not by the people of the country who will be employed at meager wages. Will the firm support a corrupt government in order to make higher profits?

Firms hope that a consideration of ethical issues during the decision-making process will be helpful in preventing or at least decreasing the frequency of unethical behavior. Having a corporate ethics policy also seems to facilitate the process of recovery after an ethical scandal—although firms may wish otherwise, unethical acts do occur and do not often go unnoticed. The lack of respect many people feel towards business today, the press's propensity for investigative reporting, and the willingness of many insiders to blow the whistle on unethical corporate behavior increase the likelihood that such behaviors will eventually be discovered. See Figure 5.2.

Ethical problems faced by marketing professionals stem from conflicts and disagreements. They tend to be relationship problems. Each party in a marketing transaction brings a set of expectations regarding how the business relationship will exist and how transactions should be conducted. For example, when you as a consumer wish to purchase something from a retailer, you bring the following expectations about the transaction: (1) you want to be treated fairly by the salesperson, (2) you want to pay a reasonable price, (3) you want the product to be available as advertising says it will and in the indicated condition, and (4) you want it to perform as promised. Unfortunately, your expectations might not be in agreement with those of the retailer. The retail salesperson may not "have time for you," or the retailer's notion of a "reasonable" price may be higher than yours, or the advertising for the product may be misleading. A summary of ethic issues related to marketing is shown in Table 5.3.

Business Week/Harris Poll

Survey of 1035 adults conducted Aug. 25–29, 2000, 1009 adults conducted June 29–July 5, 2000, 1010 adults conducted Dec. 9–12, 1999, and 1004 adults on Feb. 23–26, 1996. Results should be accurate within 3 percentage points. Results for 2000 are from June unless otherwise noted.

CORPORATE AMERICA: SOME CREDIT, MORE BLAME

American business should be given most of the credit for the prosperity that has prevailed during most of the 1990s.

	AGREE STRONGLY	SOMEWHAT AGREE	SOMEWHAT DISAGREE	DISAGREE STRONGLY	NOT SURE/ NO ANSWER
2000	26%	42%	19%	10%	2%
1996	55%*			44%*	

Business has gained too much power over too many aspects of American life.

	AGREE STRONGLY	SOMEWHAT AGREE	SOMEWHAT DISAGREE	DISAGREE STRONGLY	NOT SURE/ NO ANSWER
2000 (Aug.)	40%	32%	15%	9%	4%
2000 (June)	52%	30%	12%	4%	2%
1996	71%*			28%*	

In general, what is good for business is good for most Americans.

	AGREE STRONGLY	SOMEWHAT AGREE	SOMEWHAT DISAGREE	DISAGREE STRONGLY	NOT SURE/ NO ANSWER
2000 (Aug)	14%	33%	27%	22%	4%
2000 (June)	17%	35%	23%	24%	1%
1996	32%	39%	20%	8%	1%

How much confidence do you have in those running big business?

	2000	1999
Great deal	19%	15%
Only some	58%	69%
Hardly any	17%	13%
Not sure/No answer	5%	3%

Having large profits is more important to big business than developing safe, reliable, quality products for consumers.

	AGREE STRONGLY	SOMEWHAT AGREE	SOMEWHAT DISAGREE	DISAGREE STRONGLY	NOT SURE/ NO ANSWER
2000 (Aug.)	38%	28%	14%	17%	3%

*Question asked only agree or disagree

GORE'S BIG SCORE

At the recent Democratic convention, Vice-President Al Gore criticized a wide range of large corporations, including "big tobacco, big oil, the big polluters, the pharmaceutical companies, the HMOs." Do you agree or disagree with Gore's sentiments?

Strongly agree . . . . 39% Strongly disagree 13%
Somewhat agree . . . . . 35% Don't Know/
Somewhat disagree . . . . 9% No answer 4%

SECTOR BY SECTOR

LOW MARKS FROM CONSUMERS

How would you rate these industries in serving their consumers?

	ONLY POOR	PRETTY FAIR	GOOD	EXCELLENT	DON'T KNOW/ NO ANSWER
HMOs	43%	28%	15%	3%	11%
Tobacco companies	43%	30%	14%	5%	8%
Oil companies	39%	35%	16%	3%	7%
Insurance companies	32%	41%	21%	3%	3%

43% think HMOs serve their customers POORLY

Pharmaceutical companies	27%	37%	26%	5%	5%
Airlines	22%	41%	25%	3%	9%
Telephone companies	20%	42%	31%	6%	1%
News organizations	18%	38%	33%	6%	5%
Hospitals	15%	35%	38%	9%	3%
Entertainment companies	14%	33%	38%	9%	6%
Automobile companies	12%	42%	37%	6%	3%
Financial services firms	12%	40%	34%	5%	9%
Computer companies	4%	30%	40%	10%	16%

GOOD PRODUCTS, POOR PRACTICES

WHAT CORPORATIONS DO WELL—AND NOT SO WELL

How would you rate large U.S. companies on each of the following?

Making good products and competing in a global economy

	EXCELLENT	PRETTY GOOD	ONLY FAIR	POOR	DON'T KNOW/ NO ANSWER
2000	18%	50%	26%	5%	1%
1996	14%	44%	33%	9%	*

FIGURE 5.2 How business rates: by the numbers

While ethics deal with the relationship between buyer and seller, there are also instances when the activities of marketing influence society as a whole. For example, when you purchase a new refrigerator, there is a need to discard your old refrigerator. Thrown in a trash dump, the old refrigerator may pose a safety risk, or contaminate the soil, and certainly will contaminate the aesthetics of the countryside, thus requiring society to bear part of the cost of your purchase. This example illustrates the issue of *social responsibility*, the idea that organizations are part of a larger society and are accountable to society for their actions. The well-being of society at large should also be recognized in an organization's marketing decisions. In fact, some marketing experts stress the *societal marketing concept*, the view that an organization should discover and satisfy the needs of its consumers in a way that also provides for society's well-being. A definition for social marketing is provided by Alan Andreasen:

> *Social marketing is the adaptation of commercial marketing technologies to programs designed to influence the voluntary behavior of target audiences to improve their personal welfare and that of the society of which they are a part.*[5]

There is little doubt that the importance of social marketing is growing, and that for many marketers, it will become part of their competitive advantage.

Economic/Political Issues

Various economic forces influence an organization's ability to compete and consumer's willingness and ability to buy products and services. The state of the economy is always changing. Interest rates rise and fall. Inflation increases and decreases. Consumers' ability and willingness to buy changes. The economy goes through fluctuations. Two aspects of the economy are consumer's buying power and the business cycle.

TABLE 5.3 Ethical Issues in Marketing

Issue		Percent of Marketing Professionals Responding
Bribery	Gifts from outside vendors, payment of questionable commissions, "money under the table"	15%
Fairness	Unfairly placing company interests over family obligations, taking credit for the work of others, inducing customers to use services not needed, manipulation of others	14%
Honesty	Lying to customers to obtain orders, misrepresenting services and capabilities	12%
Price	Differential pricing, charging higher prices than firms with similar products while claiming superiority, meeting competitive prices	12%
Product	Product safety, product and brand infringement, exaggerated performance claims, products that do not benefit consumers	11%
Personnel	Firing, hiring, employee evaluation	10%
Confidentiality	Temptations to use or obtain classified, secret, or competitive information	5%
Advertising	Crossing the line between exaggeration and misrepresentation, misleading customers	4%
Manipulation of Data	Falsifying figures or misusing statistics or information, distortion	4%
Purchasing	Reciprocity in the selection of suppliers	3%

Marketing professionals were asked to describe the most difficult ethical issue they face.

Source: Lawrence B. Chonko and Shelby D. Hunt, "Ethics and Marketing Management: An Empirical Examination," *Journal of Business Research*, Vol. 13, 1985, pp. 339–359.

Consumer Buying Power

A consumer's buying power represents his/her ability to make purchases. The economy affects buying power. For example, if prices decline, consumers have greater buying power. If the value of the dollar increases relative to foreign currency, consumers have greater buying power. When inflation occurs, consumers have less buying power. A list of several aspects of consumer buying power is presented next. Each can be measured relative to a marketer's external environment.

- *Buying power:* A consumer's ability to make purchases.
- *Income:* The amount of money an individual receives from wages, rents, investments, pensions, and/or subsidies.
- *Disposable income:* The income available for spending after taxes have been paid.
- *Discretionary income:* Disposable income available for spending or saving after basic necessities (e.g., food, housing, clothing) have been purchased.
- *Credit:* An individual's ability to buy something now and pay for it later.
- *Wealth:* The accumulation of past income and other assets including savings accounts, jewelry, investments, real estate, and the like.
- *Willingness to spend:* An individual's choice of how much disposable income to spend and what to spend it on.
- *Consumer spending patterns:* Amount of money spent on certain kinds of products and services each year.
- *Comprehensive spending patterns:* The amount of income individuals allocate to expenditures for classes of products and services.
- *Product spending patterns:* The amount of income spent for specific products in a product class.

Several of these concepts are illustrated in the Newsline that follows.

NEWSLINE: EVERYONE SEEMS TO HAVE MONEY

It's been called *mystery prosperity.* The nation's economy is growing at a rate not seen since the 1960s, unemployment and inflation are the lowest in decades, and the stock market is setting records with regularity. Some economists explain our good fortune by claiming a new economy is at work, one driven by deficit reduction, low interest rates, and technological advances. Others point to things like the Asian contagion and the inevitable limits of the bull market, and wonder how long this can last (in fact it ended in 2000).

But despite market jitters, at least we can take comfort in knowing that the economy may be more stable than many fear, if only because consumer spending—which accounts for two-thirds of the nation's economic output—has been considerably muted in the past decade. Talk about unconventional wisdom. How can this be? Hasn't the media been trumpeting America's runaway spending spree?

It's true that consumer spending has been growing, but only at the aggregate level: the population is growing, the number of households is increasing, and the baby-boom generation—the youngest of which is now 35—has entered its peak spending years. But a close look at trends in spending by individual households tells a different story.

Despite low unemployment levels and rising wages, the average American household's spending has been cautious, if not downright miserly, in the last decade. The average household spent 13% less on food away from home in 1997 than in 1987, after adjusting for inflation. It spent 25% less on major appliances; 24% less on alcoholic beverages; 18% less on newspapers, books, and magazines; and 15% less on clothing.

The most important predictor of spending is lifecycle stage. Typically, households headed by twenty-somethings spend less than average on most products and services because their households are small and their incomes are low. Spending hits a maximum in middle age as family size increases and incomes peak, then falls again in older age as household size and income decline.

These stages, combined with the baby booms and busts of past decades, have made consumer marketing a complex endeavor. Add a fundamental change in the lifecycle pattern of spending, and marketers are discovering that doing business today is a lot like building a house in an earthquake zone.

Sources: "The New Consumer Paradigm," *American Demographics*, April 1999, pp. 50–58; Edwin S. Rubenstein, "Inequality," *Forbes*, January 2000, pp. 32–33; "Cutting a Pie," *Forbes*, September 4, 2000, p. 86; Susan Jacoby, "Money," *Modern Maturity*, July–August 2000, pp. 36–41.

The Business Cycle

Fluctuations in our economy follow a general pattern known as the *business cycle*. The fluctuations in economic conditions affect supply and demand, consumer buying power, consumer willingness to spend, and the intensity of competitive behavior. The four stages in the business cycle are prosperity, recession, depression, and recovery.

Prosperity *Prosperity* represents a period of time during which the economy is growing. Unemployment is low, consumers' buying power is high, and the demand for products is strong. During prosperity, consumer disposable incomes are high and they try to improve their quality of life by purchasing products and services that are high in quality and price. The U.S. economy was in a period of prosperity from 1991 to 2000. For marketers, opportunities were plentiful during prosperity, and they attempted to expand product lines to take advantage of consumers' increased willingness to buy.

Recession *Recession* is characterized by a decrease in the rate of growth of the economy. Unemployment rises and consumer buying power declines. Recession tends to occur after periods of prosperity and inflation. During a recession, consumers' spending power is low, as they are busy paying off debts incurred through credit purchases during more prosperous times. During recessions, marketing opportunities are reduced. Because of reduced buying power, consumers become more cautions, seeking products that are more basic and functional.

Depression *Depression* represents the most serious economic downturn. Unemployment increases, buying power decreases, and all other economic indicators move downward. Consequently, consumers are unable or reluctant to purchase products, particularly big-ticket items. Also, consumers tend to delay replacement purchases. Although many marketers fail during this period, insightful marketers can gain market share.

Recovery *Recovery* is a complicated economic pattern, in that some economic indicators increase while others may stay low or even decrease. Much of what happens during a recovery may be a result of intangibles, such as consumer confidence or the perception of businesses that things will get better. Tentative marketers take serious risks. Premature marketers may face dire consequences.

For marketers, an important task is to attempt to determine how quickly the economy will move into a situation of prosperity. Improper forecasting can lead some firms to overextend themselves, as consumers may be slow to change purchase habits they have been accustomed to in the more difficult economic times.

The economy is cyclical in nature. We know that the cycles will occur. We just cannot predict exactly when, or how severe the cycles will be. Assumptions must be made about money, people, and resources. For example, many organizations become less aggressive when they believe the economy is not going to grow. If they are right, they may do well. But if they are wrong, those organizations that are more aggressive can perform very well—often at the expense of the conservative organizations. Assumptions must also be made about such economic factors as interest rates, inflation, the nature and size of the workforce, and the availability of resources such as energy and raw materials.

Technology

Is the car of the future the electric car? They're called zero-emission vehicles by their advocates, but they do not have zero emissions according to some experts. While an electric car does not emit exhaust, the technology required to charge their batteries does, according to the Environmental Protection Agency.[6] Critics argue that the more electric cars that are driven, the more pollution from smokestacks at the plants that provide the electric power. You are familiar with the complaints about gas-driven automobiles, but, if the electric-powered auto is no different in terms of its impact on the environment, than there could be some interesting battles ahead between proponents of the electric car and environmental groups. In fact, some auto industry executives felt that the EPA report did not go far enough in discrediting the electric car.

Technology is the knowledge of how to accomplish tasks and goals. Technology affects marketers in several ways. First, aggressively advancing technology is spawning new products and processes at an accelerating rate that threatens almost every existing product. Second, competition continues to intensify from broad and new organizations and many substitute technologies compete with established products. Third, product innovations that result in superior performance or cost advantages are the best means of protecting or building market position without sacrificing profit margins. This is especially true in today's world, when many markets are experiencing flat or slow growth and excess capacity is commonplace.

History provides many examples of companies that have lost their competitive advantage—and perhaps even their entire business—because a competitor came into the market with a product that had superior cost advantage or performance characteristics. These examples are not limited to small or weak companies; even industrial giants like IBM, General Electric, and AT&T have seen certain parts of their markets eroded by competition that surprised them with a distinctly superior product. IBM, despite its dominant position in the computer market, lost position in the late 1970s to several smaller companies that were first to develop powerful minicomputers to replace the larger mainframe computers that were the cornerstone of IBM's business.

All organizations must make assumptions about the future in technology and its impact on their business activities. The results of technology cannot be ignored. For example, the Japanese promote the use of electronic circuits and have used them almost exclusively in their controls. However, U.S.-based organizations have been slower to change and many have continued to use electromechanical controls in their products.

Everyone enjoys thinking about the future and the kinds of technology that will evolve. Let's fast-forward a few years to see what opportunities technology will open up for marketers:

- How about ads that are targeted not to a demographic or psychographic group, but to you specifically—ads that know what you need and what you want?
- How about a house of smart appliances with Internet connections—refrigerators that tell you when you're running out of milk and dryers that know to call the repairman when they break?
- How about a cell phone that knows where you are and can direct you to a great new Korean restaurant, or a Palm handheld device that delivers streaming video right to your hand?
- How about a TV that airs a pizza ad you can order from at the click of a button, with total integration between a channel and its Web site?

INTEGRATED MARKETING 5.1

NOT IN LOVE WITH ONLINE—IMAGINE!

There are people who are Net-free, and they plan to stay that way. This seems to be especially true with many of the rich and famous. Mark McCormack, agent to Tiger Woods and tennis phenoms Venus and Serena Williams, surrounds himself with tech-savvy folks, but has never used a computer himself. Actress Daryl Hannah has a computer, but hasn't turned it on in three years. Author Harlan Ellison, who churns out novels and short stories by typing with two fingers on a manual typewriter, is simply turned off by the Internet. "It's a massive waste of time," he says. "Does Skippy peanut butter really need a Web site?"

Lest you think these are the attitudes of the slightly demented, a report conducted by Pew Internet and American Life Project indicate that half of U.S. adults are not online—and the majority of those non-users are unlikely to hit the Net any time soon:

- 57% have little or no interest in getting online.
- More than one in ten adults who are not online tried the Net before disconnection.
- More than 14% of Americans have computers but aren't online.

The results seem to contradict predictions that Internet growth will continue to boom in coming years. "It may take another generation," says Lee Rainie, director of the Pew Project, "before the Net becomes as ubiquitous and essential as the telephone and television are today."

To study the 94 million Americans who are not online, interviewers questioned 1,158 non-Internet and noncomputer users in depth. Findings included the following:

- 32%, or 31 million Americans, said they "definitely will not" go online.
- 25% say they "probably will not" venture online.
- 29% "probably will" get Internet access.
- 12% say they "definitely will" get Internet access.

Those surveyed by Pew said their primary reasons for shunning the Internet are fear and lack of interest. More than half of those not online believe that the Internet is a dangerous thing and that they are not missing anything by staying away.

Sources: Karen Thomas, "Not Everyone's E-Namored With the Net," *USA Today*, September 25, 2000, p. 3D; Dana Blankenhorn, "Hype Blasters," *Advertising Age*, June 9, 2000, pp. 58–62.

- How about underwear that knows your glucose level is rising and automatically injects you with insulin or clothing that senses a heart attack coming and tells you to take a pill?

All these miracles are possible in the amazing world of tomorrow. These are not technologies in a lab, but working prototypes, many just about to hit the market. The potential for marketers in just five years makes today's Web offerings look like a warmup act. While these services will rely on the Internet to communicate between newfangled gadgets and more intelligent servers, most of the services won't be based on HTML, for practical reasons. For example, you can't effectively run a Web browser on a cell phone screen, and you don't want one inside your shirt.

The pitfalls for marketers are also obvious. While today's Web is open, each of these new technologies has a potential gatekeeper—cell phone operators, cable companies, appliance makers, and, as noted in the Integrated Marketing box, consumers who are not enthralled with the computer.

Social Trends

The *social environment* includes all factors and trends related to groups of people, including their number, characteristics, behavior, and growth projections. Since consumer markets have specific needs and problems, changes in the social environment can affect markets differently. Trends in the social environment might increase the size of some markets, decrease the size of others, or even help to create new markets. We discuss here two important components of the social environment: the demographic environment and the cultural environment.

Demographic Changes

Whereas beliefs, values, and customs describe the characteristics of the culture and subculture, *demographics* describe the observable characteristics of individuals living in the culture. Demographics include our physical traits, such as gender, race, age, and height; our economic traits, such as income, savings, and net worth; our occupation-related traits, including education; our location-related traits; and our family-related traits, such as marital status and number and age of children. Demographic trait compositions are constantly changing, and no American, Japanese, or Brazilian is "typical" anymore. There is no average family, no ordinary worker, no everyday wage, and no traditional middle class.

Still, marketing managers must understand consumers intimately. Often, the best they can do is take a snapshot and try to understand what is happening in our culture in the early years of this century. As we see next, some trends are old; others are new. For instance, the aging of the population has been going on for several decades, but births and birth rates in recent years have been much higher than expected. Immigration is also greater than predicted, and so is the backlash against it. Interstate migration to the south and west are old trends. What is new is heavier movement from the Northeast than from the mid-West and rapid growth in the mountain states. Next, we examine nine demographic changes and how they affect marketing.

1. *Households are growing more slowly and getting older.* About half of all households are aged 45 and older and growing at an annual rate of 1% compared with nearly 2% in the 1980s. Marketing communicators must plan for a greater number of middle-aged households, consumers who are experienced and have a better understanding of price and value. These consumers should have an interest in high-quality household goods and in-home health care.

2. *The demise of the traditional family.* Married couples are a bare majority of U.S. households. Only one-third of households have children under 18, and nearly one-fourth of households are people who live alone. However, married couples dominate the affluent market as the vast majority of very high-income households are married couples. The long-term trend of high growth in nontraditional types of households and lack of growth among married couples can only mean further segmentation of an already segmented marketplace.

   A phenomenon that speaks to the change in the traditional family structure is known as the "sandwich generation." These are a growing group of adults who are caring for aging parents while raising their own children. According to a study from the National Alliance for Caregiving and the American Association of Retired Persons, there are more than 9 million Americans in this situation, 40% of them between 35 and 49. The stress of belonging to the sandwich generation is taking a toll countrywide. "All of a sudden you're struggling with this huge balancing act," says Beth Willogen McLeod, author of *Caregiving: The Spiritual Journey of Love, Loss, and Renewal.* "How do you fulfill all your roles? How do you balance your marriage, your children, your work—and elder care?"

3. *The continued increase in education.* Most adults in the United States still have not completed college (approximately 67%), but that number continues to decline. More and more people have attended some college or have an associate or technical degree. More skilled workers mean more knowledgeable and sophisticated consumers who expect more information about product attributes and benefits before making a purchase.

4. *Nonphysical jobs keep growing.* Jobs that don't require physical strength keep growing in number. Virtually all job growth during the next ten years will take place among service providers, especially in health care and social services. Because providing services requires little investment compared with producing consumer goods, we can expect continued high growth in small businesses, sole proprietorships, and other entrepreneurial activities. Also, the extremely high cost of employee benefits suggests that the use of temporary workers and independent contractors will continue to grow. Marketing managers must assess whether consumers who do not have corporate benefits will become more risk-averse because they lack the safety net of company-provided pension plans and medical insurance. If so, consumers may seek money-back guarantees or other product features that reduce risk. Marketing managers must also see whether people who work for themselves or for small firms are more time-conscious.

5. *Growing faster than expected.* About 272 million people live in the United States. This is an increase of 18 million since 1990, and most of the growth has resulted from an unforeseen boom in births. The United States had about 20.4 million births between January 1990 and December 1994. This was more than in any five-year period since the last five years of the legendary baby boom (1960 to 1964), and 6% more than in the late 1980s. The United States also experienced the highest five-year immigration total (4.6 million) since the turn of the century, an increase of 31% over the previous five years. The annual influx of nearly 1 million new residents has led to an increasingly diverse consumer marketplace, particularly among young people.

6. *The growth of minorities.* Although white non-Hispanics have been the biggest contributors to the U.S. population growth in the 1990s, Hispanics have been a

close second. The number of Hispanics in the United States increased from 22 million in 1990 to 35 million in 2000. That number is nearly twice as many new residents as were added by African-Americans and Asians. If each minority segment keeps growing at current rates, Hispanics will outnumber African-Americans in ten years. This trend will be particularly important for marketing communicators that target certain regions, because Hispanics and Asians are more geographically concentrated than African-Americans.

7. *Baby boomers become middle-aged.* More than half of Americans are aged 35 or older, and the oldest baby boomers are now aged 55. The largest ten-year age group, people aged 41–50, has been growing as it absorbs the younger half of the baby-boom generation. But the number of people in this segment reached a peak in 2000 and then started to decline. The fastest-growing age group is middle-aged people aged 45–54—the age at which income and spending peak. Middle-aged people are also the least likely of all age groups to change their residence. This combination of high growth, high income, and low mobility will provide considerable lift to discretionary spending, particularly in the categories of home furnishings, education, and insurance.

8. *People are moving south.* More than half (54%) of U.S. residents live in the ten largest states, and more than half of U.S. population growth between 1990 and 1999 occurred in these ten states. New York had the largest population of all states in 1950, but in the 1990s, fast-growing Texas pushed the barely growing New York to number three. One reason for the explosive growth in the southern states is the influx of people from other countries. More than half of the four million immigrants that located in the United States between 1990 and 1995 moved to California, Texas, or Florida.

9. *The middle class gets hammered.* According to the U.S. Census Bureau, the share of aggregate household income earned by the middle 60% of households has shrunk from 52% in 1973 to 49% 25 years later. Meanwhile, the share of such income earned by the top 20% (average income $98,600) increased from 44% to 48%. In other words, the total purchasing power of the top 20% of U.S. households now equals that of the middle 60%.[7]

Demographic Groupings

In addition to understanding general demographic trends, marketing communicators must also recognize demographic groupings that may turn out to be market segments because of their enormous size, similar socioeconomic characteristics, or shared values. We examine three examples of demographic groupings by age that have or will become dominant market segments: baby boomers, Generation X, and the baby boomlet.

The Baby Boom   The baby boom occurred from 1946 through 1964. During this 19-year time frame, 76.4 million babies were born in the United States. Today, approximately 70 million of these baby boomers are still alive. They represent about one-fourth of the total population. Because of their numbers and buying power, baby boomers have and will continue to influence the marketing mix for the services and products businesses offer and how these services and products are offered. For example, the majority of baby boomer women work full-time and view their job as a career. This trend has implications for child-care, fashion, automobiles, travel, and fast-food marketing. Health concerns will also grow as baby boomers age.

Generation X   Generation X, also known as the "baby busters" or the "shadow generation," is the group of people born from 1969 to 1980. This group has been labeled with a "slacker" stereotype. Imagine 45 million humans that are characterized as culturally illiterate, apathetic, and directionless. From a marketers' perspective, they have a total disposable income of $125 billion. In tune to the newest rage, Xers—highly steeped in a culture of sound bytes—seem to know instinctively what they want. And, more importantly, what they don't want.[8]

Unfortunately, the more marketers learn about this group, the less it appears to be a market segment. For example, Xers' lifestyles range from the 10 million who are full-time college and postgraduate students to the 15 million who are married. They are also the most radically diverse generation in history. Yet their opinions about life in the United States mirror those of the general population. For instance, 52% of Xers believe that "quality of life" is good compared with 53% of the entire population, and 64% of Xers are more "stressed about money this year," compared to 58% of the general population.

Given the diversity of Generation X, what are the possibilities that an integrated marketing strategy can be targeted to this group? The key will be finding subsegments within this 45-million-person group. For example, level of education might be a point of distinction. Those in college or with a college degree are likely to be computer-literate and can be reached by online media. Their optimism and general concern for a simpler life suggests that noncondescending marketing messages through public relations or cause-related activities would prove effective.

The Baby Boomlet   Just like the baby boomers, the group of 72 million children of the baby boomers, called the "baby boomlet" or the "echo boom," is creating new waves of change. This group spans 1975 to the present. In 1995, the boomlet had 72 million people under age 19. It is 60% larger than the baby boom. Even if 1995 is the final year for boomlet births, this generation will grow through immigration for several more decades. By 2015, the baby boomlet will again outnumber the boom.

The baby boomlets will acquire their own attitudes, often shaped by new technology and global changes. Global conversations on the Intenet will change their outlook on the world. AIDS will change their attitudes toward relationship, marriage, and family. Real-time information and the customization of the information will produce a very discerning consumer. Finally, their attitude will also be shaped by defining events. For instance, it will be a generation that expects terrorists acts, such as the Oklahoma City and the 1996 Olympics bombings. Memorable events will have a lasting effect on their outlook.

Cultures and Subcultures

All of us are part of a cultural fabric that affects our behavior, including our behavior as consumers. *Culture* is the sum of learned beliefs, values, and customs that regulate the behavior of members of a particular society. Through our culture, we are taught how to adjust to the environmental, biological, psychological, and historical parts of our environment.

Beliefs and values are guides of behavior, and customs are acceptable ways of behaving. A *belief* is an opinion that reflects a person's particular knowledge and assessment of ("I believe that . . ."). *Values* are general statements that guide behavior and influence beliefs and attitudes ("Honesty is the best policy"). A value system helps people choose between alternatives in everyday life. *Customs* are overt modes of behavior that constitute culturally approved ways of behaving in specific situations. Customs vary among countries, regions, and even families. In Arab societies, for instance, usury (payment of interest) is prohibited, so special Islamic banks exist that provide three types of accounts: non-profit accounts, profit-sharing deposit accounts, and social service funds. A U.S. custom is to eat turkey on Thanksgiving Day. However, the exact Thanksgiving Day menu may depend on family customs.

Dominant cultural values are referred to as *core values*; they tend to affect and reflect the core character of a particular society. For example, if a culture does not value efficiency but does value a sense of belonging and neighborliness, few people in the culture will want to use automatic teller machines. What do Americans value? Clearly, a catchall phrase such as the "Protestant work ethic" no longer captures the whole value system.

Core values are slow and difficult to change. Consequently, marketing communication strategies must accurately portray and reflect these values.

Secondary values also exist in any culture. Secondary values are less permanent values that can sometimes be influenced by marketing communications. In addition, secondary values are often shared by some people but not others. These values serve as a basis for subcultures.

A natural evolution that occurs in any culture is the emergence of subcultures. Core values are held by virtually an entire culture, whereas secondary values are not. A *subculture* is a group of people who share a set of secondary values. Examples include Generation X and environmentally concerned people. Many factors can place an individual in one or several subcultures. Five of the most important factors that create subcultures are:

- *Material culture.* People with similar income may create a subculture. The poor, the affluent, and the white-collar middle class are examples of material subcultures.
- *Social institutions.* Those who participate in a social institution may form a subculture. Examples include participation in marriage, parenthood, a retirement community, the army, and so on.
- *Belief systems.* People with shared beliefs may create a subculture, such as shared beliefs in religion or politics. For example, traditional Amish do not use several types of products, including electricity and automobiles. A whole set of factors has also been correlated with whether a person is a Democrat, Republican, Independent, Libertarian, or Socialist.
- *Aesthetics.* Artistic people often form a subculture of their own associated with their common interests, including art, music, dance, drama, and folklore.
- *Language.* People with similar dialects, accents, and vocabulary can form a subculture. Southerners and northerners are two traditional categories.

MARKETING CAPSULE 5.1

1. Environmental scanning refers to activities directed toward obtaining information about events and trends that occur outside the organization and that can influence the organization's decision making.
2. The following external factors affect planning:
   a. External agencies
   b. Competitors
   c. Legal and ethical factors
   d. Economic and political issues
   e. Technology
   f. Social trends

Understanding Other Cultures Around the World

Adjusting to cultural differences is perhaps the most difficult task facing marketing communicators who operate in other countries. Before entering a foreign market, a company must decide to what extent it is willing to customize its marketing efforts to accommodate each foreign market. Naturally, the more the company standardizes its effort, the less trouble it incurs and the greater the assumed profitability. But is some customization inevitable? More is said about this in a later chapter.

Forecasts of the Future

There are literally hundreds of companies and forecasters who claim to have a handle on the future. One that has an excellent track record is Roper Starch, a research firm that has been looking at trends for over 50 years. The 2000 Roper Report identified four concepts that help marketers understand Americans in the new millennium:[9]

1. *"High Pace/High Peace: Americans' high-speed lifestyles create new goals and needs"*: Silicon Valley marketers often talk about a phenomenon called "high tech–high touch"; the more technology becomes part of people's lives (tech), the more the need for personal interaction (touch). We think a similar, possibly more powerful phenomenon, is unfolding today in today's frenetic, high-speed world of drive for success, "Internet time," "24/7" business, and multitasked lifestyles. As the pace of life is picking up (high pace), there is growing desire/demand for peace. The shift to "High Pace/High Peace" is evident in the marketplace. Increasingly, brands seem to be "high-pace" (efficiency-oriented, intense brands like the Internet broker E-Trade; personalities like Microsoft chief and bestselling author Bill Gates) or "high-peace" (relaxing, spa-pace brands like Banana Republic, Canyon Ranch; personalities like spiritual leader and bestselling author the Dalai Lama. The shift is reflected in Roper data as well). Americans are working harder than ever to get ahead. Work is spilling into all corners of life: a record 39% of Americans say they often spend leisure time on work, a three-fold increase from the beginning of the decade. New technologies are making it possible to be ever more productive. Americans generally recognize that hard work is the price for getting ahead. At the same time, there is a growing yearning for peace. Most agree that the best leisure time is the time alone. But declining numbers are getting such time to rest, relax, and renew. More, instead, are feeling stressed out. This tension between high pace and high peace shows no sign that it will go away. At the same time, data suggest that there are opportunities for marketers to become a bridge to get people to both their high pace and high peace goals.

2. *"Kinnections: The movement to connection in technology, relationships, and brands"*: The increasing pace of life is not the only characteristic of America since the turn of the new century. Empowered by new technology, the strong economy, and a growing command of self-reliance and other skills, Americans have begun to reach out and take the next step to extend their sense of connection. In a whole host of areas—from communications and computing to attitudes towards family and community—connections are up. These connections are different from the past. They can be fast changing and dynamic (*kinetic*). And they appear to be part of a desire for a greater sense of association (*kinship*). The movement to connections, thus, is actually a move toward "kinnections." The results are reflected in the data. Communications technologies are taking off. This is most evident in the explosive growth of cellular communications. But it is also apparent in the computer

industry, where increasing interest in using computers to connect (e-mail, the Web) is driving interest. Many Americans say that these technologies are improving the quality of their connections, making it easier to stay in touch with friends and family, and, overall, "making life better." The growth in connections is reflected in personal relationships as well: Americans are feeling better about the family and more connected to their communities. Indeed, satisfaction with many aspects of community is at record levels. Many are pursuing spiritual connections. And this sense of connection is apparent in the marketplace as well in cause-related marketing and a greater desire for brands to go beyond the basics like quality and value (which are now expected) to connect in new ways with consumers.

3. *"Diversity/Destiny":* Diversity is destiny for America. And not just in some far-off future. The U.S. increasingly is "the world's nation": our foreign-born population has almost tripled in the past thirty years. African-Americans, Hispanics, and other minorities make up the majority of the nation's population growth in the past decade—and will account for an even larger proportion of the nation's growth in the decade to come. The result is creating new, distinctive demographic segments that must be understood. It is also changing society. America is becoming multicultural. Americans are much more appreciative of ethnic customs and traditions compared to two decades ago. Where past generations may have defined the American character in terms of pioneer heritage, Americans today see strength in our status as "a melting pot." Indeed, being a melting pot is now seen as a core source of America's greatness, almost equal to the work ethic, the free enterprise system, the Constitution and system of government, and the nation's natural splendor. Multiculturalism defines the nation's tastes in areas from food to popular music. Roper analysis shows that Americans share many basic values and concerns across racial and ethnic groups. At the same time, the data suggest that there continue to be many distinctions as well. To succeed in this year of diversity/destiny, marketers need to know both sides.

4. *"Marketing by life stage":* Marketers have traditionally relied on standard demographics to understand and predict consumer behavior. Our research shows, however, that life stage can be a more powerful predictor of consumer attitudes and behavior than traditional demographic analysis. For example, a 49-year-old woman starting a second marriage and second career may have more in common with a 29-year-old woman starting her first marriage and first career than she does with another 49-year-old woman whose last child just moved out of the house. Classifying Americans by the life events they have experienced, rather than by demographic traits, can yield insights and understanding into a market that might otherwise have been overlooked. In conjunction with *Modern Maturity*, Roper has identified seven life stage segments that demonstrate the appeal and rewards of marketing to consumers by life stage.

IN PRACTICE

Internal planning processes in marketing organizations focus on an organization's strengths and weaknesses, but organizations must also consider the impact of external environmental factors. By understanding how external elements of the marketplace affect an organization's planning process, marketers can develop strategies that capitalize on opportunities and minimize threats.

Legal and ethical issues pose complex challenges for marketers. From product liability to deregulation, the external environment varies by state and country. The Interactive Journal helps you keep up with legal and ethical issues that affect organizations. On the **Front Section**, select **Marketplace**. On the left menu in **Marketplace**, select **Law**. Here you will find articles about discrimination suits, recent legal rulings, and product liability claims. Articles are both national and international in scope.

Economic and political issues are as variable as legal issues, and are impacted by government/industry relationships, consumer spending habits, and political leadership. The Interactive Journal helps you keep up with these issues as well. On the **Front Section**, select **Politics & Policy** under **In this Section** on the left menu. Here you will find articles about pending legislation, government mandates, tax proposals, and policy directives. These articles are also national and international in scope.

Technology is rapidly changing the external environment. The Interactive Journal provides you with in-depth information and analysis on technology in **Tech Center**. From the **Front Section**, select **Tech Center**. You can use this new menu to read the latest on tech stocks and personal technology. Select **Tech Briefs** to find out what is happening with leading companies. On the right side of your screen you'll find headings with different topics. Page down to locate **Tech Resources**. Here you'll find links to **Company Profiles**, **Issue Briefings**, and a **Dot-Com Layoffs and Shutdowns** list. Select one of these links now.

The Interactive Journal also features a weekly personal technology column. Under **Free WSJ.com Sites** on the **Front Section**, select **Personal Tech**.

DELIVERABLE

Select *Microsoft* under the **Company Profiles** link in the **Tech Resources** Section of **Tech Center**. Also search the Interactive Journal by using the **Search** feature under **Journal Atlas** on the left menu for articles about *Microsoft*. Discuss the legal, ethical, and political issues in the antitrust suit filed against the company. Also discuss the implications of the suit on the company's technology.

DISCUSSION QUESTIONS

1. To what extent can marketers foresee opportunities and threats posed by the external environment? What factors can alter forecasts?
2. What steps can organizations take to ensure external elements are factored into the strategic planning process?
3. How can the information found in the Interactive Journal be utilized to help organizations take advantage of market opportunities? Divert threats?

SUMMARY

In this chapter, the importance of understanding environmental forces was discussed. Marketing decisions are affected by external agencies, competitors, regulators, the economy, technology, and the social factors. Each of these elements of the marketing environment must be monitored continuously for changes that are taking place. Changes affect the way marketers go about providing want- and need-satisfying products.

Information about external forces must be gathered for each stage of the strategic marketing planning process. The purpose of collecting and analyzing such information is to reduce the uncertainty associated with marketing decision making. While experience is an important resource, new problems or old problems that require new solutions require that marketers stay abreast of marketplace developments so that they can continue to offer successful products and service to the marketplace.

MARKETER'S VOCABULARY

External environment   Forces external to the organization that affect organization and marketing decision making.

External analysis   The identification of trends, opportunities, and threats that will influence marketing strategy and tactics.

Marketing research supplier   An external agency that specializes in the conduct of marketing research demography—the study of important population statistics such as age, income, sex, and location of people.

Business cycle   The pattern that is generally followed by a fluctuating economy.

Prosperity   A period of time during which the economy is growing.

Recession   A period of time that is characterized by a decrease in the rate of growth of the economy.

Depression   A long-lasting recession during which unemployment is very high, buying power is very low, and consumers are unwilling to spend.

Recovery   A period of time in which unemployment begins to decline, buying power increases, and consumers become more willing to purchase products.

Technology   The knowledge of how to accomplish tasks and goals.

Buying power   The ability of a consumer to make purchases.

Regulators   The set of laws, agencies, and policies established to ensure that marketers compete legally in their efforts to provide want- and need-satisfying products and services.

DISCUSSION QUESTIONS

1. Describe the role of external analysis in the strategic marketing planning process.

2. Of what importance is environmental scanning to marketing decision makers?

3. Several external forces were presented in this chapter. Describe each and provide a brief statement as to the importance of each of these to the marketing planner.

4. External agencies can provide valuable marketing services to marketing organizations. Under what circumstances do you think that a marketing organization might seek the services of an external agency like a distributor? A marketing research supplier? An advertising agency? A materials supplier?

5. Comment on the impact that the decline of mass marketing might have on marketing strategists for companies that have typically mass marketed products.

6. How should a marketing organization define its competition?

7. What role do price competition and discount promotions play in the marketing of products? Do you think that the use of these strategies has been effective from the standpoint of organizations? Customers?

8. Briefly describe the impact that each of the following has on marketing activity: regulators, the economy, and technology.

PROJECT

Since Pathfinder touched down on Mars, much has been learned about the Red Planet. But did you know that sales of Mattel's Hot Wheels Mars Rover Action Pack skyrocketed and that sales of Mars bars increased dramatically?

The activities of the National Aeronautics and Space Administration (NASA) from Alan Shepard's first space flight to today's Pathfinder have spawned many new products and spurred the sales of many products. Track key NASA events, like landing on the moon, and see which products' sales were boosted by some of these events. Also, discover what new products entered into the marketplace as a result of developments in space technology.

CASE APPLICATION

Snapple is in a financial funk.
Clearly Canadian is in a sales free-fall.
Results are mixed for Pepsi's juice line.
Coca-Cola's Fruitopia is off to a slow start.

These could have been headlines for these New Age beverages. They do accurately describe their performance. At the same time, "plain old" carbonated beverages were making a comeback after years of flat sales.

One reason cited for these results is the fading intensity of America's health kick. Consumers seem to have grown weary of sipping "all-natural" teas and juices. Many have returned to chugging sweet, fizzy colas. A second reason, according to taste researchers, is that people quickly get tired of the taste of distinctive juices and unusual teas. According to one industry expert, a third reason is that many consumers got caught up in the mystical, good-for-you, Generation X phenomenon. The phenomenon was cute and interesting for a while, but had no staying power.

A fourth reason cited for waning consumer interests is in consumer perceptions. Originally, many consumers believe that all-natural sodas, teas, and juices were healthier than brown colas. However, it has been discovered that many of these alternative beverages contain more sugar than do traditional colas.

Finally, the new generation of soft drinks has not pleased bottlers. Many bottlers spend millions of dollars to overhaul their product lines or change their distribution systems to accommodate the new soft drinks. Despite the many new products, New Age beverages have resulted in only small sales increases.

Sales of these alternative beverages are still growing, reaching a level of $5.36 billion in 1999. In that same year, the soft drink industry had total sales of about $51 billion.

Some industry experts are predicting an industry shakeout. Their reasoning is that New Age beverage sales are driven by trendy young consumers who are constantly seeking the latest drink. Tapping into this young generation, over 100 companies introduced a New Age beverage into the marketplace.

Questions:

1. Describe the external factors that have an impact on the soft drink industry.
2. How would you assess the competitive situation in the soft drink industry?
3. What marketing strategies might be appropriate for soft drink marketers in order to improve sales of New Age beverages?

REFERENCES

1. Subhash C. Jain, *Marketing Planning and Strategy*, South-Western Publishing Co., Cincinnati, OH, 1981, p. 67.
2. Robert H. Malott, 1981, "An Overdose of Lawsuits," excerpts from a speech in *Friendly Exchange*, August, 27–28.
3. Witcher, S. Karene, "A Driving Tip From Down Under: Keep Those Roos Off the Bullbar," *The Wall Street Journal*, (July 14, 1994), B1.
4. Robert J. Samuelson, "The Joy of Deregulation," *Newsweek*, (February 3, 1997), p. 39.
5. Alan R. Andreasen "Social Marketing: It's Definition and Domain," *Journal of Public Policy & Marketing*, Vol. 13(1), Spring 1994, 108–114.
6. Oscar Suris, "Electric Cars Also Pollute Air, EPA Study Says," *The Wall Street Journal*, (April 5, 1994), B1, B8.
7. Peter Francese, "America At Mid-Decade," *American Demographics*, Feb, 1995, pp. 12–31.
8. Laurie Freeman, "No Tricking the Media-Savvy," *Advertising Age*, Feb 6, 1995, p. 30.
9. "The Power to Create Competitive Advantage," *Roper Starch Worldwide*, 2000.

CHAPTER 6

MARKETING IN GLOBAL MARKETS

LEARNING OBJECTIVES

As you read through this chapter, you should develop an understanding of the following key points related to global marketing activities:

■ Global marketing is very broad in scope.

■ There are many reasons why firms chose to engage in global marketing.

■ The elements of the environment of global marketing are different than those for domestic markets.

■ Firms can enter foreign markets through a variety of strategies, each of which has advantages and disadvantages.

■ In planning marketing mix strategies, firms cannot simply copy domestic marketing mix strategies.

GOOD LUCK GETTING INTO CHINA

It's a wet morning in Old Shanghai, and Dell salesman Peter Chan is selling hard. As the Yangtze River flows by the Bund district a few floors below, Chan is getting into a flow of his own. His subject: computers and the unique benefits of Dell's direct-selling model. His customer: Xiao Jian Yi, deputy general Manager of China Pacific Insurance, a fast-growing state-owned insurance company. The audience: three of Xiao's subordinates.

Dell's aggressiveness is beginning to pay off. Not only did Dell reel in the China Pacific account, but it is also becoming a major player in China. In 1998, 36-year-old billionaire Michael Dell opened the fourth Dell PC factory in the world in Ziamen, a windswept city halfway between Hong Kong and Shanghai in China's southeastern coast. The point of Dell's push into China seems so obvious as to be a cliché: China is becoming too big a PC market for Dell, or anyone, to ignore. "If we're not in what will soon be the second biggest PC market in the world," asks John Legere, president of Dell Asia-Pacific, "then how can Dell possibly be a global player?"

Though the competition is intense, Dell is confident it has a strategy that will pay off. First, it has decided not to target retail buyers, who account for only about 10% of Dell's China sales. That way Dell avoids going head-to-head against entrenched local market leaders like Legend. "It takes nearly two years of a person's savings to buy a PC in China," notes Mary Ma, the chief financial officer of Legend. "And when two years of savings is at stake, the whole family wants to come out to a store to touch and try the machine." Dell just isn't set up to make that kind of sale yet.

One thing's for sure: the Dell model is working in China. And as long as China's PC market continues to grow, Dell is ready to grow with it.

Sources: Nell Chowdury, "Dell Cracks China," *Fortune*, June 21, 1999, pp. 120–129; Normandy Madden, "GM's Buick Rides Luxury into China," *Advertising Age*, June 24, 1999, p. 16; Carolyn Edy, "The Olympics of Marketing," *American Demographics*, June 1999, p. 47.

INTRODUCTION

Companies throughout the world have discovered that they have saturated their local market and are seeking opportunities for growth elsewhere. Ford Motors, Campbell Soup, Nestlé, Nike, and McDonald's are just a few of the companies that have had an international presence for many years. Thanks to the opening of Eastern Europe and China, the international marketplace has grown dramatically. Still, moving into other markets is tricky business and many companies have failed miserably. One thing is for sure: it requires more than taking an existing domestic marketing strategy and transplanting it in another culture.

The purpose of this chapter is to introduce you to the scope and complexity of going global with a marketing effort. In the following sections, we define global marketing and examine various aspects of the global marketing environment. Against this background, we then look at the ways in which companies typically become involved in global markets, and introduce you to the global marketing management process.

DEFINING INTERNATIONAL MARKETING

Now that the world has entered the next millennium, we are seeing the emergence of an interdependent global economy that is characterized by faster communication, transportation, and financial flows, all of which are creating new marketing opportunities and challenges. Given these circumstances, it could be argued that companies face a deceptively straightforward and stark choice: they must either respond to the challenges posed by this new environment, or recognize and accept the long-term consequences of failing to do so. This need to respond is not confined to firms of a certain size or particular industries. It is a change that to a greater or lesser extent will ultimately affect companies of all sizes in virtually all markets. The pressures of the international environment are now so great, and the bases of competition within many markets are changing so fundamentally, that the opportunities to survive with a purely domestic strategy are increasingly limited to small- and medium-sized companies in local niche markets.

Perhaps partly because of the rapid evolution of international marketing, a vast array of terms have emerged that suggest various facets of international marketing. Clarification of these terms is a necessary first step before we can discuss this topic more thoroughly.

Let's begin with the assumption that the marketing process outlined and discussed in Chapters 1–4 is just as applicable to domestic marketing as to international marketing. In both markets, we are goal-driven, do necessary marketing research, select target markets, employ the various tools of marketing (i.e., product, pricing, distribution, communication), develop a budget, and check our results. However, the uncontrollable factors such as culture, social, legal, and economic factors, along with the political and competitive environment, all create the need for a myriad of adjustments in the marketing management process.

At its simplest level, *international marketing* involves the firm in making one or more marketing decisions across national boundaries. At its most complex, it involves the firm in establishing manufacturing and marketing facilities overseas and coordinating marketing strategies across markets. Thus, how international marketing is defined and interpreted depends on the level of involvement of the company in the international marketplace. Therefore, the following possibilities exist:

- *Domestic marketing.* This involves the company manipulating a series of controllable variables, such as price, advertising, distribution, and the product, in a largely uncontrollable external environment that is made up of different economic structures, competitors, cultural values, and legal infrastructure within specific political or geographic country boundaries.

- *International marketing.* This involves the company operating across several markets in which not only do the uncontrollable variables differ significantly between one market and another, but the controllable factors in the form of cost and price structures, opportunities for advertising, and distributive infrastructure are also likely to differ significantly. Degree of commitment is expressed as follows:

  - *Export marketing.* In this case the firm markets its goods and/or services across national/political boundaries.

  - *Multinational marketing.* Here the marketing activities of an organization include activities, interests, or operations in more than one country, and where there is some kind of influence or control of marketing activities from outside the country in which the goods or services will actually be sold. Each of these markets is typically perceived to be independent and a profit center in its own right.

  - *Global marketing.* The entire organization focuses on the selection and exploration of global marketing opportunities and marshals resources around the globe with the objective of achieving a global competitive advantage. The primary objective of the company is to achieve a synergy in the overall operation, so that by taking advantage of different exchange rates, tax rate, labor rates, skill levels, and market opportunities, the organization as a whole will be greater than the sum of its parts.[1]

Thus Toyota Motors started out as a domestic marketer, eventually exported its cars to a few regional markets, grew to become a multinational marketer, and today is a true global marketer, building manufacturing plants in the foreign country as well as hiring local labor, using local ad agencies, and complying to that country's cultural mores. As it moved from one level to the next, it also revised attitudes toward marketing and the underlying philosophy of business.

Ultimately, the successful marketer is the one who is best able to manipulate the controllable tools of the marketing mix within the uncontrollable environment. The principal reason for failure in international marketing results from a company not conducting the necessary research, and as a consequence, misunderstanding the differences and nuances of the marketing environment within the country that has been targeted.

STANDARDIZATION AND CUSTOMIZATION

In 1983, Harvard marketing professor Theodore Levitt wrote an article entitled, "The Globalization of Markets," and nothing about marketing has been the same since.[2] According to Levitt, a new economic reality—the emergence of global consumer markets for single-standard products—has been triggered in part by technological developments. Worldwide communications ensure the instant diffusion of new lifestyles and pave the way for a wholesale transfer of goods and services.

Adopting this global strategy provides a competitive advantage in cost and effectiveness. In contrast to multinational companies, standardized (global) corporations view the world or its major regions as one entity instead of a collection of national markets. These world marketers compete on a basis of appropriate value: i.e., an optimal combination of price, quality, reliability, and delivery of products that are identical in design and function. Ultimately, consumers tend to prefer a good price/quality ratio to a highly customized but less cost-effective item.

Levitt distinguished between products and brands. While the global product itself is standardized or sold with only minor modifications, the branding, positioning, and promotion may have to reflect local conditions.

Critics of Levitt's perspective suggest that his argument for global standardization is incorrect and that each market strategy should be customized for each country. Kotler notes that one study found that 80% of U.S. exports required one or more adaptations. Furthermore, the average product requires at least four to five adaptations out of a set of eleven marketing elements: labeling, packaging, materials, colors, name, product features, advertising themes, media, execution, price, and sales promotion.[3] Kotler suggests that all eleven factors should be evaluated before standardization is considered.

To date, no one has empirically validated either perspective. While critics of Levitt can offer thousands of anecdotes contradicting the validity of standardization, a more careful read of Levitt's ideas indicate that he offers standardization as a strategic option, not a fact. Although global marketing has its pitfalls, it can also yield impressive advantages. Standardized products can lower operating costs. Even more important, effective coordination can exploit a company's best product and marketing ideas.

Too often, executives view global marketing as an either/or proposition—either full standardization or local control. But when a global approach can fall anywhere on a spectrum—from tight worldwide coordination on programming details to loose agreements on a product ideas—there is no reason for this extreme view. In applying the global marketing concept and making it work, flexibility is essential. The big issue today is not whether to go global, but how to tailor the global marketing concept to fit each business and how to make it work.

REASONS FOR ENTERING INTERNATIONAL MARKETS

Many marketers have found the international marketplace to be extremely hostile. A study by Baker and Kynak,[4] for example, found that less than 20% of firms in Texas with export potential actually carried out business in international markets. But although many firms view international markets with trepidation, others still make the decision to go international. Why?

In one study, the following motivating factors were given for initiating overseas marketing involvement (in order of importance):[5]

1. Large market size
2. Stability through diversification
3. Profit potential
4. Unsolicited orders
5. Proximity of market
6. Excess capacity

7. Offer by foreign distributor
8. Increasing growth rate
9. Smoothing out business cycles

Other empirical studies over a number of years have pointed to a wide variety of reasons why companies initiate international involvement. These include the saturation of the domestic market, which leads firms either to seek other less competitive markets or to take on the competitor in its home markets; the emergence of new markets, particularly in the developing world; government incentives to export; tax incentives offered by foreign governments to establish manufacturing plants in their countries in order to create jobs; the availability of cheaper or more skilled labor; and an attempt to minimize the risks of a recession in the home country and spread risk.[6]

REASONS TO AVOID INTERNATIONAL MARKETS

Despite attractive opportunities, most businesses do not enter foreign markets. The reasons given for not going international are numerous. The biggest barrier to entering foreign markets is seen to be a fear by these companies that their products are not marketable overseas, and a consequent preoccupation with the domestic market. The following points were highlighted by the findings in the previously mentioned study by Barker and Kaynak, who listed the most important barriers:[7]

1. Too much red tape
2. Trade barriers
3. Transportation difficulties
4. Lack of trained personnel
5. Lack of incentives
6. Lack of coordinated assistance
7. Unfavorable conditions overseas
8. Slow payments by buyers
9. Lack of competitive products
10. Payment defaults
11. Language barriers

It is the combination of these factors that determines not only whether companies become involved in international markets, but also the degree of any involvement.

THE STAGES OF GOING INTERNATIONAL

Earlier in our discussion on definitions, we identified several terms that relate to how committed a firm is to being international. Here we expand on these concepts and explain the rationale behind this process. Two points should be noted. First, the process tends to be ranked in order of "least risk and investment" to "greatest involvement." Second, these are not necessarily sequential steps, even though exporting is apparently most common as an initial entry.

Firms typically approach involvement in international marketing rather cautiously, and there appears to exist an underlying lifecycle that has a series of critical success factors that change as a firm moves through each stage. For small- and medium-sized firms in particular, exporting remains the most promising alternative to a full-blooded international marketing effort, since it appears to offer a degree of control over risk, cost, and resource commitment. Indeed, exporting, especially by the smaller firms, is often initiated as a response to an unsolicited overseas order—these are often perceived to be less risky.

Exporting

In general, exporting is a simple and low risk-approach to entering foreign markets. Firms may choose to export products for several reasons. First, products in the maturity stage of their domestic lifecycle may find new growth opportunities overseas, as Perrier chose to do in the U.S. Second, some firms find it less risky and more profitable to expand by exporting current products instead of developing new products. Third, firms who face seasonal domestic demand may choose to sell their products to foreign markets when those products are "in season" there. Finally, some firms may elect to export products because there is less competition overseas.

A firm can export its products in one of three ways: indirect exporting, semi-direct exporting, and direct exporting. *Indirect exporting* is a common practice among firms that are just beginning their exporting. Sales, whether foreign or domestic, are treated as domestic sales. All sales are made through the firm's domestic sales department, as there is no export department. Indirect exporting involves very little investment, as no overseas sales force or other types of contacts need be developed. Indirect exporting also involves little risk, as international marketing intermediaries have knowledge of markets and will make fewer mistakes than sellers.

In *semi-direct exporting*, an American exporter usually initiates the contact through agents, merchant middlemen, or other manufacturers in the U.S. Such semidirect exporting can be handled in a variety of ways: (1) a *combination export manager*, a domestic agent intermediary that acts as an exporting department for several noncompeting firms; (2) the *manufacturer's export agent (MEA)* operates very much like a manufacturer's agent in domestic marketing settings; (3) a *Webb-Pomerene Export Association* may choose to limit cooperation to advertising, or it may handle the exporting of the products of the association's members and; (4) *piggyback exporting*, in which one manufacturer (carrier) that has export facilities and overseas channels of distribution handles the exporting of another firm's (rider) noncompeting but complementary products.

When *direct exporting* is the means of entry into a foreign market, the manufacturer establishes an export department to sell directly to a foreign firm. The exporting manufacturer conducts market research, establishes physical distribution, and obtains all necessary export documentation. Direct exporting requires a greater investment and also carries a greater risk. However, it also provides greater potential return and greater control of its marketing program.

Licensing

Under a *licensing* agreement, a firm (licensor) provides some technology to a foreign firm (licensee) by granting that firm the right to use the licensor's manufacturing process, brand name, patents, or sales knowledge in return for some payment. The licensee obtains a competitive advantage in this arrangement, while the licensor obtains inexpensive access to a foreign market.

A licensing arrangement contains risk, in that if the business is very successful, profit potentials are limited by the licensing agreement. Alternatively, a licensor makes a long-term commitment to a firm and that firm may be less capable than expected. Or, the licensee may be unwilling to invest the necessary resources as needed to be successful. Licensing may be the least profitable alternative for market entry. Scarce capital, import restrictions, or government restrictions may make this the only feasible means for selling in another country.

Franchising represents a very popular type of licensing arrangement for many consumer products firms. Holiday Inn, Hertz Car Rental, and McDonald's have all expanded into foreign markets through franchising.

Joint Ventures

A *joint venture* is a partnership between a domestic firm and a foreign firm. Both partners invest money and share ownership and control of partnership. Joint ventures require a greater commitment from firms than licensing or the various other exporting methods. They have more risk and less flexibility.

A domestic firm may wish to engage in a joint venture for a variety of reasons; for example, General Motors and Toyota have agreed to make a subcompact car to be sold through GM dealers using the idle GM plant in California. Toyota's motivation was to avoid U.S. import quotas and taxes on cars without any U.S.-made parts.

Direct Investment

Multinational organizations may choose to engage in full-scale production and marketing abroad. Thus, they will invest in wholly owned subsidiaries. An organization using this approach makes a *direct investment* in one or more foreign nations. Organizations engaging in licensing or joint ventures do not own manufacturing and marketing facilities abroad.

By establishing overseas subsidiaries, a multinational organization can compete more aggressively because it is "in" the marketplace. However, subsidiaries require more investment as the subsidiary is responsible for all marketing activities in a foreign country. While such operations provide control over marketing activities, considerable risk is involved. The subsidiary strategy requires complete understanding of business conditions, customs, markets, labor, and other foreign market factors.

U.S. Commercial Centers

Another method of doing business overseas has come in the form of *U.S. Commercial Centers*.[8] A Commercial Center serves the purpose of providing additional resources for the promotion of exports of U.S. goods and services to host countries. The Commercial Center does so by familiarizing U.S. exporters with industries, markets, and customs of host countries. They are facilitating agencies that assist with the three arrangements just discussed.

U.S. Commercial Centers provide business facilities such as exhibition space, conference rooms, and office space. They provide translation and clerical services. They have a commercial library. They have commercial law information and trade promotion facilities, including the facilitation of contacts between buyers, sellers, bankers, distributors, agents, and government officials. They also coordinate trade missions and assist with contracts and export and import arrangements.

MARKETING CAPSULE *6.1*

1. International marketing involves the firm in making one or more marketing decisions across national boundaries.

2. The debate between standardization versus customization of the international marketing strategy is unsettled; best to consider on a case-by-case basis.

3. There are many reasons to enter an international market led by large market size and diversification.

4. There are also several reasons to avoid entering international markets, including too much red tape, trade barriers, and transportation difficulties.

5. The stages of going international are as follows: exporting, licensing, joint ventures, direct investment, U.S. commercial centers, trade intermediaries, and alliances.

Trade Intermediaries

Small manufacturers who are interested in building their foreign sales are turning to trade intermediaries to assist them in the sale and distribution of their products. These entrepreneurial middlemen typically buy U.S.-produced goods at 15% below a manufacturer's best discount and then resell the products in overseas markets. These trade intermediaries account for about 10% of all U.S. exports.[9] The trade intermediary provides a valuable service to small companies, which often do not have the resources or expertise to market their products overseas. The trade intermediaries have developed relationships with foreign countries; these relationships are time-consuming and expensive to develop.

Alliances

Heineken, the premium Dutch beer, is consumed by more people in more countries than any other beer.[10] It is also the number-one imported beer in America. Miller and Budweiser, the two largest American beer producers, have entered into global competition with Heineken, partly because the American beer market has been flat. They are doing so by forming alliances with global breweries such as Molson, Corona, and Dos Equis. Heineken has responded to the challenge, heavily promoting products such as Amstel Light and Murphy's Irish Stout. Heineken has also begun developing an alliance with Asia Pacific Breweries, the maker of Tiger Beer.

THE INTERNATIONAL MARKETING PLAN

It should be apparent by now that companies and organizations planning to compete effectively in world markets need a clear and well-focused international marketing plan that is based on a thorough understanding of the markets in which the company is introducing its products. The challenge, then, of international marketing is to ensure that any international strategy has the discipline of thorough research, and an understanding and accurate evaluation of what is required to achieve the competitive advantage. As such, the decision sequence in international marketing (see Figure 6.1) is much larger than that of domestic markets. As noted in the next Integrated Marketing box, it is also more complicated.

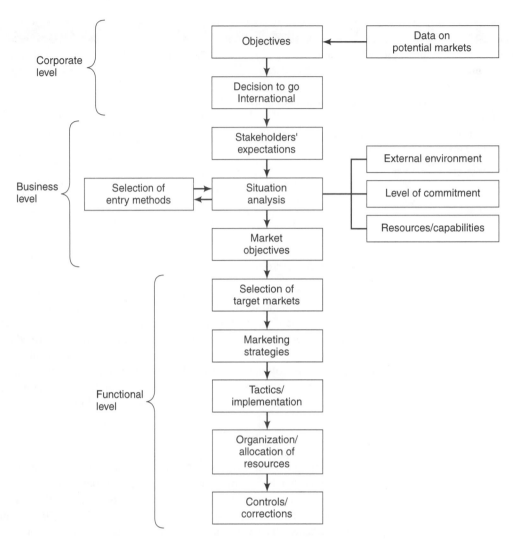

FIGURE 6.1 The decision sequence in international marketing

The Corporate Level

We begin at the corporate level, where firms decide whether to become involved in international markets and determine the resources they are willing to commit. Thus, this stage is primarily concerned with the analysis of international markets. Decisions here will be dependent on matching the results of that analysis with the company's objectives. These objectives, in turn, will be determined by the many motivating factors we have discussed in the earlier sections. The level of resources that the company is willing to commit should be determined by the strategy that is needed to achieve the objectives that have been set.

The Business Level

Business-level considerations begin with the assessment of the stakeholders involved in the business. It is important to clearly identify the different stakeholder groups, understand their expectations, and evaluate their power, because the stakeholders provide the broad guidelines within which the firm operates. In the case of international marketing, it is particularly important to address the concerns of the stakeholders in the host company.

Recall from Chapter 1 that the *situation analysis* concerns a thorough examination of the factors that influence the businesses' ability to successfully market a product or service. The results lead to a realistic set of objectives. Conducting a situation analysis in an international setting is a bit more extensive. It not only includes the normal assessment of *external environmental* factors and *resources/capabilities*, it also includes a determination of the *level of commitment* exhibited by the business, as well as possible *methods of entry*. These last two factors are interrelated in that a company's level of commitment to international markets will directly influence whether they employ exporting, a joint venture, or some other method of entry.

In turn, level of commitment and method of entry are influenced by the evaluation of environmental factors as well as resources and capabilities. The latter audits not only the weaknesses of the company, but also the strengths of the company, which are often taken for granted. This is particularly important in international markets; for example, customer brand loyalty may be much stronger in certain markets than others, and products may be at the end of their life in the domestic market but may be ideal for less sophisticated markets.

INTEGRATED MARKETING 6.1

GOING GLOBAL TAKES COORDINATION

Importing technology and the evolution of a global economy has made global marketing a reality for many American companies. Larger corporations are not alone in their pursuit of business abroad: the Department of Commerce reports that 60% of American firms exporting products today have fewer than 100 employees. American businesses have plenty of reasons to market their products in other countries. According to consulting firm Deloitte and Touche, about 95% of the world's population and two-thirds of its total purchasing power are currently located outside the U.S.

Moreover, the decision to distribute products in other countries not only opens new markets, but can also greatly expand a company's business. For example, if a U.S. bicycle manufacturer focuses only on the U.S. market, it loses the opportunity to increase revenues in countries where bicycles are a primary mode of transportation.

Global marketing can also breathe life into a foundering product, and may even extend its lifespan. Additionally, a foreign product often can command a higher price simply because consumers around the world expect foreign items to cost more.

However, implementing a global strategy requires a great deal of coordination. For example, many companies that have successfully built a strong brand in the U.S. have found that their domestic identity has little, if any, impact in markets where they are relatively unknown. An advertising campaign is one way to deal with this problem. Attaching your corporate identity to a known, respected entity in your target market is another. When FedEx, for example, wanted to increase

its name recognition in Europe, the company teamed with clothing manufacturer Benetton, an established name there. FedEx sponsors one of Benetton's formula racing cars in Europe.

Karen Rogers, manager of key customer marketing at FedEx, added that sponsoring events domestically or internationally also gives a company the opportunity to meet with perspective customers in a social setting and affords a series of spin-offs, such as promotions and product giveaways.

In distributing products globally, many American corporations team with large multinational companies that do not offer competitive products but have the resources and expertise to distribute and market those goods. This can be a cost-effective alternative to setting up operations outside the U.S.

Many small and mid-sized companies that are uncertain whether to open operations in another country investigate the possibility of using an export management company. These companies typically provide services that range from research to negotiating contracts with overseas distributors.

Sources: Dom DelPrete, "Winning Strategies Lead to Global Marketing Success," *Marketing News*, August 18, 1997, pp. 1–2; Frank Rose, "Think Globally, Script Locally," *Fortune*, Nov. 8, 1999, pp. 157–161; Lambeth Hochwald, "Are You Smart Enough to Sell Globally?" *Sales and Marketing Management*, July 1998, pp. 53–55; Erica Rasmusson, "Global Warning," *Sales and Marketing Management*, Nov. 2000, p. 17.

It is important, too, to evaluate the capacity of the firm to be flexible, adaptable, and proactive, as these are the attributes necessary for success in a highly competitive and rapidly changing world.

Undoubtedly, environmental factors have received the most attention from marketers considering international markets.

The Functional Level

Having set the objectives for the company, both at the corporate level and the business level, the company can now develop a detailed program of functional activities to achieve the objectives. Following the integrated approach employed throughout this text, each of the functional elements (e.g., finance, human resources, research) must be considered jointly. The best international marketing strategy is doomed to failure if human resources can't find and train the appropriate employees, or research can't modify the product so that it is acceptable to consumers in another country. Ultimately, this coordination between business functions is contingent on the market entry strategy employed as well as the degree of standardization or customization deemed.

Having integrated at the functional level, we next consider integration of the marketing mix elements.

Product/Promotion

Keegan[11] has highlighted the key aspects of marketing strategy as a combination of standardization or adaptation of product and promotion elements of the mix, and offers five alternative and more specific approaches to product policy:

1. *One product, one message, worldwide.* While a number of writers have argued that this will be the strategy adopted for many products in the future, in practice only a handful of products might claim to have achieved this already.

2. *Product extension, promotion adaptation.* While the product stays the same, this strategy allows for the adaptation of the promotional effort either to target new customer segments or to appeal to the particular tastes of individual countries.

3. *Product adaptation, promotion extension.* This strategy is used if a promotional campaign has achieved international appeal, but the product needs to be adapted because of local needs.

4. *Dual adaptation.* By adapting both products and promotion for each market, the firm is adopting a totally differentiated approach.

5. *Product invention.* Firms, usually from advanced nations, that are supplying products to less well-developed countries adopt product invention.

Another critical element that is closely aligned with the product and promotion is the *brand.* Anthony O'Reilly, Chairman of H.J. Heinz, believes that the communications revolution and the convergence of cultures have now set the stage for truly global marketing. The age of the global brand is at hand. For example, Heinz was looking to expand its 9 Lives cat food brand and Morris the Cat logo into Moscow. Although it's a stable and successful brand in the U. S., testing and research done by Dimitri Epimov, a local marketing manager in Moscow, led Heinz executives to make marketing changes to ensure the product's success in Russia. Namely, a fatter-looking Morris was created for packaging. Another discovery: While Americans tend to treat their kitties with tuna, Russian cat-lovers prefer to serve beef-flavored food.

As discussed earlier, product positioning is a key success factor and reflects the customer's perceptions of the product or service. However, in countries at different stages of economic development, the customer segments that are likely to be able to purchase the product and the occasions on which it is bought may be significantly different. For example, while KFC and McDonald's restaurants aim at everyday eating for the mass market in the developed countries, in less-developed countries they are perceived as places for special-occasion eating, and are beyond the reach of the poorest segments of the population. The product positioning, therefore, must vary in some dimensions. In confirming the positioning of a product or service in a specific market or region, it is therefore necessary to establish in the consumer's perception exactly what the product stands for and how it differs from existing and potential competition by designing an identity that confirms the value of the product.

Pricing

Pricing products in foreign nations is complicated by exchange rate fluctuations, tariffs, governmental intervention, and shipping requirements. A common strategy involves a marketer setting a lower price for their products in foreign markets. This strategy is consistent with the low income levels of many foreign countries, and the lower price helps to build market share. Pricing strategies are also strongly influenced by the nature and intensity of the competition in the various markets.

For these reasons, it is important to recognize at the outset that the development and implementation of pricing strategies in international markets should follow the following stages:

1. Analyzing the factors that influence international pricing, such as the cost structures, the value of the product, the market structure, competitor pricing levels, and a variety of environmental constraints
2. Confirming the impact the corporate strategies should have on pricing policy
3. Evaluating the various strategic pricing options and selecting the most appropriate approach
4. Implementing the strategy through the use of a variety of tactics and procedures to set prices
5. Managing prices and financing international transactions

Perhaps the most critical factor to be considered when developing a pricing strategy in international markets, however, is how the customers and competitors will respond. Nagle[12] has suggested nine factors that influence the sensitivity of customers to prices, and all have implications for the international marketer. Price sensitivity reduces:

- The more distinctive the product is,
- the greater the perceived quality,
- the less aware consumers are of substitutes in the market,
- if it is difficult to make comparisons,
- if the price of a product represents a small proportion of total expenditure of the customer,
- as the perceived benefit increases,
- if the product is used in association with a product bought previously,
- if costs are shared with other parties,
- if the product cannot be stored.

Finally, there are several inherent problems associated with pricing in international markets. Often companies find it difficult to coordinate and control prices across their activities in order to enable them to achieve effective financial performance and their desired price positioning. Simply, how can prices be coordinated by the company across the various markets and still make the necessary profit? Difficulty answering this question has led to two serious problems. *Dumping* (when a firm sells a product in a foreign country below its domestic price or below its actual costs) is often done to build a company's share of the market by pricing at a competitive level. Another reason is that the products being sold may be surplus or cannot be sold domestically and are therefore already a burden to the company. When companies price their products very high in some countries but competitively in others, they engage in a gray market strategy. A *gray market*, also called *parallel importing*, is a situation where products are sold through unauthorized channels of distribution. A gray market comes about when individuals buy products in a lower-priced country from a manufacturer's authorized retailer, ship them to higher-priced countries, and then sell them below the manufacturer's suggested price through unauthorized retailers.

Considerable problems arise in foreign transactions because of the need to buy and sell products in different currencies. Questions to consider are: What currency should a company price its products? How should a company deal with fluctuating exchange rates?

Finally, obtaining payment promptly and in a suitable currency from less developed countries can cause expense and additional difficulties. How should a company deal with selling to countries where there is a risk of nonpayment? How should a company approach selling to countries that have a shortage of hard currency?

Distribution and Logistics

Distribution channels are the means by which goods are distributed from the manufacturer to the end user. *Logistics*, or physical distribution management, is concerned with the planning, implementing, and control of physical flows of materials and final goods from points of origin to points of use to meet customer needs at a profit.

Essentially there are three channel links between the seller and buyer. The first link is the seller's headquarters organization, which is responsible for supervising the channel, and acts as part of the channel itself. Channels between countries represent the second link. They are responsible for getting products to overseas markets and payment in return. Finally, the third link is the channel structure (logistics) within countries, which distributes the products from their point of entry to the final consumer.

Distribution strategies within overseas markets are affected by various uncontrollable factors. First, wholesaling and retailing structure differs widely from one nation to the next. So, too, does the quality of service provided. Differences in the size and nature of retail-

---

MARKETING CAPSULE *6.2*

1. The international marketing plan includes concern for
   a. Corporate level considerations—determining the resources to be allocated
   b. Business level considerations, including:
      • assessment of stakeholders
      • the situation analysis
   c. Functional level considerations that delineate the various activities that will achieve objectives

2. The international marketing environment includes concern for:
   a. the social/cultural environment
   b. the political/legal environment
   c. the technological environment
   d. the economic environment
   e. the competitive environment

ers are even more pronounced. Retailers more closely reflect the economic conditions and culture of that country; many small retailers dominate most of these countries.

Physical distribution to overseas markets often requires special marketing planning. Many countries have inadequate docking facilities, limited highways, various railroad track gauges, too few vehicles, and too few warehouses. Managing product inventories requires consideration of the availability of suitable warehousing, as well as the costs of shipping in small quantities.

THE INTERNATIONAL MARKETING ENVIRONMENT

A number of factors constitute the international environment: social, cultural, political, legal, competitive, economic, plus technology. Each should be evaluated before a company makes a decision to go international.

The Social/Cultural Environment

The cultural environment consists of the influence of religious, family, educational, and social systems in the marketing system. Marketers who intend to market their products overseas may be very sensitive to foreign cultures. While the differences between our cultural background in the United States and those of foreign nations may seem small, marketers who ignore these differences risk failure in implementing marketing programs. Failure to consider cultural differences is one of the primary reasons for marketing failures overseas. Table 6.1 provides some illustrations of cultural differences around the world.

This task is not as easy as it sounds, as various features of a culture can create an illusion of similarity. Even a common language does not guarantee similarity of interpretation. For example, in the U.S. we purchase "cans" of various grocery products, but the British purchase "tins." A number of cultural differences can cause marketers problems in attempting to market their products overseas. These include: (1) language, (2) color, (3) customs and taboos, (4) values, (5) aesthetics, (6) time, (7) business norms, (8) religion, and (9) social structures. Each is discussed in the following sections.

Language
The importance of language differences cannot be overemphasized, as there are almost 3,000 languages in the world. Language differences cause many problems for marketers in designing advertising campaigns and product labels. Language problems become even more serious once the people of a country speak several languages. For example, in Canada, labels must be in both English and French. In India, there are over 200 different dialects, and a similar situation exists in China.

Colors
Colors also have different meanings in different cultures. For example, in Egypt, the country's national color of green is considered unacceptable for packaging, because religious leaders once wore it. In Japan, black and white are colors of mourning and should not be used on a product's package. Similarly, purple is unacceptable in Hispanic nations because it is associated with death.

Customs and Taboos
All cultures have their own unique set of customs and taboos. It is important for marketers to learn about these customs and taboos so that they will know what is acceptable and what

TABLE 6.1 Illustrations of Potential Areas of Misunderstanding Due to Differences in Cultural Norms

In Ireland, the evening meal is called tea, not dinner.

In Asia, when a person bows to you, bow your head forward equal or lower than theirs.

A nod means "no" in Bulgaria and shaking the head side-to-side means "yes."

The number 7 is considered bad luck in Kenya, good luck in the Czech Republic, and has magical connotations in Benin.

Pepsodent toothpaste was unsuccessful in Southeast Asia because it promised white teeth to a culture where black or yellow teeth are symbols of prestige.

In Quebec, a canned fish manufacturer tried to promote a product by showing a woman dressed in shorts, golfing with her husband, and planning to serve canned fish for dinner. These activities violated cultural norms.

Maxwell House advertised itself as the "great American coffee" in Germany. It found out that Germans have little respect for American coffee.

General Motors' "Body by Fisher" slogan became "Corpse by Fisher" when translated into Japanese.

In German, "Let Hertz Put You in the Driver's Seat" means "Let Hertz Make You a Chauffeur."

In Cantonese, the Philip Morris name sounded the same as a phrase meaning no luck.

In Hong Kong, Korea, and Taiwan, triangular shapes have a negative connotation.

In Thailand, it is considered unacceptable to touch a person's head, or pass something over it.

Red is a positive color in Denmark, but represents witchcraft and death in many African countries.

Americans usually smile as they shake hands. But some Germans consider smiles overly familiar from new business acquaintances. Americans shouldn't say "*Wie gehts?*" ("How goes it?"). It's also too informal for first meetings.

If you offer a compliment to a Chinese-speaking person, he or she will decline it, because disagreeing is the polite way to accept praise.

Don't say "*Merci*" ("Thanks") to a French person's compliment. You might be misinterpreted as making fun.

Italians wave goodbye as Americans beckon someone—with palm up and fingers moving back and forth; but in Oriental areas, waving with the palm down is not interpreted as goodbye, but rather, "Come here."

Offering gifts when you visit a home is expected in Japan, but in the Soviet Union it may be considered a bribe.

In Brazil and Portugal, businesspeople like to entertain foreigners in their homes. When it's time to go, the host may feel constrained to insist that the foreigner stay. Foreigners should politely take their leave.

is not for their marketing programs. Consider how the following examples could be used in development of international marketing programs:

- In Russia, it is acceptable for men to greet each other with a kiss, but this custom is not acceptable in the U.S.
- Germans prefer their salad dressing in a tube, while Americans prefer it in a bottle.
- In France, wine is served with most meals, but in America, milk, tea, water, and soft drinks are popular.

McDonalds's Corporation has opened 20 restaurants in India. Since 80% of Indians are Hindu, McDonald's will use a nonbeef meat substitute for its traditional hamburger. The likely beef substitute will be lamb, a very popular meat in India. In anticipation of its restaurant openings, McDonald's conducted extensive market research, site selection studies, and developed a relationship with India's largest chicken supplier. McDonald's has opted to market its product in India, largely because India's population of more than 900 million represents one sixth of the world's population.

Values

An individual's values arise from his/her moral or religious beliefs and are learned through experiences. For example, in America we place a very high value on material well-being, and are much more likely to purchase status symbols than people in India. Similarly, in

India, the Hindu religion forbids the consumption of beef, and fast-food restaurants such as McDonald's and Burger King would encounter tremendous difficulties without product modification. Americans spend large amounts of money on soap, deodorant, and mouth-wash because of the value placed on personal cleanliness. In Italy, salespeople call on women only if their husbands are at home.

Aesthetics

The term *aesthetics* is used to refer to the concepts of beauty and good taste. The phrase, "Beauty is in the eye of the beholder" is a very appropriate description for the differences in aesthetics that exist between cultures. For example, Americans believe that suntans are attractive, youthful, and healthy. However, the Japanese do not.

Time

Americans seem to be fanatical about time when compared to other cultures. Punctuality and deadlines are routine business practices in the U.S. However, salespeople who set def-inite appointments for sales calls in the Middle East and Latin America will have a lot of time on their hands, as business people from both of these cultures are far less bound by time constraints. To many of these cultures, setting a deadline such as "I have to know next week" is considered pushy and rude.

Business Norms

The norms of conducting business also vary from one country to the next. Here are several examples of foreign business behavior that differ from U.S. business behavior:

1. In France, wholesalers do not like to promote products. They are mainly inter-ested in supplying retailers with the products they need.

2. In Russia, plans of any kind must be approved by a seemingly endless string of committees. As a result, business negotiations may take years.

3. South Americans like to talk business "nose to nose." This desire for close phys-ical proximity causes American business people to back away from the constantly forward-moving South Americans.

4. In Japan, businesspeople have mastered the tactic of silence in negotiations. Amer-icans are not prepared for this, and they panic because they think something has gone wrong. The result is that Americans become impatient, push for a closure, and often make business concessions they later regret.

These norms are reflected in the difficulty of introducing the Web into Europe (see the next Integrated Marketing box).

Religious Beliefs

A person's religious beliefs can affect shopping patterns and products purchased in addi-tion to his/her values, as discussed earlier. In the United States and other Christian nations, Christmastime is a major sales period. But for other religions, religious holidays do not serve as popular times for purchasing products. Women do not participate in household buying decisions in countries in which religion serves as opposition to women's rights movements.

Every culture has a social structure, but some seem less widely defined than others. That is, it is more difficult to move upward in a social structure that is rigid. For example, in the U.S., the two–wage earner family has led to the development of a more affluent set of consumers. But in other cultures, it is considered unacceptable for women to work out-side the home.

INTEGRATED MARKETING 6.2

HOOKING UP IN EUROPE

Everyone in Europe vacations in August, and business is booming at Internet Train, the perhaps inappropriately named chain of Internet cafés in Florence, Italy. Just over the Ponte Vechio, the old bridge joining the Uffizi art gallery with Pallazo Pitti, there's a small storefront with 20 personal computers. Inside, people from around the world peck away at their email, communicating with friends and acquaintances from more than a hundred countries—for just 6,000 lira (about $3) per half hour.

Thousands of kilometers away in London, near Victoria Station, the scene is much the same. Stelio's Haij-Joannu, a Greek shipping tycoon and Internet entrepreneur, has created *Easy Everything*, which he claims are the world's largest Internet cafés. Haij-Joannu boasts nine Internet cafés with 3,900 PCs ready and available. "*Easy Everything* (*easyeverything. com*) is wonderful," reports Reade Fahs, CEO of London-based First Tuesday, a global Internet networking organization. "You call it an Internet café, but it's much more. Most Internet cafés are about the coffee with computers on the side. This is about 400 thin-screen computers in this very cool environment with a little coffee on the side."

Of course, the story in Europe goes far beyond email and Internet cafés. They're just the top of the innovation revolution sweeping Europe from the North to the South. Consider easyGroup, which owns *easyEverything*: easyGroup includes *easyJet.com* and *easyRentacar.com* (all properties controlled by Haij-Joannu). *EasyJet.com* bills itself as the "Web's favorite airline" and markets itself as a discount airline with steep incentives for buyers to transact online. *EasyRentacar.com* is "the world's first Internet-only rent-a-car company," he adds. He also plans to start *easyMoney.com*, offering discount mortgages online.

Still, the challenges of European Internet marketing are legion. Putting a B2C (business-to-consumer) or a B2B (business-to-business) site up in Europe is much more difficult than in the United States. Among the many complexities facing pan-European Web sites are the following:

- Developing a site for multiple languages
- Developing a site for multiple currencies
- Providing multilingual customer service
- Shipping across borders in Europe
- Handling the value-added tax (VAT)
- Coping with strict government regulatory issues
- Recruiting and retaining people in markets that prohibit or curtail stock options and other economic incentives

Sources: Henry Heilbrunn, "Interactive Marketing in Europe," *Direct Marketing*, March 1998, pp. 98–101; Michael Krauss, "Europe Forges Ahead with Web Innovations," *Marketing News*, August 14, 2000, p. 8; Michael Plogell and Felix Hofer, "No-nos in Europe," *Promo*, April 2000, pp. 23–24.

The Political/Legal Environment

The political/legal environment abroad is quite different from that of the U.S. Most nations desire to become self-reliant and to raise their status in the eyes of the rest of the world. This is the essence of nationalism. The nationalistic spirit that exists in many nations has led them to engage in practices that have been very damaging to other countries' marketing organizations. For example, foreign governments can intervene in marketing programs in the following ways:

- Contracts for the supply and delivery of goods and services
- The registration and enforcement of trademarks, brand names, and labeling
- Patents
- Marketing communications
- Pricing
- Product safety, acceptability, and environmental issues

Political Stability

Business activity tends to grow and thrive when a nation is politically stable. When a nation is politically unstable, multinational firms can still conduct business profitably. Their strategies will be affected, however. Most firms probably prefer to engage in the export business rather than invest considerable sums of money in investments in foreign subsidiaries. Inventories will be low and currency will be converted rapidly. The result is that consumers in the foreign nation pay high prices, get less satisfactory products, and have fewer jobs.

Monetary Circumstances

The *exchange rate* of a particular nation's currency represents the value of that currency in relation to that of another country. Governments set some exchange rates independently of the forces of supply and demand. The forces of supply and demand set others. If a country's exchange rate is low compared to other countries, that country's consumers must pay higher prices on imported goods. While the concept of exchange rates appears relatively simple, these rates fluctuate widely and often, thus creating high risks for exporters and importers.

Trading Blocs and Agreements

U.S. companies make one-third of their revenues from products marketed abroad, in places such as Asia and Latin America. The North American Free Trade Agreement (NAFTA) further boosts export sales by enabling companies to sell goods at lower prices because of reduced tariffs.

Regional trading blocs represent a group of nations that join together and formally agree to reduce trade barriers among themselves. NAFTA is such a bloc. Its members include the U.S., Canada, and Mexico. No tariffs exist on goods sold between member nations of NAFTA. However, a uniform tariff is assessed on products from countries not affiliated with NAFTA. In addition, NAFTA seeks common standards for labeling requirements, food additives, and package sizes.

One of the potentially interesting results of trade agreements like NAFTA is that many products previously restricted by dumping laws, laws designed to keep out foreign products, would be allowed to be marketed. The practice of *dumping* involves a company selling products in overseas markets at very low prices, one intention being to steal business from local competitors. These laws were designed to prevent pricing practices that could seriously harm local competition. The laws were designed to prevent large producers from flooding markets with very low priced products, gain a monopoly, and then raise prices to very high levels. In 1993, about 40 nations, counting the European Community as one, had anti-dumping legislation. Those in favor of agreements argue that antidumping laws penalize those companies who are capable of competing in favor of those companies that are not competitive.

Almost all the countries in the Western Hemisphere have entered into one or more regional trade agreements. Such agreements are designed to facilitate trade through the establishment of a free trade area customs union or customs market. Free trade areas and customs unions eliminate trade barriers between member countries while maintaining trade barriers with nonmember countries. *Customs Unions* maintain common tariffs and rates for nonmember countries. A *common market* provides for harmonious fiscal and monetary policies while free trade areas and customs unions do not. Trade agreements are becoming a growing force for trade liberalization; the development of such agreements provides for tremendous opportunities for U.S. companies doing business in Latin America and North America.

The creation of the single European market in 1992 was expected to change the way marketing is done worldwide. It meant the birth of a market that was larger than the United States, and the introduction of European Currency Units (Euros) in place of the individual currencies of member nations. Experience in multilingual marketing would help non-European companies succeed in this gigantic market. With new technologies such as multilingual processing programs, it would be possible to target potential customers anywhere in Europe, in any language, and in the same marketing campaign.

Progress toward European unification has been slow—many doubt that complete unification will ever be achieved. However, on January 1, 1999, 11 of the 15 member nations took a significant step toward unification by adopting the Euro as the common currency. These 11 nations represent 290 million people and a $6.5 trillion market. Still, with 14 different languages and distinctive national customs, it is unlikely that the EU will ever become the "United States of Europe."

Tariffs

Most nations encourage free trade by inviting firms to invest and to conduct business there, while encouraging domestic firms to engage in overseas business. These nations do not usually try to strictly regulate imports or discriminate against foreign-based firms. There are, however, some governments that openly oppose free trade. For example, many Communist nations desire self-sufficiency. Therefore, they restrict trade with non-Communist nations. But these restrictions vary with East-West relations.

The most common form of restriction of trade is the *tariff*, a tax placed on imported goods. Protective tariffs are established in order to protect domestic manufacturers against competitors by raising the prices of imported goods. Not surprisingly, U.S. companies with a strong business tradition in a foreign country may support tariffs to discourage entry by other U.S. competitors.

Expropriation

All multinational firms face the risk of *expropriation*. That is, the foreign government takes ownership of plants, sometimes without compensating the owners. However, in many expropriations there has been payment, and it is often equitable. Many of these facilities end up as private rather than government organizations. Because of the risk of expropriation, multinational firms are at the mercy of foreign governments, which are sometimes unstable, and which can change the laws they enforce at any point in time to meet their needs.

The Technological Environment

The level of technological development of a nation affects the attractiveness of doing business there, as well as the type of operations that are possible. Marketers in developed nations cannot take many technological advances for granted. They may not be available in lesser-developed nations. Consider some of the following technologically related problems that firms may encounter in doing business overseas:

- Foreign workers must be trained to operate unfamiliar equipment.
- Poor transportation systems increase production and physical distribution costs.
- Maintenance standards vary from one nation to the next.
- Poor communication facilities hinder advertising through the mass media.
- Lack of data processing facilities makes the tasks of planning, implementing, and controlling marketing strategy more difficult.

The Economic Environment

A nation's economic situation represents its current and potential capacity to produce goods and services. The key to understanding market opportunities lies in the evaluation of the stage of a nation's economic growth.

A way of classifying the economic growth of countries is to divide them into three groups: (1) industrialized, (2) developing, and (3) less-developed nations. The *industrialized nations* are generally considered to be the United States, Japan, Canada, Russia, Australia and most of Western Europe. The economies of these nations are characterized by private enterprise and a consumer orientation. They have high literacy, modern technology, and higher per capita incomes.

Developing nations are those that are making the transition from economies based on agricultural and raw materials production to industrial economies. Many Latin American nations fit into this category, and they exhibit rising levels of education, technology, and per capita incomes.

Finally, there are many *less developed* nations in today's world. These nations have low standards of living, literacy rates are low, and technology is very limited.

Usually, the most significant marketing opportunities exist among the industrialized nations, as they have high levels of income, one of the necessary ingredients for the formation of markets. However, most industrialized nations also have stable population bases, and market saturation for many products already exists. The developing nations, on the other hand, have growing population bases, and although they currently import limited goods and services, the long-run potential for growth in these nations exists. Dependent societies seek products that satisfy basic needs—food, clothing, housing, medical care, and education. Marketers in such nations must be educators, emphasizing information in their market programs. As the degree of economic development increases, so does the sophistication of the marketing effort focused on the countries.

The Competitive Environment

Entering an international market is similar to doing so in a domestic market, in that a firm seeks to gain a differential advantage by investing resources in that market. Often local firms will adopt imitation strategies, sometimes successfully. When they are successful, their own nation's economy receives a good boost. When they are not successful, the multinational firm often buys them out.

Japanese marketers have developed an approach to managing product costs that has given them a competitive advantage over U.S. competitors. A typical American company will design a new product, then calculate the cost. If the estimated cost is too high, the product will be taken back to the drawing board. In Japan, a company typically starts with a target cost based on the price that it estimates the market is most willing to accept. Product designers and engineers are then directed to meet the cost target. This approach also encourages managers to worry less about product costs and more about the role it should play in gaining market share. Briefly, at Japanese companies like NEC, Nissan, Sharp, and Toyota, a team charged with bringing a product idea to market estimates the price at which the product is most likely to appeal to the market. From this first important judgement, all else follows. After deducting the required profit margin from the selling price, planners develop estimates of each element that make up the product's cost: engineering, manufacturing, sales, and marketing. U.S. firms tend to build products, figure how much it costs to build the product, and then ask whether the product can be sold at a profitable price. U.S. companies tend not to assess what the market will be willing to pay.

Marketing Objectives

Having identified stakeholder expectations, carried out a detailed situation analysis, and made an evaluation of the capabilities of the company, the overall marketing goals can be set. It is important to stress that there is a need for realism in this, as only too frequently corporate plans are determined more by the desire for short-term credibility with shareholders than with the likelihood that they will be achieved.

The process adopted for determining long-term and short-term objectives is important and varies significantly, depending on the size of the business, the nature of the market and the abilities and motivation of managers in different markets. At an operational level, the national managers need to have an achievable and detailed plan for each country, which will take account of the local situation, explain what is expected of them and how their performance will be measured. Examples of objectives might be:

- Financial performance, including return on investment and profitability
- Market penetration, including sales (by volume and value), market share by product category
- Customer growth, by volume and profitability
- Distribution, including strength in supply chain, number of outlets
- Brand awareness and value
- New product introductions and diffusion
- Company image, including quality and added value (or service)

THE WALL STREET JOURNAL.

IN PRACTICE

International markets offer organizations market expansion and profit opportunities. However, entering international markets poses risks and valid reasons to avoid entering these markets exist. International marketing plans must identify the benefits and risks involved with international expansion, and detail the options for entry into the foreign market.

Deciding whether or not to adjust its domestic marketing program is a critical issue for any organization planning to expand internationally. Organizations must understand the various environmental factors affecting international marketing to determine whether a standardized or customized marketing mix will be the best strategy.

The Interactive Journal provides extensive information about world business. On the **Front Section**, select **World-Wide** from the main page.

World-Wide focuses on international news and events. You'll find information about trade agreements, international governing organizations, and regional conflicts in this section. Under the **Asia**, **Europe**, and **The Americas** headings, you'll find information specific to these regions. General news stories, financial markets activity, and technology issues are all discussed as they pertain to the specific region. For country specific information, page down to **Country News** in any of the regional sections. Using the drop down menu, you'll find links to recent news and business articles.

In the **Economy** section, you'll find an International Calendar of Economic Events. On the **Front Section**, select **Economy** from the left menu. In this section you'll also find articles about noteworthy economic developments in various countries.

Travel news is found in the **Business Fare** section of **Marketplace**. Here you'll find a Currency Converter as well as travel related business articles.

DELIVERABLE

Select one major headline in the **Asia**, **Europe**, and **The Americas** sections. Use the **Country News** menu to select the specific countries discussed and to look for additional information about the articles you've chosen. Review the articles and write a one-paragraph synopsis of each.

DISCUSSION QUESTIONS

1. How can an organization determine its best option for entering an international market?
2. What impact do international trade agreements such as NAFTA and international governing organizations such as the World Trade Organization have on decisions to expand internationally?
3. Other than the Interactive Journal, what other sources provide relevant information to organizations facing international marketing decisions?
4. What changes do you anticipate in international marketing? What countries will influence international trade?

SUMMARY

Most American firms have discovered that many opportunities exist in international marketing, as evidenced by the vast amount of goods exported by U.S.-based firms. There are many reasons why U.S. firms choose to engage in international marketing. Perhaps the most attractive reasons are the market expansion and profit opportunities afforded by foreign markets.

Basic principles of domestic marketing apply to international marketing. However, there are some differences, many of which are centered on environmental factors which affect international marketing: (1) the economic environment, (2) the competitive environment, (3) the cultural environment, (4) the political/legal environment, and (5) technological environment and the ethical environment.

Once a firm has decided to enter a particular foreign market, it must decide upon the best way to enter that market. A firm has five basic foreign market entry options, the selection of which depends largely on the degree of control that the firms wishes to maintain over its marketing program.

When a firm chooses to market its products internationally, it must decide whether to adjust its domestic marketing program. Some firms choose to customize their market programs, adjusting their marketing mix to meet the needs of each target market. Others use a standardized marketing mix. In making the decision to customize or standardize, there is a wide range of possibilities for adapting a firm's product, price, promotion, and distribution strategies.

MARKETER'S VOCABULARY

International marketing   The marketing of a company's products and/or services outside of that company's home nation.

Multinational marketing   Firms that are involved in marketing as well as production, research, human resource management and the employment of a foreign work force.

Dumping   A practice in which a firm attempts to sell discontinued products, seconds, or repaired products in overseas markets at below domestic prices.

Exchange rate   The value of one nation's currency in relation to that of another country.

Tariff   A tax placed on imported goods.

Expropriation   The act of a government taking ownership of a firm's plants.

Indirect exporting   Occurs when all of a firm's foreign sales are made through the firm's domestic sales department.

Semidirect exporting   Occurs when a firm sells products in foreign markets through agents, merchant middlemen, or other manufacturers.

Combination export manager   A domestic agent intermediary that acts as an exporting department for several noncompeting firms.

Manufacturers export agent   Similar to manufacturer's agents in domestic product setting.

Webb-Pomerene Export Association   Two or more firms that compete domestically, but work together in exporting their products.

Piggyback exporting   A situation in which one manufacturer that has export facilities and overseas channels of distribution will handle the exporting of another firm's noncompeting but complementary products.

Direct exporting   Occurs when a firm establishes an export department to sell directly to a foreign firm.

Licensing   An agreement in which a firm (licensor) provides some technology to a foreign firm (licensee) by granting the firm the right to use the licensor's manufacturing process, brand name, or sales knowledge in return for some payment.

Joint venture   A partnership between a domestic firm and a foreign firm.

Straight extension   The introduction of the same product and the same message in every foreign market.

Communication adaptation   A strategy used in foreign markets when the same product can be used to satisfy different needs, or if a product is used in a different way in foreign market.

Product adaptation   A product is changed to meet individual foreign target market needs.

DISCUSSION QUESTIONS

1. What are the reasons a firm might engage in exporting?
2. How does the economic environment affect international marketing activities?
3. How does the cultural environment affect international marketing activities?
4. How does the technological environment affect international marketing activities?
5. Briefly describe the major strategies a firm might use to enter a foreign market.
6. Why are prices often lower in foreign markets than in domestic markets?
7. What are the differences between straight extension, communication adaptation, product adaptation, dual adaptation, and product invention strategies?
8. What are the reasons why a firm might enter a foreign market by means of a joint venture strategy?
9. Briefly describe the methods of distribution used by direct exporters.
10. Why does direct investment in foreign markets afford marketers the greatest degree of control over international marketing activities?

PROJECT

Identify a U.S.-made product that is currently sold in the U.S. Develop a marketing plan for this product, assuming they plan to export to Canada.

CASE APPLICATION

UNILEVER'S GLOBAL BRAND

Unilever division Unipath is to begin the global rollout of a contraceptive product that has been 15 years in secret development and that the company is hailing as a major brand launch.

"The biggest thing to happen to contraception since the '60s," as the U.K. print and poster ads through Ogilvy & Mather Worldwide, London, describes it. Persona is the fruit of tens of millions of dollars investment.

"This is going to be a big Unilever brand," said Senior Brand Development Manager Susannah Day at its U.K. launch, backed by a $7.8 million marketing campaign that also includes an Internet site, a free phone "careline," retailer training, point of purchase displays, and direct mailings to the medical profession. O&M, a Unilever roster agency, was appointed in 1995 to create ads that would work internationally.

First evidence that all this was not mere launch puffery came at Unilever's results meeting, when Co-Chairman Niall FitzGerald revealed sparkling sales and awareness statistics and details of the product's march just into Italy and Ireland and then into the Netherlands, Scandinavia, and Germany.

In the first few weeks of the U.K. launch, Persona was the biggest selling item by value in the 1,247 stores nationwide of Boots—the retailer through which the brand was exclusively launched—and it achieved 55% consumer awareness within a month. In prelaunch research among hundreds of women in the U.K. and Germany, 30% said they were likely to buy the product.

"We expect Persona to be a mainstream form of contraception in most markets in Europe and the U.S.," notes Ms. Day. Plans are to take the brand into 20 countries by 2000, including Australia and ultimately, it is expected to go on sale worldwide. This occurred in July of 2000.

Persona works by measuring a woman's hormone levels via home urine tests and revealing the days in a month when she is least at risk of becoming pregnant. An electronic monitor records the days in a woman's cycle. On the mornings when a test is required, a yellow light flashes, asking for a stick carrying a urine sample to be inserted into the monitor. After the hormone level is measured, either a red light denoting high risk or a green light denoting low appears. Reliability is claimed to be 95%—the same as condoms.

Source: Suzanne Bedlake, "Birth of a Global Brand," *Ad Age International*, March 1997, p. 126; Rainer Hengst, "Plotting Your Global Strategy," *Direct Marketing*, August 2000, pp. 52–55; Eileen P. Moran, "Include Overseas Markets the Right Way," *Marketing News*, April 24, 2000, pp. 47–48.

Questions:

1. What will be some of the problems Persona faces as it enters markets outside of Europe?

2. The initial monitoring machine costs $78, plus $16 a month for the sticks. Will these costs present problems?

REFERENCES

1. Isobel Doole, Robin Lowe, and Chris Philips, *International Marketing Strategy*, International Thompson Business Press: London, 1999, pp. 14–15.
2. Theodore Levitt, "The Globalization of Markets," *Harvard Business Review*, May–June 1983, pp. 92–102.
3. Philip Kotler, "Global Standardization—Courting Danger," *Journal of Consumer Marketing*, Vol. 3, No. 2, Spring, 1986, pp. 13–20.
4. S. Barker and E. Kaynak, "An Empirical Investigation of the Differences Between Initiating and Continuing Exporters," *European Journal of Marketers*, Vol. 26, No. 3, 1992.
5. Ibid.
6. Anne Chen and Matt Hicks, "Going Global? Avoid Culture Clashes," *PC Week*, April 3, 2000, pp. 68–69.
7. Barker and Kaynak, op. cit.
8. Eileen Cassidy Imbach, "U.S. Commercial Centers: The Future of Doing Business Abroad," *Business America*, November, 1994, pp. 25–26.
9. Michael Selz, "More Small Firms Are Turning to Trade Intermediaries," *The Wall Street Journal*, February 2, 1995, p. B2.
10. Julia Flunn and Richard A. Melcher, "Heineken's Battle to Stay Top Bottle," *Business Week*, August 1, 1998, pp. 60–62.
11. Warren J. Keegan, "A Conceptual Framework for Multinational Marketing," *Columbia Journal of World Business*, Vol. 7, November 1973, p. 67.
12. T.T. Nagle, *The Strategies and Tactics of Pricing*, Prentice-Hall, Inc. Englewood Cliffs, N.J., 1999.

CHAPTER 7

INTRODUCING AND MANAGING THE PRODUCT

LEARNING OBJECTIVES

After reading this chapter, you should be able to:

- Look at the meaning of the term "product" from three different perspectives: the manufacturer, the consumer, and the public.
- Understand the three levels inherent in all products.
- Learn the classification systems that are used to identify products, and suggest appropriate marketing strategies.
- Clarify the difference between goods products and service products.
- Study some of the processes involved in product planning and strategy formulation: determination of product objectives and identification and resolution of factors that have an impact on the product.
- Understand the eight steps that make-up the new product development system.

JAPANESE CARS ON THE DECLINE

Japan's auto dealers have tried just about everything to revive sales. One Toyota Motor Corp. dealership in Tokyo throws monthly festivals in its parking lot and offers discounts of as much as $2,500 on new models. But potential customers such as Kai Matsuda, a smartly dressed 28 year old, isn't buying. Sure, after spending a recent Sunday touring Toyota's swank four-story Amlux showroom in Tokyo, Matsuda came away impressed. The building housed everything from rugged recreational vehicles to sleek luxury sedans such as the $37,000 Aristo. Matsuda would love to buy a new car, "if I had the money." But, with Japan's economy on the skids, he doesn't.

For Japanese carmakers preparing to roll out their new fleets at the Tokyo Motor Show, consumers such as Matsuda illustrate why 2000 was such a tough year. Despite a flurry of new launches, the recent increase in Japan's consumption tax from 3% to 5% has caused car sales to decline for six months in a row. Dealers sold 9% fewer cars in September then in the same month a year earlier and several have now fallen into the red or have gone bankrupt.

So carmakers are desperately hoping their 2000 models will boost sales. The Motor Show's new lines have the latest in breaking, engine, and transmission technology,

151

more sporty designs, and more environmentally friendly engines—including a "hybrid" car that can get 66 miles per gallon on a combination of gasoline and electricity. "Every maker is preparing new launches to keep sales from falling through the floor," says Christopher Redl, automotive analyst at ING Barrings Ltd.

But Japanese consumers are already overwhelmed with choices. "There are now over 190 car models available in the market," says Atsushi Fujii, member of the board of directors in charge of domestic sales at Nissan Motor Co. "And the average consumer can only remember about 11 of them."

Yet at the Motor Show, Japanese carmakers will be coming out with even more. Toyota wants to target young people with fun European-looking models and convertible sports car. Toyota also plans to roll out the world's first mass-produced hybrid, with sales projected at 1,000 a month. The company admits it will see the hybrid as one-third of the world's auto market by 2005. After working out the kinks in the hybrid in Japan, Toyota plans to take it for a spin in overseas markets. However, analysts worry the hybrid could cannibalize sales of other models. "Why would you want to buy a Corona when you might be able to buy a hybrid car for just about the same price?" asks Edward Brogan, automotive analyst at Salomon Brothers Inc.

In this chapter we will look at the special challenges that the marketing of products possess. Moreover, we will delineate the unique characteristics associated with products as they pass through the various stages of their lives. Particular attention will be given to the kinds of decisions that are necessary through this process.

SOURCES: Jean Halliday, "Carmakers Learn to Mine Databases," *Advertising Age*, April 17, 2000, p. S6; Emily Thorton, "Too Many Cars, Too Few Buyer," *Business Week*, October 20, 1997, p. 56; Alison S. Wellner, "Hot Wheels," *American Demographics*, August 2000, pp. 48–49; David Kiley, "Not Your Father's SUV," *American Demographics*, January 1999, pp. 44–45.

INTRODUCTION

This chapter begins our discussion of the functional areas of marketing. Why do we begin our discussion with product rather than with promotion, distribution, or pricing? The answer is quite obvious. None of those other functions serve any useful purpose without a company product that provides consumer satisfaction. Without a product, there is nothing to promote, nothing to distribute, nothing to price. This does not suggest that product is more important, rather, it is the impetus for the other marketing functions. Logically, we should start at the beginning, and the beginning of a market place is a set of correct decisions about the product offerings of the firm.

DEFINING THE PRODUCT

In essence, the term "product" refers to anything offered by a firm to provide customer satisfaction, be it tangible or intangible. It can be a single product, a combination of products, a product-service combination, or several related products and services. It normally has at least a generic name (e.g. banana) and usually a brand name (e.g. Chiquita). Although a product is normally defined from the perspective of the manufacturer, it is also important to note two other points-of-view—those of the consumer and other relevant publics.

For a manufacturer like Kraft Foods, their macaroni-and-cheese dinner reflects a food product containing certain ingredients, packaged, distributed, priced and promoted in a unique manner, and requiring a certain return on their investment. For the consumer, the product is a somewhat nutritious food item that is quick and easy to prepare and is readily consumed by the family, especially the kids. For a particular public, such as the Food and Drug Administration, this product reflects a set of ingredients that must meet particular minimum standards, in terms of food quality, storage and distribution.

Making this distinction is important in that all three perspectives must be understood and satisfied if any product will survive and succeed. Furthermore, this sensitivity to the needs of all three is the marketing concept in action. For example, a company might design a weight-reduction pill that not only is extremely profitable but also has a wide acceptance by the consumer. Unfortunately, it cannot meet the medical standards established by the Federal government. Likewise, Bird's Eye Food might improve the overall quality of their frozen vegetables and yet not improve the consumers' tendency to buy that particular brand simply because these improvements were not perceived as either important or noticeable by the consumer. Therefore, an appraisal of a company's product is always contingent upon the needs and wants of the marketer, the consumer, and the relevant publics. We define product as follows: Anything, either tangible or intangible, offered by the firm; as a solution to the needs and wants of the consumer; is profitable or potentially profitable; and meets the requirements of the various publics governing or influencing society.

There are four levels of a product: core, tangible, augmented, and promised (see Figure 7.1). We begin with the notion of the *core product*, which identifies what the consumers feel they are *getting* when they purchase the product. The core benefits derived when an overweight 45-year old male purchases a $250 ten-speed bicycle is not transportation; it is the hope for better health and improved conditioning. In a similar vein, that same individual may install a $16,000 swimming pool in his backyard, not in order to obtain exercise, but to reflect the status he so desperately requires. Both are legitimate product cores. Because the core product is so individualized, and oftentimes vague, a full-time task of the marketer is to accurately identify the core product for a particular target market.

Once the core product has been indicated, the *tangible product* becomes important. This tangibility is reflected primarily in its quality level, features, brand name, styling, and packaging. Literally every product contains these components to a greater or lesser degree. Unless the product is one-of-a-kind (e.g., oil painting), the consumer will use at least some of these tangible characteristics to evaluate alternatives and make choices. In addition, the importance of each will vary across products, situations, and individuals. For example, for Mr. Smith at age 25, the selection of a particular brand of new automobile (core product = transportation) was based on tangible elements such as styling and brand name (choice = Corvette); at age 45, the core product remains the same, while the tangible components such as quality level and features become important (choice = Mercedes).

At the next level lies the *augmented product*. Every product is backed up by a host of supporting services. Often, the buyer expects these services and would reject the core-tangible product if they were not available. Examples would be restrooms and escalators/elevators in the case of a department store, and warranties and return policies in the case of a lawn mower. Dow Chemical has earned a reputation as a company that will bend over backwards in order to service an account. It means that a Dow sales representative will visit a troubled farmer after-hours in order to solve a serious problem. This extra service is an integral part of the augmented product and a key to their success. In a world with many strong competitors and few unique products, the role of the augmented product is clearly increasing.

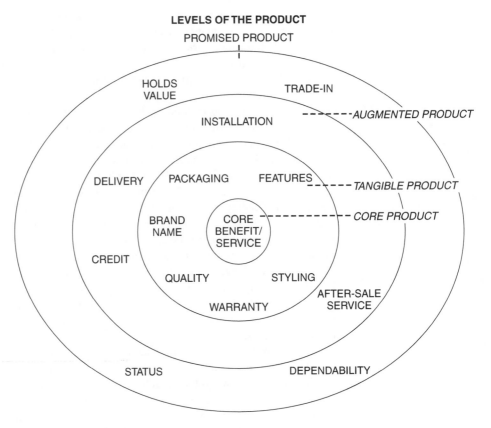

FIGURE 7.1 Levels of the product

The outer ring of the product is referred to as the *promised product*. Every product has an implied promise. An implied promise is a characteristic that is attached to the product over time. The car industry rates brands by their trade-in value. There is no definite promise that a Mercedes-Benz holds its value better than a BMW. There will always be exceptions. How many parents have installed a swimming pool based on the implied promise that their two teenagers will stay home more, or that they will entertain friends more often.

Having discussed the components of a product, it is now relevant to examine ways of classifying products in order to facilitate the design of appropriate product strategies.

CLASSIFICATION OF PRODUCTS

It should be apparent that the process of developing successful marketing programs for individual products is extremely difficult. In response to this difficulty, a variety of classification systems have evolved that, hopefully, suggest appropriate strategies. The two most common classifications are: (1) consumer goods versus industrial goods, and (2) goods products (i.e. durables and nondurables) versus service products.

Consumer Goods and Industrial Goods

The traditional classification of products is to dichotomize all products as being either *consumer goods* or *industrial goods*. When we purchase products for our own consumption or that of our family with no intention of selling these products to others, we are referring to *consumer goods*. Conversely, industrial goods are purchased by an individual or organization in order to modify them or simply distribute them to the ultimate consumer in order to make a profit or meet some other objective.

Classification of Consumer Goods

A classification long used in marketing separates products targeted at consumers into three groups: convenience, shopping, and specialty.[1] A *convenience good* is one that requires a minimum amount of effort on the part of the consumer. Extensive distribution is the primary marketing strategy. The product must be available in every conceivable outlet and must be easily accessible in these outlets. Vending machines typically dispense convenience goods, as do automatic teller machines. These products are usually of low unit value, they are highly standardized, and frequently they are nationally advertised. Yet, the key is to convince resellers, i.e., wholesalers and retailers, to carry the product. If the product is not available when, where, and in a form desirable by the consumer, the convenience product will fail.

From the consumer's perspective, little time, planning, or effort go into buying convenience goods. Consequently, marketers must establish a high level of brand awareness and recognition. This is accomplished through extensive mass advertising, sales promotion devices such as coupons and point-of-purchase displays, and effective packaging. The fact that many of our product purchases are often on impulse is evidence that these strategies work. Availability is also important. Consumers have come to expect a wide spectrum of products to be conveniently located at their local supermarkets, ranging from packaged goods used daily, e.g., bread and soft drinks, to products purchased rarely or in an emergency such as snow shovels, carpet cleaners, and flowers.

In contrast, consumers want to be able to compare products categorized as *shopping goods*. Automobiles, appliances, furniture, and homes are in this group. Shoppers are willing to go to some lengths to compare values, and therefore these goods need not be distributed so widely. Although many shopping goods are nationally advertised, often it is the ability of the retailer to differentiate itself that creates the sale. The differentiation could be equated with a strong brand name, such as Sears Roebuck or Marshall Field; effective merchandising; aggressive personal selling; or the availability of credit. Discounting, or promotional price-cutting, is a characteristic of many shopping goods because of retailers' desire to provide attractive shopping values. In the end, product turn-over is slower and retailers have a great deal of their capital tied-up in inventory. This combined with the necessity to price discount and provide exceptional service means that retailers expect strong support from manufacturers with shopping goods.

Specialty goods represent the third product classification. From the consumer's perspective, these products are so unique that they will go to any lengths to seek out and purchase them. Almost without exception, price is not a principle factor affecting the sales of specialty goods. Although these products may be custom-made (e.g., a hairpiece) or one-of-a-kind (e.g., a statue), it is also possible that the marketer has been very successful in differentiating the product in the mind of the consumer. Crisco shortening, for instance, may be considered to be a unique product in the mind of a consumer and the consumer would pay any price for it. Such a consumer would not accept a substitute and would be willing to go to another store or put off their pie baking until the product arrives. Another example might be the strong attachment some people feel toward a particular hair stylist or barber. A person may wait a long time for that individual and might even move with that person to another hair salon. It is generally desirable for a marketer to lift her product from the shopping to the specialty class (and keep it there). With the exception of price-cutting, the entire range of marketing activities are required to accomplish this goal.

Classification of Industrial Goods

Consumer goods are characterized as products that are aimed at and purchased by the ultimate consumer.[2] Although consumer products are more familiar to most readers, industrial goods represent a very important product category, and in the case of some manufacturers, they are the only product sold. The methods of industrial marketing are somewhat more specialized, but in general the concepts presented in this text are valid for the industrial marketer as well as for the consumer goods marketer.

Industrial products can either be categorized from the perspective of the producer and how they shop for the product, or the perspective of the manufacturer and how they are produced and how much they cost. The latter criteria offers a more insightful classification for industrial products.

Farms, forests, mines, and quarries provide *extractive products* to producers. Although there are some farm products that are ready for consumption when they leave the farm, most farm and other extractive products require some processing before purchase by the consumer. A useful way to divide extractive products is into *farm products* and *natural products*, since they are marketed in slightly different ways.

Manufactured products are those that have undergone some processing. The demands for manufactured industrial goods are usually derived from the demands for ultimate consumer goods. There are a number of specific types of manufactured industrial goods.

Semi-manufactured goods are raw materials that have received some processing but require some more before they are useful to the purchaser. Lumber and crude oil are examples of these types of products. Since these products tend to be standardized, there is a strong emphasis on price and vendor reliability.

Parts are manufactured items that are ready to be incorporated into other products. For instance, the motors that go into lawn mowers and steering wheels on new cars are carefully assembled when they arrive at the manufacturing plant. Since products such as these are usually ordered well in advance and in large quantities, price and service are the two most important marketing considerations.

Process machinery (sometimes called "installations") refers to major pieces of equipment used in the manufacture of other goods. This category would include the physical plant (boilers, lathes, blast furnaces, elevators, and conveyor systems). The marketing process would incorporate the efforts of a professional sales force, supported by engineers and technicians, and a tremendous amount of personalized service.

Equipment is made up of portable factory equipment (e.g., fork lift trucks, fire extinguisher) and office equipment (e.g., computers, copier machines). Although these products do not contribute directly to the physical product, they do aid in the production process. These products may be sold directly from the manufacturer to the user, or a middleman can be used in geographically dispersed markets. The marketing strategy employs a wide range of activities, including product quality and features, price, service, vendor deals, and promotion.

Supplies and service do not enter the finished product at all, but are nevertheless consumed in conjunction with making the product. Supplies would include paper, pencils, fuel oil, brooms, soap, and so forth. These products are normally purchased as convenience products with a minimum of effort and evaluation. Business services include maintenance (e.g., office cleaning), repairs (e.g. plumbing), and advisory (e.g. legal). Because the need for services tends to be unpredictable, they are often contracted for a relatively long period of time.

Goods Versus Services

Suggesting that there are substantial differences between goods products and service products has been the source of great debate in marketing. Opponents of the division propose that "products are products," and just because there are some characteristics associated with service products and not goods products and vice-versa, does not mean customized strategies are generally necessary for each. Advocates provide evidence that these differences are significant. It is the position in this book that service products are different than goods products, and that service products represent an immense market sector.

Service products are reflected by a wide variety of industries: utilities, barbers, travel agencies, health spas, consulting firms, medical care and banking, to name but a few, and they account for nearly 50% of the average consumer's total expenditures, 70% of the jobs, and two-thirds of the G.N.P. Clearly, the service sector is large and is growing. While all products share certain common facets, service products tend to differ from goods products in a number of ways.

Characteristics of Service Products

Like goods products, service products are quite heterogeneous. Nevertheless, there are several characteristics that are generalized to service products.

Intangible   As noted by Berry, "a good is an object, a device, a thing; a service is a deed, a performance, an effort." With the purchase of a good you have something that can be seen, touched, tasted, worn or displayed; this is not true with a service. Although you pay your money and consume the service, there is nothing tangible to show for it. For example, if you attend a professional football game, you spend $19.50 for a ticket and spend nearly three hours taking in the entertainment.

AD 7.1   Shoes are a traditional goods product.

Simultaneous Production and Consumption   Service products are characterized as those that are being consumed at the same time they are being produced. The tourist attraction is producing entertainment or pleasure at the same time it is being consumed. In contrast, goods products are produced, stored, and then consumed. A result of this characteristic is that the provider of the service is often present when consumption takes place. Dentists, doctors, hair stylists, and ballet dancers are all present when the product is used.

Little Standardization   Because service products are so closely related to the people providing the service, ensuring the same level of satisfaction from time to time is quite difficult. Dentists have their bad days, not every baseball game is exciting, and the second vacation to Disney World may not be as wonderful as the first.

High Buyer Involvement   With many service products, the purchaser may provide a great deal of input into the final form of the product. For example, if you wanted to take a Caribbean cruise, a good travel agent would give you a large selection of brochures and pamphlets describing the various cruise locations, options provided in terms of cabin location and size, islands visited, food, entertainment, prices, and whether they are set up for children. Although the task may be quite arduous, an individual can literally design every moment of the vacation.

It should be noted that these four characteristics associated with service products vary in intensity from product to product. In fact, service products are best viewed as being on a continuum in respect to these four characteristics. (See Figure 7.2.)

The point of this disclaimer is to suggest: (1) that service products on the right side of the continuum—e.g., high intangibility—are different from good products on the left side of the continuum, (2) that most marketing has traditionally taken place on the left side, and (3) service products tend to require certain adjustments in their marketing strategy because of these differences.

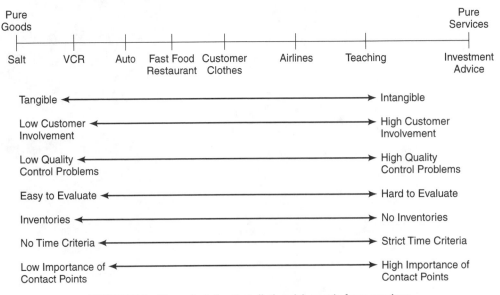

FIGURE 7.2   Characteristics that distinguish goods from services

While this discussion implies that service products are marketed differently than goods products, it is important to remember that all products, whether they are goods, services, blankets, diapers, or plate glass, possess peculiarities that require adjustments in the marketing effort. However, "pure" goods products and "pure" service products (i.e., those on the extreme ends of the continuum) tend to reflect characteristics and responses from customers that suggest opposite marketing strategies. Admittedly, offering an exceptional product at the right price, through the most accessible channels, promoted extensively and accurately, should work for any type of product. The goods/services classification provides the same useful insights provided by the consumer/industrial classification discussed earlier.

PRODUCT PLANNING AND STRATEGY FORMULATION

The ultimate purpose of this chapter is to introduce the idea that products are planned, and that a whole series of decisions go into this planning process—from the moment the product idea is first conceptualized to the day it is finally deleted. The particular label placed on the company's plan for marketing its product is the *product strategy*. It is part of the marketing strategy and should harmonize with it. Like the marketing strategy, it contains three important elements: (1) the determination of product objectives, (2) the development of product plans that will help reach product objectives, and (3) the development of strategies appropriate for the introduction and management of products.

The Determination of Product Objectives

There are a great many objectives that relate to the product management effort. Rather than attempting to provide a complete list, a discussion of the most common product objectives will provide an adequate illustration.[4]

It is safe to conclude that a universal objective is *growth in sales* as a result of the introduction of a new product or the improvement of an existing product. Certainly, there is little need to engage in either product activity unless this objective is present.

An objective related to growth in sales is *finding new uses for established products*. Since this process is generally easier than developing new products, the search for new uses of older products goes on endlessly. For example, Texas Instruments has found numerous uses for their basic product, the semiconductor.

Using excess capacity is another commonly stated product objective. This objective is prompted by the rapid turnover of products and the resulting changes in market share. Of course, such utilization is always a short-run consideration. In the long run, only those products that can generate a continuing level of profitability should be retained, regardless of the problem of excess capacity.

Maintaining or improving market share may also be an objective shared by many companies. In such cases, the emphasis of the firm is on their competitive position rather than attaining a target level of profits. Creating product differentiation is often the primary strategy employed to reach this objective.

Developing a full line of products is another typical objective. A company with a partial product line may well consider the objective of rounding out its product offerings. Often, the sales force provides the impetus for this objective in that they may need a more complete product line to offer their customers, or the resellers themselves may request a greater assortment.

Expanding a product's appeal to new market segments is a common objective. John Deere is attempting to increase its small share of the consumer power products market by aiming at suburbanites and women farmers. They have introduced a series of redesigned lawn and garden tractors, tillers, and snow blowers that are easier for women to operate.

Although this represents a limited selection of objectives, it does suggest that there must be a reason for all product-related activities. These reasons are best expressed in the form of specific objectives.

The Product Plan

Once a marketer has determined a set of product objectives, it is then possible to initiate the activities that constitute the product plan. Although there are a number of ways to look at this process, we have elected to explain this process through the product lifecycle concept (PLC). It should be noted that the value of the PLC framework as a planning tool lies at the industry and/or product category level.

The Product Lifecycle

A company has to be good at both developing new products and managing them in the face of changing tastes, technologies, and competition. Evidence suggests that every product goes through a lifecycle with predictable sales and profits, as illustrated in Figure 7.3. As such, the manager must find new products to replace those that are in the declining stage of the *product lifecycle* and learn how to manage products optimally as they move from one stage to the next.

The five stages of the PLC and their components can be defined as follows:

1. *Product development:* the period during which new product ideas are generated, operationalized, and tested prior to commercialization.

2. *Introduction:* the period during which a new product is introduced. Initial distribution is obtained and promotion is obtained.

3. *Growth:* the period during which the product is accepted by consumers and the trade. Initial distribution is expanded, promotion is increased, repeat orders from initial buyers are obtained, and word-of-mouth advertising leads to more and more new users.

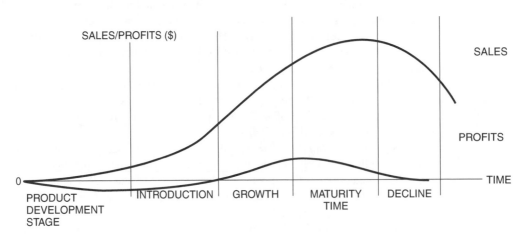

FIGURE 7.3 The product lifecycle

4. *Maturity:* the period during which competition becomes serious. Towards the end of this period, competitors' products cut deeply into the company's market position.

5. *Decline:* the product becomes obsolete and its competitive disadvantage result in decline in sales and, eventually, deletion.

It should be noted that the predictive capabilities of the product lifecycle are dependent upon several factors, both controllable and uncontrollable, and that no two companies may follow the same exact pattern or produce the same results. For example, differences in the competitive situation during each of these stages may dictate different marketing approaches. Some argue that the competitive situation is the single most important factor influencing the duration of height of a product lifecycle curve. A useful way of looking at this phenomenon is in the terms of *competitive distinctiveness*. Several years ago, Dean suggested that a separation exists between products of *lasting* and *perishable* distinctiveness. Often, new products may, upon introduction, realistically expect a long period of lasting distinctiveness or market protection—through such factors as secrecy, patent protection, and the time and cash required to develop competitive products. However, almost all new products can expect fewer than 5, 10, or 15 years of market protection.[5]

Of course, changes in other elements of the marketing mix may also affect the performance of the product during its lifecycle. For example, a vigorous promotional program or a dramatic lowering of price may improve the sales picture in the decline period, at least temporarily. The black-and-white TV market illustrated this point. Usually the improvements brought about by nonproduct tactics are relatively short-lived and basic alterations to product offerings provide longer benefits.

Whether one accepts the S-shaped curve as a valid product-sales pattern or as a pattern that holds only for some products (but not for others), the product lifecycle concept can still be very useful. It offers a framework for dealing systematically with product management issues and activities. Thus, the marketer must be cognizant of the generalizations that apply to a given product as it moves through the various stages. This process begins with product development and ends with the deletion (discontinuation) of the product.

Product Strategies

Product planning should be an ongoing process that consistently evaluates existing products, modifies where necessary, deletes products that no longer contribute to the firm, and introduces new products. Since most companies have at least one product line (and perhaps several), each containing several items, product management is a necessary activity—a daily activity. The task involves gathering the necessary data, utilizing a framework to evaluate it in light of a particular product or groups of products, selecting an appropriate strategy, and implementing that strategy. In general, there are two product strategy issues: approaches to the market and key product decisions.

Approaches to the Market

The primary task of a product is to facilitate the success of a particular market strategy. A market strategy delineates what the seller wants to accomplish relative to buyers. Strategy is partly based on the approach used to represent the product. There are three general approaches, each of which may change during the life of the product.

Product differentiation is used when a marketer chooses to appeal to the whole market by attempting to cater to the particular desires of all the buyers who hopefully would prefer his brand. This strategy is appropriate if the brand is widely popular and can be continued in general market leadership through strong promotion. Crest toothpaste is an example of a product that has successfully engaged in this strategy. Minor taste changes and formula changes have differentiated a basic product in the minds of many Crest users.

Market extension is a second approach available to the product manager. This entails attracting additional types of buyers into the market or discovering and promoting new uses of the product. Sometimes the addition of new buyers itself provides new uses for the product. 3M's Scotch tape, for example, expanded its uses when it became popular with the general consumer as well as the business consumer. Unfortunately, market extension strategies are extremely easy for competitors to copy. Thus, the brand promoting the new use is benefiting competitors as well.

Market segmentation is the final approach. As discussed in an earlier chapter, segmentation is identifying a group of consumers that tend to respond to some aspect of the market mix in a similar way. Rather than trying to appeal to the whole market, you concentrate your efforts and resources on a part of that market. The trend towards segmenting markets occurs most among branded goods. Even industrial products, such as the many varieties of diesel trucks, is an industry in which small firms survive by concentrating on some special segment of that heterogeneous total market. A company like Coca-Cola found that there were pockets of consumers that, for various reasons, did not purchase Coke. Through the introduction of Tab many years ago, followed by Diet Coke and Caffeine-Free Coke, they feel that most of the market is now covered.

Key Product Management Decisions

With every product, regardless of where it is in its lifecycle, there are certain key decisions that must be made, perhaps repeatedly. These decisions include specifying product features, package design, branding decisions, establishing related services, and legal considerations. Although these decision areas are discussed separately, it should be noted that they all interact with one another, and are monitored and modified when necessary, throughout the life of the product.

Product Features   In a functional sense, the key question is, "Does the product do what the consumer wants it to do?" Does it get clothes clean? Does it quench your thirst? Does it save you money? Some of these questions can be answered only through product research, but consumer research provides more answers.

While the development of ultra-high-speed photographic film was a research breakthrough, how the consumer perceives this benefit can be answered only by the consumer. It is possible that the product benefit is so great that it overwhelms the consumer or it is not believed by the consumer. Several new toothpaste manufacturers have recently come out with products that partially restore decayed tooth areas. They have intentionally kept this innovation very low-key, because they feared the consumer would not believe it.

Product features include such factors as form, color, size, weight, odor, material, and tactile qualities. A new car can offer thousands of alternatives when one considers the exterior and interior options. The smell of fresh bakery products or a good Italian restaurant has clearly enticed many a customer. The product must also be aesthetically pleasing. When the entire product is put together, it must create an appealing, visually attractive and distinctive need satisfier.

Packaging   With the increased importance placed on self-service marketing, the role of packaging is becoming quite significant. For example, in a typical supermarket a shopper passes about 600 items per minute, or one item every tenth of a second. Thus, the only way to get some consumers to notice the product is through displays, shelf-hangers, tear-off coupon blocks, other point-of-purchase devices, and, last but not least, effective packages. Common uses of packaging include protection, containment, communication, and utility/ease of use.[6]

Considering the importance placed on the package, it is not surprising that a great deal of research is spent on motivational research, color testing, psychological manipulation, and so forth, in order to ascertain how the majority of consumers will react to a new package. Based on the results of this research, past experience, and the current and anticipated decisions of competitors, the marketer will initially determine the primary role of the package relative to the product. Should it include quality, safety, distinction, affordability, convenience, or aesthetic beauty? For the automobile oil industry, the package has become more important to promote than product performance. To a lesser extent, this is also true for products such as powdered drinks, margarine, soft drinks, perfumes, and pet foods. In the case of Pringles, Procter & Gamble had to design a package that would protect a very delicate product. It also faced the uncertain response of retailers who have never stocked stacked potato chips before. Recall the many shapes and sizes ketchup containers have taken during the last twenty years.

Clearly delineating the role of the product should lead to the actual design of the package: its color, size, texture, location of trademark, name, product information, and promotional materials. Market leaders in the dry food area, such as cake mixes, have established a tradition of recipes on the package. However, there are other package-related questions. Do the colors compliment one another? Are you taking advantage of consumer confusion by using a package design similar to that of the market leader? Can the product be made for an acceptable cost? Can it be transported, stored, and shelved properly? Is there space for special promotional deals? Finally, various versions of the product will be tested in the market. How recognizable is the package? Is it distinctive? Aesthetically pleasing? Acceptable by dealers?

Branding   Any brand name, symbol, design, or combination of these constitutes a branding strategy. The primary function of the *brand* is to identify the product and to distinguish it from those of competitors. In addition, from the perspective of the buyer, it may simply be consistent quality or satisfaction, enhance shopping efficiency, or call attention to new products. For the seller, selecting a brand name is one of the key new product decisions, and reflects the overall position and marketing program desired by the firm. It is through a brand name that a product can: (1) be meaningfully advertising and distinguished from substitutes, (2) make it easier for the customer to track down products, and (3) be given legal protection. Also, branding often provides an interesting carryover effect: satisfied customers will associate quality products with an established brand name.

Before going any further it is necessary to distinguish several terms:

- *Brand:* a name, term, sign, symbol, design, or a combination of these that is intended to identify the goods or services of one seller or group of sellers and to differentiate them from those of competitors.
- *Brand names:* that part of a brand which can be vocalized—the utterable.
- *Brand mark:* that part of a brand which can be recognized but is not utterable, such as a symbol, design, or distinctive coloring or lettering.
- *Trademark:* a brand or part of a brand that is given legal protection because it is capable of exclusive appropriation.[7]

As was the case with product design and packaging decisions, branding requires a systematic effort at generating alternative brand names, screening them, and selecting the best alternative. However, before this process begins, a more basic decision must be made. What is the basic branding strategy to be employed? Three viable options are available.

First, a strict *manufacturer's branding policy* can be followed. This would mean that the producer refuses to manufacture merchandise under brands other than his own, although he may sell seconds or irregulars on an unbranded basis.

Second, an *exclusive distributors brands policy* could be followed. In this case, the producer does not have a brand of his own but agrees to sell his products only to a particular distributor and carry his brand name (private brands).

The final opinion is a *mixed brand policy*, which includes elements of both extremes and leads to the production of manufacturer's as well as distributor's brands. For example, Firestone sells some tires under their own brand names and some under private labels.

For most companies, both brand names and trademarks are vital in the identification of products. The design process should be guided by research; often the advertising agency is brought in to help. Brand names are mandatory if the manufacturer or distributor intends to use mass advertising. Brand names also make word-of-mouth advertising effective. Without them, repeat purchases of a particular product would be virtually impossible. Product identification through the brand name is a most important element in the product plan.

Related Services   Behind every product is a series of supporting services, such as warranties and money-back guarantees. In many instances, such services may be as important as the product itself. In fact, at times it is difficult to separate the associated services from the product features. Consequently, companies must constantly monitor the services offered by the company and its competitors.

Based on the results of data-gathering devices such as customer surveys, consumer complaints, and suggestion boxes, the product manager can determine the types of services to offer, the form the service will take, and the price charged. For example, consumers are very reluctant to purchase a stereo that can be serviced only by sending it to the factory, and paying the postage and a high service fee. Maytag, however, has been very effective in selling their appliances with service contracts and local repair. Banks are still uncertain as to whether they should charge the customer for checks, ATM use, safety deposit boxes, and overdrafts. An industrial customer might be keenly interested in related services such as prompt delivery, reliable price quotations, credit, test facilities, demonstration capabilities, liberal return policies, engineering expertise, and so forth.

Although there are a wide range of supportive services, the following are most prevalent:

1. *Credit and financing.* With the increased acceptance of debt by the consumer, offering credit and/or financing has become an important part of the total product. For certain market segments and certain products, the availability of credit may make the difference between buying or not buying the product.

2. *Warranty.* There are several types of durable products, retail stores, and even service products where warranties are expected. These warranties can provide a wide array of restitution, with a very *limited* warranty at one end of the continuum and *extended* warranties at the other. An example of the former is a VCR manufacturer that provides a 30-day warranty on the motor drive and no other coverage. The Craftsman tools division of Sears Roebuck reflects the other extreme. A broken shovel will be replaced, no questions asked, after a full summer of use. A good jewelry store has a warranty backing up every diamond ring they sell.

3. *Money-back guarantees.* The ultimate warranty is the money-back guarantee. To the customer, a money-back guarantee reduces risk almost totally. There are certain market segments (e.g., low risk takers) that perceive this service as very important. It is obvious that this service is effective only if the product is superior and

the product will be returned by only a few people. Extensive research should support this decision.

4. *Delivery, installation, training, and service.* Products that tend to be physically cumbersome or located far from the customer might consider delivery (free or a small charge) to be an integral part of the new product. Very few major appliance stores, lumberyards, or furniture stores could survive without provisions for this service. Similarly, there are products that are quite complicated and/or very technical, and whose average consumer could neither learn how to install or use it without assistance from the manufacturer. Both professional and home computer companies have been forced to provide such services. The slow development of video products or product types that have a history of breakdown and extensive maintenance must offer this service to the customer. In addition, it must be provided quickly and effectively. Although product service and maintenance has been provided to industrial customers for several years, this service is still new to many customer product manufacturers.

Product Mix Strategies   As more brands enter the market place and lock into a particular share of the market, it becomes more difficult to win and hold buyers. Other changes that occur are: (1) changes in consumer tastes and in particular, the size and characteristics of particular market segments; (2) changes in availability or cost of raw materials and other production or marketing components; and (3) the proliferation of small-share brands that reduce efficiencies in production, marketing, and servicing for existing brands. Because of factors such as these, a decision is made either to identify ways of changing the product to further distinguish it from others, or to design a strategy that will eliminate the product and make way for new products. The specific strategy to accomplish these aims may be in several general categories.

Product modification: It is normal for a product to be changed several times during its life. Certainly, a product should be equal or superior to those of principal competitors. If a change can provide superior satisfaction and win more initial buyers and switchers from other brands, then a change is probably warranted.

Yet the decision should not be approached in a haphazard manner. There are definite risks. For example, a dramatic increase in product quality might price the existing target consumer out of the market, or it might cause him/her to perceive the product as being too good. Similarly, the removal of a particular product feature might be the one characteristic of the product considered most important by a market segment. A key question the marketer must answer before modifying the product is what particular attributes of the product and competing products are perceived as most important by the consumer. Factors such as quality, functions, price, services, design, packaging, and warranty may all be determinants.

This evaluative process requires the product manager to arrange for marketing research studies to learn of improvements buyers might want, evaluate the market reception given to the competitors' improvements, and evaluate improvements that have been developed within the company. Also required is a relationship with the product research and development (R&D) department. Ideally, R&D should be able to respond quickly to the marketing department's request for product upgrading and should maintain ongoing programs of product improvement and cost reduction. Even suppliers and distributors should be encouraged to submit suggestions.

Product positioning is a strategic management decision that determines the place a product should occupy in a given market—its market niche. Given this context, the word "positioning" includes several of the common meanings of position: a place (what place does the product occupy in its market?), a rank (how does the product fare against its competitors in various evaluative dimensions?), a mental attitude (what are consumer attitudes?), and a strategic process (what activities must be attempted in order to create the optimal product position?). Thus, positioning is both a concept and a process. The positioning process produces a position for the product, just as the segmentation process produces alternative market segments. Positioning can be applied to any type of product at any stage of the life-cycle. Approaches to positioning range from gathering sophisticated market research information on consumers' preferences and perceptions of brands to the intuition of the product manager or a member of his staff.

Aaker and Shansby suggest several positioning strategies employed by marketers. A product or idea can be positioned[8]

1. By attributes—Crest is a cavity fighter
2. By price—Sears is the "value" store
3. By competitors—Avis positions itself against Hertz
4. By application—Gatorade is for after exercising
5. By product user—Miller is for the blue-collar, heavy beer drinker
6. By product class—Carnation Instant Breakfast is a breakfast food
7. By services provided—Circuit City backs up all its products

Products and brands are constantly being repositioned as a result of changes in competitive and market situations. *Repositioning* involves changing the market's perceptions of a product or brand so that the product or brand can compete more effectively in its present market or in other market segments. Changing market perceptions may require changes in the tangible product or in its selling price. Often, however, the new differentiation is accomplished through a change in the promotional message. To evaluate the position and to generate diagnostic information about the future positioning strategies, it is necessary to monitor the position over time. A product position, like sports heroes, may change readily; keeping track and making necessary adjustments is very important.

Product Line Decisions   A product line can contain one product or hundreds. The number of products in a product line refer to its *depth*, while the number of separate product lines owned by a company is the product line *width*. Several decisions are related to the product line.

There are two basic strategies that deal with whether the company will attempt to carry every conceivable product needed and wanted by the consumer or whether they will carry selected items. The former is a *full-line* strategy while the latter is called a *limited-line* strategy. Few full-line manufacturers attempt to provide items for every conceivable market niche. And few limited-line manufacturers would refuse to add an item if the demand were great enough. Each strategy has its advantages and disadvantages.

Line extensions strategies involve adding goods related to the initial product, whose purchase or use is keyed to the product. For example, a computer company may provide an extensive selection of software to be used with its primary hardware. This strategy not only increases sales volume, it also strengthens the manufacturer's name association with the owner of the basic equipment, and offers dealers a broader line. These added items tend to be similar to existing brands with no innovations. They also have certain risks. Often the company may not have a high level of expertise either producing or marketing these related products. Excessive costs, inferior products, and the loss of goodwill with distributors and customers are all possible deleterious outcomes. There is also a strong possibility that such a product decision could create conflict within the channel of distribution. In the computer example just described, this company may have entered the software business over the strong objection of their long-term supplier of software. If their venture into the software business fails, re-establishing a positive relationship with this supplier could be quite difficult.

A line extension strategy should only be considered when the producer is certain that the capability exists to efficiently manufacture a product that compares well with the base product. The producer should also be sure of profitable competition in this new market.

Line-filling strategies occur when a void in the existing product line has not been filled or a new void has developed due to the activities of competitors or the request of consumers. Before considering such a strategy several key questions should be answered:

- Can the new product support itself?
- Will it cannibalize existing products?
- Will existing outlets be willing to stock it?
- Will competitors fill the gap if we don't?
- What will happen if we don't act?

Assuming that we decide to fill out our product line further, there are several ways of implementing this decision. Three are most common:

1. *Product proliferation:* the introduction of new varieties of the initial product or products that are similar (e.g., a ketchup manufacturer introduces hickory-flavored and pizza-flavored barbecue sauces and a special hot dog sauce).

2. *Brand extension:* strong brand preference allows the company to introduce the related product under the brand umbrella (e.g., Jell-O introduces pie filling and diet desserts under the Jell-O brand name).

3. *Private branding:* producing and distributing a related product under the brand of a distributor or other producers (e.g., Firestone producing a less expensive tire for K-Mart).

In addition to the demand of consumers or pressures from competitors, there are other legitimate reasons to engage in these tactics. First, the additional products may have a greater appeal and serve a greater customer base than did the original product. Second, the additional product or brand can create excitement both for the manufacturer and distributor. Third, shelf space taken by the new product means it cannot be used by competitors. Finally, the danger of the original product becoming outmoded is hedged. Yet, there is serious risk that must be considered as well: unless there are markets for the proliferations that will expand the brand's share, the newer forms will cannibalize the original product and depress profits.

Line-pruning strategies involve the process of getting rid of products that no longer contribute to company profits. A simple fact of marketing is that sooner or later a product will decline in demand and require pruning. Timex has stopped selling home computers. Hallmark has stopped selling talking cards.

A great many of the components used in the latest automobile have replaced far more expensive parts, due to the increased costs in other areas of the process, e.g., labor costs. Using modern robotics technology has halved the manufacturing costs of several products. Through such implementation, Keebler Cookies moved from packaging their cookies totally by hand to 70% automation. Other possible ways a company might become more efficient are by replacing antiquated machinery, moving production closer to the point of sale, subcontracting out part of the manufacturing process, or hiring more productive employees.

Product Deletion   Eventually a product reaches the end of its life. This is the least understood stage of product management, because we human beings are very reluctant to think about death, even that of a product.

There are several reasons for deleting a mature product. First, when a product is losing money, it is a prime deletion candidate. In regard to this indication, it is important to make sure that the loss is truly attributable to the product and not just a quirk in the company's accounting system.

Second, there are times when a company with a long product line can benefit if the weakest of these products are dropped. This thinning of the line is referred to as *product-line simplification*. Product overpopulation spreads a company's productive, financial, and marketing resources very thin. Moreover, an excess of products in the line, some of which serve overlapping markets, not only creates internal competition among the company's own products, but also creates confusion in the minds of consumers. Consequently, a company may apply several criteria to all its products and delete those that fare worst.

A third reason for deleting a product is that problem products absorb too much management attention. Many of the costs incurred by weak products are indirect: management time, inventory costs, promotion expenses, decline of company reputation, and so forth.

Missed opportunity costs reflect the final reason for product deletion. Even if a mature product is making a profit contribution and its indirect cost consequences are recognized and considered justifiable, the company might still be better off without the product because of its opportunity cost. The opportunity cost of a mature product is the profit contribution that a new and healthy product could produce if the effort and resources being devoted to the mature item were redirected.

The final issue is actually going through a product deletion procedure. Sometimes, however, a product can be revived (see the next Integrated Marketing box).

Strategies for Developing New Products

For several decades, business has come increasingly to the realization that new and improved products may hold the key to their survival and ultimate success. Consequently, professional management has become an integral part of this process. As a result, many firms develop new products based on an orderly procedure, employing comprehensive and relevant data, and intelligent decision making.[9]

MARKETING CAPSULE 7.1

1. A product is anything, either tangible or intangible, offered by the firm as a solution to the needs and wants of the consumer, that is profitable or potentially profitable and meets the requirements of the various publics, governing, or influencing society. There is a core product, a tangible product, an augmented product, and a promised product.
2. Consumer goods are purchased for personal consumption.
3. Industrial goods are modified or distributed for resale.
4. Service products, in contrast to goods products, are characterized as being intangible and having simultaneous production/consumption, little standardization, and high buyer involvement
5. The product plan process includes the following:
   a. Determination of product objectives
   b. Development of product plans to reach objectives
   c. Development of appropriate strategies

INTEGRATED MARKETING 7.1

PUTTING LEVI'S BACK IN THE SADDLE

Levi Straus & Co. is opting for a new marketing direction. The situation is reflected by Maressa Emmar, high school sophomore from Setaukat, N.Y., and her friends, who won't wear anything from Levi's. "It doesn't make the styles we want," says Emmar, who prefers baggy pants from JNCO and Kikwear. "Levi's styles are too tight and for the older generation, like middle-aged people."

After three years of tumbling sales, layoffs, plant closing, and a failed effort to woo kids online, Levi's is gearing up for several product launches. Notes new chief executive Philip Martineau, "Levi's is a mythical brand, but our performance has been poor. We need to turn our attention back to customers and have more relevant products and marketing."

In coming months, Levi's will unveil a slew of youth-oriented fashions, ranging from oddly cut jeans to nylon pants that unzip into shorts. But Martineau is not giving up on the geezers. He wants to broaden Levi's appeal to grown-ups by extending the Dockers and Slates casual pants brands. Martineau also needs to smooth out kinks in manufacturing and shipping that prevent Levi's from rushing new products into stores.

How do you sell the idea that you're hip while not turning off the oldsters? New ads will showcase the products themselves rather than relentlessly trying to convey "attitude." A television campaign for frayed cutoff shorts shows a young woman throwing her jeans in front of an oncoming train, which slices them to cutoffs. Print will support its Lot 53 fashion-forward Levi's Engineered jeans. This new style has curved-bottom hems, slanted back pockets and a larger watch pocket to hold pagers and other electronic items.

As Levi's try to rise like a phoenix from the ashes, one of the greatest American brand icons is passing into a new era in its history. Classic Levi's Jeans may find its greatest influence, much like the American cowboy, is more myth than reality.

Sources: Michael McCarthy and Emily Fromm, "An American Icon Fades Away," *Adweek,* April 26, 1999, pp. 28–35; Alice Z. Cuneo, "Levi's Makes Move to Drop All the Hype and Push Products," *Advertising Age,* April 17, 2000, pp. 4, 69; Louis Lee, "Can Levi's Be Cool Again?" *Business Week,* March 13, 2000, pp. 144–145; Diane Brady, "Customizing for the Masses," *Business Week,* March 20, 2000, pp. 130–131.

Defining the "New" in a New Product

The determination of what constitutes a "new" product remains one of the most difficult questions faced by the marketer. Does the most recent TV model introduced by Sony represent a new product even though 95% of the product remains the same as last year's model? Are packaged salads a new product, or is the package the only part that is really new?

Indeed, companies have often been guilty of using the word "new" in conjunction with some questionable products. For example, older products have simply been marketed in new packages or containers but have been identified as new products by the manufacturer. Flip-top cans, plastic bottles, and screw-on caps have all been used to create this image of newness. Industrial companies have been guilty of similar actions. Computer manufacturers, for instance, have slightly modified some of the basic hardware or developed some software for a particular customer (banks, churches), and have felt free to claim newness. Finally, manufacturers may add an existing product to their product line and call it new, even though it is not new to the consumer.

Does technology make a product new, or features, or even the price? It is important to understand the concept of "new" in a new product, since there is sufficient evidence that suggests that each separate category of "newness" may require a different marketing strategy.

Perhaps the best way to approach this problem is to view it from two perspectives; that of the consumer and that of the manufacturer.

The Consumer's Viewpoint There are a variety of ways that products can be classified as new from the perspective of the consumer. *Degree of consumption modification* and *task experience* serve as two bases for classification. Robertson provides an insightful model when he suggests that new products may be classified according to how much behavioral change or new learning is required by the consumer in order to use the product.[10]

The continuum proposed by Robertson and shown in Figure 7.4 depicts the three primary categories based on the disrupting influence the use of the product has on established consumption patterns. It is evident that most new products would be considered continuous innovations. Annual model changes in automobiles, appliances, and sewing machines are examples. Portable hair dryers, diet soda, and aerobic dance CDs reflect products in the middle category. True innovations are rare.

Although conceptualizing new products in terms of how they modify consumer consumption patterns is useful, there is another basis for classification. *New task experience* can also be a criteria. An individual may live in a house for several years without ever having to repair a broken window. One day a mishap occurs, and Mr. Smith is forced to go to the hardware store to buy the necessary supplies required to install a new window pane. As he has no experience at all with this task, all those products are new to Mr. Smith. The glazing compound, the new glass and molding, and metal tacks, as well as the appropriate tools, are as new to Mr. Smith as a home computer. Using the model proposed by Robertson, products can also be placed on a continuum according to degree of task experience. Clearly, a product that has existed for a great many years, such as a carpenter's level, may be perceived as totally new by the person attempting to build a straight wall. In this case, newness is in the eye of the beholder.

The obvious difficulty with this classification is that it tends to be person-specific. Just because replacing a new washer in your bathroom faucet constitutes a new product for you doesn't mean it is a new product for me. However, it is conceivable that marketing research would show that for certain types of products, large groups of people have very limited experience. Consequently, the marketing strategy for such products might include very detailed instructions, extra educational materials, and sensitivity on the part of the sales clerk to the ignorance of the customer.

Another possible facet of a new task experience is to be familiar with a particular product, but not familiar with all of its functions. For example, a homemaker may have a microwave oven which she uses primarily for reheating food items and making breakfast foods. Suppose that one afternoon her conventional oven breaks and she must deliver several cakes she has donated to a church bazaar. Unfortunately, she has not baked them yet and is forced to use her microwave, a brand-new task.

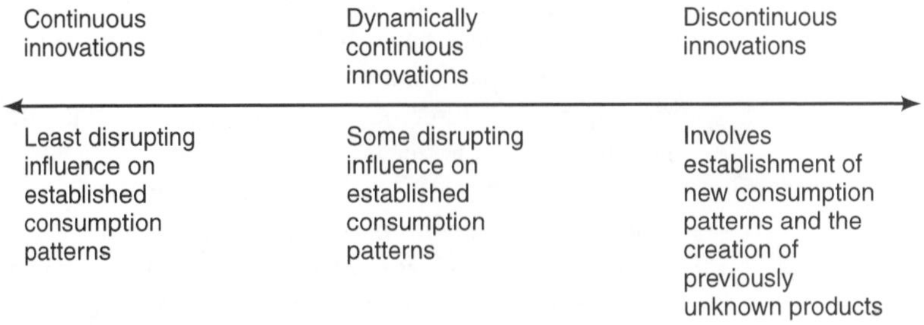

Continuous innovations	Dynamically continuous innovations	Discontinuous innovations
Least disrupting influence on established consumption patterns	Some disrupting influence on established consumption patterns	Involves establishment of new consumption patterns and the creation of previously unknown products

FIGURE 7.4 Continuum for classifying new products

Source: Thomas Robertson, "The Process of Innovation and the Diffusion of Innovation," *Journal of Marketing*, January 1967, pp. 14–19.

The Firm's Viewpoint   Classifying products in terms of their newness from the perspective of the manufacturer is also important. There are several levels of possible newness that can be derived through changes either in production, marketing, or some combination of both.

Based on a schema developed by Eberhard Scheuing, new products, from the perspective of the business, can take the following forms:[11]

1. *Changing the marketing mix:* one can argue that whenever some element of the marketing mix (product planning, pricing, branding, channels of distribution, advertising, etc.) is modified, a new product emerges.

2. *Modification:* certain features (normally product design) of an existing product are altered, and may include external changes, technological improvements, or new areas of applicability.

3. *Differentiation:* within one product line, variations of the existing products are added.

4. *Diversification:* the addition of new product lines for other applications.

A final consideration in defining "new" is the legal ruling provided by the Federal Trade Commission. Since the term is so prevalent in product promotion, the FTC felt obliged to limit the use of "new" to products that are entirely new or changed in a *functionally significant or substantial respect*. Moreover, the term can be used for a six-month period of time. Given the limited uniqueness of most new products, this ruling appears reasonable.

Strategies for Acquiring New Products

Most large and medium-sized firms are diversified, operating in different business fields. It would be unrealistic to assume that the individual firm is either capable or willing to develop all new products internally. In fact, most companies simultaneously employ both internal and external sources for new products. Both are important to the success of a business.[12]

Internal Sources   Most major corporations conduct research and development to some extent. However, very few companies make exclusive use of their own internal R&D. On the contrary, many companies make excellent use of specialists to supplement their own capabilities. Still, to depend extensively upon outside agencies for success is to run a business on the brink of peril. Ideally, the closer the relationship between the new business and existing product lines, the better the utilization of R&D will be. The National Science Foundation (NSF) (1957–77) divides R&D into three parts:

1. *Basic research:* original investigations for the advancement of scientific knowledge that do not have specific commercial objectives, although they may be in fields of present or potential interest to the reporting company

2. *Applied research:* directed toward practical applications of knowledge, specific ends concerning products and processes

3. *Development:* the systematic use of scientific knowledge directed toward the production of useful materials, devices, systems, or methods, including design and development of prototypes and processes

External Sources   External approaches to new product development range from the acquisition of entire businesses to the acquisition of a single component needed for the internal new product development effort of the firm. The following external sources for new products are available to most firms.

AD 7.2 The "Got Milk" campaign made an old product new.

1. **Mergers and Acquisitions.** Acquiring another company already successful in a field your company wishes to enter is an effective way of introducing products while still diversifying. Research suggests that mergers and acquisitions can take place between companies of various sizes and backgrounds, and that first experiences with this process tend to be less than satisfactory. Even large marketers such as General Motors engage in acquisitions.

2. **Licenses and Patents.** A patent, and the related license, arise from legal efforts to protect property rights of investors or of those who own inventions. A patent is acquired from the U.S. Patent Office and provides legal coverage for a period of seventeen years, which means all other manufacturers are excluded from making or marketing the product. However, there are no foolproof ways to prevent competition. There are two main types of patents: those for products and those for processes. The first covers only the product's physical attributes while the latter covers only a phase of a production procedure, not the product. The patent holder has the right to its assignment or license. An *assignment* is any outright sale, with the transfer of all rights of ownership conveyed to the assignee. A *license* is a right to use the patent for certain considerations in accordance with specific terms, but legal title to the patent remains with the licensor.

3. **Joint Ventures.** When two or more companies create a third organization to conduct a new business, a *joint venture* exists. This organization structure emerges, primarily, when either the risk or capital requirements are too great for any single firm to bear. Lack of technical expertise, limited distribution networks, and unfamiliarity with certain markets are other possible reasons. Joint ventures are common in industries such as oil and gas, real estate, and chemicals, or between foreign and domestic partners.

   Joint ventures have obvious application to product development. For example, small firms with technological resources are afforded an opportunity to acquire capital or marketing expertise provided by a larger firm.

The New Product Development Process

Evidence suggests that there may be as many varieties of new product development systems as there are kinds of companies. For the most part, most companies do have a formal comprehensive new product development system, and the evolution of such systems were not necessarily the result of systematic planning. The list of activities suggested in Figure 7.5 illustrates the extensiveness of this process. Because of the complexity of the process, it is important that the general guidelines of effective management be applied to new product development.[13]

Before starting our discussion of the eight-step process of new product development, a necessary caveat should be considered: a great many new products fail. Depending on definitions used for products actually introduced, failure rates range between 20 percent and 30 percent, but have been as high as 80 percent. Of more concern than the level of failure are the reasons for failure. Possibilities include: technical problems, bad timing, misunderstanding the consumer, actions by competitors, and misunderstanding the environment.

Step 1: Generating New Product Ideas

Generating new product ideas is a creative task that requires a specific way of thinking. Gathering ideas is easy, but generating good ideas is another story. Examples of internal sources are

1. *Basic research:* many companies, such as DuPont, have several scientists who are assigned the task of developing new product ideas and related technology.

2. *Manufacturing:* people who manufacture products often have ideas about modifications and improvements, as well as completely new concepts.

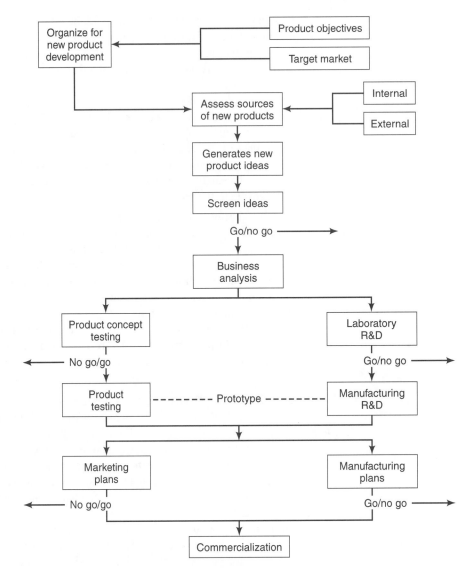

FIGURE 7.5 The new product development process

3. *Salesperson:* company salespeople and representatives can be a most helpful source of ideas, since they not only know the customer best, but they also know the competition and the relative strengths and weaknesses of existing products.

4. *Top management:* the good top executive knows the company's needs and resources, and is a keen observer of technological trends and of competitive activity.

External sources of new product ideas are almost too numerous to mention.
A few of the more useful are:

1. *Secondary sources of information:* there are published lists of new products, available licenses, and ideas for new product ventures.

2. *Competitors:* good inferences about competitive product development can be made on the basis of indirect evidence gained from salespeople and from other external sources, including suppliers, resellers, and customers.

3. *Customers:* frequently customers generate new product ideas, or at least relay information regarding their problems that new and improved products would help to solve.

4. *Resellers:* a number of firms use "councils" or committees made up of representative resellers to assist in solving various problems, including product development.

5. *Foreign markets:* many companies look toward foreign markets, especially Western Europe, because they have been so active in product development.

There are probably as many approaches to collecting new product ideas as there are sources. For most companies, taking a number of approaches is preferable to a single approach. Still, coming up with viable new product ideas is rare (see the next Newsline box).

Step 2: Screening Product Development Ideas

The second step in the product development process is *screening*. It is a critical part of the development activity. Product ideas that do not meet the organization's objectives should be rejected. If a poor product idea is allowed to pass the screening state, it wastes effort and money in subsequent stages until it is later abandoned. Even more serious is the possibility of screening out a worthwhile idea.

NEWSLINE: NEW IDEAS ARE RARE

New product ideas can come from anywhere and everywhere. It's exciting when a new product idea comes from out of the blue, prototypes test well among consumers and purchase interest scores are off the charts. But relying on the "anywhere and everywhere" approach won't do in the long run. What is required for product development are methodologies that enable us to systematically discover new product opportunities.

One such method is the *category appraisal*, which points to new product opportunities within an existing category and sometimes to opportunities in a new, adjacent category. The objective of the category appraisal study is to discover what makes the category "tick." Questions to ask include:

- What drives consumer acceptability?
- What are the strengths and weaknesses of each product in the category?
- What are the opportunities to outperform existing products?
- To what extent does brand equity play a role in product acceptability?
- Does collected data point to unexplored regions of the category "space" that new products can successfully fill?

An example from the confectionary industry illustrates this technique. The mission was to identify the properties of a new candy item for consumers who buy candy in supermarkets, convenience stores, and movie theaters. A database of in-depth sensory profile of a wide range of candy products and "liking scores" of each of those products was created. The researchers shopped 'till they dropped.

They thoroughly filled a sensory space in terms of texture, flavor, size, and appearance with 25–30 products.

A questionnaire was developed that required quantitative ratings (such as 100% scale ratings) of product attributes that were unique to some products. There were questions about hardness, chewiness, crispness, flavor intensity, degree of fruit flavor, sweetness, tartness, color, and many more. Overall liking for each product was also measured.

How well each product and brand performed—the overall liking score for each product—was not an objective of the study. The point was to discover the most generalized drivers of consumer acceptability in the confectionary category. Products were ranked by their performance and key sensory properties. Close study of the data revealed that these consumers were not the least bit influenced by brand. Overall taste was the dominant factor. Second, a new chocolate product held the most promise. Of all flavors explored, chocolate captivated consumers most. In fact, the ideal product is chocolate-filled chocolates with chocolate dipping sauce.

Sources: Jeff Braun, "Overcoming the Odds," *Marketing News*, March 29, 1999, pp. 15–16; David Fishben, "Sweet Success: Category Appraisal is Proven Source of New Ideas," *Marketing News*, March 29, 1999, pp. 15–16; Tomina Edmark, "On Your Mark," *Entrepreneur*, April 1999, pp. 161–162; Laurie Freeman, "Brach's Fruit Snacks Shapes," *Advertising Age*, June 28, 1999, pp. 5–7.

There are two common techniques for screening new product ideas; both involve the comparison of a potential product idea against criteria of acceptable new products. The first technique is a simple checklist. For example, new product ideas can be rated on a scale ranging from very good to poor, in respect to criteria such as: value added, sales volume, patent protection, affect on present products, and so forth. Unfortunately, it is quite difficult for raters to define what is fair or poor. Also, it does not address the issue of the time and expense associated with each idea, nor does it instruct with regard to the scores. A second technique goes beyond the first: the criteria are assigned importance weights and then the products are rated on a point scale measuring product compatibility. These scores are then multiplied by their respective weights and added to yield a total score for the new product idea. Table 7.1 provides an example of both these techniques for screening new product ideas.

Step 3: Business Analysis

After the various product ideas survive their initial screen, very few viable proposals will remain. Before the development of prototypes can be decided upon, however, a further evaluation will be conducted to gather additional information on these remaining ideas in order to justify the enormous costs required. The focus of the business analysis is primarily on profits, but other considerations such as social responsibilities may also be involved.

The first step in the business analysis is to examine the projected demand. This would include two major sources of revenue: the sales of the product and the sales or license of the technology developed for or generated as a by-product of the given product.

TABLE 7.1 Screening Product Ideas

		Rating						
	Weight	Very Good (5)	(4)	Fair (3)	Poor (2)	(1)	Unweighted Value	Weighted Value
Customer utilities								
- amusement	.1	X					5	.5
- comfort	.1			X			3	.3
- convenience	.2		X				4	.8
- satisfaction	.3		X				4	1.2
- easy to use	.1			X			3	.3
Ability to create effective sales appeals	.3		X				4	1.2
Price	.1				X		2	.2
Product quality	.2			X			3	.6
Product profitability	.2			X			3	.6
Attractiveness of product to customers	.1		X				4	.4
Ability to produce product in large volumes	.3	X					5	1.5
Ability of new product in helping sale of other products	.1					X	1	.1
Requires low capital investment	.3		X				4	1.2
Product can be promoted through existing advertising	.2			X			3	.6
Product can be produced in existing facilities	.3		X				4	1.2
Product can be distributed through existing channels	.3				X		3	.9
Strength of competition	.2				X		3	.6
Patent situation	.1					X	2	.2
Total Score							60	12.4

A complete cost appraisal is also necessary as part of the business analysis. It is difficult to anticipate all the costs that will be involved in product development, but the following cost items are typical:

- Expected development costs, including both technical and marketing R&D
- Expected set-up costs (production, equipment, distribution)
- Operating costs that account for possible economies of scale and learning curves
- Marketing costs, especially promotion and distribution
- Management costs

Step 4: Technical and Marketing Development

A product that has passed the screen and business analysis stages is ready for technical and marketing development. Technical development involves two steps. The first is the applied laboratory research required to develop exact product specifications. The goal of this research is to construct a prototype model of the product that can be subjected to further study. Once the prototype has been created, manufacturing-methods research can be undertaken to plan the best way of making the product in commercial quantities under normal manufacturing conditions. This is an extremely important step, because there is a significant distinction between what an engineer can assemble in a laboratory and what a factory worker can produce.

While the laboratory technicians are working on the prototype, the marketing department is responsible for testing the new product with its intended consumers and developing the other elements of the marketing mix. The testing process usually begins with the concept test. The *product concept* is a synthesis or a description of a product idea that reflects the core element of the proposed product. For example, a consumer group might be assembled and the interview session might begin with the question: "How about something that would do this? . . ."

The second aspect of market development involves consumer testing of the product idea. This activity must usually await the construction of the prototype or, preferably, limited-run production models. Various kinds of consumer preference can be conducted. The product itself can be exposed to consumer taste or use tests. Packaging, labeling, and other elements in the mix can be similarly studied. Comparison tests are also used.

Step 5: Manufacturing Planning

Assuming that the product has cleared the technical and marketing development stage, the manufacturing department is asked to prepare plans for producing it. The plan begins with an appraisal of the existing production plant and the necessary tooling required to achieve the most economical production. Fancy designs and material might be hard if not impossible to accommodate on existing production equipment; new machinery is often time-consuming and costly to obtain. Compromise between attractiveness and economy is often necessary.

Finally, manufacturing planning must consider the other areas of the organization and what is required of each. More specifically, they should determine how to secure the availability of required funds, facilities, and personnel at the intended time, as well as the methods of coordinating this effort.

Step 6: Marketing Planning

It is at this point that the marketing department moves into action again. The product planner must prepare a complete marketing plan—one that starts with a statement of objectives and ends with the fusion of product, distribution, promotion, and pricing into an integrated program of marketing action.

Step 7: Test Marketing

Test marketing is the final step before commercialization; the objective is to test all the variabilites in the marketing plan including elements of the product. Test marketing represents an actual launching of the total marketing program. But it is done on a limited basis.

INTEGRATED MARKETING 7.2

TRICKIER THAN YOU THINK

Everyone knows the fastest way to get rich is to start a dot.com business. According to the U.S. Commerce Department, traffic on the Internet doubles every 100 days. To acquire an audience of 50 million, it took radio 30 years, television 13 years, personal computers 16 years, and the Internet *four years*.

Still, marketers who go online expecting to make an "overnight killing" are in for a bruising lesson. Getting on the Web takes an investment, and once there, you have to build your Web presence and brand. And there are still technical and logistical hurdles to clear. Just ask Julie Wainwright, who got a firsthand look at the new math after the pet-products Web site she heads, Pet.com, went public in 2000. After making its debut at $11 a share, the San Francisco–based Internet company's stock rose to $14 and then promptly dropped below $3.

Volatility in the Internet business has produced a new industry—Internet consultants. As a result, a plethora of recommendations have emerged for entering an Internet business. Here are some of the suggestions:

- Keep it simple—focus on providing compelling information.
- Put customers first—understand them and meet their needs.
- Make your site web-friendly—don't assume everyone is technically competent.
- Spread the word—publicize your web address, offline as well as on the Net, by putting it everywhere you do business.
- Be ready for success—a Web site can give you more business than you can handle.

- Although e-business moves fast, managers shouldn't move carelessly—don't take risks that jeopardize reaching your goals.
- Cash-flow problems are common with Internet start-ups—project the amount of cash needed, then double it.
- Creating a true brand is specially difficult with Internet start-ups—excellent customer service, not advertising, is likely the answer.
- Deliver the goods—getting goods delivered to a customer's doorstep in a timely manner is much more complicated for Internet businesses.
- Actively monitor the customer—this ongoing dialogue leads to a deeper understanding of a customer's preferences and shopping habits, and that, in turn, leads to more personalized offerings and services.

Don't assume that the Web will solve all your problems or substitute for sound business judgment. "It is not some sort of get-rich-quick scheme," says Mark Weaver, professor of entrepreneurship at the University of Alabama. "You have to be even more a perfectionist, more meticulous, and more prepared to adjust to the changing rules of business online."

Sources: Sreenath Sreenivasan, "Wrestling with the Web," *Business Week,* May 24, 1999, pp. F16–F19; Peggy Pulliam, "To Web or Not to Web," *Internet Marketing,* June 2000, pp. 37–41; Kara Swisher, "Reality Check," *The Wall Street Journal,* April 17, 2000, p. R19; Erin Strout, "Launching an E-Business," *Sales & Marketing Management,* July 2000, pp. 89–91.

Three general questions can be answered through test marketing. First, the overall workability of the marketing plan can be assessed. Second, alternative allocations of the budget can be evaluated. Third, determining whether a new product introduction is inspiring users to switch from their previous brands to the new one and holding them there through subsequent repeat purchases is determined. In the end, the test market should include an estimate of sales, market share, and financial performance over the life of the product.

Initial product testing and test marketing are not the same. *Product testing* is totally initiated by the producer: he selects the sample of people, provides the consumer with the test product, and offers the consumer some sort of incentive to participate.

Test marketing, on the other hand, is distinguished by the fact that the test cities are to represent the national market, the consumer must make the decision herself, must pay her money, and the test product must compete with the existing products in the actual marketing environment. For these and other reasons a market test is an accurate simulation of the national market and serves as a method for reducing risk. It should enhance the new product's probability of success and allow for final adjustment in the marketing mix before the product is introduced on a large scale.

However, running a test marketing is not without inherent risks. First, there are substantial costs in buying the necessary plant and machinery needed to manufacture the product or locating manufacturers willing to make limited runs. There are also promotional costs, particularly advertising and personal selling. Although not always easy to identify, there are indirect costs as well. For example, the money used to test market could be used for other activities. The risk of losing consumer goodwill through the testing of an inferior product is also very real. Finally, engaging in a test-market might allow competitors to become aware of the new product and quickly copy it.

Because of the special expertise needed to conduct test markets and the associated expenses, most manufacturers employ independent marketing research agencies with highly trained project directors, statisticians, psychologists, and field supervisors. Such a firm would assist the product manager in making the remaining test market decisions.

1. *Duration of testing:* the product should be tested long enough to account for market factors to even out, allow for repeat purchases, and account for deficiencies in any other elements in the new product (three to six months of testing may be sufficient for a frequently purchased and rapidly consumed convenience item).
2. *Selection of test market cities:* the test market cities should reflect the norms for the new product in such areas as advertising, competition, distribution system, and product usage.
3. *Number of test cities:* should be based on the number of variations considered (i.e., vary price, package, or promotion), representativeness, and cost.
4. *Sample size determination:* the number of stores used should be adequate to represent the total market.

Even after all the test results are in, adjustments in the product are still made. Additional testing may be required, or the product may be deleted.

Step 8: Commercialization

At last the product is ready to go. It has survived the development process and it is now on the way to commercial success. How can it be guided to that marketing success? It is the purpose of the lifecycle marketing plan to answer this question. Such a complete marketing program will, of course, involve additional decisions about distribution, promotion, and pricing.

MARKETING CAPSULE 7.2

1. New product strategies begin by putting "new" on a continuum.
2. There are both internal and external sources for acquiring new products.
3. The new product development process includes the following steps:
   a. Generate new product ideas
   b. Screen ideas
   c. Perform a business analysis
   d. Technical and marketing development
   e. Manufacturing planning
   f. Marketing planning
   g. Test marketing
   h. Commercialization

THE WALL STREET JOURNAL.

IN PRACTICE

Organizations must introduce new products and manage existing products successfully to remain competitive in today's marketplace. Products are planned, and the product strategy aims to ensure that product objectives are achieved.

Unprecedented advancements in technology render shorter product life cycles. As a result, product plans must provide competitive distinctiveness.

The Interactive Journal examines product development for large and small organizations in **Marketplace**. Under the **Marketplace** heading, click on **Small Business**. This section provides articles targeted toward small and emerging businesses.

Special reports on small and emerging businesses can be found in the **Breakaway** section, also under **Small Business**.

Here you'll find more in-depth analysis about small business. The Interactive Journal also sponsors several online discussions. Click on one of the links to join an online discussion.

Return to the **Marketplace** home page and click on the **Business Focus** link on the left menu. This link directs you to articles discussing general business developments taking place in various companies.

Return to the **Front Section** and select **Starting a Business** under **Resources** in the left menu. This link sends you to the **Startup Journal**, a site designed to provide new business with a variety of tools. Navigate the bar at the top of the site for information about franchising, financing, and running a business.

ADDITIONAL SITES

Check out www.adweek.com for industry articles about advertising and brand development. The Brandweek link on the site provides weekly excerpts of headlines from the print edition.

Advertising Age is another resource for information about product strategies. Check out www.adage.com.

Business Week magazine's Web site www.businessweek.com is a comprehensive site. Daily briefings cover a wide range of topics.

DELIVERABLE

Use the Interactive Journal and Additional Sites listed here to find three articles about product development. Read each article and compare the strategies employed by the companies profiled. Why are the products successful, or why did they fail? Write a one-page brief supporting your conclusions.

DISCUSSION QUESTIONS

1. How do organizations identify product objectives when developing a product strategy? Why are these objectives important?
2. What impact do market trends have on new product development? How do organizations decide whether to introduce a new product or extend an existing product line?
3. How does the media react to new products like Apple's iMac? What about product failures like Coca-Cola's New Coke? Use the Interactive Journal to find articles about these companies and products.

SUMMARY

The ability of the organization to consistently produce new products and effectively manage existing products looms as one of the most important and difficult tasks faced by the company. This chapter provides an overview of the components that constitute a product, and the product planning process.

The process begins with the task of defining the product. In order to provide an accurate portrayal of the product, it is important to consider the perspective of the consumer, the manufacturer, and the various publics. All three perspectives must be understood and satisfied. In addition, the three components of the product are discussed. The core product identifies what the consumer expects when purchasing the product. The tangible product is reflected in its quality level, features, brand name, styling, and packaging. The augmented product is reflected by the services supporting the core/tangible product. The promised product suggests what the product delivers in the long term.

There are also several classification schemes that are useful in improving our understanding of the product into three categories: convenience, shopping, and specialty. A convenience good is one that requires a minimum amount of effort on the part of the consumer. In contrast, consumers want to be able to compare products categorized as shopping goods. Specialty goods are so unique, at least from the perspective of the consumer, that they will go to great lengths to seek out and purchase them.

Another relevant classification scheme has been applied to business goods. Three characteristics of business products are: (1) demand is derived from purchase of another product, (2) demand tends to be price-inelastic, and (3) tendency toward pure competition. Business products are classified as extractive products and manufactured products.

Goods products versus service products is the final categorization. Although there is still controversy about the validity of this separation, we contend that the differences justify adjustments in the marketing strategy for service products. Services are intangible, require simultaneous production and consumption, cannot be easily standardized, and require high consumer involvement.

This chapter continues with a discussion of the product planning process. Three elements were delineated: (1) the determination of product objective, (2) the identification and resolution of factors that have an impact on the product, and (3) the development of programs appropriate for that particular product. Examples of product objectives, as well as a discussion of the importance of product objectives, are provided. The third element of program development provides the basis for the two chapters that follow. The continuing development of successful new product looms as the most important factor in the survival of the firm. This chapter introduces the concept of "new" product as well as the process of actually producing a new product.

It is noted that what constitutes a new product must be appraised from both the consumer's point of view as well as that of the manufacturer. In the former case, newness is measured in respect to: (1) degree of consumption modification and (2) the extent of new task experience. The firm defines the product in terms of: (1) changes in the marketing mix, (2) modifications, (3) differentiation, and (4) diversification.

New products can be acquired from several internal and external sources. The firm can employ basic research, applied research, and development to develop new products. Or, they can use the external route: mergers and acquisitions, licenses and patents, and joint ventures.

MARKETER'S VOCABULARY

Product   Anything, either tangible or intangible, offered by the firm as a solution to the needs and wants of the consumer, that is profitable or potentially profitable and meets the requirements of the various publics governing or influencing society.

Consumer goods   Products purchased for personal consumption with no intention of selling to others.

Industrial goods   Products purchased by an individual or organization in order to modify the product or distribute it for a profit.

Packaging   Provides protection, containment, communication, and utility for the product.

Product lifecycle   A product planning tool that parallels the stages of the human lifecycle.

Brand   Identifies the product and distinguishes it from competitors.

Position   A strategic management decision that determines the place a product should occupy in a given market.

DISCUSSION QUESTIONS

1. What overriding objectives should be kept in mind when designing a product strategy?

2. How do the strategies of market extension and market segmentation differ?

3. Identify the steps a product manager should take in deciding how to position a product.

4. In what kind of market situation will a strategy of product differentiation be most effective?

5. What are the four product mix strategies discussed in the chapter? Name three reasons why a company might decide to alter its product mix.

6. What factors would impact a marketing manager's decision to engage in a temporary or permanent price change for a mature product?

7. How would you define the term "product"? Differentiate between the points of view of the manufacturer and the customer.

8. Distinguish between convenience goods, shopping goods, and specialty goods. Can you think of examples that belong in each category, other than those discussed in the chapter?

9. Compare and contrast the consumer's view and the firm's view of a new product.

10. Describe the steps in the new product development process. Are all these steps necessary?

PROJECT

Identify a product that you feel is in the maturity or decline stage. Determine the characteristics of this product in light of the discussion throughout this chapter. Write a 3–5 page analysis.

CASE APPLICATION

HERSHEY CHOCOLATE MILK

Hershey Foods Corp. is making an unusual move in using national TV advertising for its chocolate milk, a product that historically hasn't received much ad support. The national TV commercial, which first aired in June 1983, was shot in 12 weeks in London by Clearwater Productions. Doyle Dane Bernbach in New York developed the commercial, which has been shown nationally on a children's network and in the early fringe time period.

"The commercial's creative, it's aggressive. It breaks one cardinal rule by not mentioning this new product until 75% into the commercial. But the commercial works. We think it's unique," says Bob Jeffery, DDB VP account supervisor. He admits that the Hershey packaging also has had an important consumer impact. "The carton practically screams chocolate."

According to Hershey sales figures, Hershey chocolate milk is the number-one chocolate milk in the country. These results are indeed admirable considering the gamble Hershey took with their chocolate milk. It was the first time Hershey had attempted to sell a premixed beverage or promote a product not under its direct control. Hershey is licensing the use of its name on the chocolate milk—another big first for the company. Hershey sells powdered chocolate to large dairies, which mix the product with their milk, package it, and handle distribution. Following strict standards, Hershey has selected only certain dairies to be licensed to use the Hershey chocolate powder and label. Each dairy must follow detailed specification on mixing. To make sure there are no slip-ups, Hershey has printed a toll-free telephone number for consumers to call if they have complaints about the chocolate milk.

For Hershey, the taste of success is sweet.

Questions:

1. What type of innovation is Hershey chocolate milk?
2. How would you describe the product development process Hershey followed?
3. Describe any potential problems.

REFERENCES

1. L.P. Bucklin, "Retail Strategy and the Classification of Consumer Goods," *Journal of Marketing,* January 1963, pp. 53–54.
2. Robert G. Cooper, 1992. "New Product Success in Industrial Firms," *Industrial Marketing Management*, pp. 215–223.
3. Leonard L. Berry, "Services Marketing Is Different," *Business Magazine*, May–June 1980, pp. 19–28.
4. Brian O'Reilly, 1997. "New Ideas, New Products," *Fortune*, March 3, 1999, pp. 61–64.
5. Joel Dean, *Managerial Economics*, Englewood Cliffs, NJ: Prentice–Hall, Inc., 1951, pp. 411–412.
6. Robert J. Kelsey, "The Process of Innovation and Diffusion of Innovation," *Journal of Marketing*, January 1978, pp. 14–19.
7. Patrick Oster, "The Erosion of Brand Loyalty," *Business Week,* July 19, 1993, p. 22. Stephanie Thompson, "Brand Buddies," *Brandweek*, February 23, 1998, pp. 22–30.
8. David A. Aaker and J. Gary Shansby, "Positioning Your Product," *Business Horizons*, May–June 1982, pp. 56–62.
9. Robert G. Cooper and Elko J. Kleinschmidt, *New Product: The Key Factors to Success*, Chicago: American Marketing Association, 1990.
10. Thomas Robertson, "The Process of Innovation and Diffusion of Innovation," *Journal of Marketing*, January 1967, pp. 14–19.
11. Eberhard Scheming, *New Product Management*, Hinsdale, IL: The Dryden Press, 1974.
12. Pam Weise, "Getting Hot New Ideas from Customers," *Fortune*, May 19, 1992, pp. 86–87.
13. Abbie Griffin, "PDMA Research on New Product Development Practices: Updating Trends and Benchmarking Best Practices," *Journal of Product Innovation Management*, Vol. 14, November 1997, pp. 429–458.

CHAPTER 8

COMMUNICATING TO MASS MARKETS

LEARNING OBJECTIVES

Upon completion of this chapter, you should have an understanding of the following:

- ▨ The role of integrated marketing communication (IMC) to effectively communicate the marketer's message to its market audience.
- ▨ The definition of the four components used in IMC: advertising, personal selling, sales promotion, and public relations.
- ▨ The principles of effective communication and how they apply to marketing communication.
- ▨ The primary steps followed in designing an IMC strategy.
- ▨ The role and techniques associated with advertising.
- ▨ The role and techniques associated with sales promotion.
- ▨ The role and techniques associated with public relations.
- ▨ The role and techniques associated with personal selling.

AMERICAN EXPRESS: COMMUNICATING BIG IDEAS

Jerry Walsh has once again come up with a big marketing idea. Walsh, executive vice president of worldwide marketing for and the creative genius behind American Express, has discovered an idea that is exactly what he is looking for—something to replace the venerable "Do You Know Me?" ads and head off challenges from Visa and Diners Club. It's the ultimate in soft sell, he insists; the kind of pitch you're more likely to see on public television than on the networks. The ads don't talk to people about American Express as much as they talk to people about themselves, about their values and lifestyles. "This new campaign is going to cause tremendous excitement. It's what we do best—it's the Big Idea."

This is one in a long string of big ideas. Big ideas that have turned American Express into what some experts say is the nation's top marketer. Big ideas like the "Interesting Lives" ad campaign, which taught corporate America a whole new way of selling to women. And promotion like the company's cause-related campaign to aid the restoration of the Statue of Liberty that gave doing good deeds a gilt edge. Each time the credit card was used, the company made a donation, which netted $1.7 million for Miss Liberty and made millions for the company in fees from increased card use.

The ability of American Express to communicate to the public in new ways made it the most successful provider of credit cards, travel, and financial services. In 1993, the

American Express card (the heart of the company's business) rang up nearly $80 billion in purchases in nearly 60 million separate transactions, making it the card most used by Americans.

Much of the credit for success must go to the manner in which American Express has taken big ideas and converted them into major marketing programs. The process begins with "the hunt." Big ideas can be found anywhere, by anyone—and everybody keeps an eye peeled. The "Interesting Lives" idea, for example, was buried deep in the copy of a new "women's" ad campaign, developed by their agency Ogilvy and Mather. Since the campaign began in 1983, the number of new card members who are women has jumped from 29% to more than 50%. Moreover, notes Walsh, "Big ideas make us unstoppable because they take the high ground. There's no way to counteract big ideas without imitating them."

American Express has a very unstructured corporate environment. Consequently, every big idea needs a "champion"—someone who can charge ahead with the big idea with a minimum of restraint. Champions are allowed a free rein because management trusts their top people. Failure's no big deal at American Express. Marketing research doesn't drive the business—instinct does.

Since there are always four or five big ideas competing against each other, "battles" are inevitable. In the case of the American Express Platinum Card, the fights were particularly brutal. In meeting after heated meeting, opposing sides battled over the name, the price, the look of the card, etc. The champion of each idea openly battled each other. There are some rules, though. No one attacks anyone personally. Everyone's friends the minute the battle is over. And absolutely no politics.

In the end, Walsh's idea may not win. His big idea has some formidable foes who think it is simply too soft of a sell. Walsh is far from defeat. He's constantly drumming up support and making subtle changes in the ads themselves. Even if his idea isn't selected this time, he won't stop fighting. "My idea may retire briefly, but it won't die. We'll change it a little here, a little there, and, before you know it, it'll be reincarnated," says Walsh. "You don't win by wimping out."

Sources: Mark Padden, "Amex's Blue Card Needs More Than Good Looks to Succeed," *Future Banker,* November 1, 1999, p. 52; "Advanced Cards 101: What Makes Them So Smart and So Secure?" *Canadian Business*, August 7, 2000, p. 15; "Magic Promotes Amex Blue Business Card," *Business and Industry*, Vol. 2000, No. 95, May 17, 2000, p. 1; Michael Dumiak, "Advertising Campaigns: Amex Unrivaled in Advertising Spending," *Financial Service Marketing*, Vol. 2, No. 4, May 15, 2000, p. 8.

INTRODUCTION

The case example clearly points to one of the most difficult problems facing marketers. How can a marketer clearly and effectively communicate the story (message) in a society that is so overcommunicated that the typical consumer is both overwhelmed with the vast number of messages and annoyed at the thousands of messages that have no relevance whatsoever to that person's needs and wants? The amount of sameness, and the amount of communication clutter is so excessive, that the approach employed by American Express appears to be the only answer. Yet, as we have noted throughout this text, the needs and capabilities of marketers vary, and not all marketers are blessed with a creative genius like

Jerry Walsh. Nor do all marketers require a multimillion dollar national advertising campaign in order to reach objectives. All marketers, however, must learn to communicate their strategy to their target market.

The concept of Integrated Marketing Communication (IMC) is offered as a general framework, which can be employed by marketers in order to design a comprehensive and effective program of communication. It acknowledges the inherent differences between marketers and builds upon the reality that "every company is cast in the role of communicator." Ultimately, it is the choice of each company whether this communication process will be performed in a haphazard, unplanned way, or whether it will be guided by stated objectives and implemented through effective strategies.

This chapter introduces the concept of IMC, a framework for organizing the persuasive communication efforts of the business. Because of its visibility, many consumers feel that they already know a great deal about IMC, or at least about advertising. Most hold either a somewhat positive or negative attitude toward advertising, aggressive salespeople, coupons, and so forth. This is a case when a little bit of information can be a dangerous thing.

This chapter also provides a discussion of four of the IMC mix elements—advertising, sales promotion, public relations, and personal selling. We begin our discussion with an explanation of the role IMC plays in the marketing strategy.

THE ROLE OF IMC

The heart of every transactional exchange is communication between parties. The buyer seeks certain basic information about product features, price, quality, support service, reputation of the seller, and so forth. All this information is intended to assess how close each alternative is to meeting desired needs and wants. We seek information to reduce possible risk associated with the transaction. Presumably, the more solid the information we have, the more secure we feel in our decision. The seller also desires information. The seller wants to know whether you qualify as a buyer (i. e., do you really need the product and can you pay for it), which product features are important to you, what other choices you are considering, are you ready to buy, how much do you know about my product, and so forth. Therefore, all the parties enter a transaction with a whole set of questions they want answers to. Some of these questions are quite explicit: "How much does it cost?" Others are quite vague and may almost be subconscious: "Will this product make me feel better about myself?" All these decisions relate to the marketer's ability to integrate marketing communications (IMC).

The primary role of IMC is to systematically evaluate the communication needs and wants of the buyer and, based on that information, design a communication strategy that will (1) provide answers to primary questions of the target audience, (2) facilitate the customer's ability to make correct decisions, and (3) increase the probability that the choice they make most often will be the brand of the information provider, i.e., the sponsor or marketer.[1] Marketers know that if they learn to fulfill this role, a lasting relationship with the customer can be established.

Primary Tasks

If the marketer is to consistently and effectively communicate with consumers, three preliminary tasks must be acknowledged and achieved. First, there must be a mechanism for collecting, storing, analyzing, and disseminating relevant information. This includes information about customers (past, present, potential), competitors, the environment, trends in the industry, and so forth. The quality of communication is closely related to the quality of information. Kellogg's, for example, constantly monitors its customers through surveys and consumer panels, and keeps track of its competitors and changes in the Food and Drug Administration in order to assess the relevance of all its communication vehicles.

Second, communication is not one-way; it is a dialogue. That is, all relevant parties are actually participating in the communication process. Marketers must provide a system that constantly allows the consumer to express desires, satisfactions, complaints, and disappointments about the product, the price, the message, or the way it is distributed. There is a real tendency in large-scale marketing to view the consumer as a faceless, nameless entity, without individual needs and wants. Effective marketing communication allows direct feedback (e.g., toll-free numbers, hotlines, service departments), and actively responds by making substantial changes to address customer requests.

Finally, there must be an acknowledgement that target customers may not be the same as target audiences. While the *target market* is concerned primarily with individuals who

INTEGRATED MARKETING *8.1*

IMC—HARDER THAN YOU THINK

According to IMC guru Don Schultz, the difficulty in developing an integrated marketing communication program is in the planning. He notes that most managers have tried to integrate communication elements and activities as they were developed by various functional groups. Or they have tried to bring all the elements together once the communications concept was developed to generate one voice or a unifying brand theme that will tie all the disparate elements together.

Unfortunately, managers have been approaching the problem as one of coordination or consolidation, although integration is not at the end of the process, but at the beginning. The difficulty has been that there is not a system via which managers can develop truly integrated marketing communications.

A new approach to integration is based on the planning matrix. The matrix mantra goes like this: "From consolidate and segregate, to aggregate and integrate." The meaning is simple. Traditionally, we have tried to take a market or a category and segment it. Once we segmented the market, we then tried to apply various communication disciplines—advertising, sales promotion, or direct marketing. We tried to take activities that had been developed separately and pulled them into an integrated whole. In short, we've tried to "consolidate and segregate." Take the market, segment it, and then communicate separately to the segments.

Consider a new approach. Rather than starting with total market, start with individual customers and prospects. Aggregate them based on their behavior. Let the customers and prospects create their own groups or segments. That's aggregation. Then look at the way customers and prospects

experience marketing communications. Most consumers aren't familiar with the tightly defined marketing communications disciplines we have developed. To them, most everything we do is either an advertisement or an incentive. That's the second part of the new approach. Integrate, and most of all, simplify.

Now, the planning process is simple. At the top, we have how consumers think about and evaluate marketing communication activities. It's either a message or an incentive. We have collapsed all the very sophisticated marketing communication disciplines into what they are supposed to do: deliver a message or an incentive.

The second part of the matrix is the impact we expect the activity to have—short-term or long-term. What will be the basis for the measurement of the impact of the planned communications program? For purposes of measurement, almost everything can be considered short-term, or within the fiscal year. Long-term is anything more than one fiscal year. Building immediate sales for our product or service is short-term. Brand building is long-term. Therefore, we plan whether we'll give our target messages or incentives and the impact of those messages or incentives, either short-term or long-term.

Sources: Don E. Schultz, "A New IMC Mantra," *The Marketing News*, May 26, 1997, p. 8; Richard Linnett, "Full Court Press," *Adweek*, January 31, 2000, pp. 3–6; Don E. Schultz, "Structural Straight Jackets Stifle Integrated Success," *The Marketing News*, March 1, 1999, p. 8; Don E. Schultz, "How to Create Your Own Worst Enemy," *The Marketing News,* July 3, 2000, p. 10.

are users and potential users of the product, the *target audience* may encompass a much larger or smaller group of people. More specifically, the target audience includes all individuals, groups, and institutions that receive the marketing message and employ this information either as a basis for making a product decision or in some way employ it to evaluate the sponsoring business. Thus, the target market for E.P.T. pregnancy tests might be women between the ages of 18–34, with a college education; the target audience might also include parents of the youngest of these women, who either approve or disapprove of this product based on advertising messages, government agencies who assess the truthfulness of the product claims, and potential stockholders who determine the future success of the firm based on the perceived quality of the messages. IMC must identify all members of the target audience and must consider how the communication strategy must change in response to this membership.

In the end, the role of IMC is to communicate with target audiences in a manner that accurately and convincingly relays the marketing strategy of the firm.

Integrated Marketing Communication

Instead of a functional approach, IMC attempts to integrate these functions into a collective strategy. If conducted properly, IMC results in a more effective achievement of an organization's communications objectives. Although it is difficult to determine exactly what prompted the move to IMC, experts speculate as to several possible interrelated causes. Historically, mass media has been characterized because of its general inability to measure its results, especially sales. Recently, the availability of consumer information (especially purchase patterns) through single-source technology such as store scanners and other related technology has meant that marketers are now able to correlate promotional activities with consumer behavior. During this same period, companies have been downsizing their operations and task expectations have been expanded. This greater expectation has carried over into the client–advertising agency relationship. Agency employees can no longer remain specialists. Rather, they must understand all the functions performed for the client, as well as their own. In reality, IMC appears to be much the same as a promotional strategy, a concept that has been around for several years. Perhaps the term "IMC" has emerged due to the confusion with the term "sales promotion" and the failure of promotion to be adopted by the advertising industry. Only time will tell whether IMC will become a salient part of marketing communication. (More was said about IMC in the previous Integrated Marketing box.)

THE MEANING OF MARKETING COMMUNICATION

Defining the concept of marketing communication (MC) is not an easy task, because in a real sense, everything the company does has communication potential. The price placed on a product communicates something very specific about the product. A company that chooses to distribute their products strictly through discount stores tells the consumer a great deal. Yet if all of these things are considered communication, the following definition is offered:

> Marketing communication *includes all the identifiable efforts on the part of the seller that are intended to help persuade buyers to accept the seller's message and store it in retrievable form.*

Note that the central theme of the communication process is *persuasion*. Communication is most definitely goal-directed. It is not intended to be an arbitrary, haphazard activity. Each of the tools used in marketing communication has specific potentialities and complexities that justify managerial specialization and require directed efforts. Yet a company, even a very large one, typically does not have a specialist in each area, but only in those cases where the importance and usage frequency of the tool justify specialized competence. Historically, companies first made a separate function out of the personal selling function, later out of advertising, and still later out of public relations. The remaining tools (e.g. coupons, specials) were employed by the directors of these functional areas as needed. Although the definitions vary, the four components that make up marketing communication are as follows:

1. *Advertising:* Any paid form of nonpersonal presentation of ideas, goods, or services by an identified sponsor. Although some advertising is directed to specific individuals (as, for example, in the use of direct mail), most advertising messages are tailored to a group, and employ mass media such as radio, television, newspaper, and magazines.

2. *Personal selling:* An oral presentation in a conversation with one or more prospective purchasers for the purpose of making sales. It includes several different forms, such as sales calls by a field representative (field selling), assistance by a sales clerk (retail selling), having an Avon representative call at your home (door-to-door selling), and so forth.

3. *Public relations:* A nonpersonal stimulation of demand for a product, service, or business unit by planting commercially significant news about it in a published medium (i.e., publicity) or obtaining favorable presentation of it through vehicles not paid for by the sponsor. Although commissions are not paid to the various media, there are salaries and other expenses that mean that public relations is not a costless form of promotion.

4. *Sales promotion:* Those marketing activities that add to the basic value of the product for a limited time period and thus directly stimulate consumer purchasing and dealer effectiveness. These activities include displays, shows and exhibitions, demonstrations, and various nonrecurring selling efforts not in the ordinary routine. As the provision for an additional incentive to buy, these tools can be directed at consumers, the trade, or the manufacturer's own sales force.

THE OBJECTIVES OF MARKETING COMMUNICATION

The basic objectives of marketing communication have been reduced to three more meaningful directives: (1) to communicate, (2) to compete, and (3) to convince. The primary purpose of MC is to *communicate ideas to target audiences.* This is done through advertising, personal selling, sales promotion, and/or public relations. Principles of effective communication are intended to achieve this task. Clearly, most of marketing is communications, and it is in this context that communication is included as a purpose of MC. Moreover, whatever is communicated should be accurate, truthful, and useful to the parties involved. Because of the pervasiveness of marketing communication, it has a unique responsibility to communicate with integrity.

Helping the company to *compete consistently and effectively in the marketplace* is the second objective. For many companies, MC may offer the company its most promising marketing opportunities. Competitors may sell essentially the same product, at the same price, in the same outlets. It is only through MC that the company may be able to appeal to certain segments, properly differentiate its product, and create a level of brand loyalty that can last for many years. In addition, the prominence of extensive communication efforts on the part of competitors means that a company that did not exhibit a strong MC program would appear dull and unconvincing to the customer. Thus, MC is employed as both a defensive and offensive weapon.

The final objective of MC is to *convince*. Although this goal is most often ascribed to MC, it is the most questionable. "Convince" and "persuade" are not synonymous terms. Realistically, MC does extremely well if it presents ideas in a manner that is so convincing that the consumer will be led to take the desired action. These ideas, along with a host of other factors, will help persuade the consumer to make a particular decision. Therefore, the ability of MC to present information in a convincing manner is critical. It is also necessary to reconvince many consumers and customers. Just because a person buys a particular brand once or a dozen times, or even for a dozen years, there is no guarantee that they won't stop using the product if not constantly reminded of the product's unique benefits. Ultimately, MC objectives can be broken down into very specific tasks. The point is all MC must be guided by objectives.

In conclusion, effective marketing communication should present useful ideas (information) in a manner that makes them clearly understood (communicate), cause the consumer to believe the message is true (convince), and is as appealing or more appealing than the message delivered by competitors (compete).

HOW WE COMMUNICATE

Because communication is such an integral part of effective marketing, it is important that we provide a basic understanding of its process. Our starting point is a basic definition of human communication: a process in which two or more persons attempt to consciously or unconsciously influence each other through the use of symbols or words in order to satisfy their respective needs.

Basic Elements of Communication

The basic elements within any communication system are depicted in Figure 8.1. It includes two or more people or organizations called *communicators*. The underlying assumption of this model is that all communications (dialogue) are continuous. This factor suggests that we are constantly and simultaneously in the role of communicator and receiver. Each communicator is composed of a series of subsystems (i.e., inputs, outputs, processing). The *input subsystem* permits the communicator to receive messages and stimulus from outside as well as from the other communicator. It involves the reception of light, temperature, touch, sound and, odors via our eyes, skin, ears, nose, and tastebuds. These stimuli are intimately evaluated through a process called *perception*. Thus, we input and perceive advertising messages, a 50 cents-off coupon, the appearance and words of a salesperson, and so forth.[3]

The *processing subsystem* of a communicator includes all thought processes. As we process, we generate, organize, and reflect on ideas in response to the stimuli received. This entire process is determined not only by the stimuli just received, but also by all stimuli ever received, such as past experiences, education, health, genetics, and all other factors in our environment. Some people clearly process the humor in the Pepsi-Cola ads better than others.

The *output subsystem* includes the messages and other behaviors produced by the communicator. These include nonverbal messages, verbal messages, and other physical behaviors. All of these become input (feedback) for other people and can have both intentional and unintentional effects on them.

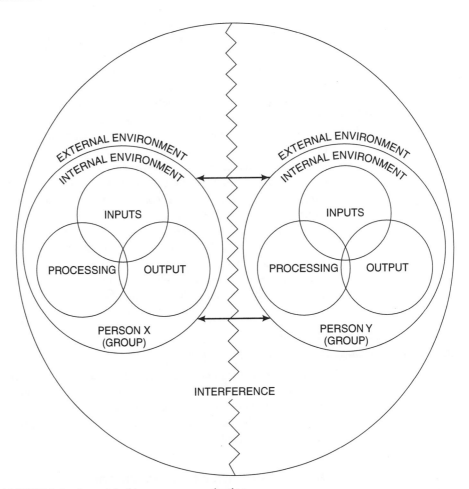

FIGURE 8.1 A model of human communication

Friend, parent, boss, client, or customer are just some of the roles we may portray in any communication process. The *nature of the role* directly affects the nature of communication. We communicate quite differently with our boss than we do with close friends. People who have known each other for a long time often devise their own communication system, which may include lots of nonverbal signals.

Finally, the communication system exists within an *environment*. The environment is everything internal and external to the communication system that can affect the system (family, school, competing advertisements, etc.). Each of the factors within the environment interacts with the communication system to a different degree. Because communication systems are open to the influence of the total environment, we can never analyze a communication event from only the point of view of the people who seem obviously involved. Everything may affect communication, positively or negatively. The latter factors may alter or distort inputs, outputs, or processing and are called interference. Interference can be generated internally (e.g., fear, love, prejudice) or externally (e.g., noise, weather, physical appearance).

MARKETING CAPSULE 8.1

1. The primary role of IMC is to systematically evaluate the communication needs and wants of the buyer and, based on that information, design a communication strategy that will: provide answers to primary questions of the target audience; facilitate the customer's ability to make correct decisions; and increase the probability that the choice they make will most often be the brand of the information provider.

2. Marketing communications is defined as a message delivery system that includes all the identifiable efforts on the part of the seller that are intended to help persuade buyers to accept the seller's message and store it in retrievable form.

3. The four components that make up marketing communication are: advertising, sales promotion, public relations, and personal selling.

4. The basic objectives of marketing communication are to: communicate, convince, and compete.

5. The elements of human communication include:
   a. The processing subsystem
   b. The output subsystem
   c. The nature of the role
   d. The environment

6. There are four types of communication systems:
   a. Interpersonal
   b. Organizational
   c. Public
   d. Mass

Types of Communication Systems

There are several types of communication systems, classified depending on the level of contact between communicators and the ability to respond to feedback.

Interpersonal Communication Systems

At the basic level of interpersonal communication systems is the *dyadic context*. A dyad consists of two people, or two major subsystems. Personal selling falls under this heading.

Organizational Communication Systems

The organizational communication context represents a much more complex system than interpersonal communication. Examples include a bank, a factory, a retail store, or the government attempting to communicate with one another. These systems include a large collection of subsystems, all organized around a common goal(s). Interactive technology has changed these types of systems in a dramatic way.

Public Communication Systems

This type of system involves communication usually from one person to a large group of people. Although everyone affects everyone else to some degree in every communication system, in a public communication context, such as a speech from a politician to people standing behind a platform of a campaign train, the speaker does most of the talking.

Mass Communication Systems

The mass communication context exists when a person/organization is communicating indirectly with a large group of people and there is even less opportunity for people to interact freely with one another and to mutually affect one another. Advertising and public relations are such mass communications.

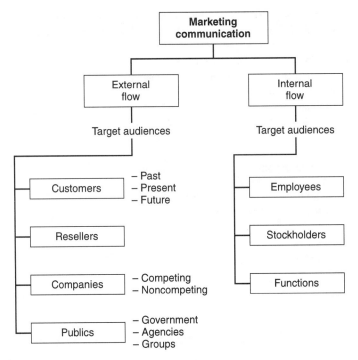

FIGURE 8.2   The flow of marketing communication

Marketing Communications

While all communication includes the same basic components depicted in Figure 8.1, marketing communication differs somewhat in two respects. First, the intent of marketing communications is to present a persuasive message, which reinforces the total offer made by the marketer. Essentially, all marketing communication attempts to create uniqueness in the mind of the target audience.

Second, marketing communication can be divided into two flows (i.e., internal and external), which are directed at different target audiences. This necessitates different communication strategies, which, never the less, must be compatible. A company cannot be telling a customer one story and stockholders another. The flow of marketing communication is depicted in Figure 8.2.

DESIGNING AN IMC STRATEGY

The design of an effective IMC strategy is a very difficult and time-consuming process that requires the efforts of many members of the marketing staff. Although there has been a great deal of variety in designing this process, the steps depicted in Figure 8.3 are most common.

As is the case with most marketing activities, IMC is guided by a set of objectives. There are numerous responses that the manager may desire from his IMC effort. Although the ultimate buyer behavior desired is product purchase, several intermediate responses may prove important as well. Examples of these intermediate responses are shown in Figure 8.4.

If there is a marketing opportunity, there must also be a *communication opportunity*. Although the role of IMC is de-emphasized in certain marketing programs, there will also be some communicative, motivational, or competitive tasks to be performed. Whether or

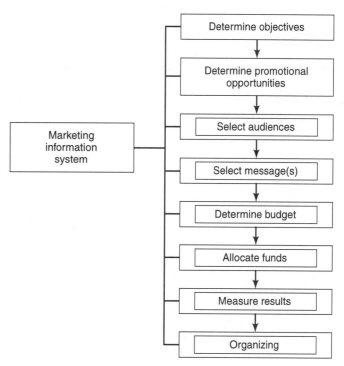

FIGURE 8.3 The IMC Strategy

not the marketing programs should rely heavily on its communication ingredient to perform such tasks depends upon the nature and extent of the opportunity. There are several conditions which, if they exist, indicate a favorable opportunity to communicate: for example, it is always easier to communicate effectively when moving with the current consumer demand rather than against it. Companies such as IBM have been actively promoting their business computers, which are increasing in popularity, rather than home computers, which are not doing as well.

The third consideration is *selecting the target audience* for the IMC. This is undoubtedly the most important factor in the IMC strategy, yet it is probably the issue that many companies slight or overlook entirely. Marketing messages must be directed at the specific target for which the overall marketing program is being designed. However, very seldom is there a single group of consumers at which to direct promotion. Many individuals affect the buying process, and the IMC program must be designed to reach all of them. In addition to the primary purchasers and users of the product, individuals who influence the purchase decision must also be considered. For example, consumers usually rely heavily upon the assistance and advice of others in purchasing such products as automobiles, interior decorating, major appliances, and physicians, to name but a few. Similarly, industrial buyers consider the advice of engineers, technicians, and even competitors. Thus it is extremely important in resolving the communication issue to identify accurately not only those who consume and buy the product but also those who influence its purchase.

Determining exactly *what to say* to the relevant audience is the fourth consideration. The heart of IMC is the transmission of ideas of marketing significance to the seller. Whether these ideas are received and perceived as intended depends in large part on the skill used in developing the communication appeal. It also depends upon the vehicle used to deliver

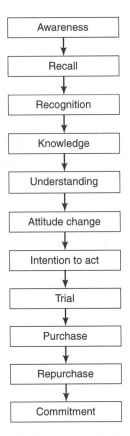

FIGURE 8.4 Goals of integrated marketing communication

the message. Whether it is the message delivered by a salesperson, a newspaper, or a point-of-purchase display, the message must facilitate reaching the communication objectives.

Money is always an important factor; a typical IMC effort is extremely expensive and is becoming more expensive every day. Keeping track of these cost elements is a full-time job. The budget for a particular IMC effort can be determined through very sophisticated computer programs or through intuitive techniques such as experience, following competition, or simply spending all you can afford. Particular budgetary approaches are summarized in Table 8.1.

Once you decide how much to spend, the amounts to be spent on personal selling, advertising, publicity, and sales promotion must be decided. After determining the major allocations, each of these figures must be broken down into much finer increments. For example, the advertising budget must be reallocated by media category, then by specific media, and finally, by particular dates, times, issues, etc.

Evaluating the effectiveness of an IMC effort is very important. Three tasks must be completed when one attempts to measure the results of IMC. First, standards for IMC effectiveness, such as retention and liking, must be established. This means that the market planner must have a clear understanding of exactly what the communication is intended to accomplish. For measurement purposes, the standards should be identified in specific, quantitative terms. Second, actual IMC performance must be monitored. To do this, it is usually necessary to conduct experiments in which the effects of other variables are either excluded or controlled. The third step in measuring IMC efficiency is to compare these per-

TABLE 8.1 Summary of Techniques: Setting the IMC Budget

Technique	General Description
Arbitrary Allocation	Management bases budget on personal experience, business philosophy, and marketing intuition
Affordability	Upper limit of budget based on available company resources
Ratio-to-sales	Amount budgeted is based on some portion of past or forecasted sales
Competitive comparisons	Budget based on amount being spent by major competitors
Experimental approach	Budget based on test market results
Objective-task method	Determine costs of reaching specific promotional objectives and sum amounts

formance measures against the standards. In doing so, it is theoretically possible to determine the most effective methods of marketing communication.

Finally, how a company *organizes* for IMC depends on the degree to which it desires to perform the communication function internally or to assign this task to outside agencies. Typically, the sales function is performed internally and the sales organization is a part of the overall, standing organizational plan. Occasionally, as when manufacturer's agents are used, outside organizations are employed to perform personal selling. Advertising services might be performed internally or externally. Sales promotion activities are usually also handled internally, although it is not uncommon for advertising agencies to be consulted in connection with sales promotion plans. The same is true for public relations.

The Promotion Mix

The manner in which the four components of IMC (i.e., advertising, personal selling, sales promotion, public relations) are combined into an effective whole is called the *IMC mix*. The promotion mix tends to be highly customized. While, in general, we can conclude that business-to-business marketers tend to emphasize personal selling and sales promotion over advertising and public relations, and that mass marketers are just the opposite, there are many exceptions. However, the following factors tend to have an impact on the particular IMC mix a company might select:

1. *Marketing/IMC objectives*: Companies that desire broad market coverage or quick growth in market share, for example, must emphasize mass advertising in order to create a dramatic and simultaneous impact.

2. *Nature of the product:* The basic characteristics of product (highly technical) suggest the need for demonstration and explanation through personal selling, or mass advertising in the case of a product with emotional appeal (perfume).

3. *Place in the product lifecycle:* Products in the introductory stage in the life cycle often need mass advertising and sales promotion, those in maturity need personal selling, and those in decline employ sales promotion.

4. *Available resources:* Companies with limited financial and human resources are often restricted to sales promotion and public relations while those with plenty of both opt for mass advertising and personal selling.[2]

The most striking fact about IMC techniques is their cross-substitutability. They represent alternate ways to influence buyers to increase their purchases. It is possible to achieve a given sales level by increasing advertising expenditures or personal selling, or by offering a deal to the trade or a deal to customers. This substitutability calls for treating the various IMC tools in a joint-decision framework.

The Campaign

Determining what particular devices to use and how to combine them in order to achieve IMC objectives is one of the greatest challenges facing the communication planner. Ordinarily, management just make use of the campaign concept. A *campaign* is a planned, coordinated series of marketing communication efforts built around a single theme or idea and designed to reach a predetermined goal. Although the term "campaign" is probably thought of most often in connection with advertising, it seems appropriate to apply the concept of a campaign to the entire IMC program.

Many types of IMC campaigns may be conducted by a company, and several may be run concurrently. Geographically, a firm may have a local, regional, or national campaign, depending upon the available funds, objectives, and market scope. One campaign may be aimed at consumers and another at wholesalers and retailers.

A campaign revolves around a *theme*, a central idea or focal point. This theme permeates all IMC efforts and tends to unify the campaign. A theme is simply the appeals developed in a manner considered unique and effective. As such, it is related to the campaign's objectives and the customer's behavior. It expresses the product's benefits. Frequently the theme takes the form of a slogan, such as Coca-Cola's "Coke is it!" Or DeBeers' "A diamond is forever." Some companies use the same theme for several campaigns; others develop a different theme for each new campaign.

In a successfully operated campaign, the efforts of all groups concerned will be meshed effectively. The advertising program will consist of a series of related, well-timed, carefully placed ads. The personal selling effort can be tied in by having the salesperson explain and demonstrate the product benefits stressed in ads. Also, the sales force will be fully informed about the advertising part of the campaign—the theme, media used, schedule of appearance of ads, appeals used, etc. The sales force will also inform the middlemen, i.e., wholesalers and retailers, about this campaign, and convince them to incorporate it into their total marketing effort. Sales promotional devices will be coordinated with the other aspects of the campaign. For each campaign, new display materials must be prepared, reflecting the ads and appeals used in the current campaign, in order to maximize the campaign's impact

---

MARKETING CAPSULE 8.2

1. Marketing communication:
   a. Is intended to be persuasive
   b. Has internal and external flows

2. The following steps are involved in designing an IMC strategy:
   a. Determine objectives
   b. Determine IMC opportunities
   c. Select audience(s)
   d. Select message(s)
   e. Determine budget
   f. Allocate funds
   g. Measure results
   h. Organize

3. Factors that most impact the IMC mix include:
   a. Marketing/IMC objectives
   b. Nature of the product
   c. Place in the product lifecycle
   d. Available resources

4. A campaign is a planned, coordinated series of marketing communication efforts built around a single theme or idea and designed to reach a predetermined goal.

at the point of sale. Personnel responsible for the physical distribution activities must ensure that adequate stocks of the product are available in all outlets prior to the start of the campaign. Finally, people working in public relations must be constantly kept aware of new products, product demonstrations, new product applications, and so forth. Of course, it is extremely important to provide enough lead time so that the public relations effort can take advantage of optimum timing.

UNDERSTANDING ADVERTISING

Undoubtedly, advertising is the promotional element that most consumers feel they know the best and hold strong opinions about. This is a result of the visibility and intrusiveness of advertising. In fact, most people have little understanding of advertising.

The Organization of Advertising

There are within the advertising industry a wide variety of means by which advertising is created and placed in media. At one extreme, an individual might write and place his own classified advertisements in a newspaper in the hope of selling his daughter's canopy bed. At the other extreme, the advertiser employs a full-service advertising agency to create and place the advertisement, retaining only the function of final approval of plans developed by that agency. Significant specialization is developed within the full-service advertising agency to discourage clients from hiring any outside vendors or other parties to perform any of the various functions involved in planning and executing advertising programs for the various advertisers that the agency serves. Another organizational possibility is a full-scale, in-house advertising department. This department may have total responsibility for all aspects of the advertisement, or some of the tasks might be optioned out to ad agencies or other types of specialty organizations, e.g., production, talent, media placement. It is not unusual for a large corporation to employ all of these possibilities or to use different agencies for different products or for different parts of the country.

Whether or not the advertiser uses an advertising agency, does his advertising in-house, or uses some combination of the two depends upon a host of factors unique to each organization: available funds, level of expertise, expediency, and so forth. Regardless of the influencing factors, a number of basic functions must be performed by someone if creative and effective advertisements are to be placed:

- What products, institutions, or ideas are to be advertised
- Who is to prepare advertising programs
- Who the organization engages and gives policy and other direction to the advertising agency, if any agency is used
- Who in the organization has the authority to develop advertising work and/or approves the advertising programs presented by the advertising agency
- Who pays the advertising bill
- Who determines the extent to which advertisements help reach the stated objectives[3]

The Advertising Department

A company advertising department can range from a one-person department to one employing 500 or more people. Regardless of the size, advertising departments share similar responsibilities:

1. Formulating the advertising program
2. Implementing the program
3. Controlling the program
4. Presenting the budget
5. Maintaining relationships with suppliers
6. Establishing internal communications
7. Setting professional standards
8. Selecting an advertising agency

The Advertising Agency

The relations between an advertising agency and a client can go on for years, although some clients do move from agency to agency. Firms such as DuPont, Procter & Gamble, Kraft, Kellogg, and General Mills rarely change agencies.

Clients employ advertising agencies because they believe that the agency can: (1) produce better-quality, more persuasive messages for their products; and (2) place these messages in the right media so that the message reaches the greater number of prospects. Clients who believe they can do better themselves set up their own in-house agencies. However, relatively few of them exist and these are in specialized fields such as retailing.

Developing the Creative Strategy

Once all the relevant facts are gathered and evaluated, the process of actually creating the advertisement is appropriate. This process is very complex, and a complete description of it is well beyond the scope of this book. However, it is possible to highlight the primary parts of this process.

To begin with, the person or persons actually responsible for the complete advertisement depends upon the advertiser's organization of the advertising function and whether an advertising agency is used. More than likely, the development and approval of advertising creation is the responsibility of the senior advertising manager within the advertiser company and, when an advertising agency is used, of the agency management. In most agencies, the responsibility is that of the senior account person, in conjunction with the senior creative person assigned to the account. The advertising effort can be divided into two elements: the creative strategy and creative tactics. The *creative strategy* concerns what you are going to say to the audience. It flows from the advertising objectives and should outline what impressions the campaign should convey to the target audience. *Creative tactics* outline the means for carrying out the creative strategy. This includes all the various alternatives available, which will help reach the advertising objectives.

The place to begin the creative strategy is to ascertain the proper *appeal* to employ in the ad. (See Table 8.2.) Identifying the appropriate appeal is just the first part of the advertising design process. The second part is to transform this idea into an actual advertisement. To say that there are a large variety of ways to do this would be a gross understatement. The number of techniques available to the creative strategist are not only vast, but the ability of more than one technique to successfully operationalize the same appeal makes this process even more nebulous.

TABLE 8.2 Primary Advertising Appeals

Product/service features	Many products have such strong technology or performance capabilities that these features can serve as a primary advertising appeal.
Product/competitive advantage	When an advertiser can determine that his product is superior, either in terms of features, performance, supporting services, or image, emphasizing a competitive advantage has proved to be a successful appeal.
Product/service price advantage	Offering a product at a reduced price or under some special deal arrangement (e.g., buy-one-get-one-free) may be the only viable appeal in a particular ad.
News about product/service	There are times when a truly new product is developed, or when an existing product is changed or improved in a substantial manner, that highlighting this single element is the core appeal.
Product/service popularity	Although the manner varies, the notion of claiming that a product is "number one" or the most popular is an appeal that has been around for a long time.
Generic approach	In such advertising, a product or service category is promoted for its own sake, but individual makes or brands of product are not singled out.
Consumer service	A popular appeal is to illustrate through the advertisement how the product may be used to best serve the needs of the consumer.
Savings through use	An opportunity to save time, money, or energy is always very appealing to consumers.
Self-enhancement	Helping us feel better about ourselves (e.g., personal care, clothing, automobiles) is an appeal that many people can't resist.
Embarrassment or anxiety	Situations that represent a threatening situation, either physically or socially, can provide the basis for an effective appeal.
Product trial	When this appeal is used, the advertiser offers a free sample, a price reduction, or some other purchase incentive to encourage consumer use or trial.
Corporate	This type of appeal presents a company or corporation in a favorable light in order to create a favorable impression or image.

Developing the Media Plan

Although the media plan is placed later in this process, it is in fact developed simultaneously with the creative strategy. This area of advertising has gone through tremendous changes; a critical media revolution has taken place.

The standard media plan consists of four stages: (1) stating media objectives; (2) evaluating media; (3) selecting and implementing media choices; and (4) determining the media budget.

Stating Media Objectives
Media objectives are normally started in terms of three dimensions:

1. *Reach*—number of different persons or households exposed to a particular media vehicle or media schedule at least once during a specified time period.

2. *Frequency*—the number of times within a given time period that a consumer is exposed to a message.

3. *Continuity*—the timing of media assertions (e.g., 10% in September, 20% in October, 20% in November, 40% in December and 10% the rest of the year).

Evaluating Media

As noted in Table 8.3, there are definite inherent strengths and weaknesses associated with each medium. In addition, it would require extensive primary research either by the sponsoring firm or their advertising agency in order to assess how a particular message and the target audience would relate to a given medium. As a result, many advertisers rely heavily on the research findings provided by the medium, by their own experience, and by subjective appraisal.

Selection and Implementation

The media planner must make media mix decisions and timing directions, both of which are restricted by the available budget. The *media mix decision* involves putting media together in the most effective manner. This is a difficult task, and necessitates quantitatively and qualitatively evaluating each medium and combination thereof.

Unfortunately, there are very few valid rules of thumb to guide this process, and the supporting research is spotty at best. For example, in attempting to compare audiences of various media, we find that A.C. Nielsen measures audiences based on TV viewer reports of the programs watched, while outdoor audience exposure estimates are based on counts of the number of automobile vehicles that pass particular outdoor poster locations. The *timing of media* refers to the actual placement of advertisements during the time periods that are most appropriate, given the selected media objectives. It includes not only the scheduling of advertisements, but also the size and position of the advertisement.[4]

Determining the Media Budget

This budget is a part of the advertising budget, and the same techniques and factors that apply to the advertising budget apply to the media budget as well.

Banner Advertisements

Before leaving the topic of advertising, both creative and media, it is important to introduce a new form of advertising—*banner advertising*. Banner ads are the dominant form of online advertising. Banner ads are graphic images in Web pages that are often animated and can include small pieces of software code to allow further interaction. Most importantly, they are "clickable," and take a viewer to another Web location when chosen.

Banner ads typically run at the top and bottom of the page, but they can be incorporated anywhere. The CASIE organization has developed a small number of standard sizes and formats. Like the Web itself, banner ads are a mixture of approaches, with elements of traditional print advertising and more targeted direct advertising. Banner ads include direct marketing capabilities. Each banner carries with it a unique identifier. This allows the Web site to track the effectiveness of the ad in generating traffic. Measurability permits ad banner pricing based on results and behavior. Click-through pricing ignores impressions and charges the advertiser based on the number of viewers that select the ad and follow it to the linking Web site.

Admittedly, the performance of banner ads to date has been less than stellar. One company, San Francisco–based Organic, has approached the problem of ineffective online advertising with a product called "expand-o." This new ad vehicle allows an advertiser to include some of its Web site's content in an expandable banner ad. At the click of a mouse, the advertisement expands to as much as five or six times its original size. For instance, an expand-o

TABLE 8.3   An Appraisal of Mass Media

Type	Strengths	Weaknesses
TELEVISION	1. Strong emotional impact 2. Mass coverage/small cost per impression 3. Repeat message 4. Creative flexibility 5. Entertaining/prestigious	1. High costs 2. High clutter (too many ads) 3. Short-lived impression 4. Programming quality 5. Schedule inflexibility
RADIO	1. Provides immediacy 2. Low cost per impression 3. Highly flexible	1. Limited national coverage 2. High clutter 3. Less easily perceived during drive time 4. Fleeting message
NEWSPAPERS	1. Flexibility 2. Community prestige 3. Market coverage 4. Offer merchandising services 5. Reader involvement	1. Short life 2. Technical quality 3. Clutter 4. Timing flexibility 5. Two-tiered rate structure
MAGAZINES	1. Highly segmented audiences 2. High-profile audiences 3. Reproduction qualities 4. Prestigious 5. Long life 6. Extra services	1. Inflexible 2. Narrow audiences 3. Waste circulation 4. High cost
OUTDOOR/ TRANSIT	1. Inexpensive 2. Flexible 3. Reminder 4. Repetition 5. Immediacy	1. Short/concise messages 2. Negative reputation 3. Uncontrollable 4. Inflexible
DIRECT MAIL	1. Flexibility 2. Develop complete/precise message 3. Supplement	1. Negative image 2. High cost per impression 3. High production costs 4. Dependent upon mailing list
SPECIALTY ADVERTISING (Directories, matchbooks, calendars, etc.)	1. Positive reinforcement 2. Segmented markets 3. Flexible	1. Wasteful 2. Expensive
INTERACTIVE	1. Flexible 2. Repetition 3. Involvement	1. Hard to measure 2. Limited market coverage 3. Uncontrollable

for Fort Washington, PA–based CDNow provides consumers with a sample of dynamically updated content housed on the music retailer's site. When the consumer clicks an arrow on the ad, it expands to show the top 10 songs in CDNow's top 100 Billboard Chart.[5]

SALES PROMOTION AND PUBLIC RELATIONS

For several years, sales promotion and public relations have been often misunderstood, mismeasured, and misused by a great many marketers. Unlike advertising and personal selling that can claim formal structures and point to obvious accomplishments, sales promotion and PR have neither. Although this situation is changing somewhat, there is still a great deal of room for improvement. In the case of sales promotion, there exists some confusion as to which activities actually fall under this heading. Are packaging, couponing, and point-of-purchase displays all sales promotion? Because the answer to this question varies from organization to organization and across situations, sales promotion is often viewed as a catch-all category that includes everything that an organization does not label advertising or public relations.

Public relations, too, is difficult to define as it deals with the ultimate intangible—creating a positive image of the company. Not only is this difficult to accomplish, but it is also virtually impossible to ascertain if you have succeeded and to what extent. An organization, for instance, might sponsor a free barbecue for a Fourth of July celebration and never really know if the money spent produced additional business. Management has a difficult time appreciating an activity that produces indirect results.

Sales Promotion: A Little Bit of Everything

As the newest member of the promotional team, sales promotion has suffered from a serious identity crisis. For example, initially the American Marketing Association defines sales promotion as, "marketing activities, other than personal selling, advertising, and publicity, that stimulate consumer purchasing and dealer effectiveness, such as displays, shows and exhibitions, demonstrations, and various non-recurrent selling efforts not in the ordinary routine."[6] In the AMA view, sales promotion supplements both personal selling and advertising, coordinates them, and helps make them more effective.[6] However, this does not provide an accurate portrayal of the role played by sales promotion. A simple way of viewing sales promotion is to say that it means *special offers*: *special* in the sense that they are extra as well as specific in time or place; offers in the sense that they are direct propositions, the acceptance of which forms a deal. Simply, it increases the perceived value of the product.

As in most aspects of marketing, the rationale of sales promotion is to provide a direct stimulus to produce a desired response by customers. It is not always clear, however, what the distinctions are between sales promotion and advertising, personal selling and public relations. For example, suppose that Pillsbury decides to tape three cans of their buttermilk canned biscuits together and sell them for a price slightly cheaper than the three sold individually. Is that a branded multipack special offer and therefore promotional? Or is it just an example of a giant-sized economy pack, and therefore a product or packaging tactic? In order to sort out which it is, the question has to be asked, is it intended to be a permanent feature of the manufacturer's product policy to have the family pack as a component of the product? If it is not, it is a sales promotion scheme.

The same sort of problem comes up when studying strategies run by firms in service industries. If a hotel offers cut-price accommodations at off-peak times of the year, is it a feature of the hotel management's pricing policy or is it a promotional tactic? If the

AD 8.1 Here's an excellent example of a sales promotion.

hotel management provides price reductions on tickets to local theaters for their guests, is it part of the product or is it a device to attract customers for a limited period only? Again, the answer can only be given once the question about performance is asked. Even then, there still tend to be elements of advertising, personal selling, public relations and sales promotion in many promotional vehicles, and this may be the right approach. A candy

AD 8.2   Example of a rebate offer.

manufacturer, for instance, has made substantial contributions of both cash and products to the local heart fund telethon. Immediately following the telethon, they run a full-page ad in several magazines describing their contributions, and describing a special rebate of 5¢ for every candy wrapper mailed in. The 5¢ can be donated to the heart fund if the customer wishes. The sales reps also have copies of this promotion to show their customers. Clearly, this strategy has all four components of the IMC mix.

Types of Sales Promotion

There are a great many techniques that are considered sales promotion. One way of organizing this myriad of techniques is in terms of audience. As shown in Table 8.4, sales promotions are directed at consumers, employees, and distributors, and dealers. While consumers attract the greatest number of sales promotion devices, the other two audiences are growing in importance. While space does not permit a discussion of these strategies, some generalizations apply to all. Specifically, the value of a sales promotion is especially prominent when a marketer is introducing a new product, especially a product with high perceived risk; is interested in creating a repeat purchase pattern for the customer; is attempting to create movement of large amounts of products quickly; is attempting to counter the strategy of a competitor; and is trying to move marginal customers to make a choice. Sales promotion cannot compensate for a poor product or ineffective advertising. Nor can it create strong brand loyalty or reverse a declining sales trend.

Public Relations: The Art of Maintaining Goodwill

Every organization engages in some form of public relations (PR). In essence, every form of communication emitted by an organization both internally and externally is perceived by various publics. In turn, these publics form attitudes and opinions about that organization, which affect their behaviors. These behaviors range from low morale on the part of the employees to product rejection on the part of consumers.

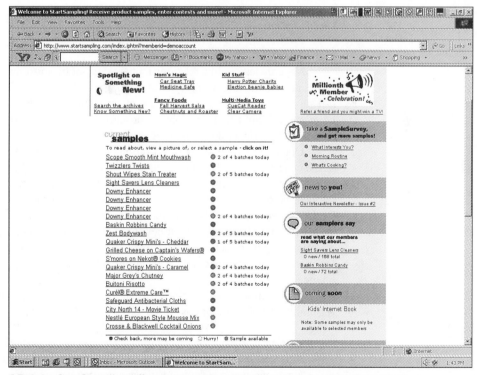

AD 8.3 StartSampling offers its more than 1.5 million members the chance to try a wide variety of samples while helping marketers more effectively connect with their target audience.

AD 8.4 Both StartSampling and FreeSamples.com have systems in place to prevent inventory depletion.

Nevertheless, public relations looms as one of the most misunderstood and mistrusted elements in marketing. Consequently, management may provide marketing in general with full support, ample scope, and time for planning, but often does not establish a role for public relations. Public relations may be brought in belatedly at advanced stages of marketing process as a peripheral area with no real purpose.

Obtaining a good working definition of public relations requires an acknowledgement of the concept's core elements. Four such elements emerge. First, the ultimate objective of PR is to retain as well as create goodwill. Second, the successful procedure to follow in public relations is to first do good, and then take credit for it. Third, the publics addressed by the PR program must be described completely and precisely. In most instances, PR programs are aimed at multiple publics that have varying points of view and needs. Consequently, the publics served should be researched just as carefully as the target audiences for an advertising campaign. Finally, public relations is a planned activity. There is an intelligence behind it.

The definition that encompasses all these considerations, and was coined at the First Assembly of Public Relations Associations in 1987, follows:

> *Public Relations practice is the art of social science in analyzing trends, predicting their consequences, counseling organization leaders, and implementing planned programs of action, which serve both the organizations and the public interest.*[7]

TABLE 8.4   Types of Sales Promotion Techniques

Audience/Technique	Description
CONSUMER	
Price Discounts	Temporary reduction in price, often at point of purchase.
Coupon offers	Certificates redeemable for amount specified.
Combination offers	Selling two products in conjunction at a lower total price.
Contests	Awarding of prizes on the basis of chance or consideration.
Rebates	Refund of a fixed amount of money.
Premiums	Tangible reward received for performing an act, normally a purchase.
Trading stamps	Certificate awarded based on purchase amount.
Sampling	Providing the product either free or for a small fee.
EMPLOYEE	
Orientation program	Introducing the employee to company facts.
Fringe benefits	Extra incentives provided by company to employee.
Institutional promotion	Messages portraying company in a positive light.
Motivational programs	Temporary incentives, e.g., contests, prizes, or awards.
DISTRIBUTOR/DEALER	
Contests	Temporary incentives offered for specific performance.
Trade shows	Central location where products are displayed/sold.
Push money/dealer loaders	Money offered for selling specified amounts of product.
Trade deals	Dealers receive special allowances, discounts, goods, or cash.

Public Relation's Publics

A *public* may be said to exist whenever a group of people is drawn together by definite interests in certain areas and has definite opinions upon matters within those areas. There are many publics, and individuals are frequently members of several that may sometimes have conflicting interests. For example, in the case of a school bond vote, a voter might be torn between feelings as a parent and as a member of a conservative economic group opposed to higher taxes; or an elderly couple, with no children now in school, might be parents of a teacher.

Public relations must be sensitive to two general types of publics: internal and external. *Internal publics* are the people who are already connected with an organization, and with whom the organization normally communicates in the ordinary routine of work. Typical internal publics in an industry are the employees, stockholders, suppliers, dealers, customers, and plant neighbors. For example, employees want good wages and working conditions, opportunities for advancement, and a secure retirement. Customers want a dependable supply of quality products provided at a fair price and supported by convenient services. Stakeholders want dividends, growth, and a fair return on their investments.

External publics are composed of people who are not necessarily closely connected with a particular organization. For example, members of the press, educators, government officials, or the clergy may or may not have an interest in an industry. The leaders of the industry cannot assume any automatic interest and, to some extent, must choose whether to communicate with these groups.

**It's the second largest state in America.
And every resident is struggling to get out.**

It's bigger than Texas, Florida or New York — but you won't find it on any map. It holds more people than Connecticut, Kentucky, Maryland, Michigan, New Jersey and Nevada combined — but it's a state of bitter uncertainty. It's home to one out of every eleven families in America. It's home to one out of every six children in America. It's home to more than 32 million desperate people trapped within its cruel boundaries. It's the state of poverty in America. And if you were poor, you'd be home by now.

POVERTY.
America's forgotten state.

Catholic Campaign for Human Development
1-800-946-4243
www.povertyusa.org

AD 8.5   The Catholic Campaign for Human Development is hoping to convey the message that one in nine Americans lives below the poverty line.

There is, of course, interaction between internal and external publics. Yet it cannot be assumed that good relations with insiders will ever be translated to outsiders without effort. An employee who is quite happy on the job may be much more interested in bowling than in the fact that the firm has just opened a new branch in Phoenix. The firm must think of what interests the external public and not what interests the firm. With employees and other internal publics, there is a fair chance that all interests may coincide because all are connected with the same organization; with an external audience, the assumption should be that the chance of such accidental coincidence of interest is slight.

Public Relations Techniques

The public relations process is quite complex and involves a wide variety of techniques. Public relations is different than any other type of promotion, because a great deal of the communication provided by a PR person must be screened and reprocessed through a third party that is not employed by the company. Therefore, if I wished for the local newspaper and television station to carry a story detailing the grand opening of my new store, I have no guarantee that either will send representatives to cover the store opening or that they will cover it the way I would have liked. Even if I were to write the story myself and send it to the newspaper, including appropriate photographs, the editor might choose not to print it or to modify it. The fact that PR is characterized by a low level of control necessitates that PR people establish a positive relationship with the various media. Without first accomplishing this goal, the tools employed by the PR person are usually doomed to failure. Various public relations techniques are described in Table 8.5.

Personal Selling and the Marketing Communication Mix

Few companies coordinate marketing communication efforts in support of the sales force. Salespeople are often separated from marketing communications specialists because of both the structure of the business and difference in perspective. Most salespeople view other marketing communication activities strictly as a means to help sell a product or company. Advertisers, sales promotion managers, and public relations experts rarely consider the needs and suggestions of salespeople, and salespeople seldom pay attention to information about a marketing communication campaign.

TABLE 8.5   Public Relations Techniques

TECHNIQUE	DESCRIPTION
News release (press release)	A prepared statement sent to various media.
Press conference	Meeting attended by media representatives for the purpose of making announcements or answering questions.
Delivering bad news	System that anticipates and handles negative events.
Publicity photographs	A prepared photo sent to various media.
Company publications	Magazines, newspapers, and newsletters produced by the company, depicting specific stories.
Open houses/tours	Providing various publics' access to plant facilities.
Meetings	Planned meeting provided for various publics, especially employees and stockholders.
Organized social activities	Company-sponsored social activities directed at employees, e.g., teams and picnics.
Participation	Company-encouraged involvement in community activities, e.g., clubs, charities.
Motion pictures/slides	Professionally produced films and slides about some aspect of the company, provided to various publics.

MARKETING CAPSULE *8.3*

1. Advertising is the marketing communication technique that provides messages to mass audiences via a creative strategy and a media strategy.

2. The organization for advertising may include an in-house advertising department or an external agency.

3. The creative strategy includes what you are going to say to the audience and the means for delivering the message.

4. Sales promotion adds value to the product, and can be targeted at consumers, salespeople, or distributors.

5. Public relations maintains or enhances goodwill with the company's various publics.

Integrating personal selling with other marketing communication elements may seriously affect that salesperson's job. Regis McKenna, international consultant, contends that although marketing technology has made salespeople more effective, it may also decrease the need for traditional salespeople who convince people to buy. As we move closer to "real-time" marketing, he believes customers and suppliers will be linked directly, so that customers can design their own products, negotiate price with suppliers, and discuss delivery and other miscellaneous concerns with producers rather than salespeople. McKenna suggests that the main role of salespeople will no longer be to "close" the sale. Instead it will be to carry detailed design, quality, and reliability information, and to educate and train clients.[8]

Don Schultz, Northwestern University professor of marketing and proponent of IMC, supports this notion of the modern salesperson. "If you create long-term affiliations, then you don't sell. You form relationships that help people buy." He observes that because products have become more sophisticated, the businesses that buy are often smaller than those that sell. "Today, I think the sales force is primarily focused on learning about the product

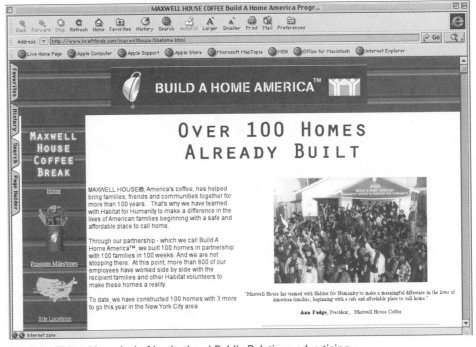

AD 8.6 This ad is typical of Institutional Public Relations advertising.

and not about the market. We're talking about flipping that around," he concludes.[9] In short, effective personal selling must focus on customer relationships.

To integrate personal selling with other marketing communication tools to forge strong customer relationships, top management should lead the integration effort. Unless managers understand what salespeople do, however, integration may not be successful. Before considering how to combine selling efforts with other marketing communication tools, we first examine the job of personal selling.

The underlying rationale for personal selling is facilitating exchange. As suggested by a personal selling expert, it is "the art of successfully persuading prospects or customers to buy products or services from which they can derive suitable benefits, thereby increasing their total satisfaction." A professional salesperson recognizes that the long-term success for the organization depends on consistently satisfying the needs of a significant segment of its target market. This modern view of selling has been called "nonmanipulative selling," and the emphasis of this view is that selling should build mutual trust and respect between buyer and seller. Benefit must come to both parties. This perspective is developed further in the Integrated Marketing box that follows.

Types of Selling

Considerable differences exist in the various kinds of selling tasks. Early writers provided two-way classification of selling jobs, consisting of *service selling*, which focuses on obtaining

INTEGRATED MARKETING 8.2

SELLING INVOLVES EVERYTHING

Salespeople have been taught for years that the key to successful selling is finding out what people need and then doing whatever it takes to fill that need. There are thousands of books and articles based on this principle alone. Recently, however, many sales professionals are discovering a better way to sell.

The real definition of selling has to do with finding out what people or businesses do, where they do it, and why they do it that way, and then helping them to do it better.

The word "need" doesn't appear in that definition at all, because there is no need associated with today's selling. A successful salesperson first asks the prospect about the company's goals before trying to fill an imagined need with the product or service being sold.

Critics of this approach say that determining what a business does is the same as determining its needs. "It's all semantics," they say. "The word 'do' is the same as the word 'need'." But it's not semantics. There is a major difference in the new sales philosophy.

What does the concept of need-driven sales really mean? For one thing, the word "need" implies that something is missing. For example, if a car has only three wheels, there is a need for a fourth. The driver of the car realizes that something is missing and stops at the nearest tire shop.

A business generally has a full complement of tires, or needed items. Even if a business needs something, it does not want a salesperson to call. The needed service or items is bought as soon as the need is recognized. In a proactive sale, the business is running smoothly when the salesperson calls. The salesperson, having been trained in a needs-driven industry, asks the prospect what is missing. The buyer replies that nothing is needed. The salesperson insists that something must be wrong, and attempts to prove that there is a solution to the "pain" the business is experiencing.

There are two possible outcomes to this scenario. The first is that no sale is made. The second is that the salesperson does uncover some deep-seated problem that can be fixed, and a sale is made. But this is an arduous process that pays off all too infrequently.

The top competitor of salespeople today is the status quo. People continue to do what they do because it works. The salesperson is a messenger of change. He or she makes a sale by helping someone improve the way they do business.

Sources: Stephan Schiffman, "Here's the Real Definition of Selling," *The Marketing News*, December 8, 1997, pp. 4–5; Diana Ray, "Value-based Selling," *Selling Power*, September 1999, pp. 30–33; Rochelle Garner, "The Ties That Bind," *Sales & Marketing Management*, October 1999, pp. 71–74.

Factor	Personal Selling	Mass Selling
Speed in a Large Audience	Slow	Fast
Cost per Individual Reached	High	Low
Ability to Attract Attention	High	Low
Clarity of Communications	High	Moderate
Chance of Selective Screening	Moderate	High
Direction of Message Flow	Two Way	One Way
Speed of Feedback	High	Low
Accuracy of Feedback	High	Low

FIGURE 8.5   Differences in personal selling and mass promotion

sales from existing customers, and *developmental selling*, which is not as concerned with immediate sales as with converting prospects to customers.

Most sales positions require some degree of both types of selling. Sales jobs can be classified on a continuum of service selling at one end to developmental selling at the other. Nine types of sales jobs are classified on this continuum (see Figure 8.6).

Service selling involves the following participants:

1. *Inside order taker*—predominantly waits on customer; for example, the sales clerk behind the neckwear counter in a men's store.
2. *Delivery salesperson*—predominately engaged in delivering the product; for example, persons delivering milk, bread, or fuel oil.
3. *Route or merchandising salesperson*—predominantly an order taker, but works in the field; for example, the soap or spice salesperson calling on retailers.
4. *Missionary salesperson*—position where the salesperson is not expected or permitted to take an order but to build goodwill or to educate the actual or potential user; for example, the distiller's missionary and the pharmaceutical company's detail person.

Low Level of Complexity

Service selling:
• Inside order taker
• Delivery salesperson
• Route or merchandising salesperson
• Missionary salesperson
• Technical salesperson

Developmental selling:
• Creative salesperson of tangibles
• Creative salesperson of intangibles

Developmental selling requiring high degree of creativity:
• Indirect salesperson
• Salesperson engaged in multiple sales

High Level of Complexity

FIGURE 8.6   A continuum of personal selling positions

5. *Technical salesperson*—major emphasis is placed upon technical knowledge; for example, the engineering salesperson who is primarily a consultant to client companies.

Developmental selling involves the following participants:

1. *Creative salesperson of tangibles*—for example, salespersons selling vacuum cleaners, refrigerators, siding, and encyclopedias.
2. *Creative salesperson of intangibles*—for example, salespersons selling insurance, advertising services, and educational programs.

Developmental selling, but requiring a high degree of creativity, involves the following participants:

1. *Indirect salesperson*—involves sales of big ticket items, particularly of commodities or items that have no truly competitive features. Sales consummated primarily through rendering highly-personalized services to key decision-makers in customers' organizations.
2. *Salesperson engaged in multiple sales*—involves sales of big-ticket items where the salesperson must make presentations to several individuals in the customer's organization, usually a committee, only one of whom can say *yes*, but all of whom can say *no*. For example, the account executive of an advertising agency who makes presentation to the *agency selection committee.* Even after the account is obtained, the salesperson generally has to work continually to retain it.

While the developmental-service and oriented classifications are helpful to better our understanding of the selling job, there are several other traditional classifications.

Inside Versus Outside Selling   Inside selling describes those sales situations in which selling takes place in the salesperson's place of business. Retail selling is inside selling. Outside selling represents situations in which the salesperson travels to the customer's place of business. Most industrial selling situations fall into this category.

Company Salespeople Versus Manufacturer Representatives   A manufacturer's representative is an independent agent who handles the related products of noncompeting firms. Generally, these agents are used by new firms or firms that have little selling expertise. Company salespeople work for a particular company and sell only the product manufactured by that company.

Direct Versus Indirect Selling   Indirect selling is characterized by situations in which people in the marketing channel are contacted who can influence the purchase of a product. This type of selling occurs in the pharmaceutical industry in which detail salespeople call on physicians in an effort to convince them to prescribe their firm's brand of drugs. Direct salespeople call on the person who makes the ultimate purchase decision.

The Selling Process

To better understand the job of a salesperson and how it should be managed, the selling process can be broken into a series of steps. Each step in the process may not be required to make every sale, but the salesperson should become skilled in each area in case it is needed. The steps are shown in Figure 8.7.

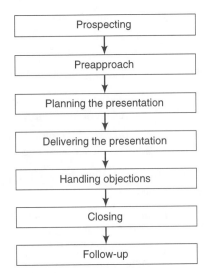

FIGURE 8.7 The selling process: steps involved

Prospecting   *Prospecting* is defined as the seller's search for, and identification of, qualified potential buyers of the product or service. Prospecting can be thought of as a two-stage process: (1) identifying the individuals and/or the organizations that might be prospects, and (2) screening potential prospects against evaluative qualifying criteria. Potential prospects that compare favorably to the evaluative criteria can then be classified as qualified prospects.

Preapproach   After the prospect has been qualified, the salesperson continues to gather information about the prospect. This process is called the *preapproach*. The preapproach can be defined as obtaining as much relevant information as possible regarding the prospect prior to making a sales presentation. The knowledge gained during the preapproach allows the tailoring of the sales presentation to the particular prospect. In many cases, salespeople make a preliminary call on the prospect for the purpose of conducting the preapproach. This is perfectly acceptable, and most professional buyers understand that such a call may be necessary before a sales presentation can be made.

Planning the Presentation   Regardless of the sales situation, some *planning* should be done before the sales presentation is attempted. The amount of planning that will be necessary and the nature of the planning depend on many factors, including: (1) the objective or objectives of the presentation, (2) how much knowledge the salesperson has regarding the buyer, buyer needs, and the buying situation, (3) the type of presentation to be planned and delivered, and (4) the involvement of other people assisting the salesperson in the sales presentation. Careful planning offers advantages for both the salesperson and the buyer. By carefully planning the presentation, salespeople can: (1) focus on important customer needs and communicate the relevant benefits to the buyer, (2) address potential problem areas prior to the sales presentation, and (3) enjoy self-confidence, which generally increases with the amount of planning done by the salesperson. In planning the presentation, the salesperson must select the relevant parts of their knowledge base and integrate the selected parts into a unified sales message. For any given sales situation, some of the facts concerning the salesperson's company, product, and market will be irrelevant. The challenge to the salesperson is in the task of distilling relevant facts from the total knowledge base. The key question here is, "What information will the prospect require before they will choose to buy my offering?"

Delivering the Presentation   All sales presentations are not designed to secure an immediate sale. Whether the objective is an immediate sale or a future sale, the chances of getting a positive response from a prospect are increased when the salesperson: (1) makes the presentation in the proper climate, (2) establishes credibility with the prospect, (3) ensures clarity of content in the presentation, and (4) controls the presentation within reasonable bounds.

Handling Objections   During the course of the sales presentation, the salesperson can expect the prospect to object to one or more points made by the salesperson. *Sales objections* raised by the prospect can be defined as statements or questions by the prospect, which can indicate an unwillingness to buy. Salespeople can learn to handle customer's objections by becoming aware of the reasons for the objections. The objections of customers include objections to prices, products, service, the company, time, or competition. The reasons for objections include that customers have gotten into the habit of raising objections, customers have a desire for more information, and customers have no need for the product or service being marketed. Salespeople can overcome objections by following certain guidelines including viewing objections as selling tools, being aware of the benefits of their products, and creating a list of possible objections and the best answers to those objections.

Closing   To a large degree, the evaluation of salespeoples' performance is based on their ability to close sales. Certainly, other factors are considered in evaluating performance, but the bottom line for most salespeople is their ability to consistently produce profitable sales volume. Individuals who perform as salespeople occupy a unique role: they are the only individuals in their companies who bring revenue into the company.

There may be several opportunities to attempt to close during a presentation, or opportunity may knock only once. In fact, sometimes opportunities to close may not present themselves at all and the salesperson must create an opportunity to close. Situations where a closing attempt is logical include:

1. When a presentation has been completed without any objectives from the prospect.

2. When the presentation has been completed and all objections and questions have been answered.

MARKETING CAPSULE *8.4*

1. Personal selling involves the direct presentation of a product or service idea to a customer or potential customer by a representative of the company or organization.

2. There are various types of selling: inside order taker, delivery salesperson, route-merchandise salesperson, missionary salesperson, technical salesperson, creative salesperson of tangibles, creative salesperson of intangibles, indirect salesperson, salesperson engaged in multiple sales.

3. The selling process includes the following steps:
   a. Prospecting
   b. Preapproach
   c. Planning for presentation
   d. Delivering the presentation
   e. Handling objectives
   f. Closing
   g. Follow-up

3. When the buyer indicates an interest in the product by giving a closing signal, such as a nod of the head.

Follow-up To ensure customer satisfaction and maximize long-term sales volume, salespeople often engage in *sales follow-up* activities and the provision for post-sale service. If a sale is not made, a follow-up may eventually lead to a sale.

Strengths and Weaknesses of Personal Selling

Personal selling has several important advantages and disadvantages compared with the other elements of marketing communication mix (see Figure 8.5). Undoubtedly, the most significant strength of personal selling is its flexibility. Salespeople can tailor their presentations to fit the needs, motives, and behavior of individual customers. As salespeople see the prospect's reaction to a sales approach, they can immediately adjust as needed.

Personal selling also minimizes waste effort. Advertisers typically expend time and money to send a mass message about a product to many people outside the target market. In personal selling, the sales force pinpoints the target market, makes a contact, and expends effort that has a strong probability of leading to a sale.

Consequently, an additional strength of personal selling is that measuring effectiveness and determining the return on investment are far more straightforward for personal selling than for other marketing communication tools, where recall or attitude change is often the only measurable effect.

Another benefit of personal selling is that a salesperson is in an excellent position to encourage the customer to act. The one-on-one interaction of personal selling means that a salesperson can effectively respond to and overcome *objections* (customers' concerns or reservations about the product) so that the customer is more likely to buy. Salespeople can also offer many specific reasons to persuade a customer to buy, in contrast to the general reasons that an ad may urge customers to take immediate action.

A final strength of personal selling is the multiple tasks the sales force can perform. For instance, in addition to selling, a salesperson can collect payment service or repair products, return products, and collect product and marketing information. In fact, salespeople are often best at disseminating negative and positive word-of-mouth product information.

High cost is the primary disadvantage of personal selling. With increased competition, higher travel and lodging costs, and higher salaries, the cost per sales contract continues to increase. Many companies try to control sales costs by compensating sales representatives based on commission only, thereby guaranteeing that salespeople get paid only if they generate sales. However, commission-only salespeople may become risk-averse and only call on clients who have the highest potential return. These salespeople, then, may miss opportunities to develop a broad base of potential customers that could generate higher sales revenues in the long run.

Companies can also reduce sales costs by using complementary techniques, such as telemarketing, direct mail, toll-free numbers for interested customers, and online communication with qualified prospects. Telemarketing and online communication can further reduce costs by serving as an actual selling vehicle. Both technologies can deliver sales messages, respond to questions, take payment, and follow up.

Another disadvantage of personal selling is the problem of finding and retaining high-quality people. First, experienced salespeople sometimes realize that the only way their income can outpace their cost-of-living increase is to change jobs. Second, because of the push for profitability, businesses try to hire experienced salespeople away from competitors rather than hiring college graduates, who take three to five years to reach the level of productivity of more experienced salespeople. These two staffing issues have caused high turnover in many sales forces.

Another weakness of personal selling is message inconsistency. Many salespeople view themselves as independent from the organization, so they design their own sales techniques, use their own message strategies, and engage in questionable ploys to create a sale. Consequently, it is difficult to find a unified company or product message within a sales force, or between the sales force and the rest of the marketing communication mix.

A final weakness is that sales force members have different levels of motivation. Salespeople may vary in their willingness to make the desired sales calls each day; to make service calls that do not lead directly to sales; or to use new technology, such as a laptop, e-mail, or the company's Web site. Finally, overzealous sales representatives may tread a thin line between ethical and unethical sales techniques. The difference between a friendly lunch and commercial bribery is sometimes blurred.

The Sales Force of the Future

What will the sales force of the year 2020 look like? Will it still consist of dependent operators who are assigned a territory or a quota? Will the high cost of competing in a global marketplace change the traditional salesperson? Although we can speculate about dramatic changes in the nature of personal selling, the traditional salesperson figure will likely remain intact for several decades. Why? Many products will still need to be sold personally by a knowledgeable, trustworthy person who is willing to resolve problems at any hour of the day.

Still, major changes in personal selling will occur, in large part due to technology. Though technology has increased selling efficiency, it has also resulted in more complex products, so that more sales calls are required per order in many industries. Also, because of the trend toward business decentralization, sales representatives now have more small or mid-sized accounts to service. Currently, companies such as Hewlett-Packard and Fina Oil and Chemical as well as many smaller companies provide laptop computers to all salespeople. Computer-based sales tracking and follow-up systems allow salespeople to track customers. This technology means that salespeople can assess customer-buying patterns, profitability, and changing needs more rapidly. Accessing this information via computer saves the salesperson time and allows customization of the sales presentation

Sales teams will continue to gain in popularity because customers are looking to buy more than a product. They are looking for sophisticated design, sales, education, and service support. A sales team includes several individuals who possess unique expertise and can coordinate their efforts to help meet the needs of the particular prospect in every way possible. The salesperson acts as a team quarterback, ensuring that the account relationship is managed properly and that the customer has access to the proper support personnel.

Procter & Gamble is one company that has adopted the team approach. P&G has 22 sales executives who coordinate the sales effort of various P&G divisions in their assigned market areas. Each manager coordinates key account teams composed of sales executives from P&G's grocery division. As many as three key account teams may sell in each market. The marketing manager supervises a logistics team composed primarily of computer systems and distribution executives. The team works closely with retailers to develop mutually compatible electronic data and distribution systems. P&G hopes the team approach will reduce the pressure for trade promotions because the team provides greater service to resellers.

Salespeople of the future will have to adjust to new forms of competition. With the increased capabilities and greater use of direct marketing, for example, salespeople must recognize that some customers will buy a product without contact with a salesperson. Product catalogs that feature everything from computers to classic automobiles are mailed directly to customers or ordered on the Internet. These often provide all the information about the product the customer needs to know. Questions can be answered through a toll-free number, an Internet comment form, or e-mail. Salespeople of the twenty-first century should either integrate direct marketing to support the selling process or offer the customer benefits not available through other marketing communications techniques.

On this very small planet, salespeople will also have to adjust to new sources of competition. Companies in Asia, South America, and Eastern Europe are introducing thousands of new products to industrialized nations every year. The salesperson of the future must know how to respond to foreign competitors and how to enter their markets. A program that integrates personal selling with other marketing communication tools will give salespeople more opportunity to act efficiently and have selling success.

NEWSLINE: NEW TOYS FOR SALES SUCCESS?

Recent technological advances have given salespeople more ways than ever to improve sales and productivity. To make technology work, however, you have to control it instead of letting it control you. Start by learning to use everyday tools (computer, fax, and e-mail) more efficiently and effectively. Once you know how to get the most out of technology, you can get more out of each workday.

- *Get a voice-mail advantage.* You can avoid time-consuming two-way phone conversations by outlining detail in voice mail. Also, if you need the person for whom you're leaving the message to take some actions, say so in the message, then say there's no need to call you back unless they have questions or problems.
- *Improve your email habits.* To avoid frequent interruptions to your workday, set aside specific, scheduled times during the day to answer your e-mail.
- *Fax casually.* When you're flooded with faxes, forget about taking the time to send replies on new sheets of paper and fill out cover sheets. Instead, simply hand-write your replies at the bottom of the fax you received and turn it around.
- *Get better acquainted with your PC.* Take an hour or so before or after work for a week to learn all of your computer's functions and how they can boost your productivity.
- *Make a sound investment.* You rely on technology every day to do your job, so it pays to spend a little more for equipment that won't let you down. Carefully assess your technology needs, then shop around for equipment that meets those needs without a lot of bells and whistles.
- *Take a break.* Overall increases in the speed of business can leave a salesperson feeling done in and turned out.

Sources: Robin Sharma, "A Technology Edge," *Selling Power*, January/February, 1998, pp. 37–38; Ginger Conlon, "How to Move Customers Online," *Sales & Marketing Management*, March 2000, pp. 27–28; Neil Rackman, "The Other Revolution in Sales," *Sales & Marketing Management*, March 2000, pp. 34–35.

THE WALL STREET JOURNAL.

IN PRACTICE

Marketing communication must communicate an organization's ideas to its target audiences, compete consistently and effectively in the marketplace, and convince consumers to buy its products. To achieve these objectives, marketers design an integrated marketing communication plan using advertising, sales promotion, public relations, and personal selling.

Marketing communication is both internal and external in scope with an array of target audiences, some small, some large. Marketing communication is also both direct and indirect. Advertising and public relations are indirect, mass communication systems, while sales promotion and personal selling are direct, interpersonal and organizational systems.

The **Marketplace** section of the Interactive Journal is an invaluable source for articles related to marketing communication. With a section dedicated for **Advertising** news, the Journal keeps readers informed of the latest trends in the field.

Marketplace Columns are the main features in the **Marketplace** section. They are regular weekly columns, offering insight into a variety of topical issues such as E-business and work and family.

The **Marketplace Extra** section is the online companion to the print edition's supplement to the Weekend Journal. Here you'll find stories about broader market trends. Astute marketers can leverage this information to learn more about consumer behavior. In turn, they can develop marketing communication strategies with more relevant and convincing messages.

CAREERS

Many marketers get their start in advertising, sales, or public relations. The Interactive Journal offers job seekers advice about finding jobs and building careers. On the **Front Section**, click on the **Careers** link under **Free WSJ.com Sites**. You'll find negotiation strategies, a career Q & A, and interviewing tips. You can also find information about writing effective cover letters and resumes.

DELIVERABLE

Read one of the featured articles in today's **Marketplace** section of the Interactive Journal. Search the Interactive Journal and other relevant sites for additional information. Identify the marketing communication strategies the company uses and argue their effectiveness. Support your conclusions with facts and chapter concepts.

DISCUSSION QUESTIONS

1. Why are organizations shifting from specialized to integrated marketing communication strategies?
2. How can organizations design marketing communication programs that keep pace with the rapid changes in technology?
3. What careers are available in advertising? Sales? Public relations? What skills are employers seeking for these positions?

SUMMARY

Marketing communication remains one of the most visible and controversial aspects of marketing. Everyday we see hundreds of ads, redeem coupons, are approached by a variety of salespeople, and are told by countless companies how good they are. This chapter introduces the persuasive arm of marketing communication. In it we suggest that since everything about a company is going to communicate something, it would be beneficial to have as much control over this process as possible. Other reasons for planning the communication effort are also discussed, as are the primary objectives: (1) to communicate, (2) to convince, and (3) to compete. The systems model of communication is discussed to clarify the general communications process. Components of this process are defined and described. Types of communications systems are described. IMC is defined from a broad perspective, and then categorized into four components: (1) advertising, (2) personal selling, (3) public relations, and (4) sales promotion. The eight-step process involved in designing an IMC strategy is discussed.

Advertising is discussed in the context of marketing communication that is targeted at mass markets. It contains a sequential process, but is highlighted through its creative strategy and media strategy.

Sales promotion and public relations are two components that are both misunderstood and misused. The second part of this chapter develops some basic concepts related to both strategies. Reasons for sales promotion and types of sales promotion are discussed. Public relations is viewed in terms of its two publics, internal and external. Several techniques used to reach these publics are proposed.

Professional selling has been defined as personal contact aimed at successfully persuading prospects to buy products or services from which they can derive suitable benefits. Selling is a major force in our economy, both in terms of employment and its impact on the success of various organizations. The product, customer, competition, and environment must all be considered in determining the relative emphasis to place on personal selling in the promotional mix. The activities of a salesperson can be broken into a series of steps called the sales process. Not all of the steps are required for every sale, but the complete process includes prospecting, preapproach, planning the presentation, the approach, delivering the presentation, handling objectives, closing, and follow-up.

MARKETER'S VOCABULARY

Advertising (consumer's perspective)   One of several incoming messages directed at the consumer, the salience of which is influenced by the emotional, physical, and need state of the individual, and the benefit of which can be information, motivation, and entertainment.

Advertising (societal perspective)   An institution of society that has the capability of informing the citizen, stimulating economic growth, and providing knowledge useful in decision making, as well as the tendency both to misallocate scarce economic resources and lead consumers to engage in behavior that may not be in their best interest.

Advertising (business perspective)   Advertising's function is primarily to inform potential buyers of the problem-solving utility of a firm's market offering, with the objective of developing consumer preferences for a particular brand.

Advertising campaign   The culmination of all the strategic, creative, and operational efforts of the people working towards a particular set of advertising objectives.

Creative strategy   Concerns what an advertiser is going to say to an audience, based on the advertising objectives. Strategy should outline what impressions the campaign should convey to the target audience.

Creative tactics   Specific means of implementing strategy.

Sales promotion   Temporary special offers intended to provide a direct stimulus to produce a desired response by customers.

Price deals   Short-term reductions in the price of a product to stimulate demand that has fallen off.

Coupon offers, certificates for a specified amount off a product.

Combination offers   Link two products together for a price lower than the products purchased separately.

Contest   A promotion that involves the award of a prize on the basis of chance or merit.

Rebates   A refund of a fixed amount of money for a certain amount of time.

Premium offers   A tangible reward received for performing a particular act, usually purchasing a product.

Consumer sampling   Getting the physical product into the hands of the consumer.

Push money   A monetary bonus paid by a manufacturer to a retail salesperson for every unit of a product sold.

Dealer loader   A premium that is given to a retailer by a manufacturer for buying a certain amount of a product.

Trade deals   Strategies intended to encourage middlemen to give a manufacturer's product special promotional efforts that it would normally not receive.

Public relations   Public relations practice is the art and social science of analyzing trends, predicting their consequences, counseling organization leaders, and implementing planned programs of action that serve both the organization's and the public interest.

Internal publics   People connected with an organization with whom the organization normally communicates in the ordinary routine of work.

External publics   People not necessarily closely connected with an organization.

Campaign   Planned series of promotional efforts designed to reach a predetermined goal through a single theme or idea.

Communication   A process in which two or more persons attempt to consciously or unconsciously influence each other through the use of symbols or words in order to satisfy their respective needs.

Federal Trade Commission (FTC)   Government agency established to protect businesses against unfair competition.

Marketing communication   Includes all the identifiable efforts on the part of the seller that are intended to help persuade buyers to accept the seller's message and store it in retrievable form.

IMC mix   Various combinations of elements in a promotional plan: advertising, sales promotion, personal selling, public relations.

DISCUSSION QUESTIONS

1. List the basic objectives of marketing communication. Why is it often difficult for promoters to reach their objectives? Provide some valid reasons why marketers should pursue these objectives.

2. Assume that top management for General Equipment, Inc. hired you to determine if a promotional opportunity exists for a fabricated part that has been developed for heavy-duty equipment. What criteria would you use as a basis of investigation?

3. Define the phrase "sales promotion." Cite some examples of how sales promotion can supplement or complement the other components of the IMC mix.

4. What steps might a public relations person take to prevent the firm from acquiring a negative public image?

5. Assume that you are the public relations director for a bank. Suppose that two people were robbed while withdrawing money from an automatic 24-hour teller machine. Develop a program in response to this incident.

6. How is the consumer's definition of advertising different from that of a businessperson's?

7. Give some examples of situations in which primary demand product advertising might be fruitful. When would selective demand product advertising be useful?

8. Assume that you have been charged with organizing an in-house advertising department for a growing consumer products company. The first task is to hire an advertising manager who will have ultimate responsibility. What responsibilities should be mentioned in the job description for this position?

9. Explain the difference between creative strategy and creative tactics.

10. List and describe the various types of appeals. Develop an appeal, as well as tactics to operationalize this appeal, for Old Spice Shave Cream.

PROJECT

Can you cite some examples of how either advertising or another form of marketing communication led you to purchase a product that did not satisfy a need? Could any form of MC (marketing communications) or gimmick lead you to repurchase it? Has MC enabled you to find a product which satisfies a personal need? How might future MC keep you loyal to a product? Write a two- to three-page response.

CASE APPLICATION

THE MICRORECORDER

One of the fastest growing industries in the United States in the past ten years has been the direct marketing of a wide variety of consumer goods and services. Today it is not unusual for most of us to shop by mail (or use some other form of direct marketing) for almost anything imaginable. Among the most well-known and successful direct marketers is Neiman Marcus, a retail department store that also discovered the additional profits of selling such unusual gifts as elephants, airplanes, and $1,000 boxes of chocolate candy—all by mail.

But Neiman Marcus is certainly not alone. There are literally thousands of companies selling via direct marketing. One of these companies is American Import Corporation. American Import was started in 1969 by Tom and Sally Struven. They started their business by importing a line of Japanese-made sports watches and selling them for $29.95 with advertisements in *The Wall Street Journal*, *The Rotarian*, *Elks Magazine*, and the *Legionnaire*. At that time, comparable watches were retailing for $49.95 to $79.95. The Struvens were successful, and in the next few years they continued to expand their product lines, compiled their own customer list, and eventually issued a shopping catalog. Although the catalog was successful, they discovered the most successful way to introduce a new item was to advertise it separately.

In early 1980, Tom and Sally Struven made arrangements to purchase 50,000 microrecorders from a Korean manufacturer. These recorders measured $1 \times 2\frac{1}{2} \times 5\frac{1}{2}$ inches and were supplied with a built-in microphone, a vinyl carrying case, a wrist strap, and a 30-minute microcassette. The microrecorder is operated by 4 AA batteries or an optional AC adapter.

This type of recorder became very popular in the past few years, particularly among businesspeople. A traveling executive or salesperson could dictate letters on the microrecorder and then have a secretary transcribe them onto letterhead. The microrecorder is also ideal as an audio notepad, substituting for paper-and pencil-notetaking.

The first microrecorder was brought to the mass market in 1975 and retailed for $400. Since then, several companies entered the market, and today there are approximately twelve major brands available through traditional retail locations. The prices of microrecorders vary by the sophistication of the individual piece of equipment; however, the retail price range is $90 to $250.

American Import Corporation decided to offer its microrecorder for $39.95. Although American Import's product was a technically simply product, it did a very capable and reliable job of performing the basic task of recording and playing back the human voice.

With several years of direct marketing experience behind them, the Struvens decided to introduce the microrecorder via direct marketing. They were planning an advertising campaign in *Barron's*, the *Wall Street Journal*, the *New York Times*, the *Chicago Tribune*, the *Los Angeles Times*, and a spot television campaign in selected markets.

The Struvens were very excited about the sales prospects of their new microrecorder, and while the media portion of their advertising campaign was rather obvious, they could not decide on the best creative approach for the product.

Several possible themes came to mind. For example, should the product be sold on the basis of its comparatively low price? Its simplicity of operation? Its flexibility of use? Its size/convenience? Perhaps they should use a competitive-comparison strategy? How about their no-risk, 30-day trial?

The products had arrived from Korea. The media schedule had been set. Shipping procedures were established. Contractual arrangements with service organizations had been made. The only obstacle between American Import Corporation and a new source of profits seemed to be the selection of the most promising creative strategy for this new minirecorder.

Questions:

1. What creative strategy would you recommend to the Struvens?

2. Suggest three alternative creative executions of the recommended strategy for a print advertisement.

REFERENCES

1. Don E. Schultz, Stanley I. Tannenbaum and Robert F. Lauterborn, *Integrated Marketing Communications*, 1993, Chicago: NTC Business Books.
2. Tom Duncan, "A Macro Model of Ingetraged Marketing Communications," *American Academy of Advertising Annual Conference*, 1995, Norfolk, VA.
3. Melanie Wells, "Many Clients Prize Agency Efficiency over Creativity," *Advertising Age*, May 16, 1994, p.28.
4. Terrance A. Shimp, *Advertising Promotion*, Fifth ed., 2000, The Dryden Press, p. 561.
5. Ann M. Mack, "Banner Daze," *Adweek*, May 22, 2000, p.86.
6. "Shaping the Future of Sales Promotion," *Council of Sales Promotion Agencies*, 1990, pp. 3.
7. "Careers in Public Relations," *Public Relations Society of America*, Summer 1989, pp.18–30.
8. Regis McKenna, "Relationship Marketing," 1991, Reading, MA, Addison-Wesley Publishing Co.
9. Don E. Schultz, "Make Communications Worth the Profits," *The Marketing News*, January 15, 2001, p. 13.

CHAPTER 9

PRICING THE PRODUCT

LEARNING OBJECTIVES

After you have read this chapter, you should develop an understanding of the following key points related to pricing:

■ The meaning of pricing from the perspective of the buyer, seller, and society.

■ The sellers' objectives in making pricing decisions.

■ The alternative pricing approaches available to the manager.

THE MCDONALD'S EFFECT

McDonald's is one humongous company. With 21,000 restaurants in 101 countries, it is everywhere—which is why the global economy is sometimes called McWorld. But back home in America, the execs that run this vast empire aren't feeling very lordly. More than ever they find they have to kowtow to the price demands of ordinary folks like Alonso Reyes, a 19-year-old Chicagoan who works at a local car dealership. Never mind that Chicago is Micky D's world headquarters—he splits his fast-food patronage between McDonald's and its arch-rival, Burger King, and counts every pennyworth of beef when deciding where to eat. So Reyes perked up when he heard that McDonald's had announced "an unprecedented value offering"—a 55-cent Big Mac that the company boasted was bad news for their competition. "Cool," said Reyes, "Coupons, specials, sales. I'll take whatever I can get."

For McDonald's top management, this pricing strategy made perfect sense. After all, declining same-store sales in the U.S. were the chain's most glaring weakness. What better way to put some sizzle in the top line than a bold pocketbook appeal?

Well, McDonald's executives should have realized that there is, in fact, a better way. But apparently they took no notice of the fallout when Phillip Morris announced deep cuts on "Marlboro Friday," or of "Grape Nuts Monday," when the Post unit of Kraft Foods kicked off a cereal price war. Predictably, "Hamburger Wednesday" sent investors on a Big Mac attack, slicing 9% off McDonald's share price in three days and dragging rival fast-food issues down with it. "It looks almost desperate," says Piper Jaffray, Inc. analyst Allan Hickok of the 55-cent come-on. Adds Damon Brundage of NatWest Securities Corp.; "They have transformed one of the great brands in American business into a commodity."

In theory, McDonald's plan will pay off, because customers only get the discount if they buy a drink and french-fries, too. Yet that gimmick-within-a-gimmick threatens to undermine pricier "Extra Value Meals," one of the chain's most successful marketing initiatives. Consumers expecting cut-rate combos won't go back to paying full price, especially if other fast-feeders discount their package deals.

Sources: Greg Burns, "McDonald's: Now, It's Just Another Burger Joint," *Business Week*, March 17, 1997, pp. 3–8; Bill McDowell, "McDonald's Falls Back to Price-Cutting Tactics," *Advertising Age*, February 3, 1997, pp. 5–7; Michael Hirsch, "The Price is Right," *Time*, February 10, 1997, p. 83; Louise Kramer, "More-Nimble McDonald's is Getting Back on Track," *Advertising Age*, January 18, 1999, p. 6; David Leonhardt, "Getting Off Their McButts," *Business Week*, February 22, 1999, pp. 84–85; Bruce Horovitz, "Fast-Food Facilities Face Sales Slowdown," *USA Today*, Wednesday, February 21, 2001, p. 3B.

INTRODUCTION

From a customer's point of view, value is the sole justification for price. Many times customers lack an understanding of the cost of materials and other costs that go into the making of a product. But those customers can understand what that product does for them in the way of providing value. It is on this basis that customers make decisions about the purchase of a product.

Effective pricing meets the needs of consumers and facilitates the exchange process. It requires that marketers understand that not all buyers want to pay the same price for products, just as they do not all want the same product, the same distribution outlets, or the same promotional messages. Therefore, in order to effectively price products, markets must distinguish among various market segments. The key to effective pricing is the same as the key to effective product, distribution, and promotion strategies. Marketers must understand buyers and price their products according to buyer needs if exchanges are to occur. However, one cannot overlook the fact that the price must be sufficient to support the plans of the organization, including satisfying stockholders. Price charged remains the primary source of revenue for most businesses.

PRICE DEFINED: THREE DIFFERENT PERSPECTIVES

Although making the pricing decision is usually a marketing decision, making it correctly requires an understanding of both the customer and society's view of price as well. In some respects, price setting is the most important decision made by a business. A price set too low may result in a deficiency in revenues and the demise of the business. A price set too high may result in poor response from customers and, unsurprisingly, the demise of the business. The consequences of a poor pricing decision, therefore, can be dire. We begin our discussion of pricing by considering the perspective of the customer.

The Customer's View of Price

As discussed in an earlier chapter, a customer can be either the ultimate user of the finished product or a business that purchases components of the finished product. It is the customer that seeks to satisfy a need or set of needs through the purchase of a particular product or set of products. Consequently, the customer uses several criteria to determine how much they are willing to expend in order to satisfy these needs. Ideally, the customer would like to pay as little as possible to satisfy these needs. This perspective is summarized in Figure 9.1.

Therefore, for the business to increase value (i.e., create the competitive advantage), it can either increase the perceived benefits or reduce the perceived costs. Both of these elements should be considered elements of price.

FIGURE 9.1 The customer's view of price

To a certain extent, perceived benefits are the mirror image of perceived costs. For example, paying a premium price—e.g., $650 for a piece of Lalique crystal—is compensated for by having this exquisite work of art displayed in one's home. Other possible perceived benefits directly related to the price–value equation are status, convenience, the deal, brand, quality, choice, and so forth. Many of these benefits tend to overlap. For instance, a Mercedes Benz E 750 is a very high-status brand name and possesses superb quality. This makes it worth the $100,000 price tag. Further, if Mark Smith can negotiate a deal reducing the price by $15,000, that would be his incentive to purchase. Likewise, someone living in an isolated mountain community is willing to pay substantially more for groceries at a local store rather than drive 78 miles to the nearest Safeway. That person is also willing to sacrifice choice for greater convenience. Increasing these perceived benefits is represented by a recently coined term—*value-added*. Thus, providing value-added elements to the product has become a popular strategic alternative. Computer manufacturers now compete on value-added components such as free delivery setup, training, a 24-hour help line, trade-in, and upgrades.

Perceived costs include the actual dollar amount printed on the product, plus a host of additional factors. As noted, these perceived costs are the mirror-opposite of the benefits. When finding a gas station that is selling its highest grade for 6¢ less per gallon, the customer must consider the 16-mile drive to get there, the long line, the fact that the middle grade is not available, and heavy traffic. Therefore, inconvenience, limited choice, and poor service are possible perceived costs. Other common perceived costs include risk of making a mistake, related costs, lost opportunity, and unexpected consequences, to name but a few. A new cruise traveler discovers she really doesn't enjoy that venue for several reasons—e.g., she is given a bill for incidentals when she leaves the ship, she has used up her vacation time and money, and she receives unwanted materials from this company for years to come.

In the end, viewing price from the customer's perspective pays off in many ways. Most notably, it helps define value—the most important basis for creating a competitive advantage.

Price from a Societal Perspective

Price, at least in dollars and cents, has been the historical view of value. Derived from a bartering system—i.e., exchanging goods of equal value—the monetary system of each society provides a more convenient way to purchase goods and accumulate wealth. Price has also become a variable society employs to control its economic health. Price can be inclusive or exclusive. In many countries, such as Russia, China, and South Africa, high prices for products such as food, health care, housing, and automobiles, means that most of the population is excluded from purchase. In contrast, countries such as Denmark, Germany, and Great Britain charge little for health care and consequently make it available to all.

There are two different ways to look at the role price plays in a society: rational man and irrational man. The former is the primary assumption underlying economic theory, and suggests that the results of price manipulation are predictable. The latter role for price acknowledges that man's response to price is sometimes unpredictable and pretesting price manipulation is a necessary task. Let's discuss each briefly.

Rational Man Pricing: An Economic Perspective

Basically, economics assumes that the consumer is a rational decision maker and has perfect information. Therefore, if a price for a particular product goes up and the customer is aware of all relevant information, demand will be reduced for that product. Should price decline, demand would increase. That is, the quantity demanded typically rises causing a downward sloping demand curve.

A *demand curve* shows the quantity demanded at various price levels (see Figure 9.2). As a seller changes the price requested to a lower level, the product or service may become an attractive use of financial resources to a larger number of buyers, thus expanding the total market for the item. This total market demand by all buyers for a product type (not just for the company's own brand name) is called *primary demand.* Additionally, a lower price may cause buyers to shift purchases from competitors, assuming that the competitors do not meet the lower price. If primary demand does not expand and competitors meet the lower price the result will be lower total revenue for all sellers.

Since, in the U.S., we operate as a free market economy, there are few instances when someone outside the organization controls a product's price. Even commodity-like products such as air travel, gasoline, and telecommunications, now determine their own prices. Because large companies have economists on staff and buy into the assumptions of economic theory as it relates to price, the classic price–demand relationship dictates the economic health of most societies. Alan Greenspan, Chairman of the U. S. Federal Reserve, determines interest rates charged by banks as well as the money supply, thereby directly affecting price (especially of stocks and bonds). He is considered by many to be the most influential person in the world.

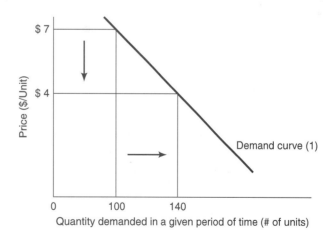

A $3 reduction in price unit would cause a 40-unit increase in the quantity demanded assuming no other variable changes.

FIGURE 9.2   Price and demand

Irrational Man Pricing: Freedom Rules

There are simply too many examples to the contrary to believe that the economic assumptions posited under the rational man model are valid. Prices go up and people buy more. Prices go down and people become suspicious and buy less. Sometimes we simply behave in an irrational manner. Clearly, as noted in our earlier discussion on consumers, there are other factors operating in the marketplace. The ability of paying a price few others can afford may be irrational, but it provides important personal status. There are even people who refuse to buy anything on sale. Or, others who buy everything on sale. Often businesses are willing to hire a $10,000 consultant, who does no more than a $5,000 consultant, simply to show the world they're successful.

In many societies, an additional irrational phenomenon may exist—support of those that cannot pay. In the U.S., there are literally thousands of not-for-profit organizations that provide goods and services to individuals for very little cost or free. There are also government agencies that do even more. Imagine what giving away surplus food to the needy does to the believers of the economic model.

Pricing planners must be aware of both the rational as well as the irrational model, since, at some level, both are likely operating in a society. Choosing one over the other is neither wise nor necessary.

The Marketer's View of Price

Price is important to marketers, because it represents marketers' assessment of the value customers see in the product or service and are willing to pay for a product or service. A number of factors have changed the way marketers undertake the pricing of their products and services.[1]

1. Foreign competition has put considerable pressure on U.S. firms' pricing strategies. Many foreign-made products are high in quality and compete in U.S. markets on the basis of lower price for good value.

2. Competitors often try to gain market share by reducing their prices. The price reduction is intended to increase demand from customers who are judged to be sensitive to changes in price.

3. New products are far more prevalent today than in the past. Pricing a new product can represent a challenge, as there is often no historical basis for pricing new products. If a new product is priced incorrectly, the marketplace will react unfavorably and the "wrong" price can do long-term damage to a product's chances for marketplace success.

4. Technology has led to existing products having shorter marketplace lives. New products are introduced to the market more frequently, reducing the "shelf life" of existing products. As a result, marketers face pressures to price products to recover costs more quickly. Prices must be set for early successes including fast sales growth, quick market penetration, and fast recovery of research and development costs.

PRICING OBJECTIVES

Firms rely on price to cover the cost of production, to pay expenses, and to provide the profit incentive necessary to continue to operate the business. We might think of these fac-

MARKETING CAPSULE *9.1*

1. Price should be viewed from three perspectives:
   a. The customer
   b. The marketer
   c. Society

2. Pricing objectives:
   a. Survival
   b. Profit

    c. Sales
    d. Market share
    e. Image

tors as helping organizations to: (1) survive, (2) earn a profit, (3) generate sales, (4) secure an adequate share of the market, and (5) gain an appropriate image.

1. *Survival:* It is apparent that most managers wish to pursue strategies that enable their organizations to continue in operation for the long term. So survival is one major objective pursued by most executives. For a commercial firm, the price paid by the buyer generates the firm's revenue. If revenue falls below cost for a long period of time, the firm cannot survive.

2. *Profit:* Survival is closely linked to profitability. Making a $500,000 profit during the next year might be a pricing objective for a firm. Anything less will ensure failure. All business enterprises must earn a long-term profit. For many businesses, long-term profitability also allows the business to satisfy their most important constituents—stockholders. Lower-than-expected or no profits will drive down stock prices and may prove disastrous for the company.

3. *Sales:* Just as survival requires a long-term profit for a business enterprise, profit requires sales. As you will recall from earlier in the text, the task of marketing management relates to managing demand. Demand must be managed in order to regulate exchanges or sales. Thus marketing management's aim is to alter sales patterns in some desirable way.

4. *Market Share:* If the sales of Safeway Supermarkets in the Dallas–Fort Worth metropolitan area account for 30% of all food sales in that area, we say that Safeway has a 30% market share. Management of all firms, large and small, are concerned with maintaining an adequate share of the market so that their sales volume will enable the firm to survive and prosper. Again, pricing strategy is one of the tools that is significant in creating and sustaining market share. Prices must be set to attract the appropriate market segment in significant numbers.

5. *Image:* Price policies play an important role in affecting a firm's position of respect and esteem in its community. Price is a highly visible communicator. It must convey the message to the community that the firm offers good value, that it is fair in its dealings with the public, that it is a reliable place to patronize, and that it stands behind its products and services.

DEVELOPING A PRICING STRATEGY

While pricing a product or service may seem to be a simple process, it is not. As an illustration of the typical pricing process, consider the following quote: "Pricing is guesswork. It is usually assumed that marketers use scientific methods to determine the price of their products. Nothing could be further from the truth. In almost every case, the process of decision is one of guesswork."[2]

Good pricing strategy is usually based on sound assumptions made by marketers. It is also based on an understanding of the two other perspectives discussed earlier. Clearly, sale pricing may prove unsuccessful unless the marketer adopts the consumer's perspective toward price. Similarly, a company should not charge high prices if it hurts society's health. Hertz illustrates how this can be done in the Integrated Marketing Box that follows.

A pricing decision that must be made by all organizations concerns their competitive position within their industry. This concern manifests itself in either a competitive pricing strategy or a nonprice competitive strategy. Let's look at the latter first.

Nonprice Competition

Nonprice competition means that organizations use strategies other than price to attract customers. Advertising, credit, delivery, displays, private brands, and convenience are all example of tools used in nonprice competition. Businesspeople prefer to use nonprice competition

---

INTEGRATED MARKETING *9.1*

HOW TO SELECT THE BEST PRICE

The Hertz Corporation knows when its rental cars will be gone and it knows when the lots will be full. How? By tracking demand throughout past six years. "We know, based on past performance and seasonal changes, what times of year there is a weak demand, and when there is too much demand for our supply of cars," says Wayne Meserue, director of pricing and yield management at Hertz. To help strike a balance, the company uses a pricing strategy called "yield management" that keeps supply and demand in check. The strategy looks at two aspects of Hertz's pricing: the rate that is charged and the length of the rental.

"Price is a legitimate rationing device," says Meserue. "What we're really talking about is efficient distribution, pricing, and response in the marketplace." For example, there are times when cars are in great demand. "It's always a gamble, but it's definitely a calculated gamble. With yield management, we monitor demand day by day, and adjust (prices as necessary)," Meserue says.

Hertz also uses length of rental as a yield management device. For instance, they established a three-night minimum for car rentals during President's Day weekend in February. "We didn't want to be turning away business for someone who wanted the car for five nights just because we had given our cars to people who came in first for one night," says Meserue, who adds that it's often better for Hertz to mandate a minimum number of days for a rental, because it ensures that cars will be rented for more days.

A smart pricing strategy is essential for increasing profit margins and reducing supply. Yet at last count, only 15% of large corporations were conducting any sort of pricing research, reports Robert Dolan, professor at Harvard Business School. "People don't realize that if you can raise your prices by just one percent, that's a big increase in your profit margin," he says. For example, if a supermarket is operating with a two-percent net margin, raising the prices by one percent will increase profitability by 33%. "The key is not taking one percent across the board, but raising it 10% for 10% of your customers," says Dolan. "Find those segments of the market that are willing to take the increase." That doesn't mean that companies can automatically pass their cost increases on to the customer, notes Dolan. If the costs are affecting an entire industry, then those costs can be passed through easily to the consumer, because competitors will likely follow the lead.

A fundamental point in smart pricing, according to Dolan: base prices on the value to the customer. As much as people talk about customer focus, they often price according to their own costs. Companies can profit from customizing prices to different customers. The value of a product can vary widely depending on factors such as age and location.

Source: Ginger Conlon, "Making Sure the Price is Right," *Sales and Marketing Management*, May 1996, pp. 92–93; Thomas T. Nagle and Reed K. Holden, *The Strategy and Tactics of Pricing*, 2nd ed., Upper Saddle River, N.J.: Prentice Hall, Inc. 1995; William C. Symonds, "'Build a Better Mousetrap' is No Claptrap," *Business Week*, February 1, 1999, p. 47; Marcia Savage, "Intel to Slash Pentium II Prices," *Company Reseller News*, February 8, 1999, pp. 1, 10.

AD 9.1 An example of nonprice competition.

rather than price competition, because it is more difficult to match nonprice characteristics. Competing on the basis of price may also have a deleterious impact on company profitability. Unfortunately, when most businesses think about price competition, they view it as matching the lower price of a competitor, rather than pricing smarter. In fact, it may be wiser not to engage in price competition for other reasons. Price may simply not offer the business a competitive advantage (employing the value equation).

Competitive Pricing

Once a business decides to use price as a primary competitive strategy, there are many well-established tools and techniques that can be employed. The pricing process normally begins with a decision about the company's pricing approach to the market.

Approaches to the Market

Price is a very important decision criteria that customers use to compare alternatives. It also contributes to the company's position. In general, a business can price itself to match its competition, price higher, or price lower. Each has its pros and cons.

Pricing to Meet Competition   Many organizations attempt to establish prices that, on average, are the same as those set by their more important competitors. Automobiles of the same size and having equivalent equipment tend to have similar prices. This strategy means that the organization uses price as an indicator or baseline. Quality in production, better service, creativity in advertising, or some other element of the marketing mix are used to attract customers who are interested in products in a particular price category,

The keys to implementing a strategy of meeting competitive prices are an accurate definition of competition and a knowledge of competitor's prices. A maker of hand-crafted leather shoes is not in competition with mass producers. If he/she attempts to compete with mass producers on price, higher production costs will make the business unprofitable. A more realistic definition of competition for this purpose would be other makers of hand-crafted leather shoes. Such a definition along with a knowledge of their prices would allow a manager to put the strategy into effect. Banks shop competitive banks every day to check their prices.

Pricing Above Competitors   Pricing above competitors can be rewarding to organizations, provided that the objectives of the policy are clearly understood and that the marketing mix is used to develop a strategy to enable management to implement the policy successfully.

Pricing above competition generally requires a clear advantage on some nonprice element of the marketing mix. In some cases, it is possible due to a high price–quality association on the part of potential buyers. But such an assumption is increasingly dangerous in today's information-rich environment. *Consumer Reports* and other similar publications make objective product comparisons much simpler for the consumer. There are also hundreds of dot.com companies that provide objective price comparisons. The key is to prove to customers that your product justifies a premium price.

Pricing Below Competitors   While some firms are positioned to price above competition, others wish to carve out a market niche by pricing below competitors. The goal of such a policy is to realize a large sales volume through a lower price and profit margins. By controlling costs and reducing services, these firms are able to earn an acceptable profit, even though profit per unit is usually less.

Such a strategy can be effective if a significant segment of the market is price-sensitive and/or the organization's cost structure is lower than competitors. Costs can be reduced by increased efficiency, economics of scale, or by reducing or eliminating such things as credit, delivery, and advertising. For example, if a firm could replace its field sales force with telemarketing or online access, this function might be performed at lower cost. Such reductions often involve some loss in effectiveness, so the tradeoff must be considered carefully.

Historically, one of the worst outcomes that can result from pricing lower than a competitor is a "price war." Price wars usually occur when a business believes that price-cutting produces increased market share, but does not have a true cost advantage. Price wars are often caused by companies misreading or misunderstanding competitors. Typically, price wars are overreactions to threats that either aren't there at all or are not as big as they seem.

Another possible drawback when pricing below competition is the company's inability to raise price or image. A retailer such as K-mart, known as a discount chain, found it impossible to reposition itself as a provider of designer women's clothiers. Can you image Swatch selling a $3,000 watch?

How can companies cope with the pressure created by reduced prices? Some are redesigning products for ease and speed of manufacturing or reducing costly features that their customers do not value. Other companies are reducing rebates and discounts in favor of stable, everyday low prices (ELP). In all cases, these companies are seeking shelter from pricing pressures that come from the discount mania that has been common in the U.S. for the last two decades.

NEW PRODUCT PRICING

A somewhat different pricing situation relates to new product pricing. With a totally new product, competition does not exist or is minimal. What price level should be set in such cases? Two general strategies are most common—penetration and skimming. *Penetration pricing* in the introductory stage of a new product's lifecycle means accepting a lower profit margin and to price relatively low. Such a strategy should generate greater sales and establish the new product in the market more quickly. *Price skimming* involves the top part of the demand curve. Price is set relatively high to generate a high profit margin and sales are limited to those buyers willing to pay a premium to get the new product (see Figure 9.3).

NEWSLINE: THE RISK OF FREE PC'S

There's no such thing as a free PC. But judging from the current flood of offers for free or deeply discounted computers, you might think that the laws of economics and common sense have been repealed. In fact, all of those deals come with significant strings attached and require close examination. Some are simply losers. Others can provide substantial savings, but only for the right customers.

The offers come in two categories. In one type, consumers get a free computer along with free Internet access, but have to accept a constant stream of advertising on the screen. In the other category, the customer gets a free or deeply discounted PC in exchange for a long-term contract for paid Internet services.

Most of these are attractive deals, but the up-front commitment to $700 or more worth of Internet service means they are not for everyone. One group that will find little value in the arrangement is college students, since nearly all schools provide free and often high-speed Net access. Others who could well end up losing from these deals are the lightest and heaviest users of the Internet. People who want Internet access only to read e-mail and do a little light Web browsing would likely do better to buy an inexpensive computer and sign up for a $10-a-month limited-access account with a service provider.

People who use the Internet a lot may also be poor candidates. That's because three years is a long commitment at a time when Internet access technology is changing rapidly. Heavy users are likely to be the earliest adopters of high-speed cable or digital subscriber line service as it becomes available in their areas.

Sources: Stephen H. Weldstrom, "The High Cost of Free PCs," *Business Week*, September 13, 1999, p. 20; Steven Bruel, "Why Talk's Cheap," *Business Week*, Septeber 13, 1999, pp. 34–36; Mercedes M. Cardona and Jack Neff, "Everything's at a Premium," *Advertising Age*, August 2, 1999, pp. 12–13.

Which strategy is best depends on a number of factors. A penetration strategy would generally be supported by the following conditions: price-sensitive consumers, opportunity to keep costs low, the anticipation of quick market entry by competitors, a high likelihood for rapid acceptance by potential buyers, and an adequate resource base for the firm to meet the new demand and sales.

A skimming strategy is most appropriate when the opposite conditions exist. A premium product generally supports a skimming strategy. In this case, "premium" doesn't just denote high cost of production and materials; it also suggests that the product may be rare or that the demand is unusually high. An example would be a $500 ticket for the World Series or an $80,000 price tag for a limited-production sports car. Having legal protection via a patent or copyright may also allow for an excessively high price. Intel and their Pentium chip possessed this advantage for a long period of time. In most cases, the initial high price is gradually reduced to match new competition and allow new customers access to the product.

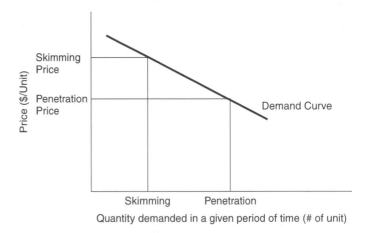

Skimming generates a higher profit margin while penetration generates greater volume.

FIGURE 9.3 Penetration and skimming: pricing strategies as they relate to the demand curve

PRICE LINES

You are already familiar with price lines. Ties may be priced at $15, $17, $20, and $22.50; bluejeans may be priced at $30, $32.95, $37.95, and $45. Each price must be far enough apart so that buyers can see definite quality differences among products. Price lines tend to be associated with consumer shopping goods such as apparel, appliances, and carpeting rather than product lines such as groceries. Customers do very little comparison-shopping on the latter.

Price lining serves several purposes that benefit both buyers and sellers. Customers want and expect a wide assortment of goods, particularly shopping goods. Many small price differences for a given item can be confusing. If ties were priced at $15, $15.35, $15.75, and so on, selection would be more difficult; the customer could not judge quality differences as reflected by such small increments in price. So, having relatively few prices reduces the confusion.

From the seller's point of view, price lining holds several benefits. First, it is simpler and more efficient to use relatively fewer prices. The product/service mix can then be tailored to selected price points. *Price points* are simply the different prices that make up the line. Second, it can result in a smaller inventory than would otherwise be the case. It might increase stock turnover and make inventory control simpler. Third, as costs change, either increasing or decreasing the prices can remain the same, but the quality in the line can be changed. For example, you may have bought a $20 tie fifteen years ago. You can buy a $20 tie today, but it is unlikely that today's $20 tie is of the same fine quality as it was in the past. While customers are likely to be aware of the differences, they are nevertheless still able to purchase a $20 tie. During inflationary periods the quality/price point relationship changes. From the point of view of salespeople, offering price lines will make selling easier. Salespeople can easily learn a small number of prices. This reduces the likelihood that they will misquote prices or make other pricing errors. Their selling effort is therefore more relaxed, and this atmosphere will influence customers positively. It also gives the salesperson flexibility. If a customer can't afford a $2,800 Gateway system, the $2,200 system is suggested.

PRICE FLEXIBILITY

Another pricing decision relates to the extent of *price flexibility*. A flexible pricing policy means that the price is bid or negotiated separately for each exchange. This is a common practice when selling to organizational markets where each transaction is typically quite large. In such cases, the buyer may initiate the process by asking for bidding on a product or service that meets certain specifications. Alternatively, a buyer may select a supplier and attempt to negotiate the best possible price. Marketing effectiveness in many industrial markets requires a certain amount of price flexibility.

Discounts and Allowances

In addition to decisions related to the base price of products and services, marketing managers must also set policies related to the use of discounts and allowances. There are many different types of price reductions—each designed to accomplish a specific purpose.

Quantity discounts are reductions in base price given as the result of a buyer purchasing some predetermined quantity of merchandise. A noncumulative quantity discount applies

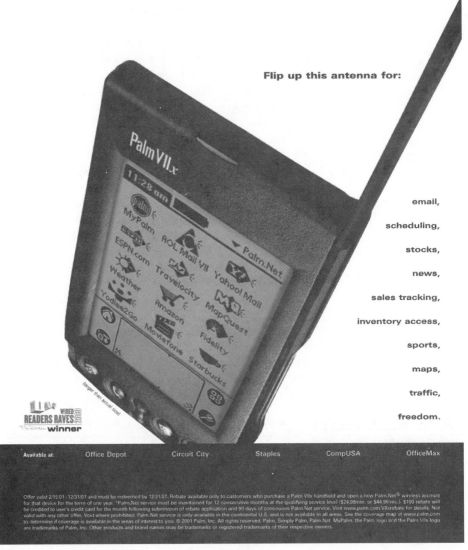

AD 9.2 A rebate can be a very effective price discount.

to each purchase and is intended to encourage buyers to make larger purchases. This means that the buyer holds the excess merchandise until it is used, possibly cutting the inventory cost of the seller and preventing the buyer from switching to a competitor at least until the stock is used. A cumulative quantity discount applies to the total bought over a period of time. The buyer adds to the potential discount with each additional purchase. Such a policy helps to build repeat purchases. Building material dealers, for example, find such a policy quite useful in encouraging builders to concentrate their purchase with one dealer and to continue with the same dealer over time. It should be noted that such cumulative quantity discounts are extremely difficult to defend if attacked in the courts.

Seasonal discounts are price reductions given on out-of-season merchandise. An example would be a discount on snowmobiles during the summer. The intention of such discounts is to spread demand over the year. This can allow fuller use of production facilities and improved cash flow during the year. Electric power companies use the logic of seasonal discounts to encourage customers to shift consumption to off-peak periods. Since these companies must have production capacity to meet peak demands, the lowering of the peak can lessen the generating capacity required.

Cash discounts are reductions on base price given to customers for paying cash or within some short time period. For example, a two-percent discount on bills paid within ten days is a cash discount. The purpose is generally to accelerate the cash flow of the organization.

Trade discounts are price reductions given to middlemen (e.g., wholesalers, industrial distributors, retailers) to encourage them to stock and give preferred treatment to an organization's products. For example, a consumer goods company may give a retailer a 20% discount to place a larger order for soap. Such a discount might also be used to gain shelf space or a preferred position in the store.

Personal allowances are similar devices aimed at middlemen. Their purpose is to encourage middlemen to aggressively promote the organization's products. For example, a furniture manufacturer may offer to pay some specified amount toward a retailer's advertising expenses if the retailer agrees to include the manufacturer's brand name in the ads.

INTEGRATED MARKETING 9.2

BEAM ME UP, SCOTTY!

You remember William Shatner, a.k.a. Captain James T. Kirk. As Kirk, he represented the epitome of integrity and professionalism. Death was better than compromise. Yet, here he is doing rather strange TV ads for Priceline.com. Inc. Why? Probably because he's being paid a ton of money, and he's having fun. Working for an apparent winner is also exciting.

We say "apparent" because transferring Priceline's patented "name your own price" system of selling airline tickets, groceries, cars, gasoline, telephone minutes, and a raft of other products is proving quite difficult. Complicating matters, several airlines and hotels are studying whether to launch Web services that could cut the legs out from under Priceline's established travel businesses.

Priceline could soon face stiff competition from its own suppliers. Hyatt, Marriott, Starwood, and Cendant—most of which sell excess hotel rooms through Priceline—are having serious discussions about starting their own company to distribute over the Internet. Essentially, these chains worry that by handing sales to Priceline, they could lose control of their customers. Several airlines have the same concerns.

To stay one step ahead, Priceline has decided to introduce 18 new products. Initially, Priceline generated 90% of its revenues from airline tickets, rental cars, and hotel rooms. By 2003, Priceline estimates that only 50% of revenues will come from these sources.

By June 2000, users were able to name their price for long-distance phone service, gasoline, and cruises. At the end of 2000, Priceline.com started selling blocks of long-distance phone time to small companies. Later, it will offer them ad space, freight services, and office equipment. New joint ventures are in the works with companies in Hong Kong, Australia, Japan, Europe, and Latin America.

Execs at Priceline say they're on the right track and that they're building a broad-based discounting powerhouse.

Sources: Pamela L. Moore, "Name Your Price—For Everything?" *Business Week*, April 17, 2000, pp. 72–75; "Priceline.com to Let Callers Name Price," *Los Angeles Times*, Nov. 9, 1999, p. 3; "Priceline to offer auto insurance," *Wall Street Journal*, Aug. 3, 2000, p. 12; "Priceline teams up with 3 phone companies to sell long distance," *Wall Street Journal*, May 2000, p. 16.

Some manufacturers or wholesalers also give prize money called *spiffs* for retailers to pass on to the retailer's sales clerks for aggressively selling certain items. This is especially common in the electronics and clothing industries, where it is used primarily with new products, slow movers, or high margin items.

Trade-in allowances also reduce the base price of a product or service. These are often used to allow the seller to negotiate the best price with a buyer. The trade-in may, of course, be of value if it can be resold. Accepting trade-ins is necessary in marketing many types of products. A construction company with a used grader worth $70,000 would not likely buy a new model from an equipment company that did not accept trade-ins, particularly when other companies do accept them.

PRICE BUNDLING

A very popular pricing strategy, *price bundling*, is to group similar or complementary products and to charge a total price that is lower if they were sold separately. Dell Computers and Gateway Computers follow this strategy by combining different components for a set price. Customers assume that these computer experts are putting together an effective product package and they are paying less. The underlying assumption of this pricing strategy is that the increased sales generated will more than compensate for a lower profit margin. It may also be a way of selling a less popular product by combining it with popular ones. Clearly, industries such as financial services and telecommunications are big users of this.

PSYCHOLOGICAL ASPECTS OF PRICING

Price, as is the case with certain other elements in the marketing mix, appears to have meaning to many buyers that goes beyond a simple utilitarian statement. Such meaning is often referred to as the *psychological aspect* of pricing. Inferring quality from price is a common example of the psychological aspect. A buyer may assume that a suit priced at $500 is of higher quality than one priced at $300. From a cost-of-production, raw material, or workmanship perspective, this may or may not be the case. The seller may be able to secure the higher price by nonprice means such as offering alterations and credit or the benefit to the buyer may be in meeting some psychological need such as ego enhancement. In some situations, the higher price may be paid simply due to lack of information or lack of comparative shopping skills. For some products or services, the quantity demanded may actually rise to some extent as price is increased. This might be the case with an item such as a fur coat. Such a pricing strategy is called *prestige pricing*.

Products and services frequently have *customary prices* in the minds of consumers. A customary price is one that customers identify with particular items. For example, for many decades a five-stick package of chewing gum cost five cents and a six-ounce bottle of Coca-Cola cost five cents. Candy bars now cost 60 cents or more, a customary price for a standard-sized bar. Manufacturers tend to adjust their wholesale prices to permit retailers in using customary pricing. However, as we have witnessed during the past decade, prices have changed so often that customary prices are weakened.

Another manifestation of the psychological aspects of pricing is the use of *odd prices*.[3] We call prices that end in such digits as 5, 7, 8, and 9 "odd prices" (e.g., $2.95, $15.98, or $299.99). Even prices are $3, $16, or $300. For a long time marketing people have attempted to explain why odd prices are used. It seems to make little difference whether one pays $29.95 or $30 for an item. Perhaps one of the most often heard explanations concerns the

AD 9.3 Winning an award is a psychological aspect of price.

psychological impact of odd prices on customers. The explanation is that customers perceive even prices such as $5 or $10 as regular prices. Odd prices, on the other hand, appear to represent bargains or savings and therefore encourage buying. There seems to be some movement toward even pricing; however, odd pricing is still very common. A somewhat related pricing strategy is *combination pricing*. Examples are two-for-one, buy-one-get-one-free. Consumers tend to react very positively to these pricing techniques.

MARKETING CAPSULE *9.2*

1. Developing a pricing strategy
   a. Nonprice competition
   b. Competitive pricing

2. New product pricing
   a. Penetration
   b. Skimming

3. Price lining means a number of sequential price points are offered within a product category.

4. Price flexibility allows for different prices charged for different customers and/or under different situations.

5. Price bundling groups similar or complementary products and charges a total price that is lower than if they were sold separately.

6. Certain pricing strategies, such as prestige pricing, customary pricing, or odd pricing, play on the psychological perspectives of the consumer.

ALTERNATIVE APPROACHES TO DETERMINING PRICE

Price determination decisions can be based on a number of factors, including cost, demand, competition, value, or some combination of factors. However, while many marketers are aware that they should consider these factors, pricing remains somewhat of an art. For purposes of discussion, we categorize the alternative approaches to determining price as follows: (1) cost-oriented pricing; (2) demand-oriented pricing; and (3) value-based approaches.

Cost-Oriented Pricing: Cost-Plus and Mark-Ups

The *cost-plus* method, sometimes called *gross margin pricing*, is perhaps most widely used by marketers to set price. The manager selects as a goal a particular gross margin that will produce a desirable profit level. Gross margin is the difference between how much the goods cost and the actual price for which it sells. This gross margin is designated by a percent of net sales. The percent selected varies among types of merchandise. That means that one product may have a goal of 48% gross margin while another has a target of 33⅓ % or 2%.

A primary reason that the cost-plus method is attractive to marketers is that they do not have to forecast general business conditions or customer demand. If sales volume projections are reasonably accurate, profits will be on target. Consumers may also view this method as fair, since the price they pay is related to the cost of producing the item. Likewise, the marketer is sure that costs are covered.

A major disadvantage of cost-plus pricing is its inherent inflexibility. For example, department stores have often found difficulty in meeting competition from discount stores, catalog retailers, or furniture warehouses because of their commitment to cost-plus pricing. Another disadvantage is that it does not take into account consumers' perceptions of a product's value. Finally, a company's costs may fluctuate so constant price changing is not a viable strategy.

When middlemen use the term *mark-up*, they are referring to the difference between the average cost and price of all merchandise in stock, for a particular department, or for an individual item. The difference may be expressed in dollars or as a percentage. For example, a man's tie costs $4.60 and is sold for $8. The dollar mark-up is $3.40. The mark-up may be designated as a percent of selling price or as a percent of cost of the merchandise. In this example, the mark-up is 74% of cost ($3.40/$4.60) or 42.5% of the retail price ($3.40/$8).

There are several reasons why expressing mark-up as a percentage of selling price is preferred to expressing it as a percentage of cost. One is that many other ratios are expressed as a percentage of sales. For instance, selling expenses are expressed as a percentage of sales. If selling costs are 8%, this means that for each $100,000 in net sales, the cost of selling the merchandise is $8,000. Advertising expenses, operating expenses, and other types of expenses are quoted in the same way. Thus, there is a consistency when making comparisons in expressing all expenses and costs, including mark-up, as a percentage of sales (selling price).

Middlemen receive merchandise daily and make sales daily. As new shipments are received, the goods are marked and put into stock. *Cumulative mark-up* is the term applied to the difference between total dollar delivered cost of all merchandise and the total dollar price of the goods put into stock for a specified period of time. The original mark-up at which individual items are put into stock is referred to as the *initial mark-up*.

Maintained mark-up is another important concept. The maintained mark-up percentage is an essential figure in estimating operating profits. It also provides an indication of efficiency. Maintained mark-up, sometimes called *gross cost of goods*, is the difference between the actual price for which all of the merchandise is sold and the total dollar delivered cost of the goods exclusive of deductions. The maintained mark-up is typically less than the initial mark-up due to mark-downs and stock shrinkages from theft, breakage, and the like. Maintained mark-up is particularly important for seasonal merchandise that will likely be marked-down substantially at the end of the season.

Although this pricing approach may seem overly simplified, it has definite merit. The problem facing managers of certain types of businesses such as retail food stores is that they must price a very large number of items and change many of those prices frequently. The standard mark-up usually reflects historically profitable margins and provides a good guideline for pricing.

To illustrate this cost-based process of pricing, let's look at the case of Johnnie Walker Black Label Scotch Whiskey. This product sells for about $30 in most liquor stores. How was this price derived?

> $5.00 production, distillation, maturation + $2.50 advertising + $3.11 distribution + $4.39 taxes + $7.50 mark-up (retailer) + $7.50 net margin (manufacturer)

Certainly costs are an important component of pricing. No firm can make a profit until it covers its costs. However, the process of determining costs and then setting a price based on costs does not take into consideration what the customer is willing to pay at the marketplace. As a result, many companies that have set out to develop a product have fallen victim to the desire to continuously add features to the product, thus adding cost. When the product is finished, these companies add some percentage to the cost and expect customers to pay the resulting price. These companies are often disappointed, as customers are not willing to pay this cost-based price.

Break-Even Analysis

A somewhat more sophisticated approach to cost-based pricing is the *break-even analysis*. The information required for the formula for break-even analysis is available from the accounting records in most firms. The break-even price is the price that will produce enough revenue to cover all costs at a given level of production. Total cost can be divided into fixed and variable (total cost = fixed cost + variable cost). Recall that *fixed cost* does not change as the level of production goes up or down. The rent paid for the building to house the operation might be an example. No cost is fixed in the long run, but in the short run, many expenses cannot realistically be changed. *Variable cost* does change as production is increased or decreased. For example, the cost of raw material to make the product will vary with production.

A second shortcoming of break-even analysis is it assumes that variable costs are constant. However, wages will increase with overtime and shipping discounts will be obtained. Third, break-even assumes that all costs can be neatly categorized as fixed or variable. Where advertising expenses are entered, break-even analysis will have a significant impact on the resulting break-even price and volume.

Target Rates of Return

Break-even pricing is a reasonable approach when there is a limit on the quantity which a firm can provide and particularly when a *target return* objective is sought. Assume, for example, that the firm with the costs illustrated in the previous example determines that it can provide no more than 10,000 units of the product in the next period of operation. Furthermore, the firm has set a target for profit of 20% above total costs. Referring again to internal accounting records and the changing cost of production at near capacity levels, a new total cost curve is calculated. From the cost curve profile, management sets the desirable level of production at 80% of capacity or 8,000 units. From the total cost curve, it is determined that the cost for producing 8,000 units is $18,000. Twenty percent of $18,000 is $3,600. Adding this to the total cost at 8,000 units yields the point at that quantity through which the total revenue curve must pass. Finally, $21,600 divided by 8,000 units yields the price of $2.70 per unit; here the $3,600 in profit would be realized. The obvious shortcoming of the target return approach to pricing is the absence of any information concerning the demand for the product at the desired price. It is assumed that all of the units will be sold at the price which provides the desired return.

It would be necessary, therefore, to determine whether the desired price is in fact attractive to potential customers in the marketplace. If break-even pricing is to be used, it should be supplemented by additional information concerning customer perceptions of the relevant range of prices for the product. The source of this information would most commonly be survey research, as well as a thorough review of pricing practices by competitors in the industry. In spite of their shortcomings, break-even pricing and target return pricing are very common business practices.

Demand-Oriented Pricing

Demand-oriented pricing focuses on the nature of the demand curve for the product or service being priced. The nature of the demand curve is influenced largely by the structure of the industry in which a firm competes. That is, if a firm operates in an industry that is extremely competitive, price may be used to some strategic advantage in acquiring and maintaining market share. On the other hand, if the firm operates in an environment with a few dominant players, the range in which price can vary may be minimal.

Value-Based Pricing

If we consider the three approaches to setting price, cost-based is focused entirely on the perspective of the company with very little concern for the customer; demand-based is focused on the customer, but only as a predictor of sales; and value-based focuses entirely on the customer as a determinant of the total price/value package. Marketers who employ value-based pricing might use the following definition: "It is what you think your product is worth to that customer at that time." Moreover, it acknowledges several marketing/price truths:

- To the customer, price is the only unpleasant part of buying.
- Price is the easiest marketing tool to copy.
- Price represents everything about the product.

Still, value-based pricing is not altruistic. It asks and answers two questions: (1) what is the highest price I can charge and still make the sale? and (2) am I willing to sell at that price? The first question must take two primary factors into account: customers and competitors. The second question is influenced by two more: costs and constraints. Let's discuss each briefly.

Many customer-related factors are important in value-based pricing. For example, it is critical to understand the *customer buying process*. How important is price? When is it considered? How is it used? Another factor is the *cost of switching*. Have you ever watched the TV program "The Price is Right"? If you have, you know that most consumers have poor price knowledge. Moreover, their knowledge of comparable prices within a product category—e.g., ketchup—is typically worse. So *price knowledge* is a relevant factor. Finally, the marketer must assess the customers' *price expectations*. How much do you expect to pay for a large pizza? Color TV? DVD? Newspaper? Swimming pool? These expectations create a phenomenon called "sticker shock" as exhibited by gasoline, automobiles, and ATM fees.

A second factor influencing value-based pricing is *competitors*. As noted in earlier chapters, defining competition is not always easy. Of course there are like-category competitors such as Toyota and Nissan. We have already discussed the notion of pricing above, below, and at the same level of these direct competitors. However, there are also indirect competitors that consumers may use to base price comparisons. For instance, we may use the price of a vacation as a basis for buying vacation clothes. The cost of eating out is compared to the cost of groceries. There are also instances when a competitor, especially a market leader, dictates the price for everyone else. Weyerhauser determines the price for lumber. Kellogg establishes the price for cereal.

If you're building a picnic table, it is fairly easy to add up your receipts and calculate costs. For a global corporation, determining costs is a great deal more complex. For example, calculating *incremental* costs and identifying *avoidable* costs are valuable tasks. *Incremental* cost is the cost of producing each additional unit. If the incremental cost begins to exceed the incremental revenue, it is a clear sign to quit producing. *Avoidable* costs are those that are unnecessary or can be passed onto some other institution in the marketing channel. Adding costly features to a product that the customer cannot use is an example of the former. As to the latter, the banking industry has been passing certain costs onto customers.

Another consideration is *opportunity costs*. Because the company spent money on store remodeling, they are not able to take advantage of a discounted product purchase. Finally, costs vary from market-to-market as well as quantities sold. Research should be conducted to assess these differences.

Although it would be nice to assume that a business has the freedom to set any price it chooses, this is not always the case. There are a variety of *constraints* that prohibit such freedom. Some constraints are formal, such as government restrictions in respect to strategies like collusion and price-fixing. This occurs when two or more companies agree to charge the same or very similar prices. Other constraints tend to be informal. Examples include matching the price of competitors, a traditional price charged for a particular product, and charging a price that covers expected costs.

Ultimately, value-based pricing offers the following three tactical recommendations:

- Employ a segmented approach toward price, based on such criteria as customer type, location, and order size.

1. Approaches to determining price include:
   a. Cost-plus and mark-ups
   b. Demand-oriented pricing
   c. Value-based approaches to pricing

- Establish highest possible price level and justify it with comparable value.
- Use price as a basis for establishing strong customer relationships.[4]

THE FUTURE OF PRICING

For too long, pricing decisions have been dominated by economists, discounters, and financial analysts. While making a reasonable profit remains a necessity, pricing must become a more strategic element of marketing. Smarter pricing, as portrayed by the value-based strategy, appears to represent the future. A case in point is the Ford Motor Co., which managed to earn $7.2 billion in 2000, more than any automaker in history. Despite a loss of market share, the key to their success was a 420,000-unit decrease in sales of low-margin vehicles such as Escorts and Aspires, and a 600,000-unit increase in sales of high-margin vehicles such as Crown Victorias and Explorers. Ford cut prices on its most profitable vehicles enough to spur demand, but not so much that they ceased to have attractive margins.

IN PRACTICE

Customers make judgments about pricing based on perceived value, not production costs. For organizations, however, pricing determines the primary source of revenue for the business. Various market segments and their respective price sensitivities must be considered when marketers decide on a pricing strategy.

Increasingly, marketers are responsible for pricing. Marketers must understand strategies previously reserved for economists and financial analysts. Questions of price points, price lining, and price bundling now fall to marketers.

What do marketers need to know to price products to maximize profits and capture market share? Break-even analyses, target rates of return, and mark-ups are a few of the processes marketers must master.

To learn more about profits and pricing, click on the Interactive Journal's link to **Money & Investing** on the **Front Section**.

In this section you'll find information about interest rates, economic conditions, and venture capital. Because interest rates affect consumer spending, it is important to understand economic indicators and their impact.

The **Business Focus** section of **Marketplace** is a good resource for articles that discuss various business marketing issues, including pricing.

Naming your own price is the strategy for Priceline.com. Customers name their own price for plane tickets, hotel rooms, and rental cars. Initially, the company relished great success. However, it has recently suffered financial losses, due in part to the "Name Your Own Price" strategy. Visit the site now at www.priceline.com.

Facilitating exchanges between customers is a successful business strategy for eBay. Calling itself "the world's online marketplace," eBay has created a trading medium for anyone interested in buying or selling items online. Items range from one-of-a-kind collectibles to everyday items such as musical instruments and sporting goods. Check out the Web site now at www.ebay.com.

DELIVERABLE

The airline industry competes heavily on price. Select two airlines and research fares for one round trip ticket on each airline, any destination. Visit several Web sites that sell airline tickets and compare fares. Compare these prices to those offered on the airlines' Web sites. Check your local newspaper for fare prices, too. Write a one-page overview of your findings.

DISCUSSION QUESTIONS

1. How do organizations decide whether to price to meet, price above, or price below competition? How do organizations measure the success or failure of their chosen strategy?
2. Are you price sensitive to any products? Do you engage in comparative shopping, searching for the "best deal"?
3. How has the Internet affected pricing strategies? How do Internet companies compete with traditional "brick and mortar" companies in pricing?

SUMMARY

The chapter begins by defining price from the perspective of the consumer, society, and the business. Each contributes to our understanding of price and positions it as a competitive advantage.

The objectives of price are fivefold: (1) survival, (2) profit, (3) sales, (4) market share, and (5) image. In addition, a pricing strategy can target to: meet competition, price above competition, and price below competition.

Several pricing tactics were discussed. They include new product pricing, price lining, price flexibility, price bundling, and the psychological aspects of pricing.

The chapter concludes with a description of the three alternative approaches to pricing: cost-oriented, demand-oriented, and value-based.

MARKETER'S VOCABULARY

Demand curve   Quantity demanded at various price levels.

Nonprice competition   Organization uses strategies other than price to attract customers.

Price war   Pricing significantly lower than competition.

Penetration pricing   Accepting a lower profit margin during the introduction of a product.

Price skimming   Price set relatively high to generate a high profit margin.

Price lining   Selling a product with several price points.

Quantity discounts   Reduction in base price given as the result of a buyer purchasing some pre-determined quantity of merchandise.

Seasonal discounts   Price discount given on out-of-season merchandise.

Cash discounts   Reduction on base price given to customers for paying cash or paying within a short period of time.

Trade discount   Price reductions given to middlemen to encourage them to stock and give pre-ferred treatment to an organization's product.

Spiffs   Prize money given to retailers to pass on to the retailer's sales personnel for selling certain items.

Price bundling   Grouping similar complementary products and charging a total price that is lower than if they were sold separately.

Mark-up   Difference between the average cost and price of a product.

Break-even price   Price that will produce enough revenue to cover all costs at a given level of production.

Value-based pricing   What that product is worth to that customer at that point in time.

DISCUSSION QUESTIONS

1. Why is price an important part of the marketing mix?

2. Who typically has responsibility for setting prices in most organizations? Why?

3. Discuss the objectives which pricing policies can be established to accomplish.

4. What conditions are necessary if a "pricing above the competition" strategy is to be successful?

5. Discuss the alternative strategies that can be adopted in new product pricing. Under what conditions should each be used?

6. List some advantages of psychological pricing. What are some of the risks?

7. What are some of the more common types of discounts and allowances and the purpose of each?

8. What is price lining? What benefits does price lining hold for customers?

9. What advantage might a uniform delivered price have for a seller?

PROJECT

Interview a marketing person responsible for pricing in their organization.
Assess the type of pricing strategy they use and why. Write a three- to five-page report.

CASE APPLICATION

UNITED TECHTRONICS

United Techtronics faced a major pricing decision with respect to its new video screen television. "We're really excited here at United Techtronics," exclaimed Roy Cowing, founder and president of United Techtronics. "We've made a most significant technological breakthrough in large screen, video television systems." He went on to explain that the marketing plan for this product was now his major area of concern and that what price to charge was the marketing question that was giving him the most difficulty.

Cowing founded United Techtronics (UT) in Boston in 1959. Prior to that time, Cowing had been an associate professor of electrical engineering at M.I.T. Cowing founded UT to manufacture and market products making use of some of the electronic inventions he had developed while at M.I.T. Sales were made mostly to the space program and the military.

For a number of years, Cowing had been trying to reduce the company's dependency on government sales. One of the diversification projects that he had committed research and development monies to was the so-called video screen project. The objective of this project was to develop a system whereby a television picture could be displayed on a screen as big as eight to ten feet diagonally. One of UT's engineers made the necessary breakthrough and developed working prototypes. Up to that point, UT had invested $600,000 in the project.

Extra-large television systems were not new. There were a number of companies who sold such systems both to the consumer and commercial (taverns, restaurants, and so on) markets. Most current systems made use of a special magnifying screen. The result of this process is that the final picture lacked much of the brightness of the original small screen. As a result, the picture had to be viewed in a darkened room. There were some other video systems that did not use the magnifying process. These systems used special tubes, but they also suffered from a lack of brightness.

UT had developed a system that was bright enough to be viewed in regular daylight on a screen up to ten feet diagonally. Cowing was unwilling to discuss how this was accomplished. He would only say that a patent protected the process and that he thought it would take at least two to three years for any competitor to duplicate the results of the system.

A number of large and small companies were active in this area. Admiral, General Electric, RCA, Zenith, and Sony were all thought to be working on developing large-screen systems directed at the consumer market. Sony was rumored to be ready to introduce a 60-inch diagonal screen system that would retail for about $2,500. A number of small companies were already producing systems. Advent Corporation, a small New England company, claimed to have sold 4,000 84-inch diagonal units at prices from $1,500 to $2,500. Cowing was adamant that none of these systems gave as bright a picture as UT's. He estimated that about 10,000 large screen systems were sold in 1996.

Cowing expected about 50% of the suggested retail-selling price to go for wholesaler and retailer margins. He expected that UT's direct manufacturing costs would vary depending on the volume produced. He expected direct labor costs to fall at higher production volumes due to the increased automation of the process and improved worker skills.

Material costs were expected to fall due to less waste due to automation. The equipment costs necessary to automate the product process were $70,000 to produce in the 0–5,000 unit range; an additional $50,000 to produce in the 5,001–10,000 unit range; and an additional $40,000 to produce in the 10,001–20,000 unit range. The useful life of this equipment was put at five years. Cowing was sure that production costs were substantially below those of current competitors including Sony. Such was the magnitude of UT's technological breakthrough. Cowing was unwilling to produce over 20,000 units a year in the first few years due to the limited cash resources of the company to support inventories and so on.

Cowing wanted to establish a position in the consumer market for his product. He felt that the long-run potential was greater there than in the commercial market. With this end in mind, he hired a small economic research-consulting firm to undertake a consumer study to determine the likely reaction to alternative retail prices for the system. These consultants took extensive pricing histories of competitive products. They concluded that, "UT's video screen system would be highly price-elastic across a range of prices from $500 to $5,000 both in a primary and secondary demand sense." They went on to estimate the price elasticity of demand in this range to be between 4.0 and 6.5.

Mr. Cowing was considering a number of alternative suggested retail prices. "I can see arguments for pricing anywhere from above Advent's to substantially below Muntz's lowest price," he said. A decision on pricing was needed soon.

Questions:

1. Should penetration pricing be used or would skimming be better?

2. What should be the base price for the new product?

REFERENCES

1. Thomas Nagle, "Pricing as Creative Marketing," *Business Horizons*, July–August 1983, pp.14–19.
2. Robert A. Robicheaux, "How Important is Pricing in Competitive Strategy?" *Proceedings of the Southern Marketing Association*, 1975, pp. 55–57.
3. Bernard F. Whalen, "Strategic Mix of Odd, Even Prices Can Lead to Retail Profits," *Marketing News*, March 1976, p. 24.
4. Peter Coy, "The Power of Smart Marketing," *Business Week*, April 10, 2000, pp. 160–162.

AD 9.4 A traditional retail ad.

CHAPTER 10

CHANNEL CONCEPTS: DISTRIBUTING THE PRODUCT

LEARNING OBJECTIVES

After reading this chapter, you should:
- Gain insight into the role of distribution channels.
- Understand the methods used in organizing channels.
- Understand the management of underlying behavioral dimensions present in most channels.
- Comprehend the elements of a channel strategy.
- Understand the tasks assigned to various channel institutions.

SAM SIGHTINGS ARE EVERYWHERE

We **began** this book with some insights on Elvis Presley and related marketing problems. Compared to Sam Walton, Elvis sightings are nonexistent. The spirit of Sam Walton permeates virtually every corner of America. This small-town retailer has produced a legacy of U.S. sales of $118 billion, or 7% of all retail sales. In the U.S., Wal-Mart has 1,921 discount stores, 512 supercenters, and 446 Sam's Clubs. Wal-Mart recently challenged local supermarkets by opening their new format: Neighborhood Markets. Overall, they have more than 800,000 people working in more than 3,500 stores on four continents.

Today, Wal-Mart is the largest seller of underwear, soap, toothpaste, children's clothes, books, videos, and compact discs. How can you challenge their Internet offerings that now number more than 500,000, with planned expansion of more than 3,000,000? Or the fact that Ol' Roy (named after Sam's Irish setter) is now the best-selling dog food brand in America? Besides Ol' Roy, Wal-Mart's garden fertilizer has also become the best-selling brand in the U.S. in its category, as has its Spring Valley line of vitamins.

So how do you beat a behemoth like Wal-Mart? One retail expert tackled this question in his autobiography. He suggests 10 ways to accomplish this goal: (1) have a strong commitment to your business; (2) involve your staff in decision making; (3) listen to your staff and your customers; (4) learn how to communicate; (5) appreciate a good job; (6) have fun; (7) set high goals for staff; (8) promise a lot, but deliver more; (9) watch your expenses; and (10) find out what the competition is doing and do something different.

The author of this autobiography: *Made in America*—Sam Walton.

Sources: Murray Raphel, "Up Against the Wal-Mart," *Direct Marketing*, April 1999, pp. 82–84; Adrienne Sanders, "Yankee Imperialists," *Forbes*, December 13, 1999, p. 36; Jack Neff, "Wal-Mart Stores Go Private (Label)," *Advertising Age*, November 29, 1999, pp. 1, 34, 36; Alice Z. Cuneo, "Wal-Mart's Goal: To Reign Over Web," *Advertising Age*, July 5, 1999, pp. 1, 27.

INTRODUCTION

This scenario highlights the importance of identifying the most efficient and effective manner in which to place a product into the hands of the customer. This mechanism of connecting the producer with the customer is referred to as the *channel of distribution*. Earlier we referred to the creation of time and place utility. This is the primary purpose of the channel. It is an extremely complex process, and in the case of many companies, it is the only element of marketing where cost savings are still possible.

In this chapter, we will look at the evolution of the channel of distribution. We shall see that several basic functions have emerged that are typically the responsibility of a channel member. Also, it will become clear that channel selection is not a static, once-and-for-all choice, but that it is a dynamic part of marketing planning. As was true for the product, the channel must be managed in order to work. Unlike the product, the channel is composed of individuals and groups that exhibit unique traits that might be in conflict, and that have a constant need to be motivated. These issues will also be addressed. Finally, the institutions or members of the channel will be introduced and discussed.

THE DUAL FUNCTIONS OF CHANNELS

Just as with the other elements of the firm's marketing program, distribution activities are undertaken to facilitate the exchange between marketers and consumers. There are two basic functions performed between the manufacturer and the ultimate consumer.[1] (See Figure 10.1.) The first, called the *exchange function*, involves sales of the product to the various members of the channel of distribution. The second, the *physical distribution function*, moves products through the exchange channel, simultaneously with title and ownership. Decisions concerning both of these sets of activities are made in conjunction with the firm's overall marketing plan and are designed so that the firm can best serve its customers in the market place. In actuality, without a channel of distribution the exchange process would be far more difficult and ineffective.

The key role that distribution plays is satisfying a firm's customers and achieving a profit for the firm. From a distribution perspective, customer satisfaction involves maximizing time and place utility to: the organization's suppliers, intermediate customers, and final

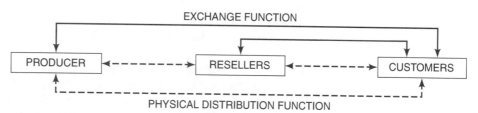

FIGURE 10.1 Dual-flow system in marketing channels

customers. In short, organizations attempt to get their products to their customers in the most effective ways. Further, as households find their needs satisfied by an increased quantity and variety of goods, the mechanism of exchange—i.e., the channel—increases in importance.

THE EVOLUTION OF THE MARKETING CHANNEL

As consumers, we have clearly taken for granted that when we go to a supermarket the shelves will be filled with products we want; when we are thirsty there will be a Coke machine or bar around the corner; and, when we don't have time to shop, we can pick-up the telephone and order from the J.C. Penney catalog or through the Internet. Of course, if we give it some thought, we realize that this magic is not a given, and that hundreds of thousands of people plan, organize, and labor long hours so that this modern convenience is available to you, the consumer. It hasn't always been this way, and it is still not this way in many other countries. Perhaps a little anthropological discussion will help our understanding.

The channel structure in a primitive culture is virtually nonexistent. The family or tribal group is almost entirely self-sufficient. The group is composed of individuals who are both communal producers and consumers of whatever goods and services can be made available. As economies evolve, people begin to specialize in some aspect of economic activity. They engage in farming, hunting, or fishing, or some other basic craft. Eventually, this specialized skill produces excess products, which they exchange or trade for needed goods that have been produced by others. This exchange process or barter marks the beginning of formal channels of distribution. These early channels involve a series of exchanges between two parties who are producers of one product and consumers of the other.

With the growth of specialization, particularly industrial specialization, and with improvements in methods of transportation and communication, channels of distribution become longer and more complex. Thus, corn grown in Illinois may be processed into corn chips in West Texas, which are then distributed throughout the United States. Or, turkeys grown in Virginia are sent to New York so that they can be shipped to supermarkets in Virginia. Channels don't always make sense.

The channel mechanism also operates for service products. In the case of medical care, the channel mechanism may consist of a local physician, specialists, hospitals, ambulances, laboratories, insurance companies, physical therapists, home care professionals, and so forth. All of these individuals are interdependent, and could not operate successfully without the cooperation and capabilities of all the others.

Based on this relationship, we define a *marketing channel* as "sets of interdependent organizations involved in the process of making a product or service available for use or consumption, as well as providing a payment mechanism for the provider."

This definition implies several important characteristics of the channel. First, the channel consists of *institutions*, some under the control of the producer and some outside the producer's control. Yet all must be recognized, selected, and integrated into an efficient channel arrangement.

Second, the channel management *process* is continuous and requires constant monitoring and reappraisal. The channel operates 24 hours a day and exists in an environment where change is the norm.

Finally, channels should have certain distribution *objectives* guiding their activities. The structure and management of the marketing channel is thus in part a function of a firm's distribution objective. It is also a part of the marketing objectives, especially the need to make an acceptable profit. Channels usually represent the largest costs in marketing a product.

FLOWS IN MARKETING CHANNELS

One traditional framework that has been used to express the channel mechanism is the concept of *flow*. These flows, touched upon in Figure 10.2, reflect the many linkages that tie channel members and other agencies together in the distribution of goods and services. From the perspective of the channel manager, there are five important flows.

1. Product flow
2. Negotiation flow
3. Ownership flow
4. Information flow
5. Promotion flow

These flows are illustrated for Perrier Water in Figure 10.2.

The *product flow* refers to the movement of the physical product from the manufacturer through all the parties who take physical possession of the product until it reaches the ultimate consumer. The *negotiation flow* encompasses the institutions that are associated with the actual exchange processes. The *ownership flow* shows the movement of title through the channel. *Information flow* identifies the individuals who participate in the flow of information either up or down the channel. Finally, the *promotion flow* refers to the flow of

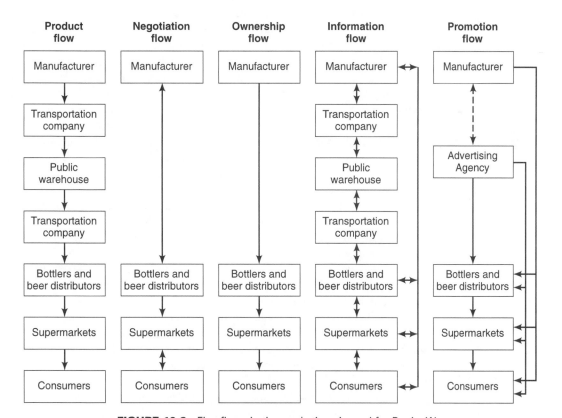

FIGURE 10-2   Five flows in the marketing channel for Perrier Water

Source: Bert Rosenbloom, *Marketing Channels: A Management View*, Dryden Press, Chicago, 1983, p. 11.[1]

persuasive communication in the form of advertising, personal selling, sales promotion, and public relations.

FUNCTIONS OF THE CHANNEL

The primary purpose of any channel of distribution is to bridge the gap between the producer of a product and the user of it, whether the parties are located in the same community or in different countries thousands of miles apart. The channel is composed of different institutions that facilitate the transaction and the physical exchange. Institutions in channels fall into three categories: (1) the producer of the product—a craftsman, manufacturer, farmer, or other extractive industry producer; (2) the user of the product—an individual, household, business buyer, institution, or government; and (3) certain middlemen at the wholesale and/or retail level. Not all channel members perform the same function.

Heskett[2] suggests that a channel performs three important functions:

1. *Transactional functions*—buying, selling, and risk assumption.
2. *Logistical functions*—assembly, storage, sorting, and transportation.
3. *Facilitating functions*—post-purchase service and maintenance, financing, information dissemination, and channel coordination or leadership.

These functions are necessary for the effective flow of product and title to the customer and payment back to the producer. Certain characteristics are implied in every channel. First, although you can eliminate or substitute channel institutions, the functions that these institutions perform cannot be eliminated. Typically, if a wholesaler or a retailer is removed from the channel, the function they perform will be either shifted forward to a retailer or the consumer, or shifted backward to a wholesaler or the manufacturer. For example, a producer of custom hunting knives might decide to sell through direct mail instead of retail outlets. The producer absorbs the sorting, storage, and risk functions; the post office absorbs the transportation function; and the consumer assumes more risk in not being able to touch or try the product before purchase.

Second, all channel institutional members are part of many channel transactions at any given point in time. As a result, the complexity may be quite overwhelming. Consider for the moment how many different products you purchase in a single year, and the vast number of channel mechanisms you use.

Third, the fact that you are able to complete all these transactions to your satisfaction, as well as to the satisfaction of the other channel members, is due to the *routinization* benefits provided through the channel. Routinization means that the right products are most always found in places (catalogues or stores) where the consumer expects to find them, comparisons are possible, prices are marked, and methods of payment are available. Routinization aids the producer as well as the consumer, in that the producer knows what to make, when to make it, and how many units to make.

Fourth, there are instances when the best channel arrangement is direct, from the producer to the ultimate user. This is particularly true when available middlemen are incompetent, unavailable, or the producer feels he can perform the tasks better. Similarly, it may be important for the producer to maintain direct contact with customers so that quick and accurate adjustments can be made. Direct-to-user channels are common in industrial settings, as are door-to-door selling and catalogue sales. Indirect channels are more typical and result, for the most part, because producers are not able to perform the tasks provided by middlemen. (See Figure 10.3.)

Finally, although the notion of a channel of distribution may sound unlikely for a service product, such as health care or air travel, service marketers also face the problem of

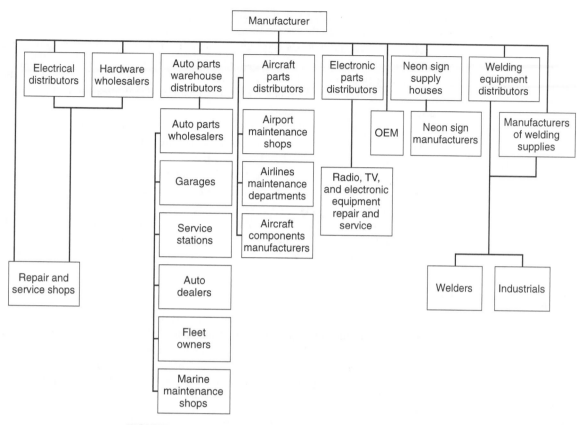

FIGURE 10.3 Marketing channels of a manufacturer of electrical wire and cable

Source: Edwin H. Lewis, *Marketing Electrical Apparatus and Supplies*, McGraw-Hill, Inc., 1961, p. 215.

delivering their product in the form, at the place and time their customer demands. Banks have responded by developing bank-by-mail, Automatic Teller Machines (ATMs), and other distribution systems. The medical community provides emergency medical vehicles, out-patient clinics, 24-hour clinics, and home-care providers. As noted in Figure 10.4 even per-forming arts employ distribution channels. In all three cases, the industries are attempting to meet the special needs of their target markets while differentiating their product from that of their competition. A channel strategy is evident.

CHANNEL INSTITUTIONS:
CAPABILITIES AND LIMITATIONS

There are several different types of parties participating in the marketing channel. Some are members, while others are nonmembers. The former perform negotiation functions and participate in negotiation and/or ownership while the latter participants do not.

Producer and Manufacturer

These firms extract, grow, or make products. A wide array of products is included, and firms vary in size from a one-person operation to those that employ several thousand people and generate billions in sales. Despite these differences, all are in business to satisfy the needs of markets. In order to do this, these firms must be assured that their products are distributed to their intended markets. Most producing and manufacturing firms are not in a favorable position to perform all the tasks that would be necessary to distribute their products directly to their final user markets. A computer manufacturer may know everything about designing the finest personal computer, but know absolutely nothing about making sure the customer has access to the product.

In many instances, it is the expertise and availability of other channel institutions that make it possible for a producer/manufacturer to even participate in a particular market. Imagine the leverage that a company like Frito-Lay has with various supermarket chains. Suppose you developed a super-tasting new snack chip. What are your chances of taking shelf-facings away from Frito-Lay? Zero. Thankfully, a specialty catalog retailer is able to include your product for a prescribed fee. Likewise, other channel members can be useful to the producer in designing the product, packaging it, pricing it, promoting it, and distributing it through the most effective channels. It is rare that a manufacturer has the expertise found with other channel institutions.

Retailing

Retailing involves all activities required to market consumer goods and services to ultimate consumers who are motivated to buy in order to satisfy individual or family needs in contrast to business, institutional, or industrial use. Thus, when an individual buys a computer at Circuit City, groceries at Safeway, or a purse at Ebags.com, a retail sale has been made.

We typically think of a store when we think of a retail sale. However, retail sales are made in ways other than through stores. For example, retail sales are made by door-to-door

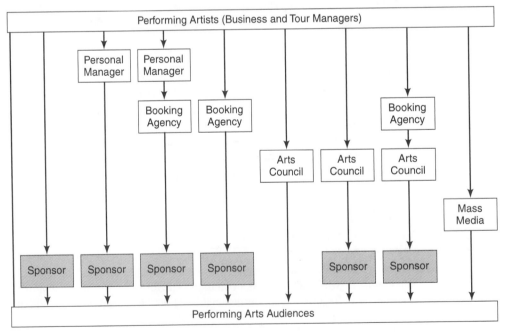

FIGURE 10.4 The marketing channels for the performing arts

Source: John R. Nevin, "An Empirical Analysis of Marketing Channels for the Performing Arts," in Michael P. Mokwa, William M. Dawson, and E. Arthur Prieve (eds.). *Marketing the Arts*, New York: Praeger Publishers, 1980, p. 204.

salespeople, such as an Avon representative, by mail order through a company such as L.L. Bean, by automatic vending machines, and by hotels and motels. Nevertheless, most retail sales are still made in brick-and-mortar stores.

The Structure of Retailing

Stores vary in size, in the kinds of services that are provided, in the assortment of merchandise they carry, and in many other respects. Most stores are small and have weekly sales of only a few hundred dollars. A few are extremely large, having sales of $500,000 or more on a single day. In fact, on special sale days, some stores have exceeded $1 million in sales.

Department Stores   Department stores are characterized by their very wide product mixes. That is, they carry many different types of merchandise that may include hardware, clothing, and appliances. Each type of merchandise is typically displayed in a different section or department within the store. The depth of the product mix depends on the store.

Chain Stores   The 1920s saw the evolution of the chain store movement. Because chains were so large, they were able to buy a wide variety of merchandise in large quantity discounts. The discounts substantially lowered their cost compared to costs of single-unit retailers. As a result, they could set retail prices that were lower than those of their small competitors and thereby increase their share of the market. Furthermore, chains were able to attract many customers because of their convenient locations, made possible by their financial resources and expertise in selecting locations.

Supermarkets   Supermarkets evolved in the 1920s and 1930s. For example, Piggly Wiggly Food Stores, founded by Clarence Saunders around 1920, introduced self-service and customer checkout counters. Supermarkets are large, self-service stores with central checkout facilities; they carry an extensive line of food items and often nonfood products.

Supermarkets were among the first to experiment with such innovations as mass merchandising and low-cost distribution methods. Their entire approach to the distribution of food and household cleaning and maintenance products was to make available to the public large assortments of a variety of such goods at each store at a minimal price.

Discount Houses   Cut-rate retailers have existed for a long time. However, since the end of World War II, the growth of discount houses as a legitimate and extremely competitive retailer has assured this type of outlet a permanent place among retail institutions. It essentially followed the growth of the suburbs.

Discount houses are characterized by an emphasis on price as their main sales appeal. Merchandise assortments are generally broad including both hard and soft goods, but assortments are typically limited to the most popular items, colors, and sizes. Such stores are usually large, self-service operations with long hours, free parking, and relatively simple fixtures.

Warehouse Retailing   Warehouse retailing is a relatively new type of retail institution that experienced considerable growth in the 1970s. Catalog showrooms are the largest type of warehouse retailer, at least in terms of the number of stores operated. Retail sales for catalog showrooms grew from 1 billion dollars in 1970 to over 12 billion today. Their growth rate has slowed recently, but is still substantial.

Franchises   Over the years, particularly since the 1930s, large chain store retailers have posed a serious competitive threat to small storeowners. One of the responses to this threat has been the rapid growth of franchising. Franchising is not a new development. The major oil companies such as Mobil have long enfranchised its dealers, who only sell the products of the franchiser (the oil companies). Automobile manufacturers also enfranchise their dealers, who sell a stipulated make of car (e.g., Chevrolet) and operate their business to some extent as the manufacturer wishes.

Planned Shopping Centers/Malls   After World War II, the United States underwent many changes. Among those most influential on retailing were the growth of the population and of the economy. New highway construction enabled people to leave the congested central cities and move to newly developed suburban residential communities. This movement to the suburbs established the need for new centers of retailing to serve the exploding populations. By 1960 there were 4,500 such centers with both chains and nonchains vying for locations.

Such regional shopping centers are successful because they provide customers with a wide assortment of products. If you want to buy a suit or a dress, a regional shopping center provides many alternatives in one location. *Regional centers* are those larger centers that typically have one or more department stores as major tenants. *Community centers* are moderately sized with perhaps a junior department store; while neighborhood centers are small, with the key store usually a supermarket. *Local clusters* are shopping districts that have simply grown over time around key intersections, courthouses, and the like. *String street locations* are along major traffic routes, while isolated locations are freestanding sites not necessarily in heavy traffic areas. Stores in isolated locations must use promotion or some other aspect of their marketing mix to attract shoppers. Still, as indicated in the next Newsline, malls are facing serious problems.

NEWSLINE: THE MALL: A THING OF THE PAST?

She was born into retail royalty, a double-decker shrine to capitalism that seduced cool customers and wild-eyed shopaholics alike to roam her exhausting mix of 200 stores. Her funky, W-shaped design was pure 1960s, as if dreamed up by that era's noted architectural whiz, Mike Brady. When her doors opened the first morning, a brass band serenaded the arriving mob.

Cinderella City, once the biggest covered mall on the planet, was a very big deal—for about six years, until the next gleaming mall came along in 1974. That's when the music stopped at Cinderella City. Soon the patrons grew scarce, the concrete began crumbling and graffiti stained some of the walls. It's not pretty, but that's the cold law of the consumer jungle. One minute you're luring shoppers from miles around to chug an Orange Julius or grab a snack at the Pretzel Hut; a few years go by, and they're planting you in the dreaded mall graveyard.

Back then, people made a day out of wandering the massive concourses and lunching in the food courts. Today, with less free time available for many people, shopping is seen as a necessity. Spending time with your family and at home is more important than spending time in a store.

The newest malls reflect the modern need for shopping speed. Covered shopping centers now come equipped with dozens of doors to the outside instead of two main entrances that usher crowds in and out through the anchor department store. That same trend paved the way for the flurry of freestanding Home Depots and TJ Maxx stores as well as discount giants like Wal-Mart. All are sapping customers from mid-market malls, already struggling. In addition to the fresh success of freestanding discount stores, the Internet is drawing off even more customers who seek to buy books or music online.

For the mall to survive, they'll have to be something different—a high-quality environment for the delivery of high touch, high experience, high margin retail goods and services: a place you go for the entertainment shopping experience.

Sources: Herb Greenberg, "Dead Mall Walking," *Fortune,* July 8, 2000, p. 304; Calmetla Y. Coleman, "Making Malls (Gasp!) Convenient," *The Wall Street Journal,* February 8, 2000, pp. B1, B2; Bill Briggs, "Birth and Death of the American Mall," *The Denver Post,* June 4, 2000, pp. D1, D4.

Nonstore Retailing   Nonstore retailing describes sales made to ultimate consumers outside of a traditional retail store setting. In total, nonstore retailing accounts for a relatively small percentage of total retail sales, but it is growing and very important with certain types of merchandise, such as life insurance, cigarettes, magazines, books, CDs, and clothing.

One type of nonstore retailing used by such companies as Avon, Electrolux, and many insurance agencies is *in-home selling*. Such sales calls may be made to preselected prospects or in some cases on a cold call basis. A variation of door-to-door selling is the *demonstration party*. Here one customer acts as a host and invites friends. Tupperware has been very successful with this approach.

Vending machines are another type of nonstore retailing. *Automated vending* uses coin-operated, self-service machines to make a wide variety of products and services available to shoppers in convenient locations. Cigarettes, soft drinks, hosiery, and banking transactions are but a few of the items distributed in this way. This method of retailing is an efficient way to provide continuous service. It is particularly useful with convenience goods.

Mail order is a form of nonstore retailing that relies on product description to sell merchandise. The communication with the customer can be by flyer or catalog. Magazines, CDs, clothing, and assorted household items are often sold in this fashion. As with vending machines, mail order offers convenience but limited service. It is an efficient way to cover a very large geographical area when shoppers are not concentrated in one location. Many retailers are moving toward the use of newer communications and computer technology in catalog shopping.

Online marketing has emerged during the last decade; it requires that both the retailer and the consumer have computer and modem. A modem connects the computer to a telephone line so that the computer user can reach various online information services. There are two types of online channels: (1) commercial online channels—various companies have set up online information and marketing services that can be assessed by those who have signed up and paid a monthly fee, and (2) Internet—a global web of some 45,000 computer networks that is making instantaneous and decentralized global communication possible. Users can send e-mail, exchange views, shop for products, and access real-time news.

Marketers can carry on online marketing in four ways: (1) using e-mail; (2) participating in forums, newsgroups, and bulletin boards; (3) placing ads online; and (4) creating an electronic storefront. The last two options represent alternative forms of retailing. Today, more than 40,000 businesses have established a home page on the Internet, many of which serve as electronic storefronts. One can order clothing from Lands' End or J.C. Penney, books from B. Dalton or Amazon.com, or flowers from Lehrer's Flowers to be sent anywhere in the world. Essentially, a company can open its own store on the Internet.

Companies and individuals can place ads on commercial online services in three different ways. First, the major commercial online services offer an ad section for listing classified ads; the ads are listed according to when they arrived, with the latest ones heading the list. Second, ads can be placed in certain online newsgroups that are basically set up for commercial purposes. Finally, ads can also be put on online billboards; they pop up while subscribers are using the service, even though they did not request an ad.

Catalog marketing occurs when companies mail one or more product catalogs to selected addresses that have a high likelihood of placing an order. Catalogs are sent by huge general-merchandise retailers—J.C. Penney's, Spiegel—that carry a full line of merchandise. Specialty department stores such as Neiman-Marcus and Saks Fifth Avenue send catalogs to cultivate an upper-middle class market for high-priced, sometimes exotic merchandise.

INTEGRATED MARKETING 10.1

THE DEATH OF RETAILING GREATLY EXAGGERATED

Recently, the MIT economist Lester Thurow suggested that e-commerce could mean the end of 5,000 years of conventional retailing if online stores can combine price advantages with a pleasant virtual shopping experience. Let's face it: the growth of malls and megastores have shown that people want selection, convenience, and low prices, and that's about it. Sure, people say they'd rather shop from the mom-and-pop on Main Street. But if the junk chain store out on the highway has those curling irons for a dollar less, guess where people go?

So a few years into the e-commerce revolution, here are a few observations and predictions:

- Online stores need to become easier to use as well as completely trustworthy.
- If people can go online and get exactly what they get from retail stores for less money, that is precisely what they will do.
- Some stores will have a kind of invulnerability to online competition; i.e., stores that sell last-minute items or specialty items that you have to see.
- Retail stores may improve their chances by becoming more multidimensional; i.e., they have to be fun to visit.

Still, not everything is rosy for e-tailers. Research provides the following insights:

- For net upstarts, the cost per new customer is $82, compared to $31 for traditional retailers.
- E-tailers' customer satisfaction levels were: 41% for customer service; 51% for easy returns; 57% for better product information; 66% for product selection; 70% for price, and 74% for ease of use.
- Repeat buyers for e-tailers was 21% compared to 34% for traditional retailers.

Suggestions to improve the plight of e-tailers include the following:

- Keep it simple.
- Think like your customer.
- Engage in creative marketing.
- Don't blow everything on advertising.
- Don't undercut prices.

While all this advice is good, the recent roller coaster ride of high-tech stocks and its disappointing results for e-tailers has completely changed the future of e-tailing. While e-tailers have spent about $2 billion industry-wide on advertising campaigns, they often devote far less attention and capital to the quality of services their prospective customers receive once they arrive on site. E-tailers are learning what brick and mortar retailers have known all along, that success is less about building market share than about satisfying and retaining customers who can generate substantial profits.

Sources: Heather Green, "Shake Out E-Tailers," *Business Week*, May 15, 2000, pp. 103–106; Ellen Neuborne, "It's the Service, Stupid," *Business Week*, April 3, 2000, p. E8; Chris Ott, "Will Online Shopping Kill Traditional Retail?" *The Denver Business Journal*, Oct. 28, 1999, p. 46A; Steve Caulk, "Online Merchants Need More Effective Web Sites," *Rocky Mountain News*, Thursday, March 8, 2001, p. 5B.

Several major corporations have also acquired or developed mail-order divisions via catalogs. Using catalogs, Avon sells women's apparel, W.R. Grace sells cheese, and General Mills sells sport shirts.

Some companies have designed "customer-order placing machines," i.e., *kiosks* (in contrast to vending machines, which dispense actual products), and placed them in stores, airports, and other locations. For example, the Florsheim Shoe Company includes a machine in several of its stores in which the customer indicates the type of shoe he wants (e.g., dress, sport), and the color and size. Pictures of Florsheim shoes that meet his criteria appear on the screen.

Wholesaling

Another important channel member in many distribution systems is the wholesaler. *Wholesaling* includes all activities required to market goods and services to businesses, institutions, or industrial users who are motivated to buy for resale or to produce and market other products and services. When a bank buys a new computer for data processing, a school buys audio-visual equipment for classroom use, or a dress shop buys dresses for resale, a wholesale transaction has taken place.

The vast majority of all goods produced in an advanced economy have wholesaling involved in their marketing. This includes manufacturers, who operate sales offices to perform wholesale functions, and retailers, who operate warehouses or otherwise engage in wholesale activities. Even the centrally planned socialist economy needs a structure to handle the movement of goods from the point of production to other product activities or to retailers who distribute to ultimate consumers. Note that many establishments that perform wholesale functions also engage in manufacturing or retailing. This makes it very difficult to produce accurate measures of the extent of wholesale activity. For purposes of keeping statistics, the Bureau of the Census of the United States Department of Commerce defines wholesaling in terms of the percent of business done by establishments who are primary wholesalers. It is estimated that only about 60% of all wholesale activity is accounted for in this way.

Today there are approximately 600,000 wholesale establishments in the United States, compared to just fewer than 3 million retailers. These 600,000 wholesalers generate a total volume of over 1.3 trillion dollars annually; this is approximately 75% greater than the total volume of all retailers. Wholesale volume is greater because it includes sales to industrial users as well as merchandise sold to retailers for resale.

Functions of the Wholesaler

Wholesalers perform a number of useful functions within the channel of distributions. These may include all or some combination of the following:

1. *Warehousing*—the receiving, storage, packaging, and the like necessary to maintain a stock of goods for the customers they service.
2. *Inventory control and order processing*—keeping track of the physical inventory, managing its composition and level, and processing transactions to insure a smooth flow of merchandise from producers to buyers and payment back to the producers.
3. *Transportation*—arranging the physical movement of merchandise.
4. *Information*—supplying information about markets to producers and information about products and suppliers to buyers.
5. *Selling*—personal contact with buyers to sell products and service.

In addition, the wholesaler must perform all the activities necessary for the operation of any other business such as planning, financing, and developing a marketing mix. The five functions listed previously emphasize the nature of wholesaling as a link between the producer and the organizational buyer.

By providing this linkage, wholesalers assist both the producer and the buyer. From the buyer's perspective, the wholesaler typically brings together a wide assortment of products and lessens the need to deal directly with a large number of producers. This makes the buying task much more convenient. A hardware store with thousands of items from hundreds of different producers may find it more efficient to deal with a smaller number of wholesalers. The wholesaler may also have an inventory in the local market, thus speeding delivery and improving service. The wholesaler assists the producer by making products more accessible to buyers. They provide the producer with wide market coverage information about local market trends in an efficient manner. Wholesalers may also help with the promotion of a producer's products to a local or regional market via advertising or a sales force to call on organizational buyers.

Types of Wholesalers

There are many different types of wholesalers. Some are independent; others are part of a vertical marketing system. Some provide a full range of services; others offer very specialized services. Different wants and needs on the part of both buyers and producers have led to a wide variety of modern wholesalers. Table 10.1 provides a summary of general types. Wholesaling activities cannot be eliminated, but they can be assumed by manufacturers and retailers. Those merchant wholesalers who have remained viable have done so by providing improved service to suppliers and buyers. To do this at low cost, modern technologies must be increasingly integrated into the wholesale operation.

Physical Distribution

In a society such as ours, the task of physically moving, handling and storing products has become the responsibility of marketing. In fact, to an individual firm operating in a high-level economy, these logistical activities are critical. They often represent the only cost-saving area open to the firm. Likewise, in markets where product distinctiveness has been reduced greatly, the ability to excel in physical distribution activities may provide a true competitive advantage. Ultimately, *physical distribution* activities provide the bridge between the production activities and the markets that are spatially and temporally separated.

Physical distribution management may be defined as the process of strategically managing the movement and storage of materials, parts, and finished inventory from suppliers, between enterprise facilities, and to customers. Physical distribution activities include those undertaken to move finished products from the end of the production line to the final consumer. They also include the movement of raw materials from a source of supply to the beginning of the production line, and the movement of parts, etc., to maintain the existing product. Finally, it may include a network for moving the product back to the producer or reseller, as in the case of recalls or repair.

Before discussing physical distribution, it is important to recognize that physical distribution and the channel of distribution are not independent decision areas. They must be considered together in order to achieve the organization's goal of satisfied customers. Several relationships exist between physical distribution and channels, including the following:

1. Defining the physical distribution standards that channel members want.
2. Making sure the proposed physical distribution program designed by an organization meets the standards of channel members.

3. Selling channel members on physical distribution programs.
4. Monitoring the results of the physical distribution program once it has been implemented.

Figure 10.5 illustrates the components of physical distribution management.

AD 10.1   Andersen appeals to both institutions and individuals.

TABLE 10.1 **Types of Modern Wholesalers**

Type	Definition	Subcategories
Full-service merchandise wholesaler	*Take title* to the merchandise and assume the risk involved in an independent operation; buy and resell products; offer a complete range of services.	• General • Limited-line
Limited-service merchant wholesalers	*Take title* to the merchandise and assume the risk involved in an independent operation; buy and resell products; offer a limited range of services.	• Cash and carry • Rack jobbers • Drop shippers • Mail orders
Agents and brokers	*Do not take title* to the merchandise; bring buyers and sellers together and negotiate the terms of the transaction: *agents* merchants represent either the buyer or seller, usually on a permanent basis; *brokers* bring parties together on a temporary basis.	*Agents* • Buying agents • Selling agents • Commission merchants • Manufacturers' agents *Brokers* • Real estate • Food • Other products
Manufacturer's sales	*Owned directly* by the manufacturers; performs wholesaling functions for the manufacturer.	
Facilitator	Perform some *specialized functions* such as finance or warehousing; to facilitate the wholesale transactions; may be independent or owned by producer or buyer.	• Warehouses • Finance companies • Transportation companies • Trade marts

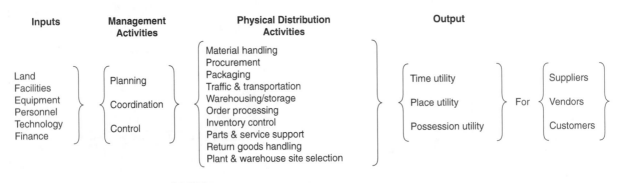

FIGURE 10.5 The physical distribution management process

1. Producers/manufacturers make or assemble the final product provided to the consumer.

2. Retailing involves all activities required to market consumer goods and service to ultimate consumers who are motivated to buy in order to satisfy individual or family needs in contrast to business, institutional, or industrial use. The various types of retailers include:
   a. Department stores
   b. Chain stores
   c. Supermarkets
   d. Discount houses
   e. Warehouse retailing
   f. Franchises
   g. Planned shopping centers
   h. Nonstore retailing

3. Wholesaling includes all activities required to market goods and services to businesses, institutions, or industrial users who are motivated to buy for resale or to produce and market other products/services. The various types of wholesalers include:
   a. Full-service merchandise wholesalers
   b. Limited-service merchant wholesalers
   c. Agents and brokers
   d. Manufacturers' sales representatives
   e. Facilitators

As you can see in Figure 10.5, successful management of the flow of goods from a source of supply (raw materials) to the final customer involves effective planning, implementation, and control of many distribution activities. These involve raw material, in-process inventories (partially completed products not ready for resale), and finished products. Effective physical distribution management results initially in the addition of time, place, and possession utility of products; and ultimately, the efficient movement of products to customer and the enhancement of the firm's marketing efforts.

Physical distribution represents both a cost component and a marketing tool for the purpose of stimulating customer demand. The major costs of physical distribution include transportation, warehousing, carrying inventory, receiving and shipping, packaging, administration, and order processing. The total cost of physical distribution activities represents 13.6% for reseller companies. Poorly managed physical distribution results in excessively high costs, but substantial savings can occur via proper management.

Physical distribution also represents a valuable marketing tool to stimulate consumer demand. Physical distribution improvements that lower prices or provide better service are attractive to potential customers. Similarly, if finished products are not supplied at the right time or in the right places, firms run the risk of losing customers.

ORGANIZING THE CHANNEL

Either through a planned process or through a natural evolution, channels of distribution reflect an observable organization structure. Three types are most common: conventional channels, vertical marketing systems, and horizontal channel systems.

Conventional Channels

The *conventional channel* of distribution could be described as a group of independent businesses, each motivated by profit, and having little concern about any other member of the distribution sequence. There are no all-inclusive goals, and in many instances, the assignment of tasks and the evaluation process are totally informal. Consequently, channel frameworks might be working against one another, tasks may go undone, and ineffective channel member relationships may last for years. Despite these deficiencies, this type of channel structure remains most common, and there are numerous examples of such networks working.

Vertical Marketing Systems

Vertical marketing systems have emerged as a solution to the problems of conventional networks. A *vertical marketing system* (VMS) comes about when a member of the distribution channel (usually the manufacturer) assumes a leadership role and attempts to coordinate the efforts of the channel so that mutually beneficial goals can be attained. Three forms of vertical integration are now common.

Administered VMS

The *administered VMS* is very close to the conventional network, but differs in that it is informally guided by goals and programs developed by one or a limited number of firms in the existing channel. This framework is the source of the concept of a *channel captain*, in that administrative skills and the power of one individual may be the driving force of the channel. Often the dominant brands, as in the case of Xerox or Procter & Gamble, are able to manifest this cooperation.

Through the recognition of a channel leader, the distribution networks function better, sales and profits are higher, product exposure improves, inventory management systems are initiated, and the coordination of promotional activities becomes a reality. An administered system is not without its problems. Often, this effort is placed on the shoulders of a single individual. Another drawback is the tendency of polarizing channel members. Businesses either become part of the VMS or remain strongly independent. Eventually these independents may find themselves at a tremendous competitive disadvantage, and may even be deprived of certain channel benefits.

Contractual VMS

There are instances when channel members wish to formalize their relationship by employing a contractual agreement, known as a *contractual VMS*. This provides additional control, and either explicitly or implicitly spells out the marketing functions to be performed by all the members of the channel. This is the most popular form of vertical marketing arrangement.

Corporate VMS

When channel members on different levels are owned and operated by one organization, *a corporate vertical marketing system* is said to exist. Such integration can be forward or backward. A manufacturer who owns the various intermediaries in its channel network has engaged in *forward* integration. A retailer who takes over the wholesaling and manufacturing tasks is *backward* integrating. This process can entail either the organization's purchasing the institutions, or establishing its own facilities. Although partial forward or backward integration is most common, total integration is becoming more popular. Manufacturers who have recently integrated through to the retail level are Dannon Yogurt, Blue Bell Ice Cream, and Pepperidge Farms. Sears and Safeway stores are two retailers that have successfully integrated backward. American Hospital Supply Corporation is an example of a wholesaler that has integrated both backward and forward.

Horizontal Channel Systems

There are instances where two or more companies are unable to acquire the capital, or don't have the technical or production know-how, to effectively market their products alone. In such cases, these companies may establish a temporary or quasi-permanent relationship in order to work with each other, and create the channel mechanism required to reach their target markets. This arrangement has been labeled a *horizontal channel* system. For example, two small manufacturers might combine their shipments to common markets in order to gain full carload transportation rates that each could not obtain separately. Another common scenario is for a large retailer to buy out several competing small retailers in order to gain entry into certain markets or with certain customers.

THE CHANNEL MANAGEMENT PROCESS

Evidence suggests that a channel should be managed just like the product, promotion, and pricing functions. This channel management process contains five steps.

Analyze the Consumer

We begin the process of channel management by answering two questions. First, to whom shall we sell this merchandise immediately? Second, who are our ultimate users and buyers? Depending upon a host of factors, including the type of product, functions performed in the channel, and location in the channel, the immediate and ultimate customers may be identical or they may be quite separate. In both cases, some fundamental questions would apply. There is a need to know what the customer needs, where they buy, when they buy, why they buy from certain outlets, and how they buy.

It is best that we first identify the traits of the ultimate user, since the results of this evaluation might determine the other channel institutions we would use to meet these needs. For example, the buying characteristics of the purchaser of a high-quality VCR might be as follows:

1. Purchased only from a well-established, reputable dealer.
2. Purchased only after considerable shopping to compare prices and merchandise characteristics.
3. Purchaser willing to go to some inconvenience (time and distance) to locate the most acceptable brand.
4. Purchased only after extended conversations involving all interested parties, including dealer, users, and purchasers.
5. Purchase may be postponed.
6. Purchased only from a dealer equipped to render prompt and reasonable product service.

These buying specifications illustrate the kinds of requirements that the manufacturer must discover. In most cases, purchase specifications are fairly obvious and can be discovered without great difficulty. On the other hand, some are difficult to determine. For example, certain consumers will not dine at restaurants that serve alcohol; others will patronize only supermarkets that exhibit definite ethnic characteristics in their merchandising. Nonetheless, by careful and imaginative research, most of the critical factors that bear on consumer buying specifications can be determined.

Knowing the buying specifications of consumers, the channel planner can decide on the type or types of wholesaler and/or retailer through which a product should be sold. This requires that a manufacturer contemplating distribution through particular types of retailers become intimately familiar with the precise location and performance characteristics of those he is considering.

In much the same way that buying specifications of ultimate users are determined, the manufacturers must also discover buying specifications of resellers. Of particular importance is the question, "from whom do my retail outlets prefer to buy?" The answer to this question determines the types of wholesalers (if any) that the manufacturer should use. Although many retailers prefer to buy directly from the manufacturers, this is not always the case. Often, the exchange requirements of manufacturers (e.g., infrequent visits, large order requirements, and stringent credit terms) are the opposite of those desired by retailers. Such retailers would rather buy from local distributors who have lenient credit terms and offer a wide assortment of merchandise.

Establish the Channel Objectives

The channel plan is derived from channel objectives. They are based on the requirements of the purchasers and users, the overall marketing strategy, and the long-run goals of the corporation. However, in cases when a company is just getting started, or an older company is trying to carve out a new market niche, the channel objectives may be the dominant objectives. For example, a small manufacturer wants to expand outside the local market. An immediate obstacle is the limited shelf space available to this manufacturer. The addition of a new product to the shelves generally means that space previously assigned to competitive products must be obtained. Without this exposure, the product is doomed.

As one would expect, there is wide diversity of form that channel objectives can take. The following areas encompass the major categories:

1. Growth in sales—by reaching new markets, and/or increasing sales in existing markets.
2. Maintenance or improvement of market share—educate or assist channel components in their efforts to increase the amount of product they handle.
3. Achieve a pattern of distribution—structure the channel in order to achieve certain time, place, and form utilities.
4. Create an efficient channel—improve channel performance by modifying various flow mechanisms.

Specify Distribution Tasks

After the distribution objectives are set, it is appropriate to determine the specific distribution tasks (functions) to be performed in that channel system. The channel manager must be far more specific in describing the tasks, and must define how these tasks will change depending upon the situation. An ability to do this requires the channel manager to evaluate all phases of the distribution network. Tasks must be identified fully, and costs must be assigned to these tasks. For example, a manufacturer might delineate the following tasks as being necessary in order to profitably reach the target market:

- Provide delivery within 48 hours after order placement
- Offer adequate storage space
- Provide credit to other intermediaries
- Facilitate a product return network
- Provide readily available inventory (quantity and type)
- Provide for absorption of size and grade obsolescence

Evaluate and Select from Channel Alternatives

Determining the specific channel tasks is a prerequisite for the evaluation and selection process. There are four bases for channel alternatives: (1) number of levels, (2) intensity at the various levels, (3) types of intermediaries at each level, and (4) application of selection criterion to channel alternatives.[3]

Number of Levels

Channels can range in levels from two to several (five being typical). The two-level channel (producer to consumer) is a direct channel and is possible only if the producer or customer are willing to perform several of the tasks performed by intermediaries. The number of levels in a particular industry might be the same for all the companies simply because of tradition. In other industries, this dimension is more flexible and subject to rapid change.

Intensity at Each Level

Once the number of levels has been decided, the channel manager needs to determine the actual number of channel components involved at each level. How many retailers in a particular market should be included in the distribution network? How many wholesalers? Although there are limitless possibilities, the categories shown in Figure 10.6 have been used to describe the general alternatives.

The intensity decision is extremely critical, because it is an important part of the firm's overall marketing strategy. Companies such as Coca-Cola and Timex watches have achieved high levels of success through their intensive distribution strategy.

Types of Intermediaries

As discussed earlier, there are several types of intermediaries that operate in a particular channel system. The objective is to gather enough information to have a general understanding of the distribution tasks these intermediaries perform. Based on this background information, several alternatives will be eliminated.

(1) *Exclusive distribution* (such as Ethan Allen and Drexel Heritage Furniture)
- The use of a single or very few outlets
- Creates high dealer loyalty and considerable sales support
- Provides greater control
- Limits potential sales volume
- Success of the product is dependent upon the ability of a single intermediary

(2) *Intensive distribution* (such as candy)—the manufacturer attempts to get as many intermediaries of a particular type as possible to carry the product
- Provides for increased sales volume, wider consumer recognition, and considerable impulse purchasing
- Low price, low margin, and small order sizes often result
- Extremely difficult to stimulate and control this large number of intermediaries

(3) *Selective distribution* (such as Baskin-Robbins)—an intermediary strategy, with the exact number of outlets in any given market dependent upon market potential, density of population, dispersion of sales, and competitors' distribution policies
- Contains some of the strengths and weaknesses of the other two strategies.
- It is difficult to determine the optimal number of intermediaries in each market

FIGURE 10.6 Levels of channel intensity

Having identified several possible alternative channel structures, the channel manager is now at a place where he or she can evaluate these alternatives with respect to some set of criteria. Company factors, environmental trends, reputation of the reseller, experience of reseller are just a few examples.

Who Should Lead

Regardless of the channel framework selected, channels usually perform better if someone is in charge, providing some level of leadership. Essentially, the purpose of this leadership is to coordinate the goals and efforts of channel institutions. The level of leadership can range from very passive to quite active—verging on dictatorial. The style may range from very negative, based on fear and punishment, to very positive, based on encouragement and reward. In a given situation, any of these leadership styles may prove effective.

Given the restrictions inherent in channel leadership, the final question is "who should lead the channel?" Two important trends are worth noting, since they influence the answer. First, if we look at the early years of marketing, i.e., pre-1920, the role of the wholesaler (to bring the producer and consumer together) was most vital. Consequently, during this period, the wholesaler led most channels. This is no longer true. A second trend is the apparent strategy of both manufacturers and retailers to exert power through size. In a type of business cold war, manufacturers and retailers are constantly trying to match each other's size. The result has been some serious warfare to gain channel superiority.

Under which conditions should the manufacturers lead? The wholesaler? The retailer? While the answer is contingent upon many factors, in general, the manufacturer should lead if control of the product (merchandising, repair) is critical and if the design and redesign of the channel is best done by the manufacturer. The wholesaler should lead where the manufacturers and retailers have remained small in size, large in number, relatively scattered geographically, are financially weak, and lack marketing expertise. The retailer should lead when product development and demand stimulation are relatively unimportant and when personal attention to the customer is important.

Evaluating Channel Member Performance

The need to evaluate the performance level of the channel members is just as important as the evaluation of the other marketing functions. Clearly, the marketing mix is quite interdependent and the failure of one component can cause the failure of the whole. There is one important difference, with the exception of the corporate VMS; the channel member is dealing with independent business firms, rather than employees and activities under the control of the channel member, and their willingness to change is lacking.

Sales is the most popular performance criteria used in channel evaluation. Sales might further be subdivided into current sales compared with historical sales, comparisons of sales with other channel members, and comparisons of the channel member's sales with predetermined quotas. Other possible performance criteria are: maintenance of adequate inventory, selling capabilities, attitudes of channel intermediaries toward the product, competition from other intermediaries and from other product line carried by the manufacturers own channel members.

Correcting or Modifying the Channel

As a result of the evaluation process, or because of other factors such as new competition, technology, or market potential, changes will be made in the channel structure. Because channel relationships have tended to be long-term, and the channel decision has such a pervasive impact on the business, great care should be taken before changing the status quo.

Terminations of channel members not performing at minimum performance standards should be employed only as a last resort. Corrective actions are far less destructive and maintain the goodwill that is so crucial in channel relationships. This requires that the channel manager attempt to find out why these channel members have performed poorly and then implement a strategy to correct these deficiencies.

Sometimes a producer decides that an entirely new channel needs to be added, or an existing one deleted. A manufacturer of camera accessories might decide that he wants to reach the skilled amateur market in addition to the professional photographer market. This would mean designing a different channel, and learning about a different set of intermediaries.

THE HUMAN ASPECT OF DISTRIBUTION

A channel of distribution by its very nature is made up of people. Ideally, a channel member should coordinate his or her efforts with other members in such a way that the performance of the total distribution system to which he or she belongs is enhanced. This is rarely the case. Part of this lack of cooperation is due to the organization structure of many channels, which encourages a channel member to be concerned only with channel members immediately adjacent to them, from whom they buy and to whom they sell. A second reason is the tendency of channel members to exhibit their independence as separate business operations. It is difficult to gain cooperation under this arrangement. Four human dimensions have been incorporated into the study of channel behavior: roles, communication, conflict, and power. It is assumed that an understanding of these behavioral characteristics will increase the effectiveness of the channel.

Role

Most channel members participate in several channels. Establishing the *role* of a channel member means defining what the behavior of the channel member should be. For example, a basic role prescription of the manufacturer may be to maximize the sales of his/her particular brand of product. This connotes that the manufacturer is to actively compete for market share, and aggressively promote his or her brand. The role prescriptions of independent wholesalers, however, are likely to be quite different. Since wholesalers may represent several competing manufacturers, his or her role would be to build sales with whatever brands are most heavily demanded by retailers. Therefore, a major issue in channel management relates to defining the role prescriptions of the various participants in order to achieve desired results. This is accomplished through a careful appraisal of the tasks to be performed by each channel member and clear communication of these roles to the members.

Communication

Channel communication is sending and receiving information that is relevant to the operation of the channel. It is critical for the success of the channel member to work to create and foster an effective flow of information within the channel. Communication will take place only if the channel member is aware of the pitfalls that await. The channel manager should therefore try to detect any behavioral problems that tend to inhibit the effective flow of information through the channel and try to solve these problems before the communication process in the channel becomes seriously distorted.

Conflict

Anytime individuals or organizations must work together and rely on each other for personal success, conflict is inevitable. *Conflict*, unlike friendly competition, is personal and direct and often suggests a confrontation. Because it is so pervasive in distribution, a great deal of research has been conducted in attempts to identify its causes, outcomes, and solutions.

There is also a need to manage conflict in the channel. This consists of (1) establishing a mechanism for detecting conflict, (2) appraising the effects of the conflict, and (3) resolving the conflict. This last consideration is most difficult to implement. Techniques such as a channel committee, joint goal setting, and bringing in an arbitrator have all been used. There are even cases when conflict is necessary. Such is the case in the e-marketplace. For example, Anne Mulcahy, President of Xerox General Markets Operation, notes, "Those that don't aggressively embrace multiple channels for multiple products will get left behind. The inherent conflict in this business model is not only a reality of business; it's a sign of a healthy company."

Power

Power is our willingness to use force in a relationship. It is often the means by which we are able to control or influence the behavior of another party. In the channel mechanism, *power* refers to the capacity of a particular channel member to control or influence the behavior of another channel member. For instance, a large retailer may want the manufacturer to modify the design of the product or perhaps be required to carry less inventory. Both parties may attempt to exert their power in an attempt to influence the other's behavior. The ability of either of the parties to achieve this outcome will depend upon the amount of power that each can bring to bear.

MARKETING CAPSULE 10.2

1. Three general alternatives exist in organizing the channel: conventional, vertical, and horizontal.
2. The steps in channel design include the following:
   a. Analyze the consumer
   b. Establish channel objectives
   c. Specify the channel tasks
   d. Select the appropriate channel from available alternatives
   e. Evaluate the results

3. Channels may exhibit several human traits:
   a. Role
   b. Communication
   c. Conflict
   d. Power

IN PRACTICE

Marketing channels connect producers and consumers by moving finished goods that are available for consumption. Channel management is a process involving careful planning and monitoring. As with other marketing functions, marketing channels have objectives that guide their activities.

To successfully manage distribution channels, marketers must analyze end consumers, establish channel objectives, specify channel tasks, select the appropriate channel, and evaluate results of the process. If these steps are executed successfully, marketers can help their organizations save costs.

Several professional and trade associations exist for channel managers and those involved in the process. The **American Society of Transportation and Logistics** (www.astl.org) is a professional organization founded in 1946 by a group of industry leaders to ensure a high level of professionalism and promote continuing education in the field of transportation and logistics.

The **National Association of Wholesalers-Distributors** (www.naw.org) comprises over 100 national line-of-trade associations, representing virtually all products that move to market via wholesaler-distributors.

The **National Retail Federation** (www.nrf.com) conducts programs and services in research, education, training, information technology, and government affairs to protect and advance the interests of the retail industry. NRF also includes in its membership key suppliers of goods and services to the retail industry.

Marketing channels can make or break Internet companies. Many Internet companies attempt to differentiate themselves by providing fast delivery of customer orders anywhere in the world. To achieve this, these companies must successfully manage their marketing channels. The Interactive Journal's **Tech Center** is an excellent source for all issues related to technology.

Keep apprised of emerging technologies, developments in specific companies, and industry trends by reading articles in **Tech Center** and **Marketplace**.

DELIVERABLE

Use the Interactive Journal to search for articles about one organization that successfully manages channels and one organization that does not. Compare the strategies of both companies and discuss what works and what does not work for each organization. Support your conclusions with concepts from the chapter.

DISCUSSION QUESTIONS

1. Why do organizations need to effectively manage their channels of distribution? What happens when they do not?
2. How does ineffective channel management affect consumers? An organization's revenue stream?
3. What role does technology play in channel management? What types of technology can organizations use to improve channel management?

SUMMARY

The complex mechanism of connecting the producer with the consumer is referred to as the *channel of distribution*. This chapter has looked at the evolution of the channel, as well as theoretical explanations for the distribution channel phenomenon. Five "flows" are suggested that reflect the ties of channel members with other agencies in the distribution of goods and services. A channel performs three important functions: (1) transactional functions, (2) logistical functions, and (3) facilitating functions. Channel strategies are evident for service products as well as for physical products. Options available for organizing the channel structure include: (1) conventional channels, (2) vertical marketing systems, (3) horizontal channel systems, and (4) multiple channel networks. Designing the optimal distribution channel depends on the objectives of the firm and the characteristics of available channel options.

The primary members of distribution channels are manufacturers, wholesalers, and retailers. Retailing is all activities required to market goods and services to the ultimate consumer. This makes retailers who perform such activities an important link in the channel of distribution for many consumer products.

Wholesaling involves all activities required to market goods and services to businesses, institutions, or industrial users who are motivated to buy for resale or to produce and market other products and services. Wholesalers provide a linkage between producers and retailers or industrial users.

Physical distribution management involves the movement and storage of materials, parts, and finished inventory from suppliers, between middlemen, and to customers. Physical distribution activities are undertaken to facilitate exchange between marketers and customers. The basic objective of physical distribution is to provide an acceptable level of customer service at the lowest possible cost. This is done using the total cost concept, which requires that all the costs of each alternative distribution system be considered when a firm is attempting to provide a level of customer service.

Channels exhibit behavior, as people do, and this behavior needs to be coordinated and managed in order to reach desired objectives. The four dimensions of behavior examined are role, communication, conflict, and power. Strategies for effective channel management include: (1) analyze the consumer, (2) establish channel objectives, (3) specify the channel tasks, (4) select the appropriate channel from available alternatives, and (5) evaluate the results. The chapter concludes with a discussion of the legal factor's impact on channels.

MARKETER'S VOCABULARY

Exchange function   Sales of the product to the various members of the channel of distribution.

Physical distribution function   Moves the product through the exchange channel, along with title and ownership.

Marketing channel   Sets of independent organizations involved in the process of making a product or service available for use or consumption as well as providing a payment mechanism for the provider.

Routinization   The right products are most always found in places where the consumer expects to find them, comparisons are possible, prices are marked, and methods of payment are available.

Retailing   Involves all activities required to market consumer goods and services to ultimate consumers.

Nonstore retailing   Sales made to ultimate consumers outside a traditional retail store setting.

Wholesaling   Includes all activities required to market goods and services to businesses, institutions, or industrial users.

Conventional channel   A group of independent businesses, each motivated by profit, and having little concern about any other member of the distribution sequence.

Vertical marketing system   Comes about when a member of the distribution channel assumes a leadership role and attempts to coordinate the efforts of the channel.

Channel role   Defines what the behavior of the channel member should be.

Channel conflict   Personal and direct friction; often suggests a potential confrontation.

Channel power   A willingness to use force in a relationship.

DISCUSSION QUESTIONS

1. Discuss the difference between the theories of the sorting concept and the postponement concept.

2. What are the five important "flows" that link channel members and other agencies together in distribution? Explain each type.

3. Define the following three channel functions: (1) transactional, (2) logistical, and (3) facilitating. What would happen to these functions if the middlemen were eliminated from the chain-linking manufacturer to consumer?

4. Why are channels of distribution important for service products?

5. Compare the characteristics of the three forms of vertical marketing systems: administered, contractual, and corporate.

6. What are the advantages to wholesalers of contractual arrangements forming cooperatives with retailers? What are the advantages to retailers?

7. What is an ancillary structure? What is its function in the distribution channel?

8. How do economic conditions of inflation, recession, and shortages impact upon the channel environment?

9. Discuss situations in which channel conflict may be desirable. How should conflict that produces negative effects be managed?

PROJECT

Starting with a well-known manufacturer, trace the various channel intermediaries employed. Draw a channel diagram.

CASE APPLICATION

CONNECTING CHANNEL MEMBERS

Brokers are in the midst of an identity crisis. Today's brokers represent more than 3,000 manufacturers, comprising nearly 60% of all commodity volume in package goods and 80% of U.S. grocery warehouse withdrawals. Many brokers rank among the top 10 vendors of their major retail customers. Much to their continuing frustration, however, many manufacturers are experimenting with some combination of broker and direct resources in an attempt to deal with the new marketplace. Some of these models are working, but managers are not.

"While each manufacturer must develop a host of different strategies to match that of individual customers, the broker has the luxury to organize his total strategy around his individual customers," says National Food Brokers Association (NFBA) president and CEO Robert Schwarze. Brokers have always been regarded for their local market expertise, but the rapid shift to micromarketing is now regarded as their opportunity to ultimately weave themselves into the very fabric of their principles' go-to-market approach.

Consumers have a lot of shopping alternatives and are taking advantage of them, which is driving manufacturers and retailers to look for consumer information to give them a competitive edge. In just a few years, as brokers have accelerated their use of data, the number of brokers having online access to syndicated data has expanded to more than 200, according to an Andersen Consulting Survey.

Traditionally, panel and retail census data have been used by manufacturers to understand the components of volume and to determine what they can do to grow volume, including the primary variables of penetration and buying rates. Now these same consumer dynamics can be used to understand retail-shopping behavior. Instead of simply measuring how many households buy a particular brand, the data measure how many shoppers who buy the brand shop at a particular retailer or retail channel. Depending on where the manufacturer fits on the scale will affect how one thinks about marketing and promotion.

"In the final analysis, understanding a retailer's position in the market is the key," said A.C. Nielsen consumer information and national sales VP Tod Hale. The knowledge about the competitive frame, including individual retailer shopper demographics, purchase behavior in a category, and measures of loyalty by account, are increasingly essential to promotional planning and evaluation. The ability to compare and contrast behavior in different accounts is essential to uncovering the opportunities.

Questions:

1. Do you see sources of conflict in this new arrangement?

2. How will role determination be determined?

REFERENCES

1. Wroe Alderson, "Factors Governing the Development of Marketing Channels," in R.M. Clewett (ed.), *Marketing Channels for Manufactured Products*, Homewood, IL: Richard D. Irwin, 1954, pp. 5–22.
2. James L. Heskett, *Marketing*, New York: Macmillan Publishing Co., Inc., 1976, pp. 265–267.
3. Roger M. Pegram, "Selecting and Evaluating Distributors," New York: The Conference Board, Business Policy Study No. 116, 1965, p. 24.
4. Louis W. Stern, and Ronald H. Gorman, "Conflict in Distribution Channels: An Exploration," in *Distribution Channels: Behavioral Dimensions*, ed. Louis W. Stern, New York: Houghton-Mifflin Co., 1969, p. 156.

PHOTO CREDITS

Chapter 1

Page 2: ©Elvis Presley Enterprises, Inc. Reproduced with permission. Page 5: ©L.L.Bean, Inc. L.L. Bean® is a registered trademark of L.L. Bean, Inc. Page 13: Courtesy Pharmaceutical Research and Manufacturers of America. Page 14: Courtesy Ball Park Franks. Page 16: From Sprint Business Homepage, www.sprintbiz.com. Courtesy Sprint. Reproduced with permission.

Chapter 2

Page 31: Courtesy Olympus America, Inc. Page 32: ©2001 Partnership for a Drug-Free America®. Page 37: Courtesy JBL, Inc.

Chapter 4

Page 83: Courtesy DISH NETWORK. ©2001 EchoStar Corporation. All rights reserved. Page 92: Courtesy UPS.

Chapter 7

Page 157: From the Stuart Weitzman ad campaign, "A Little Obsessed with Shoes," by Korey Kay and Partners. Reproduced with permission. Page 172: Courtesy ©2001 America's Dairy Farmers and Milk Processors.

Chapter 8

Page 205: Courtesy Days Inns Worldwide, Inc. Page 206: Courtesy Howe Marketing Group and Eckerd Corporation. Page 207: Courtesy StartSampling, Inc. Page 208: Courtesy FreeSamples.com. Page 210: ©2001 United States Conference of Catholic Bishops. Page 212: BUILD A HOME AMERICA™ is a trademark of KF Holdings. Reproduced with permission.

Chapter 9

Page 233: Courtesy Days Inns Worldwide, Inc. Page 238: Courtesy Palm, Inc. Page 241: ©2001 GM Corp./Campbell-Ewald. Page 251: Courtesy Aaron Office Furniture.

Chapter 10

Page 265: Reprinted courtesy Aurthur Andersen LLP. ©2001 Andersen. All rights reserved. Reproduced with permission.

INDEX

A

Acquisition of new product, 172
Advertising, 193
    appeals, types of, 200
    banner advertisements, 202–204
    business perspective, 222
    consumer's perspective, 222
    creative strategy, development of, 200
    creative tactics, 200
    defined, 190
    media plan, development of, 201–202
    organization of, 199–200
    research, 56
    societal perspective, 222
Advertising agency, 199–200
Advertising campaign, 198, 222
Advertising department, 199–200
Aesthetics, 141
AIO (activities, interests, opinions) inventories, 40
Allen, Ronald W., 99
Alliances, corporate, 133
Allowances, price, 239–240
American Airlines, 99
American Express, 185–186
American Import Corporation, 224–225
American Log Home, 44
American Marketing Association, 4, 204
Armantrout, Linda, 6
Attitude
    buyer behavior influenced by, 90–91
    defined, 49, 90, 98
Augmented product, 153

B

Baby boomers, 73, 74, 117
Baby boomlet, 118. *See also* Youth market
BankOne Leasing Corporation, 6
Banner advertisements, 202–204
Bargaining strength, 29
Barriers to market entry, 105
BBDO, 53

Beliefs, 85, 118
Bethune, Gordon M., 100
Beverage industry, 51, 124–125, 133
BlackPlanet.com, 39
Blackwell, Roger, 95
Brands/branding, 49, 84, 163–164, 167, 183
Break-even price, 243–244, 248
Brokers, manufacturers, 278–279. *See also* Distribution channels
Budget, marketing, 21, 196, 202
Budweiser corporation, 133
Business cycle, 112–113, 123
Business norms (international marketing), 141
Business services, 156
Business-to-business markets. *See* Organizational markets
Buyer
    communication needs and wants of (*See* Integrated Marketing Communication (IMC)/marketing communication)
    defined, 75
    feedback, mechanism for, 188
    motives of (*See* Motives, buyer)
    new product ideas generated by, 175
    price, view of, 227–228
Buyer behavior, 73–100
    case application, 99–100
    decision-making process, 76–81
    factors influencing, 82–91
    market exchange and, 74–75
    organizational, 91–96
    postpurchase, 81
    as problem solving, 75–91
    Wall Street Journal (wsj.com), 97
Buyer's market, 29
Buying power, 45, 106, 111–112, 117, 123
Buying task, 82–84

C

Campaigns, advertising/communication, 198–199, 222, 223
Campbell's Soup, 33
Case Corporation, 72

Cash discounts, 239, 248
Catalog marketing. *See* Direct marketing
Category appraisal, 175–176
Channels of distribution. *See* Distribution channels
Chouinard, Yoon, 80
Chrysler Corporation, 34
Coca-Cola Company, 9, 34, 162
Cognitive dissonance, 81, 98
Colors (international marketing factor), 139
Combination export manager, 131, 148
Combination offers, 209, 223
Combination pricing, 241
Commercialization of new product, 180
Common buying factors (market segment), 44
Communication, 9–10
    adaptation, 136, 149
    basic elements of, 191–192
    channel, 273
    global marketing and, 128, 136, 149
    group communications through opinion leaders, 86
    to mass markets (*See* Integrated Marketing Communication (IMC)/marketing communication)
    pricing and, 231
    types of systems, 193
Community contact, 11–12
Comparison messaging, 9
Competition, 104–106
    identification of, 10
    international marketing, 145–146
    marketing communication and, 190–191
    new product ideas from competitors, 174
    nonprice, 232–235, 248
Competitive advantage, 3, 24
Competitive analysis, 104–106
Competitive distinctiveness, 161
Competitive intelligence, 10, 11
Competitive pricing, 234–235, 245

Competitive situation, 29
Concentration strategy, 35, 49
Consumer, 8. *See also* Buyer
  advertising, perspective on, 222
  behavior (*See* Buyer behavior)
  buying power (*See* Buying power)
  credit/financing, availability of,
    164
  defined, 24, 75
  future trends, 95–96
  markets, 30
  new products, viewpoint on, 170
  protection, 108
  sampling, 209, 223
  spending patterns, 111–112
Consumer goods
  classification of, 155–156
  defined, 182
  marketing, 17
Consumer-oriented organization, 8
Contests, 209, 223
Continental Airlines, Inc., 100
Convenience goods, 155
Conventional channels, 267–268, 276
Core product, 153
Costs, as pricing factor, 227, 230–231
  break-even analysis, 243–244
  cost-plus pricing and mark-ups,
    242–243
  target rates of return, 244
  value-based pricing, 245
Cowing, Roy, 249–250
Crandall, Robert J., 99
Creative strategy, 200, 222
Creative tactics, 200, 222
Credit, consumer, 164
Cross-functional contact, 10–11
Culture
  buyer behavior and, 85
  defined, 85, 98, 118
  international markets, effect on,
    139–141
  marketing plan, effect on,
    118–121
Customary prices, 240
Customer. *See* Buyer
Customs. *See* Culture
Cyber Dialogue Data, 78

D
Data, market research
  data collection methods, 61–66
  data-mining, 68
  determining types needed, 60
  locating sources of, 60–61

processing, 66–71, 67
Dealer loaders, 209, 223
DeBeers Limited, 85
Decision-making process, 76–81,
  83–84, 98
Dell Computer Corporation, 126–127
Delta Air Lines, Inc., 99
Demand, product
  demand curve, 229, 248
  effective, 45, 50
  primary, 229
Demographics
  buyer behavior influenced by,
    84–85
  defined, 115
  marketing plan, effect on,
    115–118, 121
  market segmentation by, 36–38,
    49, 117–118
Depression, 112–113, 123
Deregulation, 107–108
Developing nations, 145
Developmental selling, 214–215
Direct exporting, 131, 148
Direct investment in foreign nations,
  132
Direct marketing, 16–17, 261–263. *See*
  also Internet
    examples, 4–5, 224–225
    sales force, effect on, 219–220
Discounts, price, 237–239, 248
Distribution channels, 20, 138–139 *See*
  also Physical distribution
  function
    case application, 277–278
    communication, 273
    conflict, management of, 274, 277
    consumer, analysis of, 269–270
    conventional, 267–268
    direct-to-user, 256
    distribution tasks, specification of,
      270
    dual functions of, 253–254
    evolution of, 254
    flows in, 255–256
    functions of, 256–257
    horizontal, 268–269
    human aspect of distribution,
      273–274
    institutional members, 254, 256
    management process, 269–273
    member performance, evaluation
      of, 272–273
    objectives, establishment of, 270
    organization of, 267–269

physical distribution, 264–267
power of members, 274, 277
producer and manufacturer,
  257–258
retailing, 258–263
role of channel member, 273, 277
selection of, 271–272
for service marketing, 256–257
Wall Street Journal (wsj.com),
  275
wholesaling, 263–264
Dolan, Robert, 232
Domestic marketing, 128
Doyle Dane Bernbach, 183
Dr. Pepper, 33
Dumping, 138, 143, 148

E
easyGroup, 142
Economic accessibility, 45, 50
Economic entity, market as, 29
Economic issues, effect on marketing
  of, 110–113, 142–145
Education and learning
  buyer behavior influenced by, 38,
    87–88, 116
  defined, 98
Elderly market, 37
Elvis Presley Enterprises, 1–2
End-use market segmentation, 41, 43
Environment, external. *See* External
  environment
Environmental scanning, 102
Ethical issues, 106–110
Ethnography, 62
European Union (EU), 143–144
Evaluation, marketing program, 21,
  196–197
Excess capacity, use of, 159
Exchange function (distribution chan-
  nels), 253, 276
Exchange process, 8, 74–75
Exchange rate, 148
Experimental research approach,
  59–60, 70
Export marketing, 128, 131, 148
Expropriation, 144, 148
External analysis, 102–104, 123, 135
External environment, 101–125
  case application, 124–125
  competitors, 104–106
  defined, 123
  economic/political issues,
    110–113, 142–144, 145
  future trends, 120–121

international markets, 139–146
legal/ethical factors, 106–110, 142–144
social trends, 115–120, 139–141
surprises, 104
technology, 113–115, 144
Wall Street Journal (wsj.com), 122
External publics, 209, 223

F
Family, buyer behavior influenced by, 87
Family lifecycle, 37–38, 87, 98, 121
Federal Trade Commission, 223
Financing, consumer, 164
Follow-up, sales, 218
Ford Motor Co., 246
For-profit marketing, 15
Franchising, 132, 259–260
Full-line product line strategy, 166
Fulton, B. Keith, 39

G
Gender, markets based on, 37
General Motors, 101–102, 104–105
Generation X, 118
Geographic market segments, 36, 44, 117
Geographic mobility, 38
Global/international marketing, 17, 126–150. *See also* Export marketing
case application, 149–150
defined, 127–128, 148
distribution and logistics, 138–139
dumping, 138
environment, 139–146
expropriation, 144
goals, setting, 146
gray market (parallel importing), 138
new product idea generation, 175
personal sales, effect on, 220
plan, 133–139
pricing, 137–138, 230
reasons for/against, 129–130, 135
stages in, 130–133
standardization and customization in, 128–129, 136–137
tariffs, 144
trading blocs and agreements, 143–144
Wall Street Journal (wsj.com), 147

Goods marketing, 13–15, 157–159
Gray market (parallel importing), 138
Gross margin pricing, 242
Group. *See* Consumer
Guarantees, product, 164–165

H
Habits, buying, 84
Haij-Joännu, Stelios, 142
Harley-Davidson, 25–26
Heineken, 133
Hershey Foods Corp., 183–184
Hertz Corporation, 232
High Frequency Marketing (HFM), 46
High-involvement decisions, 83–84, 98
Historical (case study) research approach, 60
Historical research approach, 71
H.J. Heinz Co., 136
Honda Motor Co., 17

I
Image, effect of pricing on, 231
Income, markets based on, 38
Indirect exporting, 131, 148
Indirect selling, 215
Industrial markets. *See* Organizational markets
Influences, buyer behavior, 82–91
external influences, 85–87
internal influences, 87–91
situational influences, 82–85
Informal assessment, marketing environment, 58–59, 70
Information flow, 255
Information search/processing, buyer, 77–79, 98
Inside selling, 214, 215
Institutional markets, 30
Integrated marketing. *See also* Integrated Marketing Communication (IMC)/marketing communication
defined, 11
global marketing, 135–139
Internet marketing, 78, 114, 179
pricing, 232
spying on competitors, 11
Integrated Marketing Communication (IMC)/marketing communication, 20, 185–225. *See also* Advertising; Personal selling; Public relations; Sales promotion
budget, 196
campaign, 198–199
components of, 190

customer feedback, mechanism for, 188
defined, 189–190, 223
design of, 194–199
evaluation of, 196–197
mix, 197–198, 223
objectives, 190–191
organization for, 197
planning for, 188
role of, 187–189
target audience for, 188–189
Wall Street Journal (wsj.com), 221
Internal marketing, 9, 24
Internal publics, 209, 223
International marketing. *See* Global/international marketing
Internet, 10, 16–17, 27, 115
African-American community, use by, 39
banner advertisements, 202–204
Europe, use in, 142
free services/personal computers, promotion of, 235–236
market research surveys/questionnaires, 65
new products, development of, 179
non-users, facts on, 114
retailing (e-tailers), 261–262
youth market, use by, 78
Interviews, 63–64. *See also* Questionnaires

J
Japan, 145, 151–152
Jell-O, 34, 88, 167
Joint ventures, 132, 149, 173

K
Kraft Foods, 34, 153

L
Labatt's USA, 51
Language differences (international marketing factor), 139
Learning. *See* Education and learning
Legal issues, 106–110, 142–144, 171
Less developed nations, 145
Levi Strauss & Co., 169
Levitt, Theodore, 3, 10, 128–129
Licensing, 131–132, 149, 173
Lifestyle (marketing factor), 40–41, 50, 90–91, 98, 120
Limited-line product line strategy, 166

Line extensions product lines strategies, 166–167
Line-filling product line strategies, 167
Line-pruning product line strategies, 167
L.L. Bean, 4–5
Local marketing, 17
Logistics (of distribution), 138–139
Low-involvement decisions, 84, 98
Loyalty, brand, 49, 84

M
Macromarketing, 12–13
Mail order. *See* Direct marketing
Manufactured products, 156, 257–258
Manufacturer representatives, 215
Manufacturer's export agent (MEA), 131, 148
Market. *See also* Target audience/market
  approaches to, 31–52, 161–162
  barriers to entry, 105
  defined, 28–29, 75, 98
  as economic entity, 29
  exchange (*See* Exchange process)
  extension, 162
  future of, 47
  offerings, 84
  research on, 55
  types of, 30
  undifferentiated (market aggregation), 32–33, 49
Marketing, 22
  budget, 21, 196, 202
  categories of, 12–17
  channels (*See* Distribution channels)
  concept, 8, 24
  control (evaluation), 21, 196–197
  defined, 3–6, 24
  institutions, 18
  justification for study of, 6–7
  keys to success of, 22
  management, 17–22
  mix, 19–21 (*See also* Distribution channels; Integrated Marketing Communication (IMC)/marketing communication; Price; Product)
  strategic components of, 17–22
Marketing communication (MC). *See* Integrated Marketing Communication (IMC)/marketing communication

Marketing Continuum, The, 51
Marketing organization
  capabilities of, 9
  characteristics of, 7–12
  consumer content of, 8
  cross-functional contact, 10–11
  functional-level considerations, 18
Marketing plan, 18–19, 54. *See also* Product planning and strategy formulation
  external factors (*See* External environment)
  internal focus, 102
  international marketing plan, 133–139
  media plan, development of, 201–202
  new products, 178
Marketing research, 53–72. *See also* Data, market research
  areas of research, 55–57
  case application, 72
  conducting research, 67
  cost of, 68
  defined, 70
  design for (*See* Research design)
  nature and importance of, 54–55
  preliminary investigation, 57–59
  supplier, 123
  value of, 67–68
  Wall Street Journal (wsj.com), 69
Marketing Science Institute, 56
Marketplace, 29
Market segmentation, 34–46, 49, 162
  bases of, 35–36
  competitive pricing and, 234–235
  demographic segments, 36–38
  geographic segments, 36
  identification, clarity of, 44
  new market segments, appeal to, 159–160
  organizational markets, 41–44
  psychological segments, 39–41
  qualifying customers in segments, 44–45
  single-base and multi-base segmentation, 44
  strategies, 35, 45–47
  usage segments, 38–39
  Wall Street Journal (wsj.com), 48
Market share, 159, 230, 231
Mark-ups (pricing), 242–243, 248
Martineau, Philip, 169
Maslow, A. H., 89

Mass marketing, 15–16, 193. *See also* Integrated Marketing Communication (IMC)/marketing communication
McDonald's, 226–227
MCI Communications, 68
McKenna, Regis, 212
Media
  evaluating, 202, 203
  plan, development of, 201–202
  public relations contact with, 10
Mergers, acquisition of new products through, 172
Meserue, Wayne, 232
Micromarketing, 12–13
Middle class, spending power of, 117
Miller Brewing Co., 133
Mission statements, 4, 6, 18–19
Modeling of behavior, 88
Monopoly, 29
Motives, buyer, 40, 50, 60, 88–89, 98
Mullen, David, 51
Multi-base segmentation strategy, 44, 50
Multinational marketing, 128, 148. *See also* Global/international marketing
Multiple sales, sales person engaged in, 215
Multisegment strategy, 35, 49

N
National Cattleman's Beef Association (NCBA), 62
National marketing, 17
National origin, markets based on, 38
Needs, 8
  actual/potential, 28, 44–45, 50
  defined, 75–76, 98
  identification, 76–77
  organizational buying, need recognition and description for, 93–94
  selling and, 213
Negotiation flow, 255
Neiman Marcus, 224
New products, pricing of, 230, 235–236
New products, strategies for developing, 168–180
  acquisition of new products, 171–173
  business analysis, 176–177
  category appraisal, 175–176
  commercialization, 180

consumer's viewpoint, 170
defining "newness," 169–171
Federal Trade Commission regulation, 171
generation of new product ideas, 173–175
Internet market, 179
manufacturer's viewpoint, 171
manufacturing planning, 178
marketing planning, 178
process of new product development, steps in, 173–180
screening ideas, 175–176
technical and marketing development, 178
test marketing, 178–180
Nintendo, 104–105
Nissan Motor Co., 152
Nonmarketing institutions, 18
Nonprice competition, 232–235, 248
Nonprofit marketing, 15
Nonstore retailing, 261–263, 276
Norms, 86
North American Free Trade Agreement (NAFTA), 143

O
Observational data collection, 61–63
Odd prices, 240–241
Oligopoly, 29
Online. *See* Internet
Opinion leaders, 86, 94
Organic, expand-o product of, 202–203
Organizational markets, 17, 30, 50
buying behavior, 91–96
customer types, 41, 49, 75
product types, 41, 156, 182
segmentation of, 41–44
Outside selling, 215
Ownership flow, 255

P
Packaging, 162–163, 183
Pantry (cabinet) audit, 62
Parallel importing, 138
Patagonia company, 80
Patents, 173
Patronage motives, 88
Penetration pricing, 235–236, 248
Pepsi Corporation, 9, 34, 86
Personal allowances, 239–240
Personality traits, marketing based on, 40, 49, 89–90, 98

Personal selling, 211–220
campaign, role in, 198–199
defined, 190
follow-up, 218
future trends, 219–220
process for, 215–218
strengths and weaknesses of, 218–219
technological aids for, 219–220
types of, 213–215
Pet.com, 179
Pew Internet and American Life Project, 114
Philips Petroleum, 22
Phillip Morris, 39–40
Physical distribution function, 20, 253, 264–267, 276
Piggyback exporting, 131, 148
Political issues, effect on marketing of, 110–113, 142–144
Population density, 36
Pop-up surveys, 65
PortiCo Research, 62
Positioning, 47, 165–166
defined, 183
Positive response, 45
Premium offers, 209, 223
Presley, Priscilla, 1–2
Prestige pricing, 240
Price, 20, 226–251
alternative approaches to, 242–246
break-even analysis, 243–244
bundling, 240, 248
case application, 249–250
combination pricing, 241
competitive pricing, 234–235
cost-oriented (cost-plus/mark-ups), 242–243, 248
customary, 240
customer's view of, 227–228
deals, 209, 222
demand curve, 229, 248
demand-oriented, 244
developing pricing strategy, 231–235
discounts and allowances, 237–240, 248
flexibility, 237–240
future of, 246
global markets, 137–138, 230
irrational man pricing, 230
lines/points, 237, 248
marketer's view of, 230

new products, 230, 235–236
nonprice competition, 232–235, 248
objectives, 230–231
odd, 240–241
penetration pricing, 235–236, 248
prestige pricing, 240
psychological aspects of, 240–241
rational man pricing, 229–230
skimming, 235–236, 248
societal perspective on, 228–229
target rates of return, 244
value-based pricing, 244–246, 248
Wall Street Journal (wsj.com), 247
wars, 235, 248
Priceline.com, 239
Primary demand, 229
Primary information, 60–61, 71
Private branding, 167
Probability/nonprobability samples, 66
Procter & Gamble, 219
Product(s), 20. *See also* Demand, product
adaptation, 136–137, 149
classification of, 154–159
defined, 152–154, 182
deletion, 168
delivery, installation, training, and service, 165
differentiation, 33–34, 49, 161–162
features, 162
flow, 255
goods *vs.* services, 157–159
industrial product types, 41, 156, 182
levels of, 153–154
lifecycle, 160–161, 183
modification, 165
new (*See* New products, strategies for developing)
positioning (*See* Positioning)
pricing (*See* Price)
proliferation, 167
research on, 56
specification, 94
spending patterns, 111–112
strategy (*See* Product planning and strategy formulation)
value-added elements, 228
warranties/guarantees, 164–165
Production orientation, 8
Product liability, 107

Product line decisions, 166–168
Product-line simplification, 168
Product mix strategies, 165–166
Product planning and strategy formulation, 159–184
    approaches to market, 161–162
    branding, 163–164
    case application, 183–184
    development of new products (*See* New products, strategies for developing)
    objectives, determining, 159–160
    packaging, 162–163
    product deletion, 168
    product features, 162
    product lifecycle, 160–161
    product line decisions, 166–168
    product mix strategies, 165–166
    supporting services, 164–165
    Wall Street Journal (wsj.com), 181
Profits
    pricing and, 231
    research on, 55
Projective techniques, 65–66
Promised product, 154
Promotion, sales. *See* Sales promotion
Promotion flow, 255–256
Prospecting, for sales, 216
Prosperity, 112, 123
Psychological market segments, 39–41, 49
Public relations, 10, 193, 199
    defined, 190, 208, 223
    publics of, 209–211
    techniques, 211
Purchase occasion, 38–39, 49
Pure competition, 29
Push money, 209, 223

Q
Quantity discounts, 237–239, 248
Questionnaires, 60, 63–65, 71, 80, 164, 176

R
Race, as marketing factor, 38, 39, 85, 116–117, 121
Readiness, stage of, 49
Rebates, 209, 223
Rebuys (organizational buying), 93
Recession, 112, 123
Recovery, 113, 123
Reference groups, 86–87, 98
Regional marketing, 17

Regulators, 123
Reinforcement of behavior, 88
Relationship marketing, 10
Relevant.Knowledge, 27
Religion, as marketing factor, 38, 141
Repositioning, product, 166
Research, marketing. *See* Marketing research
Research design, 59–67, 70
    anticipating results/making report, 66–67
    choosing approach, 59–60
    data collection methods, 61–66
    determining types of data needed, 60
    locating sources of data, 60–61
    sample selection, 66
Reseller markets, 30
Resellers, new product ideas generated by, 175
Retailing, 258–263, 276
    nonstore, 261–263, 276
    structure of, 259–263
Role expectations, 86
Rosso, Jean-Pierre, 72
Route salesperson, 214
Routinization, 256, 276

S
Sales. *See also* Personal selling
    growth in, 159
    new product ideas generated by salesperson, 174
    orientation, 8
    presentation, 216–218
    pricing and, 231
    research on, 55
Sales promotion, 204–207, 222
    campaign, role in, 198
    defined, 190
    internet/personal computer deals, 235–236
    research on, 56
    types of, 207, 209
Sales teams, 219
Sample selection (market research), 66
Scandinavian Airlines (SAS), 20–21
Schultz, Don, 188, 212–213
Screening, new product development, 175–176
Seasonal discounts, 239, 248
Secondary source data, 60–61, 71
Self-reporting surveys, 65–66
Seller's market, 29
Selling. *See* Sales

Semidirect exporting, 131, 148
Service products, 20, 213–215
    business services, 156
    channel distribution, 256–257
    characteristics of, 157–159
    goods compared, 13–15, 157
    supporting services, 164–165
Shopping goods, 155
Shopping malls, 260–261
Shopping orientation, 90
Single-base segmentation strategy, 44, 50
Situation analysis, 19, 135
Snowball.com, 78
Social class, 85–86, 98
Social environment, effect on marketing plan of trends in, 115–120, 139–141
Socialization, 88, 98
Social responsibility, 110
Societal marketing concept, 110
Special offers, 204–207, 209, 222–223
Specialty goods, 155–156
Spending patterns, 111–112
Spiffs, 240, 248
Spokespersons, use of, 88. *See also* Opinion leaders
SRI International, 40–41
Standard Industrial Classification (SIC), 43, 50
Storytelling, 80
Straight extension, 136, 149
Strategic planning. *See* Marketing plan
Struven, Tom and Sally, 224–225
Supplier (organizational buying), 94–95, 106
Surveys. *See* Questionnaires
Survival, pricing for, 231

T
Tangible product, 153
Target audience/market, 31, 188–189
    communicating to, 190
    selecting, 45–46, 195
Tariffs, 143–144, 148
Technical salesperson, 215
Technology, 123
    international marketing, effect on, 144
    lifestyle, effect on, 120–121
    marketing plan and, 113–115
Teen Research Unlimited, 78
Test marketing, 178–180
Time customs, as factor in international marketing, 141

Toyota Motors, 9, 128, 151–152
Trade allowances, 239–240
Trade deals, 209, 223
Trade discounts, 239, 248
Trade intermediaries, 133
Trademark, 163
Trading blocs and agreements,
    143–144
Transaction, 4, 8, 24
Trans World Airlines, Inc., 99–100

U
Ultimate users, 36–41, 49. *See also*
    Consumer
Undifferentiated markets, 32–33, 49
Unilever, 149–150
United Air Lines, 9
United Techtronics, 249–250
U.S. Commercial Centers, 132
Usage market segments, 38–39
Usage rate, 49
User status, 49

V
VALS/VALS 2, 40–42
Value-added elements, product, 228
Value-based pricing, 244–246, 248
Values, 85, 118–119, 140–141
Vehicles, electric, 101–102, 113
Vendors. *See* Supplier (organizational
    buying)
Vertical marketing system, 268, 277
Vos, Ron, 46

W
Wainwright, Julie, 179
Wall Street Journal (wsj.com)
    buyer behavior, 97
    distribution channels, 275
    external factors affecting market-
        ing plan, 122
    international marketing, 147
    marketing research, 69
    market segmentation, 48
    mass communication, 221
    overview, 23

    product planning and strategy for-
        mulation, 181
    product pricing, 247
Walsh, Jerry, 185–186
Walton, Sam, 252–253
Wants
    actual/potential, 28, 44–45
    defined, 75–76, 98
Warehouse retailing, 259
Warranties, product, 164
Wasow, Omar J., 39
Weaver, Mark, 179
Webb-Pomerene Export Association,
    131, 148
Wholesaling, 263–264, 276
    functions of, 263–264
    types of, 264, 266
Wm. Wrigley Jr. Company, 53–54
World Wide Web. *See* Internet

Y
Youth market, 36–37, 46, 73–74, 78,
    87, 118